Representing the Race

Representing the Race

A New Political History of
African American Literature

Gene Andrew Jarrett

NEW YORK UNIVERSITY PRESS
New York and London

NEW YORK UNIVERSITY PRESS
New York and London
www.nyupress.org

References to Internet websites (URLs) were accurate at the time of writing.
Neither the author nor New York University Press is responsible for URLs
that may have expired or changed since the manuscript was prepared.

Library of Congress Cataloging-in-Publication Data

Jarrett, Gene Andrew, 1975–
Representing the race : a new political history of African American literature /
Gene Andrew Jarrett.
p. cm.
Includes bibliographical references and index.
ISBN 978-0-8147-4338-6 (cloth : acid-free paper) — ISBN 978-0-8147-4339-3
(pbk. : acid-free paper) — ISBN 978-0-8147-4340-9 (e-book)
1. American literature—African American authors—History and criticism.
2. Politics and literature—United States—History and criticism. 3.
African Americans—Intellectual life. I. Title.
PS153.N5J398   2011
810.9'896073—dc22   2011011052

New York University Press books are printed on acid-free paper,
and their binding materials are chosen for strength and durability.
We strive to use environmentally responsible suppliers and materials
to the greatest extent possible in publishing our books.

Manufactured in the United States of America

c   10 9 8 7 6 5 4 3 2 1
p   10 9 8 7 6 5 4 3 2 1

Contents

Preface and Acknowledgments

Unwittingly, this book began while I was writing my first book, *Deans and Truants: Race and Realism in African American Literature* (2007), about the enormous critical and commercial expectations African American authors faced to portray their "race" in realistic ways—to demonstrate what I call racial realism. If the authors ever defied these expectations by casting not African American but "white" or "raceless" literary characters, then a host of cultural arbiters disparaged their writings as poor quality and tossed them into noncanonical dustbins. In *Deans and Truants*, I aimed to counter these practices of aesthetic judgment and canon formation that have persisted from the publications of these writings until the present day. I argued that we should revisit the circumstances, recover the writings, and redeem the authors of this anomalous tradition of "white" and "raceless" texts, a tradition that I showed to be more prevalent across history and more constitutive of African American literary identity than most of us have been led to think. When read according to other coordinates of aesthetic ideology, such as literary naturalism, science fiction, historical romance, and postmodernism, then this tradition indeed urges us to rethink canonical historiographies of African American literature that unfairly privilege writings of racial realism over those that avoid it.

In the introduction to *Deans and Truants,* I proposed a minor idea that blossomed into *Representing the Race*: the anomalous status of "white" or "raceless" kinds of African American literature had both exposed and undercut the "relationship between cultural politics and political culture" by which racial realism became a proxy for "racial progress." Consequently, the authors "suffered public criticism for shirking the political responsibilities inevitably bestowed on them as identifiable members of the race."[1] Although this statement still rings true to me, it is also a Pandora's Box: its assumption that we know exactly what we mean when we call African American literature "political" requires more space to qualify than what my study of racial realism and anomalies allowed. *Representing the Race* is that space. I retell some stories in *Deans and Truants*, among other well-known stories, from a new perspective, but I also tell new stories, all with the hope of developing an innovative political history of African American literature that overcomes the problematic ideas about race, culture, and politics that have been passed down from generation to generation and that still circulate among us today.

Saying that the growth of *Representing the Race* spans two successive moments of academic writing means that I have a lot of people to thank. Three deserve recognition above all. First, I appreciate my longtime colleague Henry Louis Gates Jr. During a conversation with me about the idea of this book, he challenged me to determine precisely how one "measures" the political value of African American literature. Posed as a question in the introduction's first sentence, Skip's challenge guided my writing for the past several years. Next, I am grateful to Madhu Dubey, another longtime colleague. Years ago, at a Woodrow Wilson Career Enhancement Fellowship Conference, held in Princeton, reuniting new assistant professors with their mentors (she was my mentor), we ate breakfast while arguing over the merits of my thesis. Ideas from that discussion still resonate with me today, as do those in her 2003 book, *Signs and Cities: Black Literary Postmodernism*, which I still regard as the model of rigorous and trenchant African American literary scholarship. Finally, I must express admiration for Kenneth W. Warren, whom I have debated both in person and in print, about African American literature. In this book, I cite and critique multiple times his work on this topic, as most critics do with influential work they take seriously. Hailing as second to none his ability to pinpoint ironic contradictions or connections among ideas that, on the surface, seem in agreement or incompatible, I hope that this book piques his interest in kind.

A number of individuals were key to bringing this book to fruition. I am indebted to Eric Zinner, editorial director of New York University Press, for encouraging me from day one and for his faith in the project. NYU Press's assistant editor, Ciara McLaughlin, shepherded the manuscript through the long peer-review process, and Despina Papazoglou Gimbel, Andrew Katz, and Martic Tulic cared for it during the copyediting process. The peer reviewers—who were anonymous, except for John Ernest, who supportively disclosed himself—provided excellent critiques and questions. Finally, I praise my literary agent, Wendy Strothman, for always paying attention to what is in my best interest as an author.

The aid I receive from my home institution, Boston University, has been outstanding. The following colleagues in the English Department I have talked to about this book, either at length or in passing: Laurence Breiner,

Julia Brown, William C. Carroll, Robert Chodat, Bonnie Costello, William Huntting Howell, Laura Korobkin, Sanjay Krishnan, Maurice S. Lee, John T. Matthews, Susan Mizruchi, Erin Murphy, Anita Patterson, Carrie Preston, John Paul Riquelme, Charles J. Rzepka, James R. Siemon, Matthew Smith, Kevin Van Anglen, David Wagenknecht, and James Winn. Of these, Mo Lee read a core section of chapter 2, on Frederick Douglass, for his 2009 *Cambridge Companion to Frederick Douglass,* and his editorial eye was, and continues to be, superb. Wonderful were my deep conversations with Mo and with Larry, Bill, Rob, Bonnie, Laura, Sanjay, Jack, Susan, Erin, JP, Chuck, Matt, David, and James Winn about the state of our profession. Graduate students John Barnard and Kerri Greenidge-Douglass were diligent research assistants. For further intellectual support, I thank my faculty colleagues in the Program of African American Studies: Allison Blakely, Mary Anne Boelcskevy, Linda Heywood, Patricia Hills, Ronald K. Richardson, and John Thornton. The program's administrator, Katy Evans, deserves special mention for making my life so much easier when I served as acting director of African American Studies in academic year 2009–2010. Finally, a number of higher administrators were instrumental to my productivity at Boston University. Virginia Sapiro, despite her busy schedule as dean of the College of Arts and Sciences and professor of political science, found time to lend me her working paper on knowledge and information as political action, which turned out to be an important reference in chapter 3. The former dean of the College of Arts and Sciences, Jeffrey Henderson; the outgoing university provost, David K. Campbell; and the outgoing associate dean for faculty, Peter Doeringer, all deserve mention here for their generosity.

A host of college and university faculty in the greater New England area have been great colleagues and supplied much food for thought over breakfasts, lunches, and dinners: at Harvard University, aside from Skip Gates, Lawrence D. Bobo, Lawrence Buell, Glenda R. Carpio, Roland G. Fryer, Werner Sollors, and John Stauffer; at Tufts University, Elizabeth Ammons, Peniel Joseph, and Christina Sharpe; at Boston College, Martin Summers; at Brown University, Rolland Murray and Daniel Kim; at Yale University, Wai Chee Dimock, Robert Stepto, and Brian Walsh. Beyond this area, the following are also personal colleagues: Houston A. Baker Jr., Herman Beavers, Adam Biggs, Daphne Brooks, Vincent Carretta, Frank Christianson, Thadious Davis, Theresa Delgadillo, Brent Hayes Edwards, Michele Elam, Guy-Mark Foster, Shelley Fisher Fishkin, Christopher Freeburg, Yogita Goyal, Lena Hill, Michael Hill, George Hutchinson, Lawrence P. Jackson, Brian Johnson, Gavin Jones, Meta DuEwa Jones, Arlene Keizer, Jacob Leland, Keith

D. Leonard, Robert S. Levine, William J. Maxwell, Koritha Mitchell, Shirley Moody-Turner, Rowan Ricardo Phillips, Marlon Ross, Mark Sanders, Cherene Sherrard-Johnson, James Edward Smethurst, Valerie Smith, Mark Christian Thompson, Jeffrey Allen Tucker, Mary Helen Washington, Ivy G. Wilson, and Richard Yarborough.

I was invited to present excerpts of this book as a lecture or a smaller paper. I am grateful to the Department of English at Grinnell College, especially Professor Shanna Benjamin, for selecting me as the third Peter Connelly Lecturer (for fall 2009), for which I delivered lectures on Thomas Jefferson and Barack Obama, the topics of chapters 1 and 6 in this book. I also thank the organizers of the Harvard University English Department's American Literature Colloquium and the Brown University English Department's "Theories of the Novel Now" conference for inviting me to speak; the feedback was great.

Last but not least, I must recognize here my closest family and friends for their love as I was writing "a book about literature and politics." My buddies Joseph and Matt are always there when I want to talk about "stuff" outside of literary studies. My mother and mother-in-law are my backbones, as are my brothers and sisters-in-law. My father and I talk the most about non-academic "stuff," again and again about why "we need to arrive" to make the world a better place. Finally, my wife, Renée, and our three children, Nyla, Noah, and Nadia, are beautiful beyond words. Renée has always calmed me when all of my projects and responsibilities gave me reason, at least in my mind, to worry. This book is as much for her as it is for all of us trying to change the world in some way.

Parts of this book have appeared previously in different form. A portion of chapter 3 appeared in sections of the introduction (which I co-wrote with Henry Louis Gates Jr.) to *The New Negro: Readings on Race, Representation, and African American Culture, 1892–1938*, ed. Gates and Jarrett (Princeton, NJ: Princeton University Press, 2007), 1–20. A portion of chapter 4 appeared in my introduction to a recent edition of Claude McKay's *A Long Way from Home* (New Brunswick, NJ: Rutgers University Press, 2007), xvii–xxxvii.

For publications whose copyright I do not own: a portion of chapter 1 appeared in an essay first published in a special issue of *Early American Literature* 46.2 (June 2011): 219–319. A portion of chapter 2 appeared in an essay first published in *The Cambridge Companion to Frederick Douglass*, ed. Maurice S. Lee, 160–72 (Cambridge: Cambridge University Press, 2009). A portion of chapter 3 appeared in an essay first published in *The Blackwell*

Concise Companion to American Fiction, 1900–1950, ed. Peter Stoneley and Cindy Weinstein, 205–27 (Malden, MA: Blackwell, 2008). And a portion of chapter 5 appeared in an essay first published in *Novel: A Forum on Fiction* 42.3 (Fall 2009): 437–42. I thank University of North Carolina Press, Cambridge University Press, Blackwell Publishers, and Duke University Press for the permission to republish material in these works.

Introduction

Toward a New Political History
of African American Literature

What is the political value of African American literature? This question has united the intellectual interests of American authors as historically far apart as Thomas Jefferson at the end of the eighteenth century and Barack Obama at the start of the twenty-first. Over the past two centuries, it has united the social interests of literary works as different as pamphlets, autobiographies, cultural criticism, poems, short stories, and novels. And it has united the rhetorical interests of intellectual debate occurring in cultural forums as remarkable as the printing press, conventions, schools, parlors, railroad cars, and courtrooms. Certainly, the lists of authors, works, and venues can go on and on, almost in an unwieldy fashion. The challenges facing anyone interested in the opening question, then, are to think about it in systematic and sophisticated ways, to learn from its history, and to understand why it is still salient today.

Measuring the political value of African American literature begins with introducing what Jefferson and Obama have in common. As we all know, both men achieved the highest political office in the United States of America. One of the nation's "Founding Fathers," Jefferson was elected its third president in 1801, after having served, most notably, as secretary of state under George Washington and then as vice president under John Adams. Two centuries later, Obama was elected the forty-fourth president in 2008, after having served in the Illinois Senate for the state's thirteenth district and then in the U.S. Senate for the state of Illinois. Prior to their careers as elected officials, both men wrote books that had been influential in shaping public opinion on the nation's democratic potential as well as on their own personal, political, and presidential qualifications. In 1776, Jefferson coauthored the Declaration of Independence, and, in 1787, he published an authoritative ethnography of early America, *Notes on the State of Virginia*. Obama released three bestselling books of autobiographical nonfiction and public policy: in 1995, *Dreams from My Father: A Story of Race and Inheritance*; in 2006, *The Audacity of Hope: Thoughts on Reclaiming the American Dream*; and in 2008, *Change We Can Believe In: Barack Obama's Plan to Renew America's Promise*. Both Jefferson and Obama invested themselves in public service; both proved their commitment to "the life of the mind," as Hannah Arendt, a political theorist, once put it.[1]

Less obvious, Jefferson and Obama both entered office as "black" presidents—but not in the customary sense of who or what they are. Jefferson's birth to a white mother from London and a white father from Virginia would suggest that he was white. Obama's birth to a white mother from Kansas and a black father from Kenya would likewise suggest that he is neither just white nor black yet both. In either case, the terms *white* and *black* connote genealogical meanings of "race" that, given our allegedly "postidentitarian" era today, threaten to oversimplify the American identities of these two storied men.[2] Nonetheless, I submit that they were "black" presidents insofar as whom they *represented*. As Jefferson was running for office, the "three-fifths compromise" or "federal ratio," thanks to a provision in the U.S. Constitution, granted a man (but not a woman, who could not yet vote) an extra three votes in the House of Representatives and the presidential Electoral College for every five slaves that he owned. The large ownership of slaves in the South accorded this region—and, indirectly, its elected officers or office-seekers—leverage in securing more electoral votes and greater political representation. Jefferson's election to the presidency benefited from the Southern advantage.[3]

Obama's election likewise benefited from securing votes from a large swath of the African American electorate. Whereas Jefferson's candidacy exploited a constitutional loophole that counted slaves while denying them the political entitlements enjoyed by white slaveholders, Obama's presidential campaign attracted African Americans in unprecedented numbers. The electoral power of African Americans and the political power of his own Democratic Party grew. Drawing on his experience as a community organizer in Chicago, he led staffers, volunteers, and Internet bloggers as they worked to register for the first time many African Americans to vote and as they reminded others how to do so again. The more experienced African American voters were persuaded to cast their ballots early on Election Day and to galvanize others to vote as well. About seventy million Americans voted for Obama in the end, helping him defeat his Republican opponent, John McCain, a senior U.S. senator from Arizona, by about ten million votes. In the history of U.S. presidential elections, Obama earned the biggest percentage and number of "black votes"—over 95 percent and sixteen million, respectively.[4]

Evidently, African Americans have been crucial to the legacies of both Jefferson and Obama. Yet an even less obvious, but equally important, story about African Americans binds them together: African American literature fueled their political imaginations. *Notes on the State of Virginia* has now become a canonical, or widely taught and analyzed, book of African American literary criticism in the academy. To be clear, "criticism" means both Jefferson's art of interpretation and his art of ridicule, such as when he claimed that two of his era's best writers of African descent, Phillis Wheatley and Ignatius Sancho, wrote literature that fell well below the stratum of reason and imagination that he had set for the political emancipation and national citizenship of slaves in the new republic. Substandard literature, in his view, disqualified Africans and their New World descendants from receiving the basic civil rights to which their fellow Anglo-American citizens were entitled.

Two centuries later, in contrast, literature supplied both the evidence and the medium by which Obama could prove not the civic worth of African Americans (for that goes without saying) but, rather, the nation's democratic promise despite and because of race. *Dreams from My Father* inspired Nobel laureate Toni Morrison so much that she remarked in a 2008 interview, "I was amazed because he writes so well. Really well, with really nice big, strong, artful sentences. But equally important was his reflection."[5] Beyond the extraordinary style and storytelling, the substance or the "reflection" of this memoir and of Obama's next book, *The Audacity of Hope,* includes explicit references to a tradition of African American writers, such as W. E. B. Du Bois, Langston Hughes, Frank Marshall Davis, Richard Wright, James Baldwin, Ralph Ellison, and Malcolm X. Pundits have, of late, ranked Abraham Lincoln and, his acquaintance, Douglass—the nation's sixteenth president and that generation's preeminent African American statesman—as Obama's foremost political role models. Obama has done little to refute that perception (especially where Lincoln is concerned). Let the full record show that, in *Dreams from My Father* and *The Audacity of Hope,* Obama also embraces African Americans who wrote on the politics of race (or racial politics, in short) as crucial to his formative understanding of this subject matter, of his ironic identity as neither just black nor white yet both, and of his biracial descent from a Kansan mother and a Kenyan father.

Fittingly, Jefferson and Obama serve as presidential bookends to this book, which I propose as one step toward a new political history of African American literature. In a number of ways I connect racial politics to African American literature. I look at African American literature's role in the political imagination, political action's role in the African American literary imagination, and, conversely, African American literature's role in political action, to the extent that it can facilitate social change. But a deeper issue of methodology must be addressed. If we accept as true the idea that historical circumstances can determine merely whether African American literature has political value, then how do we read and write literary history to account for that value, to measure it, and to trace how it has varied across genres, authors, readers, marketplaces, societies, and eras? Developing a critical historiography attuned to the political contexts of literary texts is prerequisite to my argument that literature has helped African Americans secure or improve their representation in the "formal" realms of electoral voting, governmental intervention, public policy, and law, not just in the "informal" or cultural realms where special portrayals of the "black race" aim to affect social attitudes and attain racial justice. Another part of my study involves parsing out the myths of authenticity, popular culture, nationalism, and militancy that have come to define African American political activism since the contemporary birth of Black Studies around the 1970s. We must overcome these myths to show the diverse and complex ways that African American literature—and intellectual culture generally—has not only recounted the ills of race relations but also, in some historic cases, transcended its own medium and transformed society for the better.

More specifically, I describe the "politics" of African American literature in four ways: first, by arguing that, from the late eighteenth century to the present, African American literature has come to define, demonstrate, and even succeed in political action; second, by showing that political action's informal context—its rarified production and consumption by intellectuals—does not necessarily depreciate the literature's insight or connection to the formal kinds of political action; third, by documenting the actual and virtual challenges African American writers have faced in representing racially defined communities in person and in print; and, fourth, by demonstrating that racial representation is one paradigmatic step toward reconstructing the past while overcoming the blind spots of methodology and historiography that all of us, unwittingly or not, have inherited from Black Studies. In order to achieve these goals, the stories I tell range far and wide across American culture, politics, and history. They feature the debate over racial genius in early American history, the intellectual culture of racial politics after slavery, the rise of "New Negro" politics between Reconstruction and the Harlem Renaissance, the geopolitics of African American autobiography between

World Wars I and II, the tension between copyright law and free speech in contemporary African American culture, and the political audacity of Barack Obama's creative writing. And yet one critique threads the stories together: the abilities of African American literature to transform society on multiple ideological, cultural, and political levels have not yet been treated carefully enough.

The Politics of Racial Representation

Let us now describe the problems of critical method and writing history posed by my topic of racial representation. In American history, the broadly aesthetic and political notions of representation date back to the late eighteenth century. Constitutional conventions were preoccupied with determining the degree to which elected assemblies should capture the "likeness" of their constituents while implementing their collective "will," even as the fundamental differences between the elected and the electorate were striking. In letters of correspondence, delegates to the Continental Congress, such as John Adams, William Hooper, and John Penn, conferred with each other in 1776 on whether the "most natural Substitute for an Assembly of the whole, is a Delegation of Power, from the Many, to a few of the most wise and virtuous." For literary scholar Eric Slauter, these words written by Adams in a letter to Penn reveal the historical tension between "actual" and "virtual" representation: between, on the one hand, "the desire of constituents for representatives who resembled themselves and articulated their local interests" and, on the other, "the charms of high republican theory in which the wills of the many (as well as the interests of all those persons said to lack wills of their own: children, slaves, women, white men without property, American Indians, free African Americans) were deputed to the wise and good." The paradox of representation involved a contradiction in how assemblymen acquired their social power by being at once devoted to yet also detached from their constituents, at once identifiable with yet also an idealized image of them. From the early national period onward, cultural expressions ranging from miniature portraits to literature have consistently registered the aesthetic and intellectual factors of political representation.[6]

African American literature, also from this period onward, is replete with various assumptions and anxieties about the aesthetic and political representation of not simply a social group but a "race." The political process of representing a race—or hitherto called racial representation—has a double meaning. First, it signifies the aesthetic portrayal of African Americans, and in some cases the African diaspora more broadly, in literature. Second, it signifies this group's political delegation of its collective authority to an individual person or another group. By the end of this book, I aim to have made clear that racial representation in African American literary history has consistently endeavored to overthrow racial injustice. African American writers have long been committed to exposing the white-supremacist, discriminatory, prejudicial, and inequitable degradation of African Americans on the basis of race.[7] Returning to the earlier distinctions, the "actual" representation of race means the way that representatives demonstrated an "authenticity," which, in folklorist Regina Bendix's words, alternately means "one who acts with authority," a quality suggesting that something was "made by one's hand," and, in the case of art, "the clear identifiability of the maker or authorship and uniqueness of an artifact" based on some predetermined experience and imagination of racial unity.[8] Virtual representation exposes the discrepancies between such representatives and their constituents, but, at the same time, it helps consecrate leadership by legitimizing the aesthetics and intellectualism of certain individuals, among other virtues. African American literature has been a tool of social change, addressing or redressing the attitudes of readers and stimulating social action, by balancing the actual and virtual modes of racial representation.

This claim does not sound groundbreaking; it sounds rather intuitive, as part of our common sense. It is as familiar as the ubiquitous term *cultural politics,* which E. Waldo Martin Jr. defines as "the inevitable politicization of culture and the culturalization of politics" or as "the intersection where culture and politics overlap and merge."[9] However, this definition's tautological circle only exemplifies that neither cultural studies nor literary studies has been equipped to derive the terms, concepts, and paradigms needed to generate a political methodology of African American literature. More forcefully, I state here that the instinctive political definition of African American literature is an ideological inheritance of the "black nationalist" phase of the modern civil rights movement of the past half century and that it persists only because its status as common sense lulls our desire to qualify it. We need deeper understandings of *literature* and *politics,* not to mention the stakes of intersecting the methodologies of literary studies and political studies (the latter of which I take to be either political history or political science, fields that sometimes overlap but certainly are not the same). We also need an identification of the ideological patterns and conflicts of race and politics in order to outline the development of racial representation in the styles and themes of African American literature and in the taxonomic and legal forms of African American politics. From there, we can begin to show the political determinism of literary knowledge alongside the literary determinism of political action.

To this end, I empathize with the concerns of certain leading political and literary scholars about the methodological limitations of African American literary studies. Adolph L. Reed Jr., a political scientist, has suggested that scholars of African American literature have been consistently misapplying the category of politics, "unhelpfully blur[ring] the distinction between cultural history and the history of social and political thought, such that the former has tended to substitute for the latter." More disciplined approaches, he implies, would separate culture from the issues of "legitimacy, justice, obligation, the meaning of equality, or the nature of the polity" or the issues of "demography, social psychology, political economy, or public opinion" or the issue of government.[10] In a related analysis, Kenneth W. Warren, a literary scholar, provides a nuanced and tactful way of thinking about how and why historians should distinguish between "direct black political action" and "indirect cultural politics." Direct African American political action acknowledges, in Warren's words, that "race . . . is at bottom a problem of politics and economics—of constitution making and of wielding power legislatively and economically in order to mobilize broad constituencies to preserve an unequal social order." In this context, African Americans have used activist, legislative, judicial, or public-policy means to access institutional resources and social power and to use them for their own best interests as racial subjects. Indirect cultural politics, by contrast, refers to the efforts of African American intellectuals and artists to operate "outside the political realm of direct representation—whether one did so literarily, sociologically, philosophically, administratively, or philanthropically."[11] Warren's implicit and admirable call for more accurate historical contexts that account for the cultural turn of African American politics does not decry—as much as Reed does—contemporary academic interest in cultural politics. Nonetheless, both share the assumption that "direct black political action" is more transformative than "indirect cultural politics."

Reed and Warren advance their argument in a 2010 book of scholarly essays they coedited, about "renewing black intellectual history" by revisiting "the ideological and material foundations of African American thought."[12] The academic-departmental affiliations of the editors and the volume's contributors, who all range across the fields of literary studies, political science, public policy, history, and African American studies, attest both to the cross-disciplinary importance of their inquiry and to the timeliness of putting intellectual culture and politics in their proper contexts of African American history. The book boldly questions the scholarly elitism of African American historiography, an elitism reified by its condescending appreciation of folk vernacular, authenticity, and political unity and by its neglect of historical instances in which these three racial protocols of African American community were being contested or compromised. No less elitist, such historiography has also interchanged intellectual identity and political identity. In such writings of history, the urgent social concerns articulated by African Americans in intellectual circles were, of necessity, the concerns affecting those "outside" these circles. The edited collection indicts what it calls the conceptual, institutional, and intellectual frames of reference existing today by which certain expressions of African American culture were given salience in political history:

> To be clear, our objection is not that African American studies has sacrificed intellectual integrity in pursuit of a political agenda. No scholarly endeavor can be innocent of the ideological matrices and controversies of its historical moment, least of all scholarship on human affairs. The problems with the turn in African-Americanist discourse dating all the way back to the Reagan era stem from the *way* that it links political and intellectual concerns. The presumption that the goal of scholarly intervention is to speak for black collectivity in effect posits a primary audience that lies outside the universe of fellow practitioners.

The payoffs of this critique include exposing, first, the perennial scholarly overstatements of racism and the curse of slavery, as opposed to other kinds of historical circumstances, in the lives of African Americans; and, second, the redundant references to African American "agency," such as "autonomy, community, and family," in resisting the alleged ideological and material effects of racism. Not only are these "gross, clichéd abstractions" little more than "a conceptual shorthand that ventriloquizes them [African Americans] to make a reductivist political point," they "impose[] a summary normative script onto behavior and aspirations that are certainly more complex and various." One goal of renewing African American intellectual history in the new millennium, especially with the newfound ascendance of Obama to the presidency, is to revise the more problematic notions of cultural expression and political representation, among others, in African American history, so that we can sharpen our critical terms for explaining past and current political phenomena and for anticipating what may come next.[13]

Some of the points raised by the project of Reed and Warren are well taken, but the others are as problematic as the above notions they seek to revise. Yes, I agree with the rationale behind their criticism of certain examples of African American literary studies. The recent scholarship that has perceptively assessed the political value of African American literature still may continue to understate the methodological rationales for how we theorize and historicize this literature in political terms. The problems of African American literary studies entrenched in the Reagan era, when the field consummated its academic presence, persist in both traditional and newer forms in the Obama era and remain fair game for critique.[14] Reed and Warren have helpfully distinguished literary expression from political action, while pinpointing the way certain academics have overinvested intellectual or aesthetic culture with political capital. That said, Reed and Warren wrongly privilege direct over indirect political action and underappreciate the explanatory potential in uniting culture with politics. Russ Castronovo, a fellow literary scholar, gestures to this problem as he notes how Reed, in his writings elsewhere, has resorted to "a rigid disciplinarity that upholds politics as 'an autonomous domain of social activity' that [is] thankfully immune to literary hermeneutics" and "formalist aestheticism," when "[n]either formalism nor aesthetics . . . is as formal or as historically empty as assumed."[15] Likewise, in this book, I resist such "rigid disciplinarity" and embrace, instead, an interdisciplinary mode of thinking that moves beyond the paradigms that have mischaracterized or understated the political potential of literature.

By no means is my coordination of literary studies with political studies a trivial exercise. The epistemologies and methodologies of each academic field diverge on the notion of power.[16] Jodi Dean, a political scientist, suggests that the ideal coordination would work to "expand" and "reconstitute" "the domain of politics." In this spirit, I distinguish *formal* from *informal* types of politics. Formal politics refers to the context of governmental activity, public policy, law, and social formations with which political experts, since Plato and Aristotle, have been preoccupied. Informal politics refers to the context of cultural media, representation, and subjectivity that has long intrigued literary experts. I seek an analytic balance that avoids the pitfall Dean points to: the risk of political studies "oversimplifying its accounts when it fails to acknowledge the multiplicity of political domains" and the risk of the "non-intervention" of literary studies "by presuming its political purchase in advance."[17] At the same time, I underscore a key point: whereas political representation involves actual and virtual kinds of relationships between leaders and constituents, political action involves formal and informal strategies by which these relationships become manifest and productive in the public sphere.

Especially compelling is Dean's allegation that studies of literature and culture usually presume their own political purchase. Perpetuating the critical "shorthand" that "*everything* is political," these studies overstate that everything is, to borrow a well-worn phrase, "always already" a question of power. But the shorthand happens to elide the process by which culture becomes political. Again in Dean's words, the shorthand neglects the "*how* of politics, the ways concepts and issues come to be political common sense and the processes through which locations and populations are rendered as in need of intervention, regulation, or quarantine."[18] I am concerned that certain African American intellectual contributions to political action have gone understated or misstated in the field of African American literary studies. The field has not always been as interdisciplinary in its discourse on African American political formations as its political purchase has suggested. The historical fact that African Americans have refused to take for granted the "*how* of politics" should encourage a referendum on this scholarly misstep. (This partially explains why, throughout the book, I spend much time on writers of essays or other kinds of literary nonfiction that, in effect, expound directly on this subject.) These writers have explored a number of *ideological* contexts, whereby literature could inform and transform society for the purpose of abolishing racial injustice.

By "ideology," I mean Michael C. Dawson's notion in political science. Ideology is "a world view readily found in the population, including sets of ideas and values that cohere, that are used publicly to justify political stances, and that shape and are shaped by society."[19] Dawson and Steven Hahn, a political historian, both suggest that we should distinguish the formal and informal modes of politics to describe how this social "shaping" works, and then we should regularly remind ourselves that the boundary between formal and informal African American political action is ideologically permeable.[20] Likewise, Robin D. G. Kelley, a historian, has used the informal and formal typologies of politics and contrasted them in terms of "infrapolitics" and "organized resistance." He has stated that we "need to recognize that infrapolitics and organized resistance are not two distinct realms of opposition to be studied separately and then compared; they are two sides of the same coin that make up the history of working-class resistance."[21]

Trying to describe formal and informal politics *together*, I aim to view literature—and, when applicable, broader intellectual culture—in a way sensitive to how African American writers over the past two centuries have viewed it: as an invaluable contributor to the ideology and practice of social change. I admit that my beneficial distinction of politics into formal and informal types, though now rendering explicit what has already been implicit in African American political science and history, risks at times becoming a deterministic and static taxonomy. Yet, by the end of this book, the informal and formal concepts of political action should come across as flexible and fluid. As much as political scholars have, perhaps unselfconsciously, assumed this typological dichotomy to add narrative coherence to the ideological conversations among political agents, I plan to render this dichotomy visible—and sometimes to cross-examine it—even as I deliberately use it to identify bridges between intellectual culture and political action across African American history.

Another caveat is worth mentioning here, with respect to the topic of elitism. As admirable as Dawson, Hahn, and Kelley have been for detailing the history of grassroots African American mobilization in the nineteenth and twentieth centuries, they have only at best sketched how African American political identity has emerged through cultural and intellectual formations. Not yet have they corrected the historical and present-day view that such formations are merely the legendary bastions of elitism. In this book, I plan to flesh out and correct the record, showing that racial representation has long succeeded as an intellectual and cultural genre of political action in African American history. The success has been possible even when the writers were involved in the esoteric task of revising other literary works or even in the presumably elitist task of speaking to other literary elites. To argue, as I do, that even notoriously elite African American writers have long been formally and informally invested in political action—and have been successful at it—attempts not only to pry racial politics from the grip of popular culture but also to show cases in African American intellectual history where the line separating "state elites" (political leaders) from "nonstate elites" (cultural leaders) has been quite blurry.[22] In recasting African American political history with examples of intellectual rather than popular culture, my goal is to show not that the latter is overrated but that the former is underrated. Recent history reveals that Obama's ascent to the presidency demonstrates remarkable political achievement in both intellectual and popular realms of American culture.

Historiography after Black Studies

Since the dawn of the American republic, a series of cultural, political, and legal texts by or about African Americans has realized the ideological osmosis of formal and informal types of politics, encouraging us to recast dominant histories of African American literature that have taken such permeability for granted. The following chapters of this book conduct such a revision. In brief, chapter 1 looks at the debate between Thomas Jefferson and David Walker, an African American author, over whether New World African intellectual culture, such as the literature of Phillis Wheatley and Ignatius Sancho, should be, in essence, an entrance examination to the early American polity. Chapter 2 examines the way that, in the postbellum nineteenth century, Douglass translated political action into ideologies and practices of intellectual culture in order to grapple with the repercussions of slavery, even after the "peculiar institution" was officially abolished in 1865. Referring to but also extending the historical period of chapter 2 into the next century, chapter 3 considers politics in literature, interpreting what I call New Negro politics as a paradigm, lasting from the Reconstruction of the 1870s through the Harlem Renaissance of the 1920s, in which African American authors of criticism and fiction highlighted the theme of cultural politics—such as that endorsed by Douglass—in "uplifting the race." Chapter 4 claims that the autobiographies of two African American writers, Claude McKay and Langston Hughes, written from World War I through the early part of the Cold War, document the transnational range of geopolitical activism, which used cultural expression to mobilize people for political causes and to engage political representatives at the highest levels of government and public policymaking. Chapter 5 reveals that the U.S. court of law was a recent venue in which the litigants, alongside the district and the appellate judges, of the 2001 case *SunTrust Bank v. Houghton Mifflin Company* debated and determined the transformative potential of African American literature in the realm of social change. (Here, "transformative" means *both* the political ability to change society for the sake of racial justice *and* the legal ability, under the auspices of parody, to incorporate and revise another literary work for the sake of political criticism.) In the concluding chapter, I argue that Obama, while now representing a so-called postracial phenomenon, has alternately turned in recent years away from the radical forms and toward the reconciliatory forms of African American literature written during the Black Arts, Black Power, and Black Studies Movements spanning the 1960s and the 1970s. Race was the specter of African American political history, of elder activists and politicians who were not yet ready to yield their stature to him, but their struggle still inspired his intellectual thinking and his run-up to the presidency.

My elimination of a book chapter on the decades of the 1960s and 1970s captures my belief that this famous period has dictated too much of the recent political approaches to African American literary history and that its terms need an update. In 1991, in the visionary essay "The Black Arts Movement and Its Critics," David Lionel Smith bemoaned the "paucity" of even "the most rudimentary work," not to mention the "openly hostile" and "deeply partisan" nature of scholars, on the movement. Since then, what Smith called "careful and balanced scholarship" has finally emerged, becoming what the historian Peniel E. Joseph has succinctly termed "Black Power Studies."[23] This field, in Joseph's words, "has begun to demystify, complicate, and intellectually engage demonized, dismissed, and overlooked actors and struggles by providing nuanced, well-researched, and weighty narratives that document the profound implications of black power politics for the study of African American history and U.S. history more broadly."[24] The core meaning of the Black Power Movement, popularized by Stokely Carmichael of the Black Panther Party, mostly contradicts that of the historically overlapping Civil Rights Movement (in upper case) of the 1950s through early 1960s, led by the great Martin Luther King Jr. By the late 1960s, King was conceding the rising African American interest in the Black Power Movement, but he was still consistently contrasting the "peaceful sword" of "mass nonviolent direct action" of the "southern Negro" with the "angry mood" of "black nationalism" more endemic, in his view, among "northern Negroes." Based on Christian principles, the nonviolent direction was, for King, "a more effective method and a more moral one" that he embraced for much of his political career. For this reason, he strove to correct the mainstream conception of Black Power as racial isolationism or separatism by tailoring it to suit the Civil Rights Movement's focus on the social integration of the races and on the general assistance of the poor.[25] Recently, Black Power Studies has worked to rethink the central issues of "black empowerment," "political self-determination," "racial solidarity," and "a shared history of racial oppression" in Black Power.[26]

Undoubtedly, my inspiration for writing this book arises from an unwavering appreciation of the historical salience of these central issues. At the same time, I attend to the challenge of deriving a political historiography of African American literature not beholden to the assumptions on which Black Power and its artistic and academic kin, the Black Arts and Black

Studies Movements, were understandably built. The assumptions include the definition of successful African American politics in terms of the racial authenticity of leadership; the utter ideological cohesion of racial constituencies; the primacy of popular over intellectual forms of expressive culture; and the nationalism, rather than the internationalism, of African American identity. I present an alternative historiography that looks beyond the critical methods anchored to these assumptions, held mostly in the 1960s and 1970s—assumptions that have encouraged subsequent scholars, teachers, and students to retrofit the political mantras of Black Power across African American literary history—while capturing the formal and informal nuances of political action.

To calibrate the tone of my critique, I turn to the work of Eddie S. Glaude Jr., a religion scholar who has urged the development of a "post-soul" paradigm of African American studies. In his 2007 book, *In a Shade of Blue: Pragmatism and the Politics of Black America,* he states that we need "a form of political engagement that steps out of the shadows of the black freedom struggles" of the 1960s and 1970s, which "would recognize the diversity of African American political interests."[27] Extending Glaude's periodization to as late as the 1980s in African American literary studies, I, too, welcome a plan to wrest the political historiography of African American literature from the clutches of the Black Studies era—to "step out of the shadows," in other words, and retell dominant African American storylines in a way more open-minded to the complexities and contradictions occasioned by race, even when the politics of civil rights are at stake. One benefit is that the stories behind the political rise and endurance of African American literature would only further resonate as they are passed on.[28]

With this approach in mind, let us return to my earlier summaries of each chapter in this book, this time attending to the dominant assumptions of "the black freedom struggles" that each chapter unsettles. In chapter 1, I show that the "motive" of some African Americans in the new republic was to "demonstrate black equality" in their writing of literature, an idea that many of us have come to accept, but it turns out that they also argued for political emancipation and citizenship in American identity.[29] In chapter 2, my turn to the cultural and political commentary of Douglass in the postbellum era recalls literary scholar Eric Sundquist's broad look at Douglass beyond his 1845 autobiography, *Narrative of the Life of Frederick Douglass, Written by Himself,* whose allegedly authentic voice of black nationalism the Black Studies era has overstated.[30] In chapter 3, the racial-uplift literature written by the African American elite contradicts the proletarianism and pragmatism demanded of the African American authors who were studied or who were writing during the 1960s and 1970s. In chapter 4, my focus on the transnational formations of African American geopolitical struggle between and during the world wars attempts to expand the political historiography of African American literature beyond the usual domesticity of African American cultural and political nationalism.[31] In chapter 5, Randall's novelistic critique of the racial and gender aspects of authenticity is an explicit attack on the historical confluences of sexism, patriarchy, and racial essentialism in definitions of political representation and action. Gender and sexuality cooperated in the cultural and political expressions of African American communities, in spite and because of the structures of discrimination and inequality oppressing women. From Phillis Wheatley to Alice Randall, by way of the post-Reconstruction "Woman's Era," which I discuss in chapter 3, "the gender identity of black women complicated their position as the racial subjects of black nationalist discourse"—and, I would add, of African American political discourse generally.[32] Working against the caricatures of African American women from the era of slavery to the present, Randall represents African American women in ways that echo the feminist revisions of African American historiography appearing since the rise of Black Studies, while, with an eye toward the new millennium, critiquing the privilege of racial authenticity that *both* feminist and masculinist African American literatures have in common. Finally, chapter 6 examines how Obama overcame the myths of black nationalism to develop an appreciation of the later, racially open-minded Malcolm X. As in the previous five, this chapter balances its argument with an appreciation of *agency*—or what literary scholar William J. Maxwell calls a "historically consequential self-direction"—in both the formal and informal modes of Obama's political action.[33]

The Agency of African American Literature

So crucial to my study, *agency* requires further elaboration. Racial representation, as an intellectual and cultural genre of political action, implies a demonstration of agency. As mentioned earlier, in *Renewing Black Intellectual History*, Reed and Warren critique scholarly overstatements of the role agency plays in the vicissitudes of African American political history. The critique corresponds to a concurrent debate over agency among historians of African American slavery and political action. In 2003, Walter Johnson wrote a provocative essay on the topic in order to identify the methodological stakes of a new subfield emergent within the past decade or so, called the New Social

History (represented, say, by Steven Hahn, Michael C. Dawson, and Robin D. G. Kelley, mentioned earlier). Questioning the notion that "the task of the social historian is to 'give the slaves back their agency,'" Johnson alludes to a moment from the 1960s through the 1980s when scholarship itself was politicized, when the "historical work" of determining how slaves actively resisted and overcame the system of slavery was linked to "the political project of redress" against the curse of slavery, and when such a linkage urged "white scholars to use a declaration of their alignment with Black slaves in order to signal their alignment with the ongoing struggle for Black Freedom."[34] Implicit in Johnson's definition of the New Social History is a detection of the ideological remainder of a period when, in his view, white historians were trying to affiliate with African American historians who were trying to secure a greater foothold in the American academy during the founding of Black studies.

The language of agency, or the idea that one has independent will and volition and can also act on them, has come to underwrite recent scholarly historiographies of African American humanity and social action—historiographies, I might add, whose political rhetoric has less now than before to do with a scholar's own racial identity. More important have been the stakes of narrating the history of slavery in terms of agency and what this emphasis says about the evolution of African American historiography into a crucial academic field of inquiry across the twentieth century.[35] The New Social History has grown to complicate and advance the historiography of African American slavery developed from the 1960s through the 1980s by detailing further the cultural and political pramatics of human agency.

From a longer historical perspective, I agree with Johnson that we should concentrate, in his words, on the way "enslaved people theorized their own actions and the practical process through which those actions provided the predicate for new ways of thinking about slavery and resistance."[36] Texts of intellectual culture from the era of Jefferson to that of Obama supply the evidence of how African Americans came to understand and demonstrate their own agency for social change against racial injustice, or of how they and their critics came to articulate African American political subjectivity, action, and representation. Yet I account also for the historical paradoxes and ironies of African American culture and politics: for the way that intellectualism could form cultural wedges within African American communities, but also for the way it could support political bridges within these communities, too, such as by strengthening the ideological sensitivity of their de facto or elected leaders to the problems of racism and racial prejudice. In either case, by no means were such communities victims of the political history of race, defenseless in the face of its vicissitudes. Rather, they were, and continue to be, almost always active despite and because of it.

Hopefully, my book signals a watershed moment in thinking about the political history of African American intellectual culture. I echo the reservations of Reed and Warren over the "well-embedded, commonsense form of narrative for making claims about black collective *mentalité*" afflicting political historiographies of African American intellectual culture.[37] Yet I also remember the recent admonition of John Ernest, a literary historian, that "race" and all its ideological and material constellations remain a crucial paradigm of analysis. One reason Black Studies was so adamant about its intellectual policies includes its constant need to answer questions justifying its existence and its dual attention to race and politics. Ernest calls on scholars to continue to uphold the intervention of Black Studies into American literary studies by attending to the distinctive historical conditions of African Americans (such as slavery) that have framed their awareness of race and their approaches to political action and by drawing attention to those writers and critics of African American literature who have played crucial roles in the general development of American literature. My book heeds this call. The artistic or intellectual writings by African Americans, or such writings about them, can be a centerpiece of recovering their political history as agents of social change.[38]

Let me stress here that this book is not a full political history of African American literature. It is not a comprehensive record of the ways that this tradition has evolved since slavery's end at the hands of various actors or in response to various phenomena that many of us have assumed to be broadly political. Rather, this book is a basis for such a complete history: it looks at what literary scholar David Kazanjian has called "flashpoints." A term borrowed from (the *aufblitzen* of) philosopher Walter Benjamin, a flashpoint signifies "the process by which someone or something emerges or bursts into action or being, not out of nothing but transformed from one form to another; *and,* it refers to the powerful effects of that emergence or transformation."[39] Analogous to Kazanjian's study of early American literature, my study of certain literary processes and effects of African American political agency is selective and suggestive in referring to the past, if only because my argument involves less a full rewriting of history than a full critique of historiography and an exploration of *why* and *how* one should write a history both literary and political. I am proposing a paradigm of historiography in which the principles of researching and re-presenting the past account for the literary texts and ideologies of African American writers that have connected informal to formal types of politics. Contrary to what certain critics have claimed, the "grounding of the political in the cultural" was by no means "ill-advised from start" in African American history and historiography, and a "post-identitarian conceptualization of race" is not necessarily required to realize the limitations of racial identity in political action or mobilization.[40]

In closing, I turn again to Glaude. In the preface to *In a Shade of Blue,* he talks about his participation in a summer 2006 town-hall meeting in Texas, alongside two celebrated experts on racial politics, media host Tavis Smiley and religion scholar Cornel West. One topic of discussion was the relationship between "knowledge" and "action." In response to a person who asserted that "knowledge without action is useless" and that "we must *do* something with that knowledge," Glaude responded with the questions "What if we understand knowledge not as separate from doing, but rather as a *consequence* of it? What if knowledge is simply the fruit of our undertakings?" Borrowing the language of philosopher John Dewey, these questions constitute the premise of *In a Shade of Blue*: the philosophical tradition of Anglo-American pragmatism, of which Dewey was a pioneer, may help us to explain and overcome some of the "conceptual problems that plague contemporary African American political life."[41] The interdisciplinary questions through which Glaude resolves the undertheorized relationship between knowledge and African American political action are useful in converse terms: What if we understand doing as a consequence of knowledge? What if our undertakings are simply the fruit of knowledge? What does it take for knowledge to motivate or work on behalf of political action?

The answers to these questions are far from straightforward, especially when the knowledge in question develops from the reading of literature. In their most precise and sophisticated forms, the answers require a reconsideration, as I have already suggested, of the definitions and assumptions in connecting cultural expression to political action and in arguing that the former may cause the latter while informing and transforming society. To begin this reassessment, we must deduce that talking about politics is tantamount to talking about power, especially in regard to African Americans, whose status as a "minority" group automatically implies a power relation to a "majority" group. The symbols in African American cultural expression that develop and shape knowledge and attitudes may likewise imply the power relation.[42] As literary scholar Suzanne Gearhart suggests, "The question of minority cultures is inseparable from a question of power, or at least when we speak of a minority culture today it seems to me that what we have in mind are cultural groups whose members are not only fewer in number than those of the cultural majority but who are also relatively disempowered with respect to members of a more powerful majority culture or group."[43] Two centuries ago, Jefferson's Enlightenment generation reasoned that African Americans were inferior and should be circulated and exchanged as commodities in the global capitalist economy of slavery and the slave trade. According to Frederick Douglass, although American slavery formally ended in 1865, as an "old monster" it could persist in "new," ideological "form" and become even more dangerous unless antislavery work continued—but also adjusted—to counteract it.[44] Action against the racism that endorsed slavery, in other words, needed to assume multiple political forms to succeed. African American literature turned out to be one of those forms.

1

The Politics of Early African American Literature

In fall 1780, Thomas Jefferson, as governor of Virginia and as a recently elected member of the American Philosophical Society, began drafting the twenty-three "queries" or chapters of *Notes on the State of Virginia*. Jefferson wrote the book in response to a questionnaire sent to him and the rest of the republic's twelve governors by François Marbois, the secretary of the French Legation in the United States, who was requesting cultural, historical, scientific, economic, geographic, and political information about the states. From the first to the final published editions of the manuscript, a process that began in Paris in 1785 and ended with an authoritative version in 1787, *Notes* turned out to be a thoroughgoing naturalist ethnography of Virginia. Amid this analysis, in "Query XIV," Jefferson claims that the poems of "Phyllis Whately [*sic*]" are "below the dignity of criticism." Equally relevant, the literature of Ignatius Sancho, a fellow black writer of Wheatley's generation, also lacks "reason and taste" and, "in the course of its vagaries, leaves a tract of thought as incoherent and eccentric as is the course of a meteor through the sky."[1]

Regarding this infamous criticism, scholars have long held that the racism of Jefferson mirrored the racism of the broader Western Enlightenment, a philosophical movement spanning both the American and European sides of the Atlantic, the former featuring the so-called Founding Fathers; the latter, Immanuel Kant and David Hume, among others. In *Notes*, Jefferson states his belief that the "race of Negroes brought from Africa" are naturally, or inherently, inferior and that the limited production and quality of their literature serves as evidence (77). Presumably, the subsequent nature of black-authored literature developed in response to Jefferson and his Enlightenment brethren. Henry Louis Gates Jr., one of the leading scholars on race and Jefferson, has recently said that "Jefferson's comments about the role of their literature in any meaningful assessment of the African American's civil rights became the strongest motivation for blacks to create a body of literature that would implicitly prove Jefferson wrong. This is [Phillis] Wheatley's, and Jefferson's, curious legacy in American literature." The response of blacks to Jefferson and the Enlightenment, Gates concludes, helped to determine the "political motive" of the African American literary tradition.[2]

Declaring the political origin of African American literature is tricky. The premise of Gates's conclusion arises intact from the first book he wrote on the subject and published in 1989, *Figures in Black: Words, Signs, and the "Racial" Self,* which, according to one of its book reviewers, Kenneth W. Warren, suffers from a paradox. In Gates's endeavor to derive a racially authentic literary theory, he condemns the social-science approaches, cultivated in the Black Studies era of the 1970s and early 1980s, neglecting the literariness of African American creative writing. Yet, as Gates treasures the *political* authenticity of African American authors from the eighteenth century until the present, he arguably treats their literature in similarly nonliterary ways. The notion of Wheatley's political motives, then, can be just as untenable as the methodological critique used to derive it.[3]

A second flaw shows that the political myth of literary origins is neither an isolated nor an old case. Even cutting-edge scholarship has floated this myth, which reduces the complexity of African American literary history to a scenario of cause and effect: to the idea that the "political motive" of Wheatley and early African American authors—"early," in the sense of those writing in the late eighteenth and early nineteenth centuries—reacted almost directly to the racism of Jefferson and his fellow Founding Fathers. The paradigm of causation—or the idea that racism spurred the formation of racial politics—has framed certain recent literary and political historiographies of race and slavery in early America. David Kazanjian, a literary scholar of this period, said, in a recent debate held on this topic in the journal *Early American Literature,* "the terms of this debate were poorly posed, caught as they were in a mechanical understanding of historical causality. It seems to me that slavery and race are usefully understood as coextensive formations feeding off of one another and requiring genealogical investigations of effects, rather than discrete entities functioning either as cause or [as] effect and requiring presumptively positivist searches for a singular origin."[4] Frances Smith Foster, another such scholar, has expressed more general reservations over the kinds of African American literary studies that have aimed to "offer a definitive or comprehensive survey of origins or of development." Often, these studies write or rewrite histories that "require facts or observations and conclusions that are then selected, organized, and emphasized."[5] The complementary points made by Kazanjian and Foster are clear. Whereas Kazanjian urges us to avoid the political historiography of race and slavery according to causation, Foster suggests further that this historiography has already conspired in a teleology that uses a political effect of race, such as the instituting of antebellum antislavery societies, to explain early American phenomena, such as African American print culture.

In this chapter, I examine a crucial but, for now, simple-sounding question implied by the diagnoses of Kazanjian and Foster: How do we assess the political value of literature written by Africans and their descendants in the New World? Before we can surmise that such literature was political insofar as it aimed to confront racism, before we can reach conclusions on the literature's political effects and success—before we can do any of these things, we should take a closer look at how the notions of *literature* and *politics* themselves resonated in debates held at the time. The debates, it turns out, featured white and black intellectuals alike—not simply authentically black political agents of social change—whose *politicizations* of early African American literature did not necessarily correspond to the scales of racism and radicalism, respectively. Rather, the politicizations meditated on the implications of literacy and intelligence for the ability of the African diaspora to govern itself and to represent itself as an official constituency with collective interests.

Early African American literature emerged at a time when culture and politics were almost one and the same in the written and social constitutions of government. Two close readings, one on Jefferson's *Notes* and the other on its 1829 critique, David Walker's *Appeal to the Coloured Citizens of the World, but in Particular, and Very Expressly, to Those of the United States of America,* support this claim. In *Notes,* Jefferson's dismissal of the ability of blacks to reason and imagine, and then to produce exceptional literature, was so reprehensible that, of course, subsequent generations of black writers sought to refute it. But Jefferson's hypothesis on black literary or intellectual inferiority was not what he wanted to prove ultimately. Still held today, the inference that blacks sought to refute the hypothesis through literature happens to misstate Jefferson's logic, which turned out to be just one among several corollaries in *Notes,* just one among several incidental steps toward proving that reason and imagination were prerequisite to the induction of any society into the early American polity. Jefferson's disparagement of Phillis Wheatley certainly interlocks with a broader critical tendency—evident in reviews of her 1773 book, *Poems on Various Subjects, Religious and Moral*—to view hers as merely "imitative" of the poetry written by whites. In a sense, the way that Wheatley's poetry was "slavish," or subservient to traditional literary forms, reaffirmed her legal subjectivity as a slave (because she was not manumitted until five years later). Subtended by the romantic notions of literary genius and originality, allegations of black imitativeness demonstrated, in the words of literary historian Eric Slauter, "the new language of cultural racism."[6] I spend less time on Jefferson's own literary racism—after all, he says very little about Wheatley and Sancho—than on its implied intercorrelations of genius, race, and political representation.

Walker recognized the trajectory of Jefferson's logic when other historians and writers of his time did not. My analysis of Walker's *Appeal* enables us to qualify a political genealogy of early African American literature. Better than any other black writer of his generation, Walker rebuts the cultural and political implications, as opposed to the premise, of Jefferson's condemnation of Wheatley. Representative examples of black intelligence accredit, rather than discredit, the case for black political enfranchisement. Moving beyond the prominent black commentary on Jefferson's fear of divine retribution for the nation's enslavement of blacks, Walker also incorporates the jeremiad into *Appeal* in order to achieve several rhetorical goals: to insulate his critique from theistic reprobation; to rebut authoritatively the religious ideologies that had underwritten slavery; and while citing *Notes* line by line, to identify the self-contradiction that Jefferson shares with those who advocate religious egalitarianism even as they withhold it from black slaves.

Walker attempts to debunk Jefferson's prescription of reason and imagination for political citizenship by taking advantage of his membership in an educated black elite whose broad grasp of Western history and whose access to the resources of print culture enhanced its authority in the public sphere. In fact, while critical of the racism of Enlightenment rationality, Walker nonetheless belonged to a broader American movement at the turn into the nineteenth century in which blacks (and whites, including Jefferson) were going as far back as the ancient, classical traditions of Greece and Rome to define a usable intellectual past and tailor it to fit current political agendas.[7] Written "in behalf of freedom," as put by African American abolitionist Henry Highland Garnet's preface to an 1848 edition, *Appeal* embodies intellection and assumes the format of four "articles" (or chapters) imitating what Kazanjian has rightly called "the very legal and governmental speech acts—such as the Declaration of Independence and the Constitution."[8] Walker rightly predicted that the impending political controversy surrounding *Appeal* would lead to a host of commercial challenges. The historical record of regional authorities trying to suppress *Appeal*'s circulation—which spanned Virginia, South Carolina, and Georgia—confirms Walker's prescience.[9] The supposed blasphemy lay in how Walker borrowed the very historical analogies of *Notes,* suggesting that blacks, if unshackled, could demonstrate the political potential whose existence Jefferson was so eager to deny. *Appeal* is singular as much for its precise refutation of Jefferson on this issue as for expressing Walker's own concession, ironically, that "ignorance" and "wretchedness" have stunted the political growth of blacks (32). Education can help blacks overcome these flaws.

The payoff of my comparative reading of Jefferson and Walker is twofold. First, we are poised to affirm a political genealogy of African American literature in which the doctrine of racial uplift, or the idea of elevating the African diaspora in intellectual and cultural ways, began prior to the 1865 emancipation of slaves. Racial uplift was not exclusively a phenomenon of the postemancipation nineteenth century, though its ideological entrenchment during this period set the terms of racial representation in African American literature for generations to come. Rather, this doctrine began in the preemancipation era and, for that matter, even before the antebellum era, in direct engagement with Founding conceptions of intellectual and political agency.[10] Second, we are poised to marry in a special way formal with informal realms of political action, such as action in law and government with action in intellectual culture. The longstanding oppositionality of racial politics versus racism in early American literary criticism mischaracterizes the contact between formal and informal politics as the solitary argument for proving that writing literature alone was enough for blacks to disprove white allegations of their intellectual inferiority. I recommend that we refrain from this simplified political view of early African American literature. When extracted from the teleological presumptions retrofitted from our contemporary time, the antonymic relationship between literary excellence and intellectual inferiority turns out to have emerged from a more complex genealogy of race and racism peculiar to early American political culture. Indeed, when David Ramsey, a white historian, wrote to Jefferson and lamented that *Notes* "depressed the negroes too low," we should couple these words with those of David Walker, who attempted, in 1829, to critique Jefferson's "depressing" disqualification of blacks from American emancipation and citizenship, not just from the canon of American literature.[11]

Toward a Political Genealogy of Race and Racism

Describing the political genealogy of early African American literature potentially opens the proverbial can of worms, if a 2006 roundtable published in *Early American Literature,* mentioned earlier, is any indication. Entitled

"Historicizing Race in Early American Studies" and featuring the eminent scholars Joanna Brooks, Philip Gould, and David Kazanjian, the roundtable reveals the fault lines of disagreement on how to historicize the construction of race and how to historicize the politics of race.[12] The journal's current editor, Sandra M. Gustafson, invites the roundtable scholars "to think about the theoretical implications of their work for an understanding of 'race' in the early period."[13] In response, the scholars outline their methodologies of race and literary history by reciting and elaborating the arguments of their books, all published in 2003: Brooks's *American Lazarus: Religion and the Rise of African American and Native American Literatures,* Gould's *Barbaric Traffic: Commerce and Antislavery in the Eighteenth-Century Atlantic World,* and Kazanjian's *The Colonizing Trick: National Culture and Imperial Citizenship in Early America.*

To begin with, Brooks argues that the philosophical and practical impact of race on oppressed groups was quite evident. The very racial "concepts of 'Blackness' and 'Indianness' were essentially Euro-American inventions imposed upon people of color of various African and indigenous American ethnic affiliations to advance the economic and political dominance of whites." Gould does not necessarily underplay this racial impact, but he does suggest that the meaning of race itself demonstrates a "far greater elasticity" than what Brooks permits. Interpreting "race in context of the historical formations of sentimentalism and capitalism," Gould considers the mutual influence of transnational and transgeneric literatures alongside "ideologies of race that are themselves unstable."[14] Above all, the studies of Brooks and Gould proceed from different assumptions about the ideological construction and material tractability of race in early America. (Implicit in Kazanjian's words on the debate, which I quoted earlier, he stands somewhere between these two positions.)

Measuring the tractability of race leads to a submerged, though no less important, disagreement between Brooks and Gould on the criteria by which we should assemble a literary archive of early America. Should we examine the lives and literatures of the alleged perpetrators of racial discrimination, or those of the alleged victims, in order to historicize the meaning of race? What is at stake in studying white imaginations of race as opposed to black experiences of racism? Gould rightly points out that cataloging the archive merely in these terms neglects the ideological current of racism through the minds and actions of both whites and blacks. Yet Brooks also correctly asserts that reducing racism to merely an ideology threatens to ignore its actual devastation of minority groups.

Despite Brooks's and Gould's different approaches to historicizing race, they agree that the racial paradigm of human difference stood at the center of how the authors and subjects of primary texts negotiated, accumulated, and allocated political power in the early republic. Gould senses this agreement when he asks, "What does it mean, for example, to say that [Phillis] Wheatley is 'free'? Or that she emancipates herself *as* a writer? The field is still in the process of engaging such questions. I would argue, as I think Brooks does, that addressing such questions necessitates thinking through the different registers on which the very terms 'liberty' and 'slavery' signified."[15] We must also study how early American literature served as the site of such thought, in which race, nature, slavery, politics, emancipation, liberty, and citizenship are defined in their contemporary terms, not retrofitted from our own.[16] If we accept this precaution, how do we establish the political genealogy of early African American literature?

First, we should examine the way in which the political genealogy of race and racism underwrote in early America the fundamental relationship between intellectual culture and political representation. By "fundamental," I do not simply mean in the basic sense that examples of intellectual culture, such as literature, motivated the political action of its readers or that such action necessarily inspired writers to engrave certain forms and themes in the literature. Rather, I mean that intellectual culture and political representation were so inextricably interwoven in early America that defining one without the other was nearly impossible. In a recent study of the cultural origins of the U.S. Constitution, to which I have already referred a couple times, Eric Slauter proves that during the eighteenth century, there was a "shifting desire to see politics as an effect of culture and culture as an effect of politics," a view in which "a science of politics . . . took as a central tenet that the empirical manners, customs, taste and genius—in a word, what I have called the 'culture'—of a people must be taken into account in determining what constituted the most 'natural' government for that people."[17] The culture of a people was crucial to deciding the governmental formations that they served and that, in turn, served them. The Constitution, prima facie a historical documentation and ongoing revision of the laws and governmental apparatuses of the United States, recorded the cultural identity of a people. In the early versions of the Constitution, people were grappling with the mission of this document as well as with such corollary issues as aesthetics and intellect, race and representation, slavery and natural science, the secular and the divine. Based on this premise that cultural expressions and exchanges communicated crucial political information in the early national period, I am now prepared to argue, more precisely, that early American narratives about African American literature in particular pivoted on the perceived aesthetic and intellectual failings of a handful of blacks, but only to the extent that these failings allegedly portended the incapability of this elite class to represent itself, much less its race, in the realm of formal government.

Second, we must take a closer look at what it meant for early white and black American intellectuals to politicize African American literature. The politicization occurred regardless of the author's race, intent, and choice of literary forms and themes. Phillis Wheatley, Francis Williams, Lucy Terry, Jupiter Hammon, Lemuel Haynes, and George Moses Horton petitioned for racial equality both in their social activism on slavery and constitutional higher law and in their individual demonstrations of literary excellence.[18] Pamphlets were a flexible literary technology—which historians Richard Newman, Patrick Rael, and Philip Lapsansky have called "something between a broadside and a book"—that African Americans used to deliver a range of public statements, in a host of literary and rhetorical forms, and on a range of subjects. Thus, we should not restrict the authorship and texts of this genre merely to the term "pamphlets of protest," although the term does describe a substantial number of the texts of early African American print culture.[19] The pamphleteers were not always or necessarily focused on race and politics. As Frances Smith Foster stresses, "these people of African descent were concerned about slavery and the slave trade, but these were not their only, nor always their primary, issues. They also worked to communicate physical and metaphysical realities and to develop their moral, spiritual, intellectual, and artistic selves. They wrote about civil rights, economic enhancement, love, and marriage," among many, many other things.[20] In sum, the racial identity of authorship was not always a reliable predictor of the political nature of early African American literature. Nor were the literary intentions and productions always reliable indicators of it. A consequence of our modern-day retrospection, the taxonomic insecurity of these political definitions deserves a deeper investigation into why contemporaneous readers regarded early African American literature as "political" in the first place.

The roundtable discussion in *Early American Literature* shows the political stakes in portraying the era's intellectual readers as an interracial community. But how do we compare and contrast white readers and black readers without getting stuck, in Gould's words, in "the traditional critical binary between hegemony and subversion"? How do we do so also without forgetting, in Brooks's words, that "people of color in early America recognized their common experiences and conditions and, consequently, reclaimed racial categories as a basis for collective identification and action toward emancipation"?[21] To some degree, the interracial antagonism was unavoidable. Dating back to the debate between "Rusticus" and "Africanus" on the natural order of race and the legitimacy of slavery in the March and April 1790 issues of the *United States Gazette*, white and black writers more likely jockeyed against each other, rather than within their respective racial groups, to make their voices heard in the literary press.[22] The historical record further confirms that the slave trade, slavery, and systemic racism had a deleterious impact in the New World, especially on Africans and African Americans whose literary productions were likely to accrue political value despite their intentions or contentions. Yet and still, to repeat an earlier point, the racial identities of these authors did not predict their relationships to racism. Even in *Notes*, Jefferson himself equivocates on the maintenance of slavery, and in *Appeal*, Walker does the same on the subject of racial uplift. The occasional ambiguity of their writings undermines the notion that the literate African American community, Walker included, was perfectly resolute in understanding and expressing uplift or that the Anglo-American community, Jefferson included, was equally resolute in condemning it.

Recent scholarship on Jefferson and Walker has begun moving us toward grasping the political complexity of early African American literature. Regarding Jefferson, Jordan Stein, a literary scholar, has noted that Harriet Beecher Stowe, in her 1857 preface to Frank J. Webb's novel *The Garies and Their Friends*, poses a question that echoes Jefferson's thesis in *Notes*: "Are the race at present held as slaves capable of freedom, self-government and progress?" Stowe's connection of "freedom and *self*-government" was a preemancipation principle for uplifting and instilling political agency in blacks.[23] The literary historian John Ernest has also noted that certain black authors realized the gravity of Jefferson's political, not merely his literary, claims. *Notes* was "nearly as important as the Declaration of Independence," of which Jefferson happened to be a principal author in 1776.[24] Remarkably, *Notes* seeks to deny the political agency of blacks, even as the Declaration of Independence declares it for the new republic as a whole. Black writers, understandably, could not allow Jefferson's hypocrisy to go unrequited. Finally, Frank Shuffelton, a Jefferson specialist, has added that *Notes* was a byproduct of "an invisible, informal learned society of [Jefferson's] own devising, one that answered his needs for both information and friendship" as he circulated the manuscript for peer review.[25] The book encapsulates Jefferson's own thinking, sensibilities, and anxieties, to be sure, but also a worldview of racial politics peculiar to his intellectual circle.

Although a host of scholars have written on Jefferson and race, few have written both at length and critically on Jefferson's interpretation of early African American literature.[26] Just as few have written in such a way on David Walker, and even fewer on Walker's critique of Jefferson.[27] One explanation for the latter fact is the longstanding appreciation of the generic and historical meanings of *Appeal,* not so much its palpable antagonism toward one man. First, *Appeal* participates in an early pamphleteering tradition—including Richard Allen and Absalom Jones's 1794 "A Narrative of the Proceedings of the Black People during the Late Awful Calamity in Philadelphia," Daniel Coker's 1810 "Dialogue between a Virginian and an African Minister," James Forten's 1813 "Series of Letters by a Man of Colour," and Prince Saunders's 1818 "An Address before the Pennsylvania Augustine Society"—that spoke equally well to white and black constituencies.[28] Second, *Appeal* demarcates the historical threshold between two eras. It arrives at the conclusion of an early national period, when the minds of black authors still tilted toward questions about the Founding Fathers, yet also at the inception of an antebellum period, invigorating black abolitionists with invectives of racial nationalism, inspiring them to oppose the rising American Colonization Society, and broadening the rhetorical possibilities of the pamphlet form as slavery became increasingly untenable for the nation.

The historical dimensions of *Appeal,* moreover, should not distract us from the clarity of Walker's focus on Jefferson. Although quite thin (comprising about thirty thousand words, spread over a preamble and four articles), the pamphlet cites Jefferson about twenty times explicitly (such as by name, in reference to *Notes,* and through quotations) and implicitly (such as in reference to Jefferson's colleagues). The early articles of *Appeal,* constituting about one-quarter of the book's entire length, speak to Jefferson most directly, with a rhetorical assault by turns relentless, unequivocal, and vitriolic, perhaps the hallmarks of revolutionary or insurrectionist rhetoric ever since. Yet the most sustained and influential study of Walker, published by Peter P. Hinks in 1996, exemplifies how one can spend too much time overemphasizing Jefferson's arguments for black inferiority without detailing adequately their political insinuations.[29] We should borrow a page from Walker, whose refutation of black inferiority per se was the least of his concerns in 1829. After all, he already embodied the refutation. More salient was his critique of the cultural and political implications of Jefferson's racially derogatory calculus of black genius in *Notes.* For Walker, *Notes* was one of the "writings for the world" in which Jefferson's "assertions," unless checked, hardly "will pass away into oblivion unobserved by this people and the world" (*Appeal,* 26). Walker's rebuttal of the political disqualification of African Americans calibrated black revolutionary lexicon with a constructive criticism of *Notes*'s limitations.

My connection of Jefferson's *Notes* to Walker's *Appeal* might seem a perpetuation of what has been roundly denounced—routing a political discussion of the African American literary tradition through the antebellum period of the 1830s and 1840s. For a long time, abolitionism and the slave narrative have both preoccupied scholars, whereas only recently have we reckoned with the transatlantic trope of the "genius in bondage," including writers of African descent who were writing in English yet not necessarily affiliated with American abolitionism. Any ascription of the term "African American" to this trope thus should proceed carefully, for it verges on a methodological failure to account accurately for the British or larger Anglophone contexts within which Wheatley, Sancho, Olaudah Equiano, and other writers of their generation came to be "black."[30] Nonetheless, as we shall now see, Jefferson's disparagement of Wheatley and Sancho does raise primarily *American* questions about the politics of racial representation, and it does warrant a closer look at how antebellum authors, such as Walker, were some of the first in line to address the questions squarely.

"Proofs of Genius": Thomas Jefferson's Notes on the State of Virginia

As mentioned in this book's introduction, the politics of racial representation signifies, among other things, the expression, negotiation, and distribution of power according to both formal and informal types of politics. Literary scholar Matthew Cordova Frankel comes closest to engaging this idea in the context of early America: "Jefferson's racialist speculations, most particularly his extended disquisitions on the 'lesser beauty' and depreciated imaginative capacities of African slaves, shape his understanding of the freed slave's representative potential. In full light of his racial theories, Jefferson's appraisal of the restricted aesthetic products of African labor amplifies the perceived limitations of the slave's incorporation into the state."[31] Whereas the Declaration of Independence argues for the "right" of American citizens to independence, *Notes* argues whether they have the "capacity" to exercise it, and whether they could become a "representative citizen" capable of reconciling the paradox of "standing apart from his constituents by virtue of any direct legislation yet capable of embodying in his imagination a harmonized population."[32]

Jefferson's racial speculations used "sublime" iconography of the representative white citizen who was negotiating and overcoming the New World wilderness. Also useful was the prevailing iconography of the blighted black subject who was far less than ideal and who was by no means a national representative. Theories of natural and social law at the time were denying slaves representative citizenship. Slaves were being disregarded as inferior to other races, for the prevailing laws and letters dislocated them (as well as ex-slaves alike) from the new republic. To be fair, Jefferson does say in *Notes* that slavery is a "blot in our country" and, in an optimistic tone, that republican laws have been drafted considering "the perpetual prohibition of the importation of slaves." This law "will, in some measure, stop the increase of this great political and moral evil, while the minds of our citizens may be ripening for a complete emancipation of human nature" (94). Yet he does conclude that, until that prohibition comes to pass, blacks do not have the capacity for formal political representation and governance in the New World. Literature is one proof of that.

Jefferson initiates this argument in *Notes* when he contrasts the environments and inhabitants of America from those of Europe, a rhetorical maneuver patriotic during the Revolution, which lasted from about 1775 to 1783. "Query VI," though subtitled "a notice of the mines and other subterraneous riches, its trees, plants, fruits, &c," stratifies and describes the human races, while combining the methodologies of natural science and social science, such as physiology (or the study of human features, activities, and development) and sociology (or the study of these issues along with social institutions and relations) (28). A "proud theory" encourages Jefferson's analysis of "the Man of America, both aboriginal and emigrant," particularly the differences between and among Anglo-American whites and such racial minorities as Indians and Negroes, or what we now take to be Native Americans and African Americans (71). Reading the faculties of the "Man of America" in terms of the natural sciences intrigues Jefferson:

How has this "combination of the elements and other physical causes" [such as inhospitable weather and precipitation] . . . been arrested and suspended, so as to permit the human body to acquire its just dimensions, and by what inconceivable process has their action been directed on his mind alone? To judge of the truth of this, to form a just estimate of their genius and mental powers, more facts are wanting, and great allowance to be made for those circumstances of their situation which call for a display of particular talents only. (66)

Jefferson's "proud theory" of American nationalism inspires the revisionist attempt, coordinated by him and some of his peers, to rescue the flagging intellectual reputation of Anglo-American Virginians in the late eighteenth century.[33] To raise the profile of these Virginians, he observes their competition and defines them in racial terms: the minority population of Native Americans and African Americans. Eyewitness accounts and scholarly research led him to conclude that Virginia's Native Americans are equal to whites, except for a couple stereotypical differences: the "Indian man," due to a general lack of "habituat[ion] to labor," has small hands and wrists (65). Social idiosyncrasies peculiar to the "Indian man" also result from unique native origins (and, by inference, from his response to an invading British empire). In much the same way that the Native American "is neither more defective in ardor . . . than the white reduced to the same diet and exercise, . . . his vivacity and activity of mind is equal to ours in the same situation" (63, 64). But Jefferson goes on to admonish, "Before we condemn the Indians of this continent as wanting genius, we must consider that letters have not yet been introduced among them" (68). Jefferson indicts the cultural environment and historical circumstances for the appreciable limitations of Native Americans, even as he implies that this group has evolved to be fundamentally inferior to whites.

Jefferson does not excuse the limitations of African Americans.[34] Again, as a natural-cum-social scientist, he speculates on and stereotypes their physical and behavioral tendencies: "Negroes have notoriously less hair than the whites; yet they are more ardent" (66). As a consequence of their ancestry or heredity, blacks are inherently inferior to whites, according to "Query XIV," a chapter on "the administration of justice and description of the laws" in America (137). Resuming his typology of blacks, Jefferson notes "the real distinctions which nature has made" among strange physical features (145). From exteriority to interiority is his next rhetorical shift, a transition that distinguishes Notes from the mostly climatological explanation of racial difference propounded by his era's French naturalists, including Georges Louis Leclerc, Comte de Buffon, author of the influential multi-volume book Natural History (published between 1749 and 1778) to which Jefferson responds directly.[35] Typology, again, becomes the sine qua non of Jefferson's discrediting of black intellect. "Comparing them by their faculties of memory, reason, and imagination, it appears to me that in memory they are equal to the whites; in reason much inferior, as I think one could scarcely be found capable of tracing and comprehending the investigations of Euclid; and that in imagination they are dull, tasteless, and anomalous" (146). Black intellect is rudimentary in two respects: it has the capabilities merely to detect the environment—"their existence appears to participate more in sensation than reflection"—and store the information gleaned from it (146). In any case, blacks lack the sophistication to generate and synthesize information, much less comprehend the abstract, philosophical writings of Euclid, the Greek mathematician. Several pages later in "Query XIV," Jefferson is blunter still: blacks are "inferior in the faculties of reason and imagination" and "inferior to the whites in the endowments of both body and mind" (150–51).

The thread of argument on black inferiority traces back eight chapters, to "Query VI," in which Jefferson's transatlantic comparison of the so-called Old World and the New World draws natural and social as well as intellectual differences between the inhabitants of the two continents. The "Indians" of America, as mentioned earlier, are "wanting genius," for "letters have not yet been introduced to them" (68). But he then adopts a historical analogy, about how the societies north of the European Alps, due to the influx of "Roman arms and arts," were "swarming with numbers." One should surmise that as "numbers produce emulation," they "multiply the chances of improvement, and one improvement begets another" (68). Jefferson also states his belief that, aside from his era's preeminent English mathematician, Isaac Newton, born in Lincolnshire's Woolsthorpe-by-Colsterworth, the region north of the Alps has produced few, if any, "good poets," "able mathematicians," or "great inventors in arts or sciences" (68). Social circumstances, in other words, do not always explain the development of a civilization, or the traits and tendencies of those within it.

By the same token, just as the Alps have not noticeably distinguished the cultures of certain European populations, Nature is not "a Cis or Trans-Atlantic partisan," as implied by Buffon in *Natural History*. In rebutting Buffon, Jefferson becomes as much an emblem of American intellectual patriotism as, ironically, the Frenchman-turned-American St. Jean de Crèvecoeur (or John Hector St. John). Jefferson affirms the prestige of his national culture in the double face of Europe's condescension and, consequently, America's potential lack of self-esteem. French naturalism deserves scrutiny for applying "this new theory of the tendency of nature to belittle her productions on this side of the Atlantic" (69). The infancy of American civilization means that the nation has a long way to go before it can become truly competitive in the arts and humanities, although, aside from England, no European nation can genuinely claim an elite intellectual history.

The natural, social, and intellectual stages of Jefferson's transatlantic argument anticipate his ultimate tethering of "genius" to "action":

As in philosophy and war, so in government, in oratory, in painting, in the plastic art, we might show that America, though but a child of yesterday, has already given hopeful *proofs of genius*, as well of the nobler kinds, which arouse the best feelings of man, which call him into action, which substantiate his freedom, and conduct him to happiness, as of the subordinate, which serve to amuse him only. We therefore suppose that this reproach is as unjust as it is unkind; and that of the geniuses which adorn the present age, America contributes its full share. (70; italics mine)

The "noble" forms of genius accumulate political prestige when they call "man" "into action," "substantiate his freedom," and "conduct him to happiness." The term *political*, as I use it, overlaps with the previous language coauthored by Jefferson in 1776, when the (Thirteen United States) Declaration of Independence was ratified. At the outset, the document asserts that "it becomes necessary for one people to dissolve the political bonds which have connected them with another" and "that all men are created equal, that they are endowed by their Creator with certain unalienable Rights, that among these are Life, Liberty and the pursuit of Happiness."[36] If we take the "Creator" in the Declaration of Independence to be equivalent to "Nature" in *Notes*, we see that Jefferson is deriving a multilayered caveat of human inequality—at once natural and racial, and *therefore* intellectual and political—applying to blacks.

In "Query XIV," Jefferson elaborates the caveat of racial inequality in legal and political terms. In his discussion of the Report of the Revisors, which intended to revise Virginia's laws, he admits that slaves are treated as property, "distributable among the next of kin, as other moveables" (144).[37] But Jefferson mentions a "proposition" or "amendment" "prepared, to be offered to the Legislature whenever the bill should be taken up": the newborn slaves "should continue with their parents to a certain age, then be brought up, at the public expense, to tillage, arts or sciences, according to their geniuses, till the females should be eighteen, and the males twenty-one years of age, when they should be colonized" and sent away to a "proper" place, and when they should be declared "a free and independent people" (144–45). Jefferson was one of the founders of this political theory of colonizing blacks, and his discourse laid the seeds by a few decades for the establishment, in 1816, of the American Colonization Society, among other organizations, to repatriate blacks to the African colony of Liberia. The ACS sought to avert further social conflict between blacks and whites in America, to encourage Christian missionary activity in Africa, and to profit from the global capitalism that an American presence in the region could facilitate.[38] But the recolonized slaves never were free and independent, in the analogous way that the white citizens of the thirteen American colonies never were until the American Revolutionary War. (The race of the European colonists empowered them, of course, to seize their independence when the time arrived.) Shorn of the religious and capitalist rhetoric, Jefferson's argument in *Notes* for black emancipation without political enfranchisement promotes racial separatism, with a trembling eye toward preserving civic peace despite the resentment of the slave, who "may not as justifiably take a little from one who has taken all from him, as he may slay one who would slay him?" (150).

Ironically, Jefferson condones the recolonization and upbringing elsewhere of newborn slaves in the "arts or sciences, according to their geniuses," but refuses to imagine this prospect on American soil. The political presence of blacks is too problematic:

> [D]eep-rooted prejudices entertained by the whites; ten thousand recollections by the blacks of the injuries they have sustained; new provocations; the real distinctions which nature has made; and many other circumstances, will divide us into parties, and produce convulsions, which will probably never end but in the extermination of the one or the other race. To these objections, which are political, may be added others, which are physical and moral. (145)

Jefferson explains the "physical and moral" traits of blacks in "Query VI," but only as a prerequisite to the corollary thesis mentioned earlier, that they are capable of only the retention of information, not reason and imagination. As Frankel puts it, "Jefferson's picture of the black imagination not only depicts the slave as outside the bounds of political consensus but also as essentially lacking the cognitive rudiments through which consensus might be attained."[39] Stated in passing and as a matter of fact, Jefferson's denigration of the literature of New World Africans becomes all the more devastating when seen as but a stepping stone toward a denigration of their political potential. Blacks who were writing literature when *Notes* was being circulated far and wide had to deal with its profane declaration that they have produced not one literary work promising their intellectual equality with whites.

Coming from a Founding Father, Jefferson's condescension toward blacks must have been a specter. Perhaps the specter was as haunting as that of English intellectuals, who looked down on colonial America, roiled Jefferson, and inspired the defensive rhetoric of *Notes*. Blacks could be downgraded not just below whites but also below Native Americans, who could "astonish you with strokes of the most sublime oratory; such as prove their reason and sentiment strong, their imagination glowing and elevated." In contrast, Jefferson insists, "never yet could I find that a black had uttered a thought above the level of plain narration" (147), again conjuring the idea of rudimentary storage, processing, and regurgitation of information. Despite blacks' experiences as slaves, their failed attempts at producing poetry (in the elite sense) confounded Jefferson even more. "Misery is often the parent of the most affecting touches in poetry. Among the blacks is misery enough, God knows, but no poetry" (147). Curiously, the subsequent disclaimer about Phillis Wheatley and Ignatius Sancho, which I have already discussed at the outset, shows Jefferson trying to don the hat of literary criticism atop those of the natural and social sciences. Jefferson's detour through black-authored literature reinforces the previous "European Alps" claim: the cultural environment is not more reliable than racial blood in predicting human superiority or inferiority. Blood predicts the "natural" incapabilities of slaves, just as it had predicted the natural capability of Roman slaves (a "race of whites") to uplift themselves in the arts and sciences, despite their own downtrodden political status (150).[40]

In the decades after Jefferson published *Notes,* his opinions on the intellectual and political capabilities of African Americans varied, but they remained relatively consistent in their correlation of true genius with Anglo-Saxon ancestry. In an August 31, 1791, letter to Benjamin Banneker, an African American mathematician, Jefferson's tone shifts from the earlier tone of his 1787 analogy of Roman slaves, which implies that inherited "nature," not so much environmental "condition," had "produced the distinction" of artistic and scientific intelligence (*Notes,* 149). In the letter, Jefferson sounds more hopeful:

Nobody wishes more than I do to see such proofs as you exhibit, that nature has given to our black brethren talents equal to those of the other colors of men, and that the appearance of want of them is owing only to the degraded condition of their existence both in Africa and America. I can add, with truth, that no one wishes more ardently to see a good system commenced for raising the condition, both of their body and mind, to what it ought to be, as fast as the imbecility of their present existence, and other circumstances which cannot be neglected, will admit.[41]

Over time, the kind of resignation expressed in *Notes* tempers Jefferson's hope that "the degraded condition" could be an isolated factor. In his August 25, 1814, letter to a fellow Virginian who sympathized with the plight of slaves, Jefferson declares that African Americans are "as incapable as children of taking care of themselves," much less governing and representing themselves in the political world.[42] A decade and a half later, when David Walker released a pamphlet attacking *Notes*, he was targeting such ongoing racial myths to which Jefferson clung.

"To Refute Mr. Jefferson's Arguments Respecting Us": *David Walker's* Appeal to the Coloured Citizens of the World

David Walker is arguably the first black author to critique *Notes* in Jefferson's own terms. He calls on "those who know and feel, that we [blacks] are MEN as well as other people; to them I say, that unless we try to refute Mr. Jefferson's arguments respecting us, we will only establish them." After all, "Mr. Jefferson was one of as great characters as ever lived among the whites" (*Appeal,* 26). By focusing on Walker's response to Jefferson, I am not saying, as historian Bruce Dain may be implying about a recent scholarly trend, that "refuting *Notes* [was] the starting point of African American race writing." After all, even Dain himself recalls that quite the opposite occurred, that "Jefferson in effect was reacting to a Phillis Wheatley, to her very existence and her accomplishments, however much he denigrated them."[43] Instead, I am saying, first, that *Notes* was one of the first intellectual documents that defined in both racial and political terms the writings of African Americans and, second, that Walker played a groundbreaking role in interpreting the broader meaning of Jefferson's political statements on racial representation.

Walker begins to dismantle Jefferson's political logic by identifying the racial discrimination of Christianity that inspired many whites to support slavery. The Protestant wing of the African American Press, whose coordination of pamphlets and broadsides, printers and distributors, alongside reading societies and churches, fused religious and political discourses on race relations, categorizes Walker's mode of critique.[44] The role that Christian theology played in white intellectual and political rationales for slavery or colonization indeed deserved indictment. Racial hierarchy and paternalism descended especially from Christianity to organize social relations between masters and slaves and to implant the ethos of industry and obligation in slave communities. Proslavery advocates, with assistance from their biased exegeses of the Holy Bible, justified the peculiar institution as natural and consistent with the social structure and industry espoused in free society. Walker combated the overall mission of proslavery advocates.[45]

On his way toward reprimanding Jefferson for writing *Notes,* Walker questions the racist ways in which proslavery advocates manipulated scripture. The third article of *Appeal,* "Our Wretchedness in Consequence of the Preachers of the Religion of Jesus Christ," declares that "pure and undefiled religion, such as was preached by Jesus Christ and his apostles, is hard to be found in all the earth." Showing here an evidently racial explanation of religion, he blames "Europeans in Europe" for being in "violation" of the sinless preachers, and "American ministers" for sending puritanical missionaries to Africa to "convert the heathens." In America, the ministers deserve further blame for "keep[ing] us and our children sunk at their feet in the most abject ignorance and wretchedness that ever a people was afflicted with since the world began" (47–49). The racial hypocrisy of the Old and New Worlds, as Walker sees it, recurs in the way many whites selected certain parts of the Bible to support slavery. In multiple footnotes, Walker refers to the books in the Bible—such as to Revelations, the last and most apocalyptic book—amid a series of homiletic calls for whites to repent for their racial sins. In doing so, he advances the black intellectual tradition of exploiting the fears of Jefferson and other anxious whites of national doomsday.

The authority of directly referring to or quoting from the Bible is very important to Walker's criticism of Christian proslavery advocacy in *Appeal.* The preamble addresses his *"dearly beloved Brethren and Fellow Citizens,"* assures them that the absolute truth inspiring him is impervious to detraction, and accuses his critics of bias: "against all accusations which may or can be preferred against me, I appeal to heaven for my motive in writing," not to those who have mischaracterized biblical scripture (12). Walker goes on to describe himself as the embodiment of truth, motivated alternately by individualism, patriotism, and religion: "The sources from which our miseries are derived and on which I shall comment, I shall not combine in one, but shall put them under distinct heads and expose them in their turn; in doing which, keeping truth on my side, and not departing from the strictest rules of morality, I shall endeavor to penetrate, search out, and lay them open for your inspection. If you cannot or will not profit by them, I shall have done *my* duty to you, my country and my God" (13). In putting "truth on [his] side," Walker draws a moral line between himself and those he represents, on one side, and presumably those whom he calls his "enemies," on another (22, 71, 72). The ethical stance substantiates the observation of Ian Finseth, a literary scholar, that Walker consistently "substitutes morality for intellect as the criterion of natural superiority," while arguing that the historical impropriety of whites invalidates Jefferson's acclaim of their intellectual superiority in *Notes*.[46]

The rhetorical turn of *Appeal* to higher law reflects what literary scholar Willie J. Harrell Jr. calls a core feature of the jeremiad, another genre of the Afro-Protestant Press, which turned out to be "the first literary development of African-American writers in antebellum America."[47] Again, the scholarly discourse of literary origins is debatable, but the jeremiad does enfold progressive theology within antislavery political critique. The jeremiad is both galvanizing as well as apocalyptic, both "the call to consciousness and action" and "engaged in gradually elevating Blacks and forging within them a collective awareness of their destiny."[48] Whereas postemancipation African American literature complicates and even downplays the revolutionary dimension of racial "elevation" or uplift, Walker's *Appeal*, at the threshold between the early and the antebellum eras, capitalizes on revolutionary discourse to spur abolitionism. Walker refuses to leaven his harsh moral criticism of Jefferson, even though that Founding Father's genuine fear of divine retribution for American slavery convinced William Hamilton and William J. Watkins, two renowned African American orators, to soften theirs. Sharpening Walker's criticism of Jefferson's *Notes*, theology cooperated with, if not served, political action in secular American culture.[49] For this reason, *Appeal* targets as racist bedfellows both back-to-Africa colonizationists (his contemporary foes) and Jefferson (his historical foe).

Early in *Appeal*—such as in the first article, "Our Wretchedness in Consequence of Slavery"—Walker's supplication attends to Jefferson's conclusion that blacks are inferior to whites. Recall that, in Jefferson's eyes, although the environment has constrained African Americans at least as much as it has Native Americans, that excuse is negligible. Walker picks up on this discrepancy in racial treatment:

> Have [whites] not, after having reduced us to the deplorable condition of slaves under their feet, held us up as descending originally from the tribes of *Monkeys* or *Orang-Outangs*? O! my God! I appeal to every man of feeling—is this not insupportable? Is it not heaping the most gross insult upon our miseries, because they have got us under their feet and we cannot help ourselves? Oh! pity us we pray thee, Lord Jesus, Master.—Has Mr. Jefferson declared to the world, that we are inferior to the whites, both in the endowments of our bodies and of minds? It is indeed surprising, that a man of such great learning, combined with such excellent natural parts, should speak so of a set of men in chains. (20)

A few pages later, Walker follows up on this point by connecting Jefferson's degradation of blacks to his naturalist theory of racial genius. He recites the very lines in "Query XIV" of *Notes,* quoted earlier, in which Jefferson claims that the slaves of the Romans "were often their rarest artists. They excelled too in science, insomuch as to be usually employed as tutors to their master's [sic] children. . . . [B]ut they were the race of whites. It is not their *condition* then, but *nature,* which has produced the distinction" (*Appeal,* 26; Walker's italics; quoting *Notes,* 149).

Jefferson's sentences—or, more precisely, Walker's own quotation of them— are significant for at least three reasons. First, as I have already pointed out, a contradiction arises between the Roman analogy with its implied dismissal of environmental influence and Jefferson's discouragement elsewhere in *Notes* of a similar "condemnation" of Native Americans for their inferior status is a consequence of their deprivation of "letters"(68). Second, Walker's quotation of these lines is part of a larger revisionist historiography in *Appeal,* one that shifts the genealogical prestige of civilization from the Romans and Greeks to the Egyptians, from the white race of Europe to the black race of Africa. Third, and most relevant to my argument, Jefferson's racial stratifications along naturalist axes compelled Walker and other African American writers to react in writing. The concern determined, once again in Finseth's words, "the ways in which antislavery representations of the relationship between racial and national history drew upon scientific and quasi-scientific concepts of human and nonhuman 'nature.'"[50] Though less scientific than James McCune Smith, a contemporary African American intellectual and abolitionist, Walker still derives a remarkable kind of racial representation (or what Finseth calls "blackness") focused on "a reallocation of political and economic resources—that is, to bring about true freedom."[51]

Walker attacks Jefferson's deduction that reason and imagination should be political preconditions of representative citizenship. True, the second article of *Appeal,* "Our Wretchedness in Consequence of Ignorance," grants Jefferson's hypothesis that the highest standards of reason and imagination are rare among blacks. Yet this concession does not negate Walker's moral celebration of blacks for inspiring the nation's political reform, despite their enslavement. Incredulous over Jefferson's audacity, Walker once again quotes lines from "Query XIV" of *Notes,* such as the statements that blacks are "inferior in the faculties of reason and imagination" and "inferior to the whites in the endowments of both body and mind." This "unfortunate difference of colour," Jefferson goes on to say, "and perhaps of faculty, is a powerful obstacle to the emancipation of these people" (150–51). *Appeal* rebuts this point by countering the Roman history that Jefferson uses and by proposing that slaves, once unfettered, could ascend in political stature:

Every body who has read history knows, that as soon as a slave among the Romans obtained his freedom, he could rise to the greatest eminence in the State, and there was no law instituted to hinder a slave from buying his freedom. Have not the Americans instituted laws to hinder us from obtaining our freedom? Do any deny this charge? Read the laws of Virginia, North Carolina, &c. Further: have not the Americans instituted laws to prohibit a man of colour from obtaining and holding any office whatever, under the government of the United States of America? Now, Mr. Jefferson tells us that our condition is not so hard, as the slaves were under the Romans!!!! (27)

Walker's revisionist historiography—or his rewriting of Jefferson's history of the Roman slave in *Notes*—exposes the collusion of informal and formal laws in early America's racial politics. The publication of *Appeal* coincides with the Northern inception of black abolitionism, which realized that, in the words of historian Tunde Adeleke, "though slavery had become sectional, racism was national."[52] However conflicted the black abolitionist movement may have been between pacifism and antagonism, it recognized the need to confront racial oppression in both legal and illegal forms, in both institutional and ideological contexts, all of which demanded considerations of nonviolent racial uplift more so than the tactic of violence rationalized by the insurrectionism of John Brown, a white radical abolitionist who led the unsuccessful 1859 raid on Harpers Ferry, Virginia, to liberate the town's slaves; Henry Highland Garnet, a black clergyman; Nat Turner, the slave who led the miraculous 1831 slave revolt in Southampton County, Virginia; and even Walker himself.

Pacifism, it was true, gave way to antagonism in desperate times. Even one of the most diplomatic statesmen of his generation admitted in his third autobiography, published first in 1881, *The Life and Times of Frederick Douglass,* that when all else failed politically he became more open-minded to Brown's ethos and, later, more resigned to the Civil War's calamitous resolution of slavery.[53] In *Appeal,* Walker likewise claims that blacks, after years of slavery, now "glory in death" and that "as Mr. Jefferson wisely said, [whites] have never *found us out*—they do not know, indeed, that there is an unconquerable disposition in the breasts of blacks, which when it is fully awakened and put in motion, will be subdued, only with the destruction of the animal existence." In short, "kill or be killed," in two senses: inflict or suffer harm, sacrifice others or the self, instead of enduring slavery any further (36–37; italics in the original).

Referring to Jefferson in revolutionary rhetoric indicates the depth of Walker's deliberation over not only the role *Notes* played in the violent mythology of blacks but also the critical method he must use in *Appeal* to counteract it. The sarcasm in Walker's cross-examination of Jefferson's problematic reasoning enables him, as an activist, to taunt the Founding Father and become the worst political insubordinate. The tone reveals that Walker recognizes the ironic contradictions between what Jefferson represents and what he says in *Notes,* on the one hand, and his political complicity in perpetuating American slavery, on the other. The language of violence or suicide puts Walker in the same category of insurrectionists as he stokes the fears of Jefferson and whites in America about what divine intervention has in store for them, including the potential desire of blacks to "slay" whites once liberation gives them a chance (*Notes,* 150).

Yet Walker surely knew that violence was not a winning practical strategy for the abolitionist movement. The numerical minority of blacks in the American population meant that black violence, without broad white assistance, likely would have triggered overwhelming counterattack, been suppressed, and exacerbated antiblack vehemence. (Later, the 1831 and 1859 slave rebellions led by Turner and Brown, respectively, failed as a consequence of this circumstance.) What was more, the violence contradicted the intellectualism of moral suasion that black leaders were hoping to demonstrate, the Christian benevolence in loving neighbors and enemies, and the gradual pacifism encouraged by the abolitionism of William Lloyd Garrison and Quaker activists. Walker, Douglass, and other black writers or activists such as Garnet and Martin Delany were expressing ambivalent attitudes toward black violence against whites, even as their most high-flown rhetoric, revolutionary and nationalistic alike, suggested otherwise.[54] Even though my earlier phrase "kill or be killed" still works as a shorthand for Walker's militancy, he still also believed, in more complex philosophical ways, that blacks were capable of political representation, if given the chance and the means.

The educational differences within the African American community, however, caused Walker to waver occasionally in his refutation of Jefferson's political prognosis for blacks. He was certain of the political promise of African Americans (once unfettered), but he was less certain of the proof that blacks would know exactly what to do once they attained political franchise. In the second article of *Appeal,* Walker details a few examples of "ignorant" and "wretched" conduct—such as the disrespectful conflict within and between the black families of slave communities or the criminal activities of certain blacks—that had heightened white anxieties over black insurrection (32–36). More revealing is Walker's lamentation over the hurdle of illiteracy in black political advancement, which compels him to say, "Men of colour, who are also of sense, for you particularly is my appeal designed." He urges these intelligent men to "enlighten" the more ignorant and wretched "brethren" who "are not able to penetrate [*Appeal*'s] value" (40).

The educational disparities within and among black communities (both free and enslaved) forced Walker to mobilize blacks through a "trickle down" version of racial uplift, which used the public circulation of literature within free communities as well as the "underground communication networks" within slave communities to broadcast information. As Walker's biographer, Peter P. Hinks, notes, the "big fear of the authorities in the South was that the arrival of the *Appeal* would introduce subversive ideas into their communities, and stimulate increased efforts of the slaves to communicate among themselves and extend their networks—that its impact would be organizational as well as ideological."[55] Walker was knowledgeable enough to distinguish between audience (a large group which includes both the literate and the illiterate, who acquired information firsthand, secondhand, and so forth) and readership (a smaller, more exclusive group which includes primarily the literate, who may help circulate acquired information elsewhere). As the subtitle of *Appeal* says, Walker was capable of communicating with "the Slaves of the United States of America" and of "awaken[ing] in the breasts" of his "afflicted, degraded and slumbering brethren" (12–13). Yet he knew that he must communicate also with intellectual readers, for speaking to the slaves alone faced a plethora of complications, such as the high rate of illiteracy and the limitations of circulating literature through slave communities. Given his assertion that he wrote *Appeal*'s four articles, "together with [his] Preamble, dedicated to the Lord for your inspection, in language so very simple, that the most ignorant, who can read at all, may easily understand," *Appeal* betrays Walker's true motivations (81).

Although Walker was poised to represent the race, he did not see himself as part of it. I return to *Appeal*'s second article on ignorance and wretchedness to show the highest degree of his intellectual condescension, beginning with his story of some black children who attend school but still learn only "a little more about the grammar of their language than a horse does about handling a musket" (42). At this point, Walker proceeds to tell a long story about his interview with an elderly black man on education, which deserves quotation in its entirety:

I promiscuously fell in conversation once, with an elderly coloured man on the topics of education, and of the great prevalency of ignorance among us: Said he, "I know that our people are very ignorant but my son has a good education: I spent a great deal of money on his education: he can write as well as any white man, and I assure you that no one can fool him," &c. Said I, what else can your son do, besides writing a good hand? Can he post a set of books in a mercantile manner? Can he write a neat piece of composition in prose or in verse? To these interrogations he answered in the negative. Said I, did your son learn, while he was at school, the width and depth of English Grammar? To which he also replied in the negative, telling me his son did not learn those things. Your son, said I, then, has hardly any learning at all—he is almost as ignorant, and more so, than many of those who never went to school one day in all their lives. My friend got a little put out, and so walking off, said that his son could write as well as any white man. Most of the coloured people, when they speak of the education of one among us who can write a neat hand, and who perhaps knows nothing but to scribble and puff pretty fair on a small scrap of paper, immaterial whether his words are grammatical, or spelt correctly, or not; if it only looks beautiful, they say he has as good an education as any white man—he can write as well as any white man, &c. The poor, ignorant creature, hearing, this, he is ashamed, forever after, to let any person see him humbling himself to another for knowledge but going about trying to deceive those who are more ignorant than himself, he at last falls an ignorant victim to death in wretchedness. I pray that the Lord may undeceive my ignorant brethren, and permit them to throw away pretensions, and seek after the substance of learning. (43–44)

Walker criticizes the son to deflate the elder's thrill, which stems more from low expectations (such as having merely beautiful penmanship) than from high expectations (such as making sure that the penned language signifies grammatical proficiency). For Walker, penmanship is only ink deep, while language requires an intellectual depth that comes principally through education. Such criticism may have been harsh and warranted the disaffection of certain readers. Earlier in *Appeal,* Walker states, "what I write, I do it candidly, for my God and the good of both parties," black and white (35). His high expectations sacrifice racial camaraderie for racial progress. Walker's condescension to the elderly man, furthermore, is a symptom of the symbolic paradox of political leadership that characterized black proponents of racial uplift over the next century: the notion of being extraordinary, of demonstrating enough leadership to emerge from and speak on behalf of a black constituency, yet also the notion of being ordinary, of demonstrating enough racial empathy to mitigate the practical detachment implied by this emergence.

To conclude, Jefferson's politicization of the black subject in the New World substantiated (but did not make correct) his condemnation of Wheatley and Sancho. They were two of the best literary authors the African diaspora had to offer, aside from Olaudah Equiano, at the turn into the nineteenth century. In America, they were not so different from whites, in the sense that both groups were proceeding to establish their literary traditions in the face of broad Western skepticism (which includes the "Old World" of Europe). While, quite simply, a routine reaffirmation of one's own sense of superiority by alleging another's inferiority, Jefferson's degradation of black writers and culture was, in addition, a systematic deduction that blacks were unqualified for emancipation, political representation, and national citizenship. In *Notes,* Jefferson's portrayal of blacks as a less than ideal or representative subject supports his conclusion that they should either remain in their subservient state of enslavement or undergo colonization outside the country.

This chapter has linked two topics that hitherto have been tenuously connected in literary scholarship: first, Jefferson's premise of black inferiority, discussed at the outset of this chapter, and, second, his solution urging for the deportation of blacks from American territory to an outside colony, which, in 1821, became the African nation-state of Liberia. I have surmised that Jefferson *needed* to disqualify blacks from political representation *in order to* avoid emancipating them from slavery and then granting them formal citizenship on American soil. To justify extraterritorial colonization as political emancipation, he resorted to certain problematic assumptions and theories about racial representation, not merely the threat of insurrection, partly flowing from his denigration of the intelligence and literature of blacks, and not to mention from the Enlightenment belief that blacks are inferior in body and mind.[56] Jefferson communicated this desire across his published papers, including *Notes* and the autobiography, essays, and letters of correspondence he wrote while a statesman. Yet *Notes* was his first sustained treatise on the topic and was the most tractable statement on racial politics for early and antebellum African American authors. Walker's rebuttal of Jefferson presaged a postbellum argument by black authors of racial uplift about that simultaneously informal and formal relationship between intellectual culture and racial politics. In *Appeal,* Walker implies that intellectual culture, such as Jefferson's *Notes,* reflected and influenced the American polity on an ideological level—in the world of ideas and attitudes.

In light of this comparative close reading, we can return to a question posed earlier, regarding the 2006 debate in *Early American Literature.* A core concern was whether we should emphasize either the perpetrators or the victims of racism in order to historicize the meaning of race and establish a proper literary archive of early America. I claim that we must realize the complexity of this contrast: such perpetrators and victims of racism—say, Jefferson and Walker—ideologically overlapped in privileging intellectual culture within conceptions of political representation and self-governance. As meaningful as Phillis Wheatley's poetry may have been in her time and continues to be in ours, equally, if not more, meaningful was the way that she became a flashpoint for a broader intellectual debate over genius, race, and representation at the turn into the nineteenth century. Jefferson's derogation of Wheatley's poetry may be called racist, but to call it only that would be to reduce the complexity of how its political poignancy drew strength from the intellectual and cultural elitism of government.

2

The Intellectual Culture of Racial Politics after Slavery

Frederick Douglass laments in his 1871 essay "The New Party Movement" that African Americans in the South must fear "not the written law, which cannot execute itself, but the unwritten law of a powerful [Democratic] party, perpetually executing itself in the daily practices of that party." Ideological slavery, not the corporal kind of the preemancipation era, means that ideas and discourse could "render" African Americans only a "little better than slaves to a community, by being proscribed, limited, oppressed, and doomed to poverty and ignorance as effectually as though laws were passed ordaining their degradation."[1] An African American writer, critic, editor, orator, and social activist, Douglass was communicating his frustration with the real-world, practical effects of "the unwritten law," an emotion that fueled his mixed opinion, also expressed in the essay, on the political status and outlook of his race in the United States. Ever since African Americans' constitutional emancipation from slavery in 1865, they had enjoyed unprecedented success in law and politics as the South underwent governmental reconstruction in the wake of the Civil War. During this same period, though, they had also reeled from attacks on their civil rights, along with the rise of the Democratic Party. Together, these two circumstances had gradually stripped African Americans of legal and political power. Ever mindful of this history, Douglass concludes that the unwritten laws of racial injustice and chauvinism may be as palpable as those written by the very local, state, and federal levels of government.

In this chapter, I explore these ideas of Douglass by interpreting a representative selection of his letters, speeches, and essays written or published after 1865, a corpus less often examined by scholars than his third autobiography, first published in 1881, *The Life and Times of Frederick Douglass,* which I discuss, too. In the writings, Douglass tells us that political action must use an intellectual approach to shaping cultural ideas, attitudes, and behaviors, not only an electoral approach to increasing governmental representation, in order to vanquish the ideological repercussions of slavery after emancipation. Undoubtedly, the efforts of African Americans to negotiate, secure, and share social power were a direct function of the degree to which they could vote, hold office, register an affiliation with a political party, have their delegates confirmed at conventions, and serve on juries. Yet African American political action prevailed in intellectual culture—and necessarily so. Political theories of racial genius, partially descendant from the kind Thomas Jefferson derived in the early national period, persisted in both electoral politics and cultural politics, with the goals of discrediting the promise of African American political representation and sustaining white supremacy. Douglass and other African American writers of his generation recognized this fundamental linkage of racist politics and intellectual culture, critiqued it in their writings, outlined strategies for overcoming it as a race, and, at times, participated in social activism to implement their strategies. Despite philosophical differences, the slave-narrative and early-modern autobiographies of Harriet Jacobs, Booker T. Washington, and Douglass show that the African American acquisition of literacy and literary skill became political according to a teleology of racial uplift, or a belief that the more education African Americans received, the more likely they were to accumulate and distribute power across their racial communities while assimilating to the nation.[2] Certainly, the illiteracy and general lack of formal education among many African Americans limited the practicality of racial-uplift teleology. But the roles literacy and literature played in informing and transforming individuals, institutions, organizations, and interest groups on behalf of African American enfranchisement cannot be understated.

Although the political impact of African American print culture was vulnerable to romantic mythology (as in the autobiographies just listed), it had long demonstrated the ability to transform society, even when its mode of expression had resulted in occasional miscommunication between writers and readers and in occasional racial misrepresentation. Postmodernism may be partially responsible for the current kind of historiography that devalues the political power of print culture. The paradigm challenges the notion that, if print is assumed to be transformative at all, literature is as socially transformative as other kinds of new cultural media, such as the Internet, film, television, radio, and so on. "In the postmodern period," according to Madhu Dubey, a leading expert on postmodernism, "print culture is often deemed to be on the verge of extinction insofar as it is associated with individualist, elitist, and hierarchical ideologies, whereas the new technologies are said to be more amenable to the claims of diverse social constituencies." How, then, can we ever claim "the social legitimacy of print culture"?[3] Postmodern anxieties can fuel scholarly resistance to the historical idea that, again in Dubey's words, "the dehumanization of African-Americans was essential to the definition of universal humanity in print modernism."[4] Resistance of this sort, I hypothesize, can skew historiography enough to distort the transformative effects of African American literature over the past two centuries. While I second the general resistance of recent African American literary postmodernism to certain tenets of Black Studies, this chapter on Douglass anticipates and addresses a potential historiographical skepticism (inherent to this very resistance) over the transformative power of print literacy and literature in the ideological and material settings of postbellum racial politics.[5]

The Politics of Racial Genius in the Nineteenth Century

In the nineteenth century, racial genius remained a central trope in political representation and government. Descendant from Jefferson's political calculus of racial genius, the oppressive social and cultural edicts persisted both before and well after emancipation, even in the most mundane circumstances of African American life. As I detailed in the previous chapter, in "Query VI" of *Notes on the State of Virginia* (1787), Jefferson claims that, "[b]efore we condemn the Indians of this continent as wanting genius, we must consider that letters have not yet been introduced among them."[6] Gateways toward the civilization held so sacrosanct in early America, literacy and letters alike may be defined broadly enough to include the rudimentary ability to read and write as well as the ability to apply acquired knowledge to the method of critique. To be fair, Jefferson recognized Phillis Wheatley and Ignatius Sancho as exceptionally literate African Americans. Yet these writers were neither literary nor reproducible enough, in his view, to permit African American political empowerment at any level of government.[7]

How do we show that such a political theory of racial genius was resurfacing throughout the nineteenth century? First, we must affirm the extent to which African Americans were trying to turn a host of difficult historical circumstances into opportunities for political enfranchisement. In the nineteenth century, African American social agency, consciousness, and mobilization developed in four major stages: slavery, the Civil War, Reconstruction, and Redemption/Nadir. Historian Steven Hahn has stated that enslaved African Americans were neither "nonpolitical, prepolitical, [n]or protopolitical" as a consequence of their deprivation of the citizenship and the elective franchise that Congress and the amended Constitution had given them shortly after emancipation. Rather, despite the social strictures of the South and the North, African American communities had marshaled the cultural and religious resources for political action. The mobilization of the communities included the creation of paramilitary defense organizations, strategic alliances with whites in the Democratic Party, and policies of emigration to certain countries outside the United States or of migration to certain states within it. In any political way they could, African Americans protected and advanced themselves.[8] Next, the Civil War spurred the rebellion of slaves on plantations. Fleeing their masters in large numbers, slaves joined the Union army, helping overthrow the opposing Confederate army and devastating the Confederate defense of slavery. Constitutional amendments and the Civil Rights Acts emancipated and enfranchised African Americans, enabling them to reconstitute their enslaved communities as freed communities while adjusting to the country's changing legal and political landscapes.

By the Civil War's end, the emancipation of slaves and the enfranchisement of all African Americans signaled a new age of Reconstruction. The ratifications of the Constitutional amendments that Congress passed during the radical reconstruction of the South created a number of opportunities. The Thirteenth Amendment emancipated African Americans from slavery in 1865, at the end of the Civil War, paving the way, in 1868, for the Fourteenth Amendment's certification of citizens' rights and its protection of the due process and human equality of African Americans in a court of law. The Fourteenth Amendment also granted citizenship to everyone born or naturalized in the United States and aimed to protect their entitlement to the immunities and privileges of citizenship. At the same time, this amendment was a refutation of the three-fifths compromise: it penalized a state for denying or abridging a citizen's right to vote in any presidential, congressional, or local election. The Fifteenth Amendment in 1870 (along with the Nineteenth in 1920) was needed to declare the rights of citizens to vote, regardless of their "race, color, or previous condition of servitude" (and their "sex"). Hence, the voting rights of African Americans (and, eventually, women) were secured.[9] Finally, the Civil Rights Acts of 1866, 1871, and 1875, respectively, further protected the citizenship of African Americans, guarded their civil rights from the Ku Klux Klan, and demanded their equality of treatment in public spaces. Between the Civil War's end and the late 1870s, the Union army deployed troops in the South to uphold these new legal and political guidelines, hoping to augur a more racially equitable, or "New," South.[10]

The subsequent period of Redemption rolled back African American civil rights. Led especially by whites born and reared in the "Old South" who still demanded African American subservience and reacted to Reconstruction with disgust and anger, Redemption coincided with the controversial presidential election of 1876. The Democratic candidate, Samuel J. Tilden, won the popular vote yet lost the Electoral College to the Republican candidate, Rutherford B. Hayes. The congressional resolution of the constitutional crisis—because the writers of the Constitution had failed to foresee the electoral discrepancy that Tilden faced—was the Compromise of 1877. The Republican Party agreed to withdraw the federal army from the South in exchange for the Democratic Party's concession to Hayes of the nineteenth presidency of the United States. The consequences of the agreement were remarkable. Over four million former slaves were left vulnerable to violent white supremacists and the rise of Jim Crow intimidation. The rate of African Americans being lynched, among other kinds of racial terror, skyrocketed. The Republicans scaled back their fight for African American civil rights. And African Americans lost their foothold in Congress and state government. For these reasons, Reconstruction's end in the late 1870s through the turn into the twentieth century became known as Redemption from the perspective of white Southern racists, and as the "Nadir," the "Dark Ages of Recent American History," and the "Decades of Disappointment" from the antithetical perspective.[11] Adding insult to injury, in 1883, the U.S. Supreme Court ruled that the 1875 Civil Rights Act, which ordered equal treatment in public accommodations, was unconstitutional.

Embedded in this racist politics of the nineteenth century, especially in the South, were intellectual machinations to uphold white supremacy. Electoral politics merged with intellectual politics, a marriage designed to withstand the mounting pressure to enfranchise African Americans. Literacy was one major precondition for political citizenship. Electoral and governmental officials routinely tested the literacy of African Americans to assess, and often to dismiss, their worthiness for political representation and government. The low rates of literacy, reading comprehension, and literary skill in African American communities supported a broad postbellum argument, waged by white supremacists, that these communities were so intellectually inferior that they should be disqualified from any kind of political franchise. As the historian Leon F. Litwack notes, prior to emancipation, "Slaveholders, legislatures, and the courts deemed black illiteracy essential to the internal security of the white South. . . . If black people needed to be persuaded of the compelling importance of learning, they had only to look around them.

Power, influence, and wealth were associated with literacy and monopolized by the better educated class of southern whites."[12] Customs hardened to bar African Americans from learning how to read and write and how to grasp, in sophisticated ways, the complexities of daily life.

Following in the footsteps of such customs, laws passed in the antebellum era—the period roughly between the founding of American antislavery societies in the early 1830s and the moment of the Civil War in the early 1860s—anticipated the direct correlation of learning to read and write with political franchise and helped to formalize the prohibition of African American literacy. The historian Heather Andrea Williams has shown that "antiliteracy" laws were designed to short-circuit the attempts of African Americans to write their own passes to freedom, read inspiring literature, access or communicate with political networks beyond their own communities, and enhance their understanding of their own oppressed condition. One of the first antiliteracy acts was passed in South Carolina in 1740: "Whereas the having of slaves taught to write, or suffering them to be employed in writing, may be attended with great inconveniences, *Be it enacted,* That all and every person and persons whatsoever who shall hereafter teach or cause any slave or slaves to be taught to write, or shall use or employ any slave as a scribe in any manner of writing hereafter taught to write, every such person or persons shall for every such offence forfeit the sum of one hundred pounds of current money." Equivalent laws were enacted later in this state, in 1800 and 1834; in Virginia, in 1819 and 1849; in Mississippi, in 1823; in Georgia, in 1829 and 1833; in Louisiana, in 1830; in North Carolina, in 1830; in Alabama, in 1831 and 1856; and in Missouri, in 1847.[13]

Oppressed under such cultural and legal circumstances, African American writers documented the legacy of discrimination against African Americans who attempted to acquire literacy or who demonstrated high intelligence. Most notably, Douglass, in his 1845 autobiography, revisits the consternation of his former master, Mr. Auld, who learned that his wife was teaching young Frederick the alphabet and warned her of literacy's irreversible corruption of the slave: "If you give a nigger an inch, he will take an ell. A nigger should know nothing but to obey his master—to do as he is told to do. Learning would SPOIL the best nigger in the world."[14] The economic and political interests of slavery focused on maintaining the ignorance of slaves to the basic moral unfairness of their plight and to the complex ways that lawmakers, judges, and politicians alike had deprived them of their natural rights as human beings. For slaves, learning to read and write was an important means of self-enlightenment regarding these issues. For ex-slave autobiographers, such as Olaudah Equiano, Douglass, Harriet Jacobs, William Wells Brown, and Booker T. Washington, print-based learning and communication were crucial to developing political consciousness, sometimes with an eye toward implementing public policies on behalf of slave and free African American communities.

Although these and other African American writers may be culpable for, at times, overly romanticizing the political value of literacy in their narratives of slavery, freedom, and social ascent, the remarkable establishment and enhancement of laws and customs prohibiting or regulating African American literacy justify their hyperbole. Upon the emancipation of slaves, the penalties levied on anyone who taught African Americans how to read and write merely shifted their target onto the freed African Americans themselves. After African Americans were granted the right to vote, and after some of them demonstrated exceptional literacy to enter the ballot booth, laws were passed raising the cognitive or intellectual standards from basic reading to critical sophistication. Historian C. Vann Woodward has stated that an "understanding clause," along with such restrictions as a "grandfather clause" or a "poll tax," was passed in the constitutions of South Carolina, Louisiana, North Carolina, Alabama, Virginia, Georgia, and Oklahoma between 1895 and 1910. The "literacy qualification," by certifying the right of African Americans to vote in booths located in these states, worked, rather successfully, to shape the electorate and prioritize political issues that happened to benefit the constituents of those administering the tests. Other stories of intellectual tests of African Americans' sophistication include requests that they provide "a reasonable interpretation" of a state constitution, answer questions that could be gleaned only after reading historical sources, and even translate into English foreign languages such as Chinese.[15] Unsurprisingly, newly enfranchised African Americans went to their respective election booths, eagerly looking forward to vote, but frequently faced insurmountable obstacles, such as white electoral officials who tested their literacy or general intelligence. More often than not, African Americans failed the exams; their abilities to read and write, as well as to reason and imagine, suffered disrepute; and they lost the right to political franchise.

The exasperation of African American writers of the nineteenth century finds language in David Walker's 1829 *Appeal*, discussed in the previous chapter. Rather insecurely, Walker acknowledges the discrepancy in "attainments" between whites and African Americans and describes what African Americans must do to overcome their cultural and intellectual disadvantages and gain political power:

Mr. Jefferson's very severe remarks on us have been so extensively argued upon by men whose attainments in literature, I shall never be able to reach, that I would not have meddled with it, were it not to solicit each of my brethren, who has the spirit of a man, to buy a copy of Mr. Jefferson's "Notes on Virginia," and put it in the hand of his son. For let no one of us suppose that the refutations which have been written by our white friends are enough—they are *whites*—we are *blacks*. We, and the world, wish to see the charges of Mr. Jefferson refuted by the blacks *themselves*.[16]

In issuing a clarion call for African Americans to confront the ideological capital of *Notes,* Walker also appreciates the capital that they can leverage if they commit to developing, among themselves and their (male) progeny, a tradition of cultural and political criticism indicting the deleterious ideas of Jefferson and his fellow Founding Fathers.

In the couple of decades after the publication of Walker's *Appeal,* African American writers likewise critiqued *Notes.* Often, they referred to "Query XVIII," in which Jefferson asks some of his most vexed questions on the democratic meaning and the potential repercussions of slavery:

And can the liberties of a nation be thought secure when we have removed their only firm bases, a conviction in the minds of the people that these liberties are the gift of God? That they are not to be violated but with his wrath? Indeed I tremble for my country when I reflect that God is just: that his justice cannot sleep for ever: that considering numbers, nature and natural means only, a revolution of the wheel of fortune, an exchange of situation, is among possible events: that it may become probable by supernatural interference![17]

Notable African American authors, intellectuals, and abolitionists of the antebellum era capitalized on Jefferson's fears of recrimination (both social and divine) for the nation's complicity in slavery. William Wells Brown, in his 1853 novel, *Clotel,* quotes from "Query XVIII" and calls attention to Jefferson's "trembling," in addition to his philandering with and fathering of slaves: "But, sad to say, Jefferson is not the only American statesman who has spoken high-sounding words in favour of freedom, and then left his own children to die slaves."[18] Needless to say, Jefferson's illicit sexual relations and interracial progeny have become an undying source of controversy in subsequent African American history. William Hamilton and William J. Watkins also used Jefferson's forecast of national apocalypse (despite its deeply colonialist motives) as a rhetorical lever to condemn the nation's moral turpitude. Daniel Coker probed a broad white anxiety, reflected in Jefferson's, over the upcoming catharsis and redemption awaiting Ethiopia's children in the New World.[19] Finally, James McCune Smith indicted the theories of racial psychology and physiology that Jefferson pursues elsewhere in *Notes*. In Smith's 1859 essay "On the Fourteenth Query of Thomas Jefferson's Notes on Virginia," he challenges Jefferson's conclusion that the alleged mental and physical differences between the races make them socially irreconcilable.[20] In preemancipation African American literature, Smith's stands as one of the most sustained critiques of the racial premise of *Notes* and Jefferson's specter over the African American presence in American "civilization." Yet, beyond critiquing Jefferson's book literally and point by point, African Americans later in the nineteenth century built intellectual culture that counteracted the prevailing allegations of inferior African American literacy, intelligence, literature, and political representation. Indeed, after the Civil War, Frederick Douglass described not only the ideological assumptions of slavery that persisted even after the peculiar institution itself was abolished but also the political cornerstones needed so that this intellectual culture could survive at least as long.

"In What New Skin This Old Snake Will Come Forth Next": Frederick Douglass on the Postbellum Ideology of Slavery

Fomenting social movements determined the political tractability of African American literature. Douglass, in deriving an intellectual methodology after slavery to understand this correlation, described social change in both formal and informal contexts. The franchise of African Americans was almost always under attack by both the written and unwritten laws of racial discrimination. For political empowerment, Douglass knew that African Americans had to confront laws and government on their own terms. State constitutions, alongside malicious legislative, judicial, and social practices, could well compromise the federal application of the constitutional amendments and congressional statutes that were mandated in Reconstruction.[21] The party system of political representation also failed to account perfectly for African American interests. In an 1868 essay, "The Work before Us," Douglass claims that the Democratic Party seeks voters among "those classes of the American people who are proud of their contempt for humanity—who scout benevolence and brotherly kindness as the weakest nonsense" (207). Yet the Democratic Party's disdain for Reconstruction did not automatically compel Douglass to align himself with the Republican Party. Even before the Republican Party's elected majority began to decline at all levels of government in the 1872 elections, he had voiced skepticism about its commitment to racial justice. In "The New Party Movement," he notes that the Republican Party "came into existence to oppose the aggressions of slavery . . . and to abide the consequences of such opposition even to the extent of defending the Union." But the abolition of slavery and the success of the Union army in the Civil War should not rationalize the party's abdication of its egalitarian obligations. After all, through ideological means, "slavery still finds a refuge in Southern sentiment and in the Democratic Party" (255).

Also published in 1871, Douglass's essay "Politics an Evil to the Negro" echoes the case that politics is "one of the most important levers that can be employed to elevate his race," contrary to the racist claim, mimicked by the essay's title, that politics corrupts it (273). First and foremost, African American enfranchisement is the goal. In 1865, Douglass received an invitation to celebrate, alongside the Colored People's Educational Monument Association, the memory of recently assassinated president Abraham Lincoln. In response, he wrote a letter stressing "the immediate, complete, and universal enfranchisement of the colored people of the whole country." He goes on to say that the "great want of the country is to be rid of the Negro question, and it can never be rid of that question until justice, right and sound policy are complied with" (169–70). For Douglass, African American men (but not women) deserved the right to "the ballot," "the right to keep and bear arms" as part of paramilitary self-defense, and the right to intermingle with whites: "enjoying the same freedom, voting at the same ballot-box, using the same cartridge-box, going to the same schools, attending the same churches, traveling in the same street cars, in the same railroad cars, on the same steamboats, proud of the same country, fighting the same foe, and enjoying the same peace and all its advantages."[22] Legislation and the court of law could remedy many of these racial inequities and divisions.

Formal political action of this sort, though, could not always overcome the unwritten, ideological laws of racism. Sensing this, Douglass favored a flexible notion of politics, in which representations and exercises of power could manifest themselves in both formal and informal ways. His best statement on this issue appears in essays he wrote in support of women's suffrage.[23] In one essay, "Woman Suffrage Movement" (1870), Douglass's argument for women's suffrage contains the concepts he needed to reaffirm the case for African American suffrage:

If woman is admitted to be a moral and intellectual being, possessing a sense of good and evil, and a power of choice between them, her case is already half-gained. Our natural powers are the foundation of our natural rights; and it is a consciousness of powers which suggests the exercise of rights. The power that makes her a moral and an accountable being gives her a natural right to choose the legislators who are to frame the laws under which she is to live, and the requirements of which she is bound to obey. . . . Unless it can be shown that woman is morally, physically, and intellectually incapable of performing the act of voting, there can be no natural prohibition of such action on her part. (232–33)

Just as the rebuttal of the moral, physical, and intellectual inferiority of women was central to asserting that they deserved the elective franchise, the refutation of such inferiority in African Americans was equally central to arguing that African Americans deserved it, too.[24]

Douglass's theory of power applied as well to the informal political factors of women's suffrage. In another 1870 essay, "Woman and the Ballot," he translates the notion of power across a variety of social and material contexts: "Power is the highest object of human respect. Wisdom, virtue, and all great moral qualities command respect only as powers. Knowledge and wealth are nought but powers. Take from money its purchasing power, and it ceases to be the same object of respect. We pity the impotent and respect the powerful everywhere. To deny woman her vote is to abridge her natural and social power, and deprive her of a certain measure of respect" (237). In abstract terms, the accumulation or distribution of power worked in dialectical relation to the elective franchise, representing the ideological narratives of social, cultural, and intellectual life—in sum, the symbolic capital of "natural rights," "wisdom," "virtue," "all great moral qualities," "respect," "knowledge," and "wealth." Ideological narratives of this kind underwrote Douglass's moral philosophy of political egalitarianism, which insisted that the pursuit of justice should embrace the Constitution while guiding African American political action. One year after emancipation, Douglass published an essay, "Reconstruction," supporting this point: the Constitution "knows no distinction between citizens on account of color. Neither does it know any difference between a citizen of a State and a citizen of the United States. Citizenship evidently includes all the rights of citizens, whether State or national" (204). As broadened and strengthened through amendments, constitutional egalitarianism framed Douglass's conception of African American politics.

Corruption devalued the transformative potential of African American political action, however. In the postbellum years, Douglass bemoaned the murder and mayhem that African Americans suffered at the hands of whites, in addition to the material, real-world proof of socioeconomic inequities between the two groups.[25] The lack of law and civil rights enforcement prompted him to argue, in "The Need for Continuing Anti-slavery Work" (1865), that slavery had continued in the postbellum era as ideological phantasmagoria: "It has been called by a great many names, and it will call itself by yet another name; and you and I and all of us had better wait and see what new form this old monster will assume, *in what new skin this old snake will come forth next*" (169; italics mine). Five years later, in an essay aptly entitled "Seeming and Real," Douglass portrays the discrepancy between law and custom as the reason for racial injustice and as a conundrum of legal and political theory: "[L]aw on the statute book and law in the practice of the nation are two very different things, and sometimes very opposite things" (227). The discrepancy between egalitarianism and the inhumane practices of many whites impugned the "practical value" of government documents such as the Constitution. As literary and legal scholar Deak Nabers notes, the Constitution's reputation as the "supreme law of the land" obscured the degree to which it "states" or "accounts" for laws but does not automatically "enact" them.[26] The constitutional progression from egalitarian theory to written word to social impact followed a long, circuitous, ideological road, comprising several divisions and kinds of political labor on the parts of U.S. leaders and their constituencies.

In addition to formal politics, Douglass recognized other ways for African Americans to overcome the minimal enforcement of the Reconstruction mandates. One way included the development of certain social, cultural, and intellectual strategies that could circulate ideas to the benefit of African American empowerment. Public meetings and reading groups were small-scale examples of mobilization in which illiterate and intellectual African Americans alike could interact and discuss racial politics. Larger-scale examples included conventions—state constitutional conventions and labor conventions—in which African Americans could reach consensus on how to communicate their interests to politicians. Political scientist Michael C. Dawson has stated that "the antebellum Negro Convention movement of the first half of [the nineteenth] century can be viewed as the first major forum for black ideological debate."[27] This movement continued into the age of Reconstruction, when "the first opportunity for African Americans [existed] to combine ideological debate with high levels of political activity and mobilization."[28] Ideological debate within and among the races provided a social and cultural complement to the formal laws of Reconstruction.

Douglass underscored the importance of conventions to African American social empowerment. In "The Southern Convention" (1871), he criticizes the *Union*, a Republican newspaper in Macon, Georgia, for opposing the "fact of the wronged, outraged, and down-trodden colored people of the South calling a convention [of Colored Citizens in Columbia, South Carolina] for the purpose of consulting as to the best means of bringing themselves up from the degrading position they have been forced into by slavery" (251). Twelve years later, at a convention for African American men held in Louisville, Kentucky, he delivered an address that fleshes out the political meaning of conventions. Contrary to the multitude of critics denouncing African American assembly, Douglass cherished it as one of the "safety-valves of the Republic":

[F]irst, because there is a power in numbers and in union; because the many are more than the few; because the voice of a whole people, oppressed by a common injustice, is far more likely to command attention and exert an influence on the public mind than the voice of single individuals and isolated organizations; because, coming together from all parts of the country, the members of a National convention have the means of a more comprehensive knowledge of the general situation, and may, therefore, fairly be presumed to conceive more clearly and express more fully and wisely the policy it may be necessary for them to pursue in the premises. Because conventions of the people are in themselves harmless, and when made the means of setting forth grievances, whether real or fancied, they are the safety-valves of the Republic. (376–77)

In this address Douglass provides one of his most sustained analyses of the labor, capitalism, education, banking system, civil rights, human equality, and political ambition of African Americans. The case for African American conventions contributed to his broader theory that the nation was "governed by ideas as well as by laws" ("The United States Cannot Remain Half-Slave and Half-Free," 358). Conventions optimized the expression, circulation, and critique of the egalitarian principle of social justice, permitting the widest cross-section of African American communities to congregate in one place for the express purpose of exchanging ideas. Conventions were one of the most influential forums for African American self-empowerment.

Other kinds of African American political activity existed in print culture, such as in the intellectual cultivations of literacy and the African American press (or the periodicals edited or owned by African Americans) and in the founding of monuments, institutions of higher education, reading groups, and literary societies. The communicative salience of African American print literacy has been well documented.[29] More relevant to our purpose is the mid-nineteenth-century rise of the African American press that Douglass appreciated and mastered as an organ of political action. From 1870 to 1874, Douglass owned and edited the *New National Era,* a weekly newspaper where he routinely espoused the virtues of the African American press and condemned the fallacies or improprieties of other newspapers on the race question.[30] Yet he shot an arrow across the bow of conventional thinking in 1891, when he stressed that "the colored Press [should] say less about race and claims to race recognition, and more about the principles of justice, liberty, and patriotism" ("The Negro Press," 469). Eric Sundquist, a literary historian, explains that Douglass's rhetoric gravitated across his life toward the principles of the original framers of the Constitution and Declaration of Independence and away from the racial radicalism that could characterize his abolitionist and early postbellum political work.[31] Portraying "late Douglass" as consistently egalitarian in political ethos would accurately make him the forerunner to a special African American tradition of political philosophy including Ida B. Wells, W. E. B. Du Bois, and Martin Luther King Jr. Yet portraying "midlife Douglass" also in these terms, while using his 1866 essay "Reconstruction" as evidence, would be just as accurate.[32] The attribution of "the principles of justice, liberty, and patriotism" to the African American press showed Douglass's longtime commitment to reaching these goals to the benefit of all humanity.

Cultural monuments further helped mount the ideological attack on the unwritten laws that oppressed African Americans. Shortly after Lincoln's assassination on April 15, 1865, W. J. Wilson wrote a letter to Douglass inviting him to enroll as an officer of the Educational Monument Association (associated with the National Lincoln Monument Association, chartered in May 1865) and to support its plan to erect the National Lincoln Monument Institute in memory of Lincoln's leadership in emancipating African Americans. While a genuine supporter of Lincoln, Douglass wrote back declining the invitation and questioning the association's plan to depend on the philanthropy of "white men," rather than both the funds and the manual labor of African Americans, to "build" the institute: "A monument of this kind, erected by the colored people—that is, by the voluntary offerings of the colored people—is a very different thing from a monument built by money contributed by white men to enable colored people to build a monument" (172). Monuments captured the negotiation between the races over social power that had been played out in the political arenas of national life. The abilities of African Americans to fund and create their own cultural institutions demonstrated a particular claim to social power that was crucial to their broader claim to national citizenship. Eleven years later, Douglass reiterates this point in his speech "Oration in Memory of Abraham Lincoln," an introduction to the Freedmen's Monument, located in Washington, D.C., in memory of Lincoln, declaring, "[W]e, the colored people, newly emancipated and rejoicing in our blood-bought freedom, . . . have now and here unveiled, set apart, and dedicated a monument," whose traits capture "something of the exalted character and great works" of Lincoln (311). Monument culture and political culture were one and the same.

Douglass also recognized the political meaning of schools. In "Howard University" (1870), he venerates the D.C.-based university, which, though located in "the city which knew [colored] people only as property," had arisen as "an Institution of learning, vieing [sic] in attractiveness and elegance, with those of the most advanced civilization, devoted to the classical education of a people which, a few years ago, the phrenologist, archaeologists and ethnologists of the country, told us . . . were wholly incapable of acquiring even a knowledge of the English language" (234). The sign of civilization extended from the literature written by African Americans to the monuments and schools established by them.[33] At the 1865 inauguration of the Douglass Institute in Baltimore, Maryland, Douglass refused to mince words when he stated, "[The edifice] is destined to play an important part in promoting the freedom and elevation of the colored people of this city and State, and I may say of the whole Union" (175). Once again, we see that African American cultural establishments can serve a political cause, as long as their ideological attack on racial injustice and chauvinism empowered African Americans in the process.

Literary societies empowered African Americans by promoting print literacy, encouraging learning and intellectual exchange, spawning reading cultures, and attending to the racial-political concerns of the era. Since the founding in 1881 of the D.C.-based Bethel Historical and Literary Association, it was, according to literary historian Elizabeth McHenry, a "public or 'popular' forum that permitted a growing middle and upper class to mingle and converse and encouraged them to engage one another in healthy and productive debate on the political matters that affected them most directly."

Bethel was "a prototype of the post-Reconstruction black public sphere, and, at the same time, a model for the development of African American literary societies nationwide."[34]

"The Race Problem," a scarcely examined 1890 speech Douglass delivered to Bethel and a full house of rapt listeners in D.C.'s Metropolitan A.M.E. Church, deserves extended discussion here. More than any other postbellum speech by Douglass, "The Race Problem" expounds on the political value of literary society and explains the political struggle over public ideas and discourse that had contributed to the ideological enslavement of African Americans. Bethel was an ideal setting for Douglass's political announcement, "It is an institution well fitted to improve the minds and elevate the sentiments not only of its members, but of the general public. Nowhere else outside of the courts of law and the Congress of the United States have I heard vital public questions more seriously discussed."[35] In this social context "outside" the formal realm of politics, he tells a number of ironic stories. First, the Christianity practiced by whites, to begin with, argued that all humanity is equal before God, even as it theologized the inferiority of African Americans. Next, the U.S. government's recruitment of men into the military, though urgent, assigned African Americans subservient duties, if they were even enlisted at all. Third, marriage was a social and cultural cornerstone of the country, yet certain laws forbade African Americans themselves (as well as affianced African Americans and whites) to enter it. Finally, educational leaders and institutions touted the importance of literacy and learning yet denied African Americans access to them. Douglass portrayed these as examples of the unfailing hypocrisy of many whites and, to a lesser extent, African Americans who shared their racist views.

Above all, Bethel must help in the ideological war against the Race Problem, a discourse that was circulating in both formal and informal contexts of political activity. Douglass's ideological emphasis, to reiterate, stemmed from a moral philosophy that held truth and justice sacred. "Truth is the fundamental, indispensable, and everlasting requirement in obtaining right results," he asserts in the speech. "No department of human life can afford to dispense with truth." For this reason, he despises the "advantage to error . . . which is often employed with marked skill and effect in the presentation to the minds of men of what may be called half truths for whole truths" (3, 5). History suggests that Douglass's words were symptomatic of the larger concern, among African American writers and intellectuals in the late nineteenth century, with the racist information that popular culture was circulating throughout all levels of American society. The hybrid amalgam of truths and falsehoods in this information heightened the political anxieties of elite African American society over its public representations. Yet a closer look at Douglass's speech to Bethel indicates a more critical and nuanced perspective on what a rising African American intellectual at the time, W. E. B. Du Bois, in 1903, called "ever an unasked question": "How does it feel to be a problem?"[36]

In the 1890 speech, Douglass expresses reservations over this kind of question. "I object to characterizing the relation subsisting between the white and colored people of this country as the Negro problem, as if the Negro had precipitated the problem, and as if he were in any way responsible for the problem" (5). The problem with the "Negro-Problem" discourse was the "offensive associations" of the words "Negro" and "Problem" that downplayed full truths, played up half truths, interspersed utter lies, and, with the help of the powerful in society, succeeded in "confusing the moral sense of the nation and misleading the public mind" (5, 8). Douglass describes it more poignantly when he concludes, "Problem, problem, race problem, negro problem, has . . . f[l]itted through their sentences in all *the mazes of metaphorical confusion*" (8; italics mine).

Combining at once the modes of rebuke and intellectual inquiry, Douglass's "criticism" of the ideological language, metaphors, rhetoric, and creativity of racism does not overstate the political power of "sentences." Rather, his criticism measures exactly their influence both within and without the literary societies, monuments, schools, and institutes that had been working to shape the way African Americans understood and accessed the political process. Again, at the level of sentence, Douglass recommends "employing the truest and most agreeable names to describe the relation which at present subsists between ourselves and the other people of the country" (5). Yet terminological revision is not enough. The revised language and ideas must correspond to a reformed political psyche in which the majority of whites could live alongside emancipated African Americans. This nation must deal with the legal abolition of corporal slavery not by, consciously or subconsciously, devising unwritten laws that instituted ideological slavery but instead by developing "sufficient moral stamina to maintain its own honor and integrity by vindicating its own Constitution and fulfilling its own pledges" (8). Douglass's unwavering, patient faith that "truth, justice, liberty, and humanity will ultimately prevail" (16) could have been seen—and, today, still might be seen—as too idealistic and out of touch with the contemporary realities of African America. Nonetheless, his moral and political philosophies ended up sustaining him from his early youth to his death—through the eras of bondage and emancipation, through the amendments and rollbacks of the Constitution, through the congressional changes in party leadership, through the ideological persistence of slavery. And, at every moment, he was a stalwart leader in the political war on the laws of racism, both written and unwritten.

"The Elite of the Land": The Politics of Statesmanship

So far, I have shown that, in the nineteenth century, African Americans resorted to various social, cultural, and intellectual tactics to counteract the "unwritten laws" of racial oppression. To reiterate Steven Hahn's points: the strategies included the development of biological and social "kinship," "labor" practices, "circuits of communication and education," the black church, emigration and migration societies, and paramilitary organizations. Generally, African Americans succeeded in employing these methods to conjoin both formal and informal types of political action.[37] Douglass gestured to the public meetings, literacy and reading groups, the African American press, conventions, monuments, schools, and literary societies as the key arenas of informal political action whereby African Americans could conduct the ideological work that the legal and legislative mandates of the Constitution and Congress could not accomplish alone.

Douglass further argued that the "ideas and values" of racism undermined the influence of constitutional and congressional egalitarianism. Although abolished by the Thirteenth Amendment, the principles of slavery were so ingrained in American society and culture that they persisted, in Douglass's eyes, after 1865 in ideological form. During the postbellum period, racism constituted the language, ideas, and representations of the "Race Problem"; inspired the violent and prejudicial conduct of many whites; and influenced even the actions of some African Americans, such as Booker T. Washington, who, ironically, shared the views of these whites.[38] For this reason, Douglass's work in racial politics neither assumed the sole form of abolitionism nor ended with emancipation. Rather, it continued afterward, as he declared the importance of government, law, and public policy to empowering African American communities; the need for African Americans to confront racism through emendations to law and governance; and the realization that such changes required the cultural and intellectual enhancement of political conventions and language.

The irony of Douglass's notion of "the unwritten law" is that the law *was* written, but as ideological "script," told and retold as narrative. Michael C. Dawson states that all ideologies "seek to define and control debates by providing a 'script' of scenarios with which to think about the political world." By implication, "the racial order" of the United States, which, in the nineteenth century, had long "assigned racial groups various degrees of citizenship rights, legal status, relationships to the security apparatus, [and] places in the economy," also consisted of "a script about the moral unworthiness of African Americans as justification for the denial of citizenship rights and exclusion from broad sectors of civil society."[39] Since then, the political conflicts preoccupying African Americans have involved a competition of ideological scripts to determine the dominant narratives of racial identity and race relations in the United States.

Thus far, I have recovered a postbellum oeuvre of Douglass—his letters, speeches, and essays—that most scholars (except biographers) tend to subordinate to his third autobiography, first published in 1881, *The Life and Times of Frederick Douglass,* which covers almost his entire life. *Life and Times* does touch on our issues in question, though not as fully or as theoretically as the essays, since the book is most obligated to retelling his life story. More importantly, *Life and Times* enables us to see—more deeply than his non-autobiographical essays—how Douglass himself, as a statesman, sought to achieve a symbolism that exploited the complementary relationship of formal and informal politics.

Late in *Life and Times,* Douglass mentions the several invitations he received to run for elected office. Though honored, he realizes the problems awaiting him if he ever followed this path:

The adoption of the fourteenth and fifteenth amendments and their incorporation into the Constitution of the United States opened a very tempting field to my ambition, and one to which I should probably have yielded had I been a younger man. I was earnestly urged by many of my respected fellow-citizens, both colored and white, and from all sections of the country, to take up my abode in some one of the many districts of the South where there was a large colored vote and get myself elected, as they were sure I easily could do, to a seat in Congress—possibly in the Senate. That I did not yield to this temptation was not entirely due to my age, for the idea did not square well with my better judgment and sense of propriety. The thought of going to live among a people in order to gain their votes and acquire official honors was repugnant to my self-respect, and I had not lived long enough in the political atmosphere of Washington to have this sentiment sufficiently blunted to make me indifferent to its suggestions. I do not deny that the arguments of my friends had some weight in them, and from their standpoint it was all right; but I was better known to myself than to them. I had small faith in my aptitude as a politician, and could not hope to cope with rival aspirants. My life and labors in the North had in a measure unfitted me for such work, and I could not have readily adapted myself to the peculiar oratory found to be most effective with the newly-enfranchised class. In the New England and Northern atmosphere I had acquired a style of speaking which in the South would have been considered tame and spiritless, and consequently he who "could tear a passion to tatters and split the ear of groundlings" had far better chance of success with the masses there than one so little boisterous as myself.

Upon the whole I have never regretted that I did not enter the arena of Congressional honors to which I was invited.[40]

Despite Douglass's political philosophy that informal and formal types of political action must complement each other in social change, he perceives elected office as unattractive to him, who was, at that time, probably the most politically powerful African American in the postwar nation prior to the phenomenal ascent of Booker T. Washington in the century's last decade. Running for elected office was too opportunistic, insulting, idiosyncratic, and trendy for Douglass to take it seriously. Aside from personal distaste, elected office also did not guarantee him the political power he needed or deserved in the public sphere. To repeat, the rollback of Reconstruction and the decline of the Freedmen's Bureau, among other African American political institutions, as W. E. B. Du Bois once so eloquently argued, negated the real-world effect of African American elected officials.[41] Douglass measured his political impact in terms divorced from his own electoral potential, through which a delegable authority of racial representation could have gained credence.

Douglass preferred to gravitate toward the electoral success of his peers. The historic bond between Douglass and Abraham Lincoln proves this point. On March 4, 1865, the date of Lincoln's second inauguration, Douglass attended a reception at the executive mansion, where he found himself, as one of the first African Americans invited to it, in rare and exclusive company. "I had for some time looked upon myself as a man," he remarks in *Life and Times,* "but now in this multitude of the *élite* of the land, I felt myself a man among men" (265). Later, policemen who were standing at a doorway to the mansion's interior and who were unaware of Douglass's stature accosted him until he announced his acquaintance with Lincoln, and until another authoritative white attendee had recognized him and demanded his admission. Once inside, Lincoln made Douglass feel at home: "Recognizing me, even before I reached him, he exclaimed, so that all around could hear him, 'Here comes my friend Douglass.'" After a small exchange of pleasantries, Douglass "passed on, feeling that any man, however distinguished, might well regard himself honored by such expressions, from such a man" (266).

Such episodes in *Life and Times* telescope Douglass's political philosophy, on the translations of political power beyond the formal realm, through his impressions of statesmanship. As a statesman, Douglass was an expert in the art of government, practically and philosophically understood. I must emphasize here the distinction between calling Douglass a racial representative and a statesman. In the closing years of his accomplished life as a racial leader, Douglass stated that he wrote literature for a people "not allowed to speak for themselves, yet much misunderstood and deeply wronged." But this statement begins with a condescending clause: "Time and events have summoned me to stand forth both as a witness and an advocate for a people long dumb" (*Life and Times*, 375). To a degree, he was correct, if we put his condescending attitude to the side. Slavery had outlawed African Americans from acquiring print literacy and had crippled their educational institutions to such an extent that, in the postbellum years, they suffered intellectual handicaps. Hence, Douglass (in his later years) and Booker T. Washington both agreed that African Americans should learn the basic methods of reading and writing—not so much the sophisticated methods of critical reading and creative writing—and the skills of industrial labor (ibid., 203). However, African American writers, including Douglass and Washington, also "misunderstood and deeply wronged" the race, even as they (with the exception of Washington) indicted whites for committing such misdeeds against it. The countless ways that elite African American writers failed to speak accurately on behalf of their imagined African American constituents suggest that their representations of the race have just as often been acts of misrepresentation.[42] But the theoretical problem of racial misrepresentation does not diminish the political power Douglass still accumulated as a statesman. The political power that accompanied his symbolism of statesmanship offset the practical limitations of political power that had crippled African American elected officials and that would have afflicted him had he, too, run for and held office. The historian Philip Dray puts it best in his summary of the challenges that these officials faced in the era of Reconstruction, and he guides our thinking on what Douglass could have faced if he had followed the same political path:

In Congress, the forces of resistance were aligned almost perpetually against them. Without seniority, they could neither head nor wield influence within prominent committees and had to struggle to leverage power as best they could. One handicap was their want of entrenched political support. With the exception of Robert Smalls [member of the U.S. House of Representatives from South Carolina's Fifth and Seventh Districts] and John Roy Lynch [also a member, from Mississippi's Sixth District], most were not natives of the districts they represented, and their constituencies, while substantial, tended to be comprised of voters of modest means. Thus they lacked the capability enjoyed by other members of Congress to call upon established political networks in their home districts or states, and in Washington were often forced to rely on white allies whose own influence might rise or wane unexpectedly.[43]

Fortunately for Douglass, his clout was not so tied to inconsistent white support. Statesmanship shielded him because its political prestige allowed him to abscond from the formal elections and geographic constituencies that generally held politicians accountable to special interests. His second autobiography, *My Bondage and My Freedom* (1855), and *Life and Times* overlap in their discussions of the "statesmen" that he encountered during his nearly two-year sojourn in England shortly after the release of his first autobiography, *Narrative of the Life of Frederick Douglass,* in 1845.[44] (The blasphemy of his antislavery discourse in *Narrative*, Douglass and others believed, endangered his safety in America and required his quick departure abroad [*Life and Times,* 164]). The trip to England gave Douglass the opportunity of "becoming acquainted with educated people and of seeing and hearing many of the most distinguished men of that country" (*Life and Times,* 165). The quintessential statesmen happened to be members of British Parliament: Richard Cobden and John Bright were "the rising statesmen of England . . . [who] possessed a very friendly disposition toward America"; Daniel O'Connell, a leader of the Irish political aspiration for Catholic Emancipation, was a "transatlantic statesman [who] bore a testimony more marked and telling against the crime and curse of slavery"; Lord (Henry Peter) Brougham, another member of Parliament and an advocate of the abolition of the slave trade, was an experienced and versatile debater; and Sir John Bowering was a gifted linguist and a translator and anthologist of poetry (166, 168, 169, 170). In much the same way that Douglass's own statesmanship transcended political materialism, the various philosophical and intellectual distinctions of these men happened to supersede the political purchase of Parliament.

Since that trip to England, Douglass had encountered a host of Americans whom he also deemed statesmen, even though he disagreed with some of them on public policy and had disavowed any equivalent commitment he could have shared to political office. They include Lewis Cass, a former commander in the War of 1812 and a proslavery, Democratic U.S. senator from Michigan; John Caldwell Calhoun, another proslavery, Democratic advocate who served as vice president under both John Quincy Adams and Andrew Jackson and as U.S. senator from South Carolina; Lincoln, the sixteenth and first Republican president of the United States who had proclaimed the emancipation of all slaves; James Abram Garfield, an antislavery, Republican U.S. senator from Ohio and the twentieth president of the United States; William Henry Seward, an antislavery, Republican governor, a U.S. senator from New York, and the secretary of state under Lincoln; and Charles Sumner, an antislavery, Republican U.S. senator from Massachusetts and one of the leading supporters of Reconstruction (199, 211, 219, 297, 348). Douglass also admired certain women he met in his life, in England and America, such as Mary Howitt, a British Quaker and famous poet, writer, editor, and translator; and Harriet Beecher Stowe, an antislavery leader and the author of the influential 1852 novel *Uncle Tom's Cabin* (170, 201). Contrary to Douglass, whose symbolic authority as a statesman was preferable to the electoral and coalitional insecurity of fellow African Americans in government, the above white men (but not the white women, who could not yet run for office) benefited from the actual way that their statesmanship and governmental offices mutually reinforced their political authority. Despite the racial double standard, these individuals still exhibited the kind of qualities Douglass revered. Some were "calm, cool, deliberate," like President Lincoln; their intellect was "exalted" and "matured," like a philosopher or a historian of constitutional higher law; and their dispositions were "wise and patriotic," like President Garfield's (211, 254, 297, 348).

Biographies support the probability that Douglass shared some of the personal qualities of these men and women.[45] They also confirm that he was a statesman in action and spirit, supporting the contemporary thesis of Herbert J. Storing, an influential political scientist, historian, and philosopher, who has argued convincingly that Douglass, regardless of his race, belonged to a tradition of statesmen that, by the late nineteenth century, included Thomas Jefferson, John Marshall, John C. Calhoun, and Lincoln.[46] I agree. The statesmanship of Douglass that we can infer throughout *Life and Times* captures a special discourse of racial representation accounting for the symbolic and practical exercises of African American political power in postslavery America, even while the unwritten law of white supremacy worked to mitigate them in these very terms.

3

New Negro Politics
from Reconstruction to
the Harlem Renaissance

From Reconstruction to the Harlem Renaissance, the symbolic transition of the "Negro" from "Old" to "New" is one of the more compelling stories of the competition of ideological scripts, especially as they pertain to racial representation, in the United States.[1] In 1923, the Reverend Reverdy C. Ransom wrote a poem, "The New Negro," capturing the trope of the New Negro in all its complexity and optimism:

> Rough hewn from the jungle and the desert's sands,
> Slavery was the chisel that fashioned him to form,
> And gave him all the arts and sciences had won.
> The lyncher, mob, and stake have been his emery wheel,
> TO MAKE A POLISHED MAN of strength and power.
> In him, the latest birth of freedom,
> God hath again made all things new.
> Europe and Asia with ebbing tides recede,
> America's unfinished arch of freedom waits,
> Till he, the corner stone of strength
> Is *lifted into place and power.*
> Behold him! dauntless and unafraid he stands.
> He comes with laden arms,
> Bearing rich gifts to science, religion, poetry and song.[2]

Many intellectuals and scholars specializing in nineteenth- or twentieth-century African American literature have told this story, or some variation or part thereof, about New Negro politics, or the way that intellectual culture, in collaboration with formal politics, has helped to "lift" Negroes into the "place and power" that they, as human citizens, rightly deserved.[3] New Negro politics accounts for a cultural formation that sought to overcome the prevailing theme, in more mainstream culture, that African Americans were inferior and unassimilable in American "civilization." Manifest in contexts of literature—as well as in those of drama, illustrations, and speeches—New Negro politics sought to prove that African Americans, then described as a race, could be uplifted in moral, educational, and cultural ways. The proof lay in the images of uplifted African Americans that permeated African American intellectual culture. The feature was a reincarnation of the political rhetoric of miniature portraiture in early America. The literary historian Eric Slauter states that "certain aesthetic assumptions about likeness, resemblance, and form structured American political thought at its foundational moment."[4] I would add that these assumptions were adopted and revised to develop a cultural basis for African American political thought a century later, when racial representation continued to counteract the widespread impression that African Americans were unworthy of political enfranchisement.

African American intellectuals used literature to explain or critique racial uplift and its cultural implementation as political action.[5] Focusing on criticism and fiction, this chapter shows that the correlation between African American communities and racial-uplift ideology had translated into special rhetorical, aesthetic, and thematic features constituting the political tradition of African American literature at the turn into the twentieth century. Of course, there is a pitfall in calling African American literature any kind of "tradition," as I have throughout this book. My assertion that racial uplift characterizes a political ideology of African American literature does not intend to homogenize the literature's goals, an act that past scholars have warned against.[6] Nor do I wish, necessarily, to segregate such African American literature from, say, Anglo-American literature, which, at the turn into the twentieth century, has more often been associated with such genres as realism, naturalism, local color, and regionalism. As literary scholar Michele Elam astutely notes, scholarly focus on "what one might call a racial anxiety of influence by both blacks and whites tends to disavow the complex ways both traditions at times mutually inform each other."[7] Nor, finally, am I suggesting that the permutations of racial-uplift literature automatically bespeak, within the African American literati, an intergenerational "anxiety of influence," as the succession from "Old Negro" to "New Negro" implies.[8] Rather, I seek to reveal the patterns of political ideology in African American literary history, or the way that select writers distinguished the formal and informal codes of racial uplift in their derivation of an African American political subjectivity. The mere communication between African American

writers and their readers was a profoundly political one, in that a reciprocal relationship existed between the literary dissemination of information
among readers and the strategic enhancement of their social power.

Informing society was indeed as much a political act as *transforming* society. In the 1958 classic *The Human Condition,* political theorist Hannah Arendt
turns to Greek political history to argue that "most political action . . . is indeed
transacted in words" and that "finding the right words at the right moment"—
or what I regard as a default goal of literary writing—"quite apart from the
information or communication they may convey, is action."[9] More recently,
political scientist Virginia Sapiro similarly notes that we must regard information—whether it be the units of knowledge or the processes of communicating
or receiving them—not merely as a precursor to but, rather, as a crucial form
of social participation in a civil polity.[10] Marc Howard Ross, another political
scientist, qualifies this assertion, stating that cultural organizations—and cultural expressions, I should add—circulate information and, in doing so, may
solve a number of "political problems" to "bolster group solidarity and effective mobilization." Such organizations and expressions help people to distinguish their "membership and sphere of operation within the context of the
contemporaneous political setting," to address "the political need for intense
internal communications among the group's constituent parts," and to establish the "mechanisms for decision making" as well as the "authority for implementing decisions for speaking, where appropriate, on behalf of the group."[11]

To a certain degree, Ross's outline corresponds to what I aim to prove in
this book. In the first two chapters, I have defined the political implications
of African American culture for the new republic and for postbellum America. In this chapter, I tackle the question, What does a political historiography of the commercial marketplace and the racial representations associated
with African American literature both entail and reveal? The publication and
circulation of racial-uplift literature at the turn into the twentieth century
happened to be a political enterprise. The literature relayed information to
and empowered readers and their communities about the possibilities and
problems of African American mobilization.

New Negro Criticism from Anna Julia Cooper to Alain Locke

In some of the ideological scripts of the United States—to paraphrase
the previous chapter's conclusion on Frederick Douglass's 1890 speech "The
Race Problem"—racism becomes manifest as the "offensive associations"
and "metaphorical confusion" of actual "sentences" circulating in American

culture. Unsurprisingly, Douglass and other African American writers of his and the next generation had confronted these sentences with their own. From the late nineteenth century to the Harlem Renaissance, African American literature of racial uplift took up this battle cry as an ideological tradition seeking to transform society by redressing racism. Contrasting the transformative potential of racial-uplift literature directly with that of law, government, and public policy, however, is the intuitive but not always the best way of assessing that literature's political value. Rather than pitting formal and informal practices of African American political action *against* each other, and then passing judgment on which is more valuable, a more sensible approach would be to view these practices as *complementary* in a single enterprise of social change. In doing so, we may see that an ideological resistance to racism partially determines the political value of racial-uplift literature. In the press, the literary marketplace, the institutes of higher education, and the literary societies, racial-uplift literature rooted and routed ideological scripts of New Negro politics, such as one script about the historical role of intellectualism in informal political debates and another about the role of literature in setting their rhetorical terms.

Racial uplift outlines the parameters of what could be thought of as *New Negro criticism*. This historical tradition comprises essays that explicitly mention the term "New Negro," alongside those that do not but were, nonetheless, equally involved in the wider critical conversation on race, representation, and African American culture. An array of essays written by sophisticated critics, historians, and thinkers anchored political meaning to artistic or cultural portrayals of race. In the 1892 book *A Voice from the South: By a Black Woman of the South,* Anna Julia Cooper critiques the fiction of William Howells, the "dean" of American literature in the late nineteenth century, for caricaturing African Americans and oversimplifying their lives and struggles. Although his literary contemporaries Albion Tourgée and George Washington Cable, in her view, drew more realistic images of African Americans, Cooper still concludes that "an authentic portrait, at once aesthetic and true to life, presenting the black man as a free American citizen, not the humble slave of [Harriet Beecher Stowe's 1853 novel] *Uncle Tom's Cabin*—but the *man,* divinely struggling and aspiring yet tragically warped and distorted by the adverse winds of circumstance, has not yet been painted."[12]

As critical as Cooper and other African American intellectuals were of racist cultural portrayals, and although Cooper was a pioneer for demanding more education, civic rights, and political responsibilities for African American women, racial-uplift ideologues still subscribed to what historian Kevin

Gaines has called the "ostensible universal but deeply racialized ideological categories of Western progress and civilization."[13] The categories associated the West and the ideas of human progress and civilization with the accomplishments and class privileges of Anglo-Saxon whites. The discourse of racial uplift tended to portray African American aspirations to respectability as jointly racial and socioeconomic. Such African American "uppity" desires threatened white supremacy and the maintenance of socioeconomic hierarchy among the races. By contrast, to many African American proponents of uplift, those desires were a natural byproduct of their race's perceived assimilation to larger American society.

What is more, African American leaders had to balance the promise of modernity, racial progress, and increasing national acceptance with the reality that whites still remained anxious over African American stereotypes. Certain individual, societal, and institutional strategies of racism denied African Americans their entitlement to human freedom, in both the sense of constitutional philosophy and the sense of literal mobility and personal expression. And if the problems across the color line were not enough to discourage African American leaders, consider the problems they faced within the race: the project of racial uplift rested on a tension between, on the one hand, the "Talented Tenth" model of African American elites and, on the other, a racial constituency these elites consistently exaggerated as an inferior group, a status that rationalized the importance of racial uplift in the first place.[14] According to Marlon Ross, a literary historian, several dominant New Negro cultural genres, "or authoritative modes of expression," examined this *problématique* of racial uplift, including "new-century race treatises," "anthologies (race tracts and albums)," "New Negro personal narratives (autobiographical and fictional)," and "professional sociological studies."[15] These modes deepen our understanding that African American cultural expressions resonated in various political ways at the turn into the twentieth century.

The writings of W. E. B. Du Bois and Booker T. Washington—and the ways that their readers had compared and contrasted them—remarkably influenced the expression of racial uplift in African American literature, although Du Bois, as I shall soon show, adjusted his outlook on politics and culture during the Harlem Renaissance. In his 1903 collection of essays *The Souls of Black Folk: Essays and Sketches,* Du Bois incorporates various artistic forms—including epigraphs of poetry, bars of music, block quotations of lyrics, and lyrical prose—to punctuate his sometimes autobiographical and always polemical comments about racial uplift. In Washington's *Up from*

Slavery: An Autobiography (1901), there is not as much of an explicit concern with literary aesthetics. Rather, the attention to form appears in the range and type of revisions the book needed over several editions, as it moved from appealing to an almost exclusively African American readership to a more mainstream, white one. The first edition of Washington's autobiography, *The Story of My Life and Work,* published in 1900, was so fraught with errors in style, diction, and typography that it endangered Washington's goal of representing himself—and, by extension, his race—in a respectable way. *Up from Slavery,* the edition canonized today, corrects these problems.[16] *The Souls of Black Folk* and *Up from Slavery* had put Du Bois and Washington in the best rhetorical positions to uplift the race and convince readers that theirs was a project worth undertaking. A century later, these books have come to represent their diverging political philosophies. Washington supposedly advocates a gradual, accommodationist, industrial-school brand of racial uplift, not unlike the kind Douglass advocated later in life.[17] In contrast, Du Bois's book, especially the third chapter, entitled "Of Mr. Booker T. Washington and Others," critiques this approach as kowtowing to racism. More intellectually ambitious and abstract strategies of racial advancement are needed, Du Bois suggested.[18]

As the twentieth century progressed, Du Bois's critical work expanded in scope, as when he aligned the international, imperialist war being waged in Europe with the domestic war of racial politics being waged at home, in the United States. In a 1919 editorial published in the *Crisis,* Du Bois decries the wartime mistreatment in France of African American troops, who were being unfairly accused at home and abroad of raping women, among other atrocities. The admirable participation of African American soldiers in an international struggle on behalf of the United States and its European allies against the German military, according to Du Bois's testimony, could not alleviate the soldiers' concerns that their home country "represents and gloats in lynching, disenfranchisement, caste, brutality and devilish insult" of the darker-skinned race. Consequently, African Americans did not desire just to "*return from fighting*" but to "*return fighting*" on behalf of "Democracy."[19] Du Bois's political-warrior mentality resonated among other African American intellectuals, including Hubert H. Harrison in his 1920 book, *When Africa Awakes: The "Inside Story" of the Stirrings and Strivings of the New Negro in the Western World.* Harrison argues that the New Negro must embrace a "Race-First" philosophy that realizes the importance of direct political representation and action: "*The new Negro race in America will not achieve political self-respect until it is in a position to organize itself as a politi-*

cally independent party."[20] Outlined in a chapter entitled "The New Politics: The New Politics for the New Negro," Harrison further contends that African Americans must "demand, not 'recognition,' but representation": "we are out to throw our votes to any party which gives us this, and withhold them from any party which refuses to give it"—the refusing party at this time was the Republican Party.[21]

The publications of Du Bois and Harrison, among others, did not discourage accusations that the New Negro was politically meaningless. In "The New Negro Hokum" (1928), Gustavus Adolphus Stewart laments that African Americans secure governmental positions that are at best "second-rate," without influence.[22] The iconoclastic cynicism of this article betrays Stewart's disingenuousness. Rhetorically, it resembles an article, published a couple years earlier, that likely served as the model: George Schuyler's "The Negro-Art Hokum" (1926), in which Schuyler similarly masks his own true beliefs in the Negro's political salience.[23] Schuyler's iconoclastic campaign, it turns out, began amid the public debate over Alain Locke, his ambassadorial status, and his two edited collections, both released in 1925, "Harlem: Mecca of the New Negro" (the March 1 issue of the *Survey Graphic*), and its later edition in book form, *The New Negro: An Interpretation*. Locke's romantic construction of the New Negro neglected the depth and diversity of African American struggle, and Schuyler used satire to expose his failing.

New Negro criticism probed the foregoing political complexities of African American society as it tried to distinguish aesthetics and politics. An ideological conflict existed within the program of racial uplift. From one perspective, the wartime and postwar New Negro was undergoing an evolution toward political action; from the other, this figure was undergoing a "devolution into culture hero," as literary scholar Barbara Foley puts it, and thus away from political action.[24] Similar to mine thus far, Foley's contrast unsettles the conventional scholarly story of the Negro apolitically moving from Old to New in the nineteenth and twentieth centuries. The New Negro we often attribute to Locke's romantic imagination could also have been, in the words of literary historian Henry Louis Gates Jr., a "militant, card-carrying, gun-toting Socialist who refused to turn the other cheek."[25] Modern political culture revolved about the contradictory personifications of the New Negro. Again, in Foley's words, "In the revolutionary crucible of 1919, the term *New Negro* signified a fighter against both racism and capitalism; to be a political moderate did not preclude endorsement of at least some aspects of a class analysis of racism or sympathy with at least some goals of the Bolshevik Revolution."[26] In periodicals ranging from the *Call, Liberator,* and the *Worker's Monthly* to the *Negro*

World, Messenger, and the African Blood Brotherhood's *Crusader,* antiracist discourse portrayed the New Negro, through a class frame of analysis, as a political activist of both national and international stature.

Evidence supports my claim that Locke's popular collections shifted New Negro ideology from political radicalism to romantic culturalism, an ideological turn pivoting on proclamations that African American art and culture were undergoing rebirths of extraordinary proportions. Although only a glimmer in some of Locke's earlier, pre-Renaissance writings and lectures, he relatively succeeded in disengaging African American culture from radicalism in *The New Negro* by revising certain essays he chose for the book while omitting others from it that conjured up radical sentiment. He succeeded in suppressing the idea that the New Negro was radical in both tone and purpose.[27] Portrayed as ahistorical, lower-class, and authentic, the "folk" served as a romantic metonym of the African American community, facilitating Locke's turn from racial antagonism to racial amelioration. The concomitant decline in the production and consumption of left-leaning New Negro politics turned out to be an accurate compass for the direction of modern political culture in the United States.[28]

New Negro politics reflected historical phenomena, philosophical debates, and cultural genres. In 1924, Du Bois called the collective emergence of talented African American authors a remarkable "younger literary movement," younger than his own literary generation of Paul Laurence Dunbar and Charles W. Chesnutt, that was revising the norms of class, society, and sexuality. One year later, Locke, the putative dean of this movement, likewise recognized a "younger generation" of African American writers for whom racial experience provided the material for their creative expression. The movement, he also argued, coincided with the advancement of Anglo-American writers toward more accurate—if less Old Negro—portrayals of African Americans. For Locke, such images portrayed sensitivity, tact, and realism, unlike the minstrel images found in the so-called plantation tradition of Anglo-American literature in the postbellum nineteenth century or in the equally racist and more violent images found in early twentieth-century Anglo-American literature.[29]

During the Renaissance, a debate also raged over art versus propaganda. The central point of contention appeared between Du Bois and Locke. In 1926, Du Bois remarked that the desire of African Americans to conform to mainstream public expectations led them to cling to obsequious attitudes, to perpetuate false racial stereotypes, and to settle into political ambivalence or complacency. He advocated a Negro art in which the apostle of "beauty" intertwined with the apostles of "truth," "goodness," "justice," "honor," and what was "right." In the end, art should express propaganda so that it could "gain[] the right of black folk to love and enjoy," an entitlement that should go hand in hand with African American political demands for fair, humane treatment in the United States and around the world.[30] Du Bois's disregard, in his words, of the "wailing of the purists" anticipated and tried to preempt Locke's position on art and propaganda. Locke's 1928 essay "Art or Propaganda?" reveals his long-held belief that propaganda must implicitly accept perceptions of African American inferiority to build its refutation of it.[31] Propaganda also was an inevitable limitation of African American self-expression and creativity in the arts. For the next decade, Locke continued this line of argument, admonishing the new proletarian wave of African American writers "not to ignore or eliminate the race problem, but to broaden its social dimensions and deepen its universal human implications."[32] The debate between Locke and Du Bois about art versus propaganda encapsulated the conflicting views and even fractured the African American intellectual community in the post–World War I era.[33]

Racial-Uplift Fiction from Pauline Hopkins to Rudolph Fisher

In the end, African American intellectuals from Anna Julia Cooper to Alain Locke varied in their critical understandings of New Negro politics. Yet there was collective agreement in the field of New Negro criticism that artistic portrayals of "race" should aspire to acceptable standards of historical realism and political diplomacy. The success of this project hinged on the expertise of African American artists as well as cooperative race relations. African American writers debated the implications of this situation in their fiction by examining the ideological and practical dimensions of racial uplift. Periodicals were a major venue for such argument and analysis, in addition to books.[34] The emphasis of *Colored American Magazine, Voice of the Negro,* and *Horizon* on how to exploit the literary marketplace to achieve political goals marked a decided postbellum departure of African American intellectual discourse from the abolitionist rhetoric found in earlier, antebellum periodicals such as *Anglo-African Magazine, Freedom's Journal, National Reformer, Mirror of Liberty,* and *Douglass' Monthly.* This turn comprised a growing African American intellectual focus on the responsibility of African American literature to racial uplift and on the kind of forms and themes that could best facilitate the expression and impact of this doctrine. The turn also captures a time when African American leaders and uplifters linked informal to formal political exercises of racial representation.

I must stress here that African American artists and intellectuals, though well aware of the extent and limitations of this turn, did not turn *away* from political action, although the rhetorical departure of that political action from abolitionism may suggest this much. Rather, the turn signals a means by which African American cultural and intellectual elites examined and articulated discourses of racial uplift that political activists, theoretically, could later adopt and deploy, even though the post-Reconstruction, Jim Crow rollback of African American civil rights was derailing the mission. Moreover, this turn could be seen as a further demonstration of how African Americans inherited and capitalized on what Amy L. Blair, a literary scholar, has called the cultural ideology of "reading up," where "upwardly-mobile members of the middle class were being encouraged to read as a means of social and economic success . . . as long as they enter[ed] into an identificatory relationship with the right figures in the right books."[35] African American writers exploited the vicarious and reciprocal relationship between uplifted African American characters and readers within elite, middle-class, and intellectual communities in order to enhance the political effect of their literature.

African American cultural and political thought thrived on this literary hermeneutic. Literary historians Abby Arthur Johnson and Ronald Maberry Johnson have stated that "black artists and intellectuals have debated the function of Afro-American literature: should it serve the aesthetic tastes of the individual writer, or should it advance the interests of Afro-Americans as a group. Some writers favored art-for-art's sake, or approximations of that emphasis; others articulated the need for art-for-people's sake, as they termed it."[36] Analysts of racial-uplift literature realized its potential for communicating African American collective interests, although the stratification of this racialized society, as a consequence of class, culture, and literacy, meant that uplift would consistently subtract the underprivileged from its formula for racial progress.

The exigency of racial uplift motivated some editors of African American periodicals to publish literature alluding to African American social marginalization, economic disfranchisement, and political disempowerment, while others did not place as much emphasis on these themes and published, instead, literature that, in numinous writing style, implied the collective racial progress of African American writers in the realm of belles lettres. In the "Editorial and Publishers' Announcements" of a May 1902 issue of *Colored American Magazine*, Pauline Hopkins, the magazine's editor and serial contributor of essays and fiction, expressed optimism over the future of the

African American literati. "Our short stories, by our Race writers," she states, "are becoming more and more literary in style, and we shall soon see an era of strong competition in the field of letters."[37] Dedicated to being a periodical "of," "by," and "for" African Americans, one that sought to strengthen "the bonds of racial brotherhood," *Colored American Magazine* was geared toward publishing fiction that achieved these ends, which, theoretically, should educate and elevate African American readers.[38] The periodical was also largely consistent, at the turn into the twentieth century, with, to reiterate Blair's point, a "peculiarly American," if mostly middle-class, sensibility, a "fixation on and idealization of upward mobility."[39] One year prior to Hopkins's statement, William Stanley Braithwaite, an eminent African American author and anthologist of poetry, was even more optimistic and prophetic. He predicted that an African American literary movement would come to pass, one whose global recognition and esteem would be commensurate with those of past international literary movements. He asserted, "[W]e are at the commencement of a 'Negroid' renaissance," which "will have in time as much importance in literary history as the much spoken of and much praised Celtic and Canadian renaissance."[40] That movement turned out to be the Harlem, or New Negro, Renaissance of the 1920s.

African American writers also understood the central role of literary style in demonstrating racial uplift. That style needed to be respectable in its exclusion of dialect and in its inclusion of themes of African American civilization in the postbellum New World.[41] At the same time, and especially in the pages of African American periodicals, this literature needed to help advance the social activism of the African American intelligentsia, to mobilize African American readers to commit to serious thought or social action, and to educate African Americans who could not read but could still participate in reading societies and acquire information secondhand. In Hopkins's editorial capacity at *Colored American Magazine,* she encouraged African American writers to refine a pedagogy of racial uplift that would "*develop the men and women who will faithfully portray the inmost thoughts and feelings of the Negro with all the fire and romance which lie dormant in our history,* and, as yet, unrecognized by writers of the Anglo-Saxon race."[42] Applying this mantra to her literary work, she devised a form of sensationalism in the magazine novels she published between 1901 and 1903—*Hagar's Daughter: A Story of Southern Caste Prejudice*; *Winona: A Tale of Negro Life in the South and Southwest*; *Of One Blood: Or, the Hidden Self*—that accommodated both racial uplift and one of the most popular genres of nineteenth-century American literature.[43]

Fiction was the primary literary means of racial uplift. According to literary scholar Hazel V. Carby, Hopkins, for one, "regarded fiction as a particularly effective vehicle of instruction as well as entertainment. Fiction, Hopkins thought, could reach the many classes of citizens who never read history or biography, and she created fictional histories with a pedagogic function: narratives of the relations between the races that challenged racist ideologies."[44] Similar to antebellum domestic novels, Hopkins's magazine fiction featured lurid details that were intended to elicit intense curiosity and emotion from its readers, while portraying reading societies that were both literary and political. Her fiction showed that the sensational African American dime novels and story papers of her era riveted readers enough to deliver a social message, while overcoming the narrative discontinuities that plagued serializing a story. Literary serials and print media nonetheless played crucial roles in the popular dissemination and digestion of political ideas.[45]

Not all racial uplift appeared in fiction, of course, but the genre was a popular and effective medium for the development and sustenance of that ideological discourse. Paul Laurence Dunbar inscribed racial uplift in his poetry, but he did so even more in his short stories. His reputation as the nation's first de facto African American poet laureate overshadows the fact that he, alongside Charles W. Chesnutt, was one of the most prodigious African American creative writers of racial uplift of his generation. Between 1890 and 1905, Dunbar wrote or published more than one hundred short stories. Several of these stories focus on the strengths and weaknesses of African American electoral politics and its relationship to racial uplift. Consistent with this emphasis in his essays, the stories illustrate the extent of Dunbar's interest in the African American political issues and debates of his era.[46]

At the turn into the twentieth century, novels were just as convenient as short stories for African American writers to explore the meaning of racial uplift. Despite their length and complexity, most of these novels have one thing in common: a brief yet informative scene of informal political action, when the characters debate over racial uplift, progress, or politics. These scenes illustrate the collision of political didacticism (the kind found in speeches and essays) and literary exigency (such as moving the narrative along). Sometimes the scenes appear out of place, slowing down the story to a crawl; but they still help turn the plot in a certain direction, while revealing, at the very least, an author's awareness of the political issues, debates, and actions that were stimulating race relations in the real world.

Frances Ellen Watkins Harper's 1899 novel, *Iola Leroy, or Shadows Uplifted*, stands out for depicting African American elites in racial-uplift activism.

Historically, this class of individuals, in Kevin Gaines's words, "made uplift the basis for a racialized elite identity claiming Negro improvement through class stratification as race progress, which entailed an attenuated conception of bourgeois qualifications for rights and citizenship."[47] Racial-uplift discourse, as articulated by the special scenes in Harper's novel, recalls political speeches delivered before an intellectual audience or in political debate between intellectuals. Set during the Civil War and Reconstruction, *Iola Leroy* traces the struggles of a woman, the title character, who learns that, despite her wealthy white Southern ancestry, her mother is a mulatto. The mythical but legalized so-called one-drop rule of racial identity makes her African American, though. Prior to this moment, Iola, as a child, is an "unintentional" passer, unaware of her legal identity as an African American.[48] Once this information leaks out, Iola is enslaved. After her manumission during the war, various struggles with racism compel her to become more active in African American intellectual and political circles.

In the novel's closing chapter, "Friends in Council," we encounter one of these circles. Harper depicts "pleasant, spacious parlors" that were "filled to overflowing with a select company of earnest men and women," including professors, clergy, and medical doctors, "deeply interested in the welfare of the race."[49] At a key moment in this conversation, one of the attendees reads a poem that calls out the visceral distractions of the African American masses: "Have you no other mission / Than music, dance, and song?" It then becomes uplifting and directive: "Go, muffle all your viols; / As nerves learn to stand."[50] Even though the poem is outside the interactive ebb and flow of the conversation, it shows the intervention of *Iola Leroy*: while speaking on racial oppression, the poem still enunciates the intellectual interests of an exclusive African American society. "Friends in Council" is one of several scenes in *Iola Leroy* in which Harper incorporates feminist and political speeches and articles to achieve historical verisimilitude and rhetorical effect.[51]

Also published in 1899, Sutton Griggs's *Imperium in Imperio* is as much a work of fiction as it is, in the words of its subtitle, "a study of the Negro race problem" that connects political rhetoric to racial uplift. The novel focuses on an underground network of racial-uplift ideologues, led by the president of the Imperium, Bernard Belgrade, against whom Belton Piedmont, his adviser, competes for the Imperium's leadership. Both men deliver speeches that paint two philosophical extremes: political militancy and conservative assimilationism. To begin with, we learn from the novel's narrator, Berl Trout, that "[t]he Congress of the Imperium was called and assembled in special session at the

Capitol building just outside of Waco." Trout is informing us, as readers, that we will receive valuable political information: "the secret deliberations of the Imperium are herein disclosed for the first time."[52] In the session, Bernard delivers a speech focused on industrialism, education, the judicial system, and politics and concludes with a call for war against the U.S. government. The speech's militancy is most ironic, given that Bernard hails from a prosperous family in which his mother was a quadroon, his father was white, and his consequent light skin and privilege help to propel him to and through Harvard. In contrast, to the dismay of the faithful Imperium Congressmen, Belton offers a point-by-point counterargument that criticizes the Imperium's militancy, despite, again ironically, the racism he has suffered as a result of his dark skin color. The Imperium's execution of Belton for treason captures Griggs's critique of racial uplift—namely, that it does not go far enough politically to remedy the problems African Americans face in the United States.

The portrayals of the Imperium speeches recall the equally poignant reprint in *Up from Slavery* of Washington's 1895 address at the Cotton States and International Exposition in Atlanta, Georgia. At this event, Washington succeeded in amazing both white philanthropists and African American leaders (who, though, were consistently more skeptical than whites) with his oratory. By extension, *Up from Slavery* broadens his base of white political support by transcribing the eloquent speech in the elegant prose of his autobiography. Some readers admitted to crying while reading *Up from Slavery,* and others claimed that it was as powerful as the Holy Bible.[53] Both *Imperium in Imperio* and *Up from Slavery* climax when the speeches consummate racial-uplift activity. By investing the written word with an oratorical quality, Griggs's novel captures what literary scholar Arlene A. Elder has called "the aesthetic dilemmas of his predecessors in their attempts to sound an authentic voice through the strategies of nineteenth-century popular fiction."[54] The books of Griggs and Washington typify the tendency of African American literature to incorporate the special scenes of historical realism, rhetorical devices, and political debate to authorize a vision of racial uplift.

Beyond sharing narrative and rhetorical forms with *Up from Slavery,* however, *Imperium in Imperio* examines Belton's political deficiencies in order to wage an exceptional critique of Washington's brand of patriotism and, indirectly, to call into question the Tuskegee leader's dismissal of African American political aspirations. Literary scholar Stephen Knadler states that Griggs's novel pinpoints how Belton's "sentimental" and "nostalgic" devotion to the United States reflects the sentimental kind of national citizenship demonstrated by the Citizen Tom, a cultural trope akin not solely to Uncle Tom, the subservient protagonist of Harriet Beecher Stowe's 1852 novel, *Uncle Tom's Cabin*, but also to the "Old Negro" figures of the plantation tradition of Anglo-American literature.[55] Griggs's novel arrives at a time when Washington, in his 1899 book on the Spanish-American War, *The Future of the American Negro*, was reviving the language of his 1895 Atlanta speech, which was encouraging "those of the white race" to "cast down" their "buckets"—or, in other words, to depend on "the most patient, faithful, law-abiding, and unresentful people that the world has seen." In his view, African Americans were "ready to lay down [their] lives, if need be, in defense of [whites]," interweaving their "industrial, commercial, civil, and religious" lives with whites, even as "[i]n all things that are purely social [the races] can be as separate as the fingers." Washington appreciated everything except the political goals of Reconstruction in his notion of "mutual progress" between the races.[56]

A few years later, *The Future of the American Negro* continues the philosophy of accommodation in its description of the Spanish-American War (which lasted from April to August 1898). In the war, Theodore Roosevelt's Rough Riders, who, on July 24, captivated the mainstream media by storming into Sevilla, Cuba, and inciting the Battle of Las Guasimas with Spain, obscured the simultaneous presence of the Tenth Cavalry of African American soldiers. The obscurity raised concerns among certain American observers that the African American soldiers were torn between serving their country and revolting against its racism. Seeking to assuage these concerns, again mostly among his white constituents, Washington states,

> When during our war with Spain, the safety and honour of the Republic were threatened by a foreign foe, when the wail and anguish of the oppressed from a distant isle reached our ears, we find the Negro forgetting wrongs, forgetting the laws and customs that discriminate against him in his own country, and again choosing the better part. . . . In the midst of all the complaints of suffering in the camp and field during the Spanish-American War, suffering from fever and hunger, where is the official or citizen that has heard a word of complaint from the lips of a black soldier?[57]

In *Imperium in Imperio*, the philosophic tension in Griggs's depiction of Belton as well as in the record of Washington's alleviation of public anxieties over African American insurrection, to borrow Knadler's words again, conceivably illustrates the era's "crisis in patriotic black political subjectivity that arose when African Americans were called to silence their protest in support of the troops and the spread of an American-style democracy overseas."[58]

Yet I would add that Griggs's critique must be associated more directly with the era's African American intellectual debate over the meaning of political franchise. In *The Future of the American Negro,* only a few sentences after highlighting the faithfulness of the African American soldier, Washington addresses the "truth" that "the efforts on the part of [the Negro's] friends and the part of himself to share actively in the control of State and local government in America have not been a success in all sections." Washington blames the African American overemphasis on "politics and the holding of office," to the neglect of personal development of "property, economy, education, and Christian character"—a complaint that reappears in *Up from Slavery,* published two years after *The Future of the American Negro.*[59] An unwavering retort, *Imperium in Imperio* is nothing less than an assertion of an alternative government in which African Americans could develop their own nationalist identity, precisely because their newfound constitutional rights were being disrespected and curtailed in post-Reconstruction America.

The African American contemporaries of Sutton Griggs likewise painted scenes of intellectual debate to determine the exigency of political office. In Hopkins's 1900 novel, *Contending Forces: A Romance Illustrative of Negro Life North and South,* about the relationship between racial genealogy and the inheritance of wealth, she depicts print literacy and intellectual societies in ways that punctuate political themes and views. A "sewing-circle," depicted in chapter 8, seeks to contradict an idea presented by the character Arthur Lewis, the principal of an African American industrial institution in Louisiana, that "women should be seen and not heard, where politics is under discussion" (126). In vogue among Boston's African American middle class, the sewing-circle enabled influential African American women to examine and discuss politics without the intrusion of men. In one parlor, the women debate "the place which the virtuous woman occupies in upbuilding a race" (148). One of the attendees, Mrs. Willis, a politician's widow, seeks to refute claims that African American women are automatically inferior moral beings and lack virtue, due to their African ancestry. She incorporates what literary scholar Cathryn Bailey calls "the language of bourgeois Victorian womanhood," which pervaded postbellum American women's literature and celebrated virtuous white womanhood, even as Mrs. Willis indicts its racist assumption that virtuous African American womanhood is inherently "a contradiction in terms."[60] Mrs. Willis encourages the other women in the circle—who are brainwashed into believing otherwise—to realize that the "civilization" of African American women in America does not sacrifice their inherent virtue, especially when this process forces them into situations that compromise their legitimacy or morality. One of the attendees, Sappho Clark, a radiant yet mysterious beauty, doubts the argument's implications. Mrs. Willis reiterates, nonetheless, that the enforced servitude of Africans and their descendants says more about the enslavers than the enslaved: namely, that "the civility of no race is perfect whilst another race is degraded" (*Contending Forces*, 150).

Coincidentally, Sappho attends another meeting, held by the American Colored League of New England's African American leaders, where this issue arises again. Amid discussions revolving around the necessity for political agitation against white supremacy and those selfish "contending forces" fracturing the African American community from within, a man named Lycurgus (Luke) Sawyer tells the story of an illegitimate girl born to a woman whom her uncle raped (246). The woman was an octoroon, and the uncle was a white man who believed that women with one drop of Negro blood knew nothing of virtue and were designed by God to be the concubines of white men (261). At the end of this story, and at perhaps the most melodramatic moment in *Contending Forces*, Sappho faints, because it turns out that she is the illegitimate child and that she is keeping it a secret, perhaps committing a sin, as she continues to pass for a white woman. Literary scholar Sean McCann has observed that "[a]t the moment when Sappho faints, she ceases to work as Hopkins's 'political mouthpiece' and becomes . . . a vessel of history," someone whose "task for the contending forces of Boston" is "first to represent the struggle to recover a bitter history and second to deliver this imperiled heritage to the men whom Hopkins pictures as the truly important agents of 'racial development.'"[61] Sentimentalism, coupled with the prevailing sexism of African American mobilization, diminishes the political potential of Sappho's agency, in the analogous way, as we shall soon see, that the prevailing racism of human evolutionary thought restricts Dr. Miller's potential in Charles W. Chesnutt's 1901 novel, *The Marrow of Tradition*. Nonetheless, we must recognize the broader importance of the tropes and themes of revisionist African American historiography from which the unwitting sexist complicity of Hopkins emerges. For Hopkins, the sewing-circle and the meeting of the American Colored League serve two roles in *Contending Forces*. First, they allow Hopkins to isolate the political discussions of racial uplift from the novel's narrative exigencies. Second, and almost paradoxically, Hopkins subtly interweaves the very plot of Sappho's life to show that, on the one hand, white male predators of African American women and, on the other, the rationale for the enslavement and the continued postbellum oppression of African Americans both work to undermine African American women's moral claims to virtue as well as their claims to social power in both formal and informal realms of politics.

In *The Marrow of Tradition*, Chesnutt concentrates on the political disempowerment of African Americans by merging fiction and history. To reveal the strategy and harm of racism, he uses actual history to discuss the politics and problems of racial uplift. Set in a Southern town called Wellington, the novel re-creates the buildup to whites' massacre of African Americans in Wilmington, North Carolina, in November 1898, which Chesnutt investigated in the aftermath and which, due to the white media's bias across the country, deserved, he felt, a more accurate, albeit literary, historiography.[62] To be sure, as faithfully as Chesnutt depicted the historical antagonism between African American political agency and white supremacy, I should note that his literary vision (or revision) of African American political history still occasionally succumbs to white-supremacist ideology. "Physiological whiteness," as literary scholar Ryan Jay Friedman puts it, had accrued enough "cultural prestige" to form the basis of the "rights and dignities" of citizenship in Jim Crow America.[63] Still, *The Marrow of Tradition* aims to depict the degree to which the social, economic, and political visibility of racial uplift, personified by the African American middle class, threatened white supremacy.

In a key scene set in the office of Wellington's newspaper, the *Morning Chronicle*, three white men meet, as they routinely do, to talk about politics: Major Philip Carteret, the newspaper's editor; Captain McBane, a former overseer; and General Belmont, an aristocrat. The men represent the prevailing view among white racists that African Americans are unfit to "participate in government" and are a "menace" to the "commonwealth." Their "limited education," "lack of experience," "criminal tendencies," and "hopeless mental and physical inferiority to the white race" mean that their uplift is impossible.[64] Six months later, the campaign for white supremacy initially planned by the men is flagging. To drum up support, the major begins publishing columns in the *Morning Chronicle* reiterating the problem of racial uplift and its social, economic, and political threat to white privilege and the nation. When he meets again with the captain and the general to update them on the campaign's progress, the major reads an editorial published in a local African American newspaper that considers the white anxiety over miscegenation a problem because it is used to justify the mass lynching of African Americans. Especially blasphemous in the New South, the article, along with the men's written response to it, energizes the white Republican base, if not also incites the larger body of white supremacists.

The Marrow of Tradition enables Chesnutt to touch on a host of issues and events that were also very real concerns in the New South during the buildup to the riots. They include the disagreements among whites in the Republican and Democratic parties on the nature and implications of African American political growth; the vitriol and violence of white supremacists as they sought to intimidate white sympathizers with, and African American leaders of, racial uplift; the Southern adoption of such discriminatory schemes as the "grandfather clause," which restricted suffrage to citizens, particularly whites, whose fathers and grandfathers could legally vote during the era of slavery; and the differences in racial-political activism between the middle-class and lower-, planter-class segments of white society. All of these were mechanisms by which whites coped with the extent to which racial uplift, as literary scholar Bryan Wagner puts it, "reconfigured the visual field of [Wellington] by initiating changes in local architecture, neighborhood demographics, and sidewalk etiquette." Such reconfiguration damaged "the epistemology of white supremacy" and, at the same time, underwrote an ideological "crisis in white identity."[65] Racial uplift was a field of political ideology in which African American intellectuals could define their positions within the race, in contrast to other, if "lesser," African Americans. It was also a field in which the intellectuals had to define and assert their claims to civilization in the face of certain whites' sense of entitlement and in the face of their consistent resorting to hostility and violence to secure social privilege.

After the golden age of racial-uplift fiction in the 1890s, it continued to examine the expression of white antagonism toward African American political agency. During the Harlem Renaissance, African American authors of novels about racial uplift tended to echo Du Bois's side of the debate with Alain Locke, namely, that African Americans interested in uplift faced several pitfalls in trying to meet the expectations of whites. These novelists took this argument one step further, focusing on the role of such African American conformity in the problems afflicting the material realization of racial uplift. Through this line of reasoning, African American authors questioned not so much the theoretical and political value of racial uplift as the potential failures and hypocrisies in how some African Americans and whites practiced it. Certainly, African American novelists had critiqued racial uplift long before the Harlem Renaissance. In *The Sport of the Gods* (1902), Dunbar satirizes the African American intellectual community as a group of gamblers and night owls who frequent the Banner Club, where Joe Hamilton, the novel's protagonist, suffers a moral decline. Anticipating novels that would appear during the Harlem Renaissance, *The Sport of the Gods* suggests that

African American intellectuals, the supposed bastions of proper values in the racial-uplift program, could be quite indistinguishable from those often accused of ethical malfeasance.

Other novels published before the Harlem Renaissance, though, cast a critical eye toward racial uplift in another way: through the theme of passing. Literary scholar Werner Sollors explains that "passing" refers to the way that one crosses "any line that divides social groups." Usually, in the nineteenth and the first half of the twentieth centuries, it pertained to African Americans racially passing for whites in "modern social systems in which, as a primary condition, social and geographic mobility prevailed, especially in environments such as cities or crowds that provided anonymity to individuals, permitting them to resort to imaginative role-playing in their self-representation."[66] African Americans who intended to pass for white—those who could manipulate their appearance and behavior enough to do so—exploited the social performativity and ambiguity of racial identity to achieve two main goals, as long as their original identities were not discovered: the social privileges and the material, economic benefits already enjoyed by white society; and the protection from racist violence and discrimination that members of this society inflicted on African Americans.[67]

Racial passing implicitly unsettled the African American solidarity of racial uplift. The long-term program of racial uplift, a program that worked gradually through the cultural and moral influence of whites, as well as through the political processes of social activism, public policy, and governmental intervention, could not match the attractive immediacy that racial passing afforded. Passing was a dangerous route toward individual freedom; it was an offense incurring great punishment if discovered. Yet that was a risk countless African Americans were willing to take.

Racial passing has political implications that connect to one of the finer points in this book: the degree to which race predicts—or, at the very least, explains—one's expression of political ideology. The historical persistence of the so-called one-drop rule rationalized the arbitrariness of racial identification and exacerbated the subjective unreliability of identifying political behavior in terms of race. As literary scholar Kenneth W. Warren puts it in his perceptive analysis of Roxy's being "as white as anybody" in Mark Twain's 1894 novel, *Pudd'nhead Wilson,* "Given that race is a social construction, it might be just as accurate to describe Roxy as being as black as anybody. But if everybody is as black or as white as everyone else then maybe the problem is that nobody is as white or black as she [or he] seems."[68] Although an imperfect indicator of cultural and political behavior, race had nevertheless been conceived in uplift literature as a reasonable indicator of a specific experience of human difference.

In Harper's *Iola Leroy*, the title character's embrace of an authentic African American heritage and political agency in the face of white supremacy explains her reluctance to pass racially, even though physiologically (in light of her light skin color) and culturally (her high degree of refinement) she is quite capable of assimilating to certain kinds of white society. In doing so, she shares the strategy of Hopkins (in *Contending Forces*) in wedding an assertion of African American ancestry with an expression, in the words of literary scholar Michael Borgstrom, of a "specifically female form of social activism by subverting traditional gender roles," in effect choosing "a public life dedicated to service to other blacks" and "the role of the tragic mulatto."[69] Racial-uplift fiction suggests that participating in a definable African American political community can provide one way for the passable "mulatto" to overcome the naturalistic "tragedy" of racial intermixture often propounded in post-Reconstruction American literature.

Despite this opportunity for political redemption, the African American literature of racial passing meditated on and expressed an ambivalent attitude toward the automatic sociological connection of race to human experience, since the color ambiguities of race at once reinforced and contradicted the Jim Crow segregation intrinsic to human experience. Put another way, race had determined as much as it had contradicted the literary tradition of political ideology out of which racial-uplift literature—and, perhaps, African American literature generally—formed. The political determinism of such literature was an ideological byproduct of a *societas*, whose original Latin usage, in Hannah Arendt's words, "had a clear, though limited, political meaning; it indicated an alliance between people for a specific purpose."[70] The racism in white-supremacist ideology thus decided the political orientation of even the most racially ambiguous characters within African American literature.

The barrage of racist treatment compels the unnamed protagonist of James Weldon Johnson's *The Autobiography of an Ex-Coloured Man* to pass for white. First published anonymously in 1912 and then under Johnson's name in 1927, the novel, like previous racial-uplift novels, incorporates a climactic scene in which a debate between various parties by turns was "miscellaneous," "drifted toward politics," and then, "as a natural sequence, turned upon the Negro question," upon whether once race can be truly superior to another.[71] In the wake of this conversation, amid the protagonist's first exposure to a Southern African American community, he remarks that he has a greater appreciation for, because he tries to identify with, racial-uplift literature:

[The American Negro's] efforts to elevate himself socially are looked upon as a sort of absurd caricature of "white civilization." A novel dealing with coloured people who lived in respectable homes and amidst a fair degree of culture and who naturally acted "just like white folks" would be taken in a comic-opera sense. . . . However, . . . the future Negro novelist and poet [have the opportunity] to give the country something new and unknown, in depicting the life, the ambitions, the struggles, and the passions of those of their race who are striving to break the narrow limits of traditions.[72]

The genre of racial-uplift literature frames the protagonist's optimistic view of not only his own life as a person publicly identified as African American but also the lives of African Americans generally, a group that tries to overcome the social, economic, and institutional inequities that hinder its collective advancement. As the protagonist fathers the two children of his white wife, to whom he discloses his racial identity but who then dies with his secret, he chooses to pass for a white man to spare his family the stigma of being racially blackened, so to speak. The protagonist appreciates race men, especially Booker T. Washington, "who are publicly fighting the cause of their race" and "who are making history and a race," but his admittedly "small and selfish" act to maintain his status as a white man indicts the limitations of racial-uplift ideologues: "these men have the eternal principles of right on their side, and they will be victors even though they should go down in defeat."[73] Put more pessimistically, a victory in the ethical world could not guarantee a victory in the political world.

During the Harlem Renaissance, African American intellectuals echoed the sentiments of the narrator of *The Autobiography of an Ex-Coloured Man*—namely, that the success or failure of racial uplift results from how well African American leaders, especially Washington, attracted white political leaders, patrons, and philanthropists. The debate at the turn into the twentieth century over Washington's philosophy of racial uplift was, for a long time afterward, the subject of much partisanship within the African American intellectual community. In 1903, Du Bois resisted the philosophy of accommodation espoused by the "Tuskegee Machine" in chapter 3 of *The Souls of Black Folk*. Two years later, Anna Julia Cooper, at the cost of her job as principal of a African American school in Washington, D.C., likewise refused to subordinate academic to industrial education.[74] Yet Charles S. Johnson, the influential founder and editor of *Opportunity: A Journal of Negro Life*, wrote an essay at the height of the Renaissance, in 1928, that more agreeably attributes the Harlem Renaissance's interracial dynamic to the long-term achievement of Washington's social philosophy.[75] To be fair, the storied philosophical distance separating Washington and Du Bois—even including the one I referred to previously—may be misleading or overstated. The substance of Washington's appeals, such as the need for the political alliance of white patrons and African American leaders, did not pose a problem for Du Bois. As Adolph L. Reed Jr., a political scientist, puts it,

> Both Washington and Du Bois accepted the essential model of social hierarchy that prevailed in the society and maintained that "uplift" of the black population entailed an elite-driven accretion of the characteristics of "civilization." This conception of uplift in turn implied an approach to social problems in general and to group organization in particular that connected with the general black population only as an object of social engineering. Therefore, the substantive alliances required to realize its programmatic agendas had to be sought outside the race.[76]

The obsequious nature of Washington's pleas, as well as their monopolization of the philanthropic resources of white corporate capitalism, offended and frustrated Du Bois. Hopkins experienced firsthand the political power and loyalties of Washington when she was dismissed at the same time that he assumed control of the periodical she had long edited, *Colored American Magazine.* He then directed the paper to appeal more to white readers, a portion of whom did not aggressively support its mission of African American solidarity. In this situation, as Hopkins saw it, Washington's commitment to the racial-supremacist sensibility of white patronage undermined the progress of African American cultural and political policies.[77]

Writers of the Harlem Renaissance, including Nella Larsen, recognized and further critiqued the misstep in Washington's political philosophy. In Larsen's 1928 novel, *Quicksand,* the light-skinned African American protagonist of African American and Danish ancestry, Helga Crane, begins a remarkable journey in her life: she leaves her teaching post at a Southern institution similar to Alabama's Tuskegee Institute; abandons her well-to-do, African American middle-class fiancé; and proceeds to move from the South to Chicago, Harlem, Copenhagen, and finally back to Alabama, where she struggles with the new demands of work, love, marriage, and motherhood. The novel opens with images reminiscent of Washington's *Up from Slavery,* an autobiography that portrays its author and the Tuskegee Institute as excessively utilitarian and disciplinarian in upholding cleanliness, good behavior, and manual industry. Helga complains about "the strenuous rigidity of conduct" required in "this huge educational community" in the South called Naxos.[78] (Tellingly, "Naxos" is an anagram of "Saxon," as in "Anglo-Saxon.") In Naxos, Helga resents the African American deference to whites' insistence on moderate racial uplift, the philosophical "system" that turns Naxos into "a machine," "a show place in the black belt, exemplification of the white man's magnanimity, refutation of the black man's inefficiency."[79] The gradual realization of "the trivial hypocrisies and careless cruelties which were, unintentionally perhaps, a part of the Naxos policy of uplift", jades Helga's vision of the viability of racial uplift.[80]

Quicksand turns out to be one of several Harlem Renaissance novels that expose the pitfalls of white involvement in racial uplift. These novels are consistent with studies that show that white patronage and philanthropy had occasionally proven complicit in preserving white supremacy, in treating African Americans in racist ways, and in perpetuating the idea that African Americans were inherently inferior and always in need of elevation or civilization. By definition, patronage meant the support of a cultural idea through the actual funding of individual artists, artistic groups, or cultural institutions, whereas philanthropy entailed a more long-term, humanitarian focus. In any case, a condescending relationship formed between patron and client, donor and recipient. And during the Harlem Renaissance, such power relationships were quite often sexual, not only racial.[81]

Jessie Fauset's *There Is Confusion* (1924) closes with a stinging indictment of the racial inequity exploited by white philanthropy. Written in response to T. S. Stribling's *Birthright* (1922), which captured for Fauset Anglo-American literature's misrepresentation of the Negro, *There Is Confusion* seeks to portray, with relative accuracy, how Philadelphia's African American middle class embraces racial heritage and kinship and how it struggles with the legacy and current realities of racism.[82] In Fauset's novel, we encounter respectable African American characters who are self-made and upstanding—aspiring artists, professionals, and World War I patriots. One of the patriots, Peter Bye, meets on an overseas battlefield one Dr. Meriwether Bye, a white physician who turns out to be Peter's uncle. When the two men talk with each other, Meriwether confesses his guilt in enjoying, during his unwitting years, family wealth from owning slaves and its concomitant privileges. Learning these facts devastates him. He decides to commit himself to the medical corps, hoping that, by giving up his life, he can repay his "debt" (246). While trying to discourage Meriwether from bearing the entire guilt of Anglo-America, Peter admires the man's devotion to freedom. Much later, when Peter returns to Philadelphia after the war, he remembers Meriwether's appeal: "'And just as you black men helped us, Bye,' he used to say, 'there're plenty of white men to help you. You don't know it; for one thing, you've shut your mind to us. Oh, you're not to blame, lots of us aren't to be trusted; most of us, I'm afraid. But we're ignorant and incredulous. Show us what manhood means, Bye" (282). But thereafter, as the opportunity arises for Peter to trust a white person, "his old demon of dislike and suspicion flar[ed] up in him" (295).

Two years after Meriwether's death, Peter's great-granduncle (or Meriwether's grandfather), called "Old Meriwether," visits Peter and his family at their Philadelphia home. In their wending conversation, we learn that Old Meriwether had an African American brother named Joshua Bye, whose African American descendants include Isaiah (the son), Meriwether (the grandson), and Peter (the great-grandson). Old Meriwether and Joshua were the sons of Aaron Bye, the white patriarch of what came to be the wealthy Bye estate in Bryn Mawr, Pennsylvania. Old Meriwether's white side of the family, in a sense, inherited the wealth, but Joshua's black side did not. Joshua was Aaron Bye's illegitimate son, presumably born to an African American woman who was his slave and mistress. Guilt and compassion urge Old Meriwether to support his African American great-great-grandnephew, Peter's son, whom he considers the last of the Byes. Old Meriwether offers to take the boy to live with him in Paris and Vienna, where the boy would be free from America's racism and, eventually, inherit Old Meriwether's fortune. Yet Old Meriwether refuses to acknowledge publicly his kinship with the boy; it would do no good to the boy to know that "Aaron Bye's blood flowed in his veins" (297) or that the boy was essentially African American.

Peter rejects the offer, for a few reasons. First, for Peter to hand his son over to Old Meriwether upon the promise of gifts and money undermines his integrity as a supportive father, even though he and his wife, Joanna (Marshall), are financially struggling as new parents. What is more, to hand the son over unsettles the pact made between Peter and Joanna—namely, that their children should be "brave" and "plucky" enough to live in America and not expatriate to another country, which, according to the novel, was the growing trend at that time (285). *There Is Confusion,* in its narrative and genealogical complexity, concludes that even when familial connections justify whites' financial support of their mixed-race progeny, this support can indirectly preserve the status quo of uneven power relations between the races.

In *The Walls of Jericho* (1928), Rudolph Fisher similarly exposes the problem of white patronage and philanthropy in the program of racial uplift. But in the novel's central section, entitled "Uplift," he satirizes the very scene of the Harlem Renaissance—the theme of the club, which appeared in several novels of the era—to illustrate the ways that whites, along with African Americans, have become "professional uplifters," or experts in exploiting the program for their own advantage.[83] Agatha Cramp, a white benefactor and public servant, epitomizes this group. Although she has committed herself to humanitarian causes, among which is the elevating of African Americans, she has difficulty imagining them as anything more than "alien, primitive people" who have not yet earned the humanity to which she and her own race lay claim (67). Miss Cramp's stereotypes work to maintain the distance between herself and African Americans, a distance that protects her sense of privilege and keeps them in their place as a group constantly and interminably in need elevation.

At a costume ball annually held at the Manhattan Casino and sponsored by an uplift organization called the General Improvement Association, the fact that an African American lawyer could pass for white and shorten this very distance appalls Miss Cramp. Given how the ball is organized, one would suspect that she could not succumb to this kind of deception. The casino is divided into two main sections: the large dance floor, where "just ordinary respectable people or [working-class] rats" (72), all of whom are African American, congregate; and the upper tier, where "dickties and fays" (73)—or, respectively, well-to-do African Americans and a sprinkling of their white acquaintances and guests—hang out. Sitting among this upper-class society of spectators, profiteers, and uplifters, Miss Cramp observes all around the casino the people she seeks to uplift but expresses concern about whites' descending to commingle with African Americans in such an intimate setting. At this point, Miss Cramp encounters Fred Merrit, that passable African American lawyer who looks "with great suspicion and distrust upon all visitors who came to Harlem 'socially'" (106). A lively and subtly contentious discussion begins between the two, in which the white woman confides her exoticization and deprecation of African Americans, while the African American man, passing as white, finds his suspicion and distrust of whites affirmed. Sarcasm tinges his words enough to fool her into believing that he agrees with her opinions of African Americans. But the inflection also enables him, through his experience of living as an African American, to critique these opinions as wrongheaded and as symptomatic of the hypocrisy of white uplifters. When Miss Cramp eventually learns that Merrit is African American, she realizes that, unwittingly, she has just carried on an intellectual conversation and even flirted with a member of a race she had disregarded as nothing more than a society of servants and specimens.

Comparable to the sort of reaction Fisher probably hoped to provoke from the readers of *The Walls of Jericho*, Miss Cramp's devastation advances the novel's intervention into racial-uplift debate by demonstrating what was at stake in the program's incorporation of white patronage and philanthropy. By the end of the novel, readers are presented an image of what Phillip Brian Harper, a literary scholar, has called "a united and socially-solidified black community," a utopianism "arguably essential to the viability of any progressive political vision."[84] In the next chapter, I examine the extent to which the diversity of political affiliations and geographic movement within this community complicates the strategies of racial and class uplift as well as the ability of literature to implement them.

4

The Geopolitics of African American Autobiography between the World Wars

The autobiographies of Claude McKay and Langston Hughes do not record any personal interaction between the two writers, but the texts do tell us that they corresponded in literature and letters. While admiring each other's work from afar, they similarly connected race, class, and transnationalism to geopolitics, or to geographically contingent forms of politics. In McKay's 1937 autobiography about his life after World War I, *A Long Way from Home,* he recalls a "genteel-Negro hostility" to a novel about African American lower-class and bohemian life that he had published nine years earlier, in 1928, *Home to Harlem.*[1] The hostility expressed toward McKay resembles the way literary critics disparaged Hughes's "primitive Negro poems" in his 1927 collection, *Fine Clothes to the Jew.* Just as McKay suggested a camaraderie with Hughes, the converse occurred a decade earlier, in a couple letters from Hughes to McKay in 1925 and 1928. In them, Hughes praises his elder as "the best of the colored poets" and *Home to Harlem* as "the finest thing 'we've' done yet," in which "we" represents the two authors among the African American literati.[2] By the time of Hughes's second autobiography, *I Wonder as I Wander: An Autobiographical Journey,* about his life in the 1930s but appearing in 1956, he had already published a full-length autobiography in 1940, along with a number of essays, remembering McKay's accomplishments.[3]

The small number of available exchanges between the two writers, coupled with the homage Hughes pays to McKay's generation, explains the ostensible one-sidedness of the admiration. In their autobiographies, however, the mutual respect indicates a shared argument: that art, as it helped to uplift the race, could combat racism and capitalism in the United States and around the world. McKay and Hughes were as much agents of political and class reform as they were literary travelers; they employed what literary scholar Michelle Ann Stephens has called "the perspective of a traveling black subject" to achieve a geopolitical and transnational form of African American literature.[4] In this chapter, I suggest that both *A Long Way from Home* and *I Wonder as I Wander* show that their authors participated in the Communist (with a capital *C*, in reference to the official organization) or left-wing, "radical" parties while writing and thinking about literature as an informal strategy to influence societies at home and abroad.

A Long Way from Home covers McKay's life from the end of World War I to circa 1933, when his recalcitrance annoyed members of the Harlem Renaissance intelligentsia, including James Weldon Johnson and Alain Locke. McKay likened his journeys to truancy or vagabondage—to a broadening of his perspectives on the Harlem Renaissance, race relations, and the cultural impetus of social action.[5] He understood the paradoxical unity and tension between the "red" and the "black," between the class-based and race-based strategies of social mobilization, which sharpened his vision of human difference and imbued his literature with political import. His 1919 poem "If We Must Die" arose especially from a political sympathy he shared with radical programs; its thematic universalism, though, reflects his public detachment from the specters of the Communist Party or, more broadly, from an oversimplified political identity.[6]

According to *I Wonder as I Wander*, a memoir spanning from 1931 to 1938, Hughes shared McKay's literary geopolitics, or his opinions on how literature could communicate and inflect formations of social activism within and across regions. On the surface, the fact that these writers held common literary and geopolitical interests contradicts the fact that they held contrasting obligations to the Harlem Renaissance. Biographer Wayne F. Cooper states that McKay was a "rebel sojourner," absent from Harlem proper as he traveled the world.[7] By expressing reservations over McKay's lack of commitment to the prevailing African American cultural politics, the Renaissance's leaders overlooked his remarkable theoretical study of both race and class in the global development of political groups, such as the radical Left and the Communist Party. In contrast, Johnson and Locke praised Hughes for embodying what the Harlem Renaissance stood for. Even Hughes admitted that he longed for Harlem, where he resided in 1921 and 1922. Also, in 1926, Hughes published his now-canonized essay "The Negro Artist and the Racial Mountain" in celebration of the city's efflorescence.[8] The discrepancy in the canonical statures of McKay and Hughes, nonetheless, belies their political kinship on the global issues of race and class.

My readings of McKay's and Hughes's autobiographies enable us to answer a question that follows from the previous chapter: How can we broaden our domestic model of the politics of African American literature to account for transnational points of reference? In the century after American slavery officially ended, this political tradition has shown African American authors telling stories of personal and racial uplift, their migrations across the country, their achievement of a sophisticated sense of racial identity, and their entitlement to American citizenship.[9] *A Long Way from Home* and *I Wonder as I Wander* depart from this tradition in one crucial respect: the travels of their authors around and beyond the United States had stimulated their imagining and writing of literature as both geopolitical and anti-imperialist. McKay and Hughes alike exemplified what we could call authors of a geopolitical as well as a transnational genre of autobiography.[10] In limning the political dimensions of the genre, I am not so preoccupied with proving and measuring the aesthetic value of political art (though I do gesture to its possibility in my analysis of McKay's poem "If We Must Die," I do not so much in my analysis of Hughes's works). Rather, I am focused on how the authors represented themselves and their art as political (in the informal sense) while representing others (in official, delegable capacities) on behalf of international social change.

Portraying autobiography as history is certainly fraught with complexity. Any study of *A Long Way from Home* and *I Wonder as I Wander* must treat the authors, among other recognizable figures in the books, as both self-serving literary personae and approximations of historical reality.[11] The autobiographies oscillate between fact and fiction, documentation and fabrication; their selective representations of memory play up certain storylines while playing down others for the sake of narrative exposition. The autobiographies are not transparent windows into McKay's and Hughes's lives and circumstances but, instead, texts with special rhetorical identities, illustrated in the factual discrepancies between the autobiographies and historical record. Discrepancies exist between what McKay says in *A Long Way from Home* and what he says in his nonfictional books of 1923 and 1925, *Negroes in America* and *Trial by Lynching: Stories about Negro Life in North America*. They also exist between what Hughes says in *I Wonder as I Wander* and what he says in the more sympathetic communist material (with a lowercase *c*, in reference to the class and political theory) located in his 1950s private archive of letters and in excised autobiographical texts.[12] Still, the autobiographies invite us to appreciate history—to look at transnational movement as not only voluntary, which is the impression McKay and Hughes give, but also enforced, which is the impression we must discern. (In the case of Hughes, global curiosity and cultural politics motivated him to travel, but McCarthyism and wider anticommunist sentiment in the United States during the Cold War made his residence in the country untenable.)[13] *A Long Way from Home* and *I Wonder as I Wander* are thus as revealing literarily as they are historically.

My comparative readings of the texts and contexts of the two autobiographies have several implications. First, they encourage an archival recovery of *A Long Way from Home*. Published in his late forties, it was the first of several books by McKay in the last decade of his life, the others being *Harlem: Negro Metropolis* (1940) and *My Green Hills of Jamaica,* which was written in 1946 (but not published until 1979) and reflects on the cultural, political, and intellectual contexts of his early literary career, the Harlem Renaissance, and his global travels. Next to Hughes's first autobiography, *The Big Sea* (1940), McKay's *A Long Way from Home* provides one of the most unflattering exposés of the Harlem Renaissance. Unfortunately, McKay's book has not yet received as much scholarly and classroom attention as has Hughes's, even though it provides an equally intriguing and informative analysis of identity, art, race, and geopolitics between the world wars.[14]

Next, my focus on Hughes's *second* autobiography, *I Wonder as I Wander,* as opposed to the first, *The Big Sea,* arises from my belief that it may provide more information about his stance on political art than what we have learned from traditional biographical overviews of his life.[15] True, *The Big Sea* talks about Hughes's initial geopolitical awareness. As a young lad, he stopped selling a radical newspaper, *Appeal to Reason.* He learned that doing so could get him and his African American readers "in trouble." Later, in high school, he interacted with a Jewish girl of "foreign-born" parents who were more "democratic" and less "anti-Negro" than Anglo-American families and who let him read such radical newspapers as the *Socialist Call* and the *Liberator*—of which McKay was once an editor, by the way. Many students in Hughes's school celebrated the Bolshevik Revolution, forcing school officials to crack down on the lack of Americanism that this joy suggested.[16] Finally, while a student, Hughes wrote a short story, "Mary Winonsky," that addressed the reaction in American urban newspapers to Bolshevism.[17] But *I Wonder as I Wander* gives us a clearer sense of his crucial geopolitical associations with radical, left-wing organizations from World War I through the Cold War.[18] I do not mean to understate the ideological insight of the two definitive biographers of McKay and Hughes, Wayne F. Cooper and Arnold Rampersad. If anything, Cooper and Rampersad have illuminated the factual discrepancies—and there are quite a few—between what McKay and Hughes say in their autobiographies and the personal and historical facts confirmed by scholars. In this chapter, though, I pay more attention to the degree to which the autobiographical rhetoric of McKay and Hughes belongs to the political genealogy of African American literature that I have so far examined in this book.

"The Great Current Running through the World": Claude McKay's A Long Way from Home

McKay was one of the most prolific and sophisticated writers of the first half of the twentieth century. The celebration of his 1919 poem "If We Must Die" and the critical praise of his 1922 volume of poetry, *Harlem Shadows,* combined to anoint him one of the greatest living American poets of African descent since Paul Laurence Dunbar. Soon afterward, Alain Locke, the so-called dean of the Harlem Renaissance, characterized McKay as a promising "youth" of New Negro modernism. Alongside writers such as Jean Toomer, Countee Cullen, and Hughes, McKay starred in the groundbreaking collections of 1925, edited by Locke: the "Harlem: Mecca of the New Negro" issue of the *Survey Graphic* and its expanded version, *The New Negro: An Interpretation.* That we tend to associate McKay with the Harlem Renaissance should surprise no one.

Yet a number of facts complicate McKay's association with the Harlem Renaissance. As mentioned earlier, he was absent from Harlem proper during the movement. From 1919 to 1921, he toured London; and from 1923 to 1934, he traveled to parts of Soviet Russia, Berlin, Paris, Marseilles, Barcelona, Tangier, and Morocco. Second, McKay's iconoclastic approach to literature and culture alienated him from the Harlem Renaissance intelligentsia. Third, unlike the more apolitical members of the Harlem Renaissance, as we shall soon see, he became a Marxist-informed radical. In the United States, he read and contributed to political magazines; abroad, he did the same, while attending conferences on the 1917 Bolshevik Revolution. McKay was a "rebel sojourner," not only an associate, of the Harlem Renaissance, an idea that comes across in his documentation, in *A Long Way from Home,* of the multiple native and residential homes he cherished. His first home was Jamaica, where (in Clarendon Parish) he was born and where he lived until he left in 1912. Having achieved a mere "local reputation as a poet," he abandoned Jamaica because he could not benefit there from the "bigger audience," the "high achievement," and the "great currents of life" he believed were available in New York City. He especially enjoyed living in Harlem, his first home away from home. After working long hours and many weeks on the railroad, he often felt a "physical joy of getting back to the city that was home" (*A Long Way from Home,* 9). Harlem was the psychic and emotional point of reference he longed for, whether as an interstate, domestic worker on the Pennsylvania Railroad or later as an international traveler.

For McKay, being "a long way" from his native or residential homes implied geographic as well as psychological and spiritual distance. In words that anticipated Hughes's *I Wonder as I Wander,* McKay blamed his early "lust to wander and wonder," his "spirit of the vagabond," for his dropping out of Kansas State College in the spring of 1914.[19] He "had no desire to return home" to Jamaica (9). Even "domestic partnership," such as marriage, detracted from the possibilities of physical mobility: "I had wandered far and away until I had grown into a truant by nature and undomesticated in the blood" (118). McKay felt at home only while traveling. The farther away he got from his native or residential home, the closer he came to a full understanding of himself as a politician, creative writer, and literary aesthetician.

McKay's self-understanding in these terms began prior to his global travels, when he was a fledgling writer and editor and when he was oscillating between the proverbial philosophies of art for art's sake and art for society's sake. One day at the office of the *Liberator,* where he was working as one of the magazine's editors, he came across some poems that e.e. cummings had submitted for possible publication. McKay showed them to the acting editor in chief (the editor in chief, Max Eastman, was out of the office), who condemned them for being decadent. The longstanding mission of the *Liberator,* which had succeeded the *Masses* in February 1918, stated that literature should contribute to the cause of social revolution. In McKay's editorial tenure at the *Liberator,* it would seem that he tried to separate his literary identity from his political identity, but his own writing—as opposed to his magazine editing—of literature revealed a more intricate relationship between the two. Ideally, he wanted to detach one from the other, rejecting the notion of "a proletarian, or a bourgeois, or any special literature or art" and instead embracing the idea that "whenever literature and art are good and great they leap over narrow group barriers and periods to make a universal appeal." When it came to the idea of proletarians writing literature, he acknowledged that "it was much easier to talk about real proletarians writing masterpieces than to find such masterpieces" (110).[20] While he appreciated the community of proletarian authors with which he identified himself, in other words, their literature still needed to compete for the universal title of masterpiece. Yet McKay really could not detach politics from aesthetics. Contradicting his notion of the universal masterpiece, he also, at times, thought that audience and historical factors determined the aesthetic excellence of literature and that aesthetics did not and could not exist in an apolitical vacuum. Reading the many African American newspapers recounting the incessant racial strife and lynchings enraged McKay, in the end shaping his poetry and fueling the geopolitical thrust of his literary aesthetics.

McKay was otherwise well aware of the difference between the theoretical power of political discourse and the material influence of political action. Between 1919 and 1921, England's International Club first immersed him in the radical political theories of such "dogmatists and doctrinaires" as socialists, communists, trade unionists, and journalists (57). He was compatible with the Marxists he met, for political activities in Jamaica and the United States had already, if informally, prepared him for Marxist thought.[21] British exposure to political radicalism inspired him to publish poems and essays in the *Workers' Dreadnought,* edited by women's suffragist and British socialist Sylvia Pankhurst. McKay also studied how to place Karl Marx's philosophy of social organization in historical context and to grasp why intellectuals and politicians of the early twentieth century had found his writings so appealing.[22] But reading Marx did not fully teach McKay how to be a political activist. Marx "belonged even more to the institutions of learning than to the street corners from which [he] had so often heard his gospel preached" (58). In the cold, snow-laden streets of Moscow in 1922, that very distinction between intellectual thought and daily life struck McKay as he interacted with the many Russians who knew more about poverty and hunger than about "the true nature of Communism," only that Vladimir "Lenin was in the place of the Czar and that he was a greater Little Father" (125). Figuring out how to overcome the disconnection between theoretical intellection and the practical world did not come easy to McKay until he met "Comrade Vie," a multilingual, foreign revolutionary who helped to refine McKay's radical perspectives and to focus his activist energies.

McKay's desires to probe and critique doctrines were a key part of his intellectual nature and his socialization in the international circles of formal politics. At a 1922 London reunion with members of the International Club (the year of the Fourth Congress of the Communist International), McKay disaffiliated from the Communist Party, although, ironically, he still gravitated to a friend whom he described as "not a fanatic or dogmatist" and with whom he had "often waxed satirical about Communist orthodoxy" and "discussed the idea of a neo-radical magazine in which nothing in the universe would be held sacred" (123). The Third Communist Internationale (or the Comintern) confused McKay's attachment to the principles of the Communist Party with his membership in the organization. At times against his will, he was treated as if he were a Communist Party delegate or representative.

Once, upon entering the Bolshoi Theater in Moscow to watch a play about proletarian society and culture, McKay endured being manhandled by ushers who had been ordered to whisk him onto the stage near Max Eastman and Gregory Zinoviev, chairman of the Comintern. Disoriented and unprepared to say anything, McKay rejected Zinoviev's invitation to speak. When Eastman chimed in, arguing that meeting public expectations should override individual self-interest and that, consequently, McKay should speak on behalf of the "Negro workers of America," the annoyed writer responded that he approached geopolitical organizations "as a writer, and not an agitator" (136). Despite his reluctance, public expectations and political urgency thrust him into situations of formal politics more involved than he desired.[23] With McKay's celebrity came privileges that were accorded only to the delegates, privileges that he relished, even though they, in turn, came from confusion over his exact status within the Communist movement. Despite his voiced reluctance to separate his literary and political activities, official political distinction enabled him to tour the world and secure the cultural capital required for his travel both among the radical societies of Europe and in the provinces of Russia. McKay's international literary celebrity would have been impossible without his official status in political radicalism. Touring Russia in the wake of his cultural rise enhanced his self-understanding as an internationalist.

Internationalism also determined McKay's intellectual approach to race and class, which he tried to prioritize in the Communist movement. Trapped proverbially between a rock and a hard place, he knew that certain members of the intelligentsia, such as Jewish American educator and critic Joel Elias Spingarn, demoted socialist radicalism in favor of a race-based radicalism benefiting the political interests of African Americans. He also knew, though, that Communist radicals argued that "it was impossible for any man to be pro-Negro and anti-radical" at the same time (116). The "Negro Problem" had to be traced to its origins in racism as well as in the consequences of class where everyone, regardless of racial background, belonging to a common disadvantaged group could unite in a common political cause. By tackling this conundrum in A Long Way from Home, McKay's concerns predated the intersection of race, class, and politics in the second half of the

1945 autobiography, *Black Boy,* where Richard Wright talks about his life in Chicago from 1926 to 1936. (In 1977, Harper and Row released the second half of *Black Boy* as *American Hunger.*) But, unlike Wright, who concentrates here on the American domestic setting, McKay imagines in his own autobiography transnational political events in which blacks and reds, race and class, could take center stage.

McKay's transnational racial politics was timely. During and in the decade after World War I, political agitation (with regard to both class and race) escalated on both national and international fronts. In 1919, the summer was "red" in two senses, according to literary scholar Barbara Foley, "signifying at once the political repression of leftists and the bloody suppression of black rebellion."²⁴ In March of that year, Vladimir Ilyich Lenin founded the Comintern, rode communism's wave of popularity after the 1917 Bolshevik Revolution, and declared the need for a concerted effort to globalize communist thought. Later, in the summer and autumn of that year, hundreds of African Americans died in at least thirty race riots. Violence between the races ravaged many sections of the United States, including Elaine, Arkansas; Chicago; and Washington, D.C. Historical coincidence underlined the ideological coincidence of these events.

London first exposed McKay to the potential cultural definition of racial politics, in the context of his stimulated internationalism. The International Club, mentioned earlier, was only one of two clubs where McKay took solace. To survive London, a city he assailed time and again for its racism, he also frequented a club for colored soldiers where he could discuss the issues of race and culture, while distributing well-known African American periodicals: the *Crisis,* the *Messenger, Negro World,* the *Pittsburgh Courier,* and the *Chicago Defender.* The social comfort of these two clubs—one for radical leftists, the other for colored soldiers—mirrored his comfort in a political philosophy that linked race to class. William J. Maxwell, an expert on McKay and his times, states that the author's indoctrination into Marxism cultivated his views on class consciousness in African American political action and on racial consciousness in international communism.²⁵ In due time, McKay attempted to modify Marxist theory in his 1923 book published in Russia, *Negry v Amerike* (translated as *The Negroes in America*). One of the first monographs theorizing the relationship between race and class, *The Negroes in America* indicted the Marxist and communist neglect of race in transnational political organization.

Race elevated McKay's authority in radical societies. Taking advantage of his own dark skin color, he claimed that he was authentically black—more pure-blooded than the lighter-skinned intellectuals and political activists encircling him. To enjoy the privilege of attending Communist Party congresses, he realized, behaving like a "typical Negro," like one who looked African American as well as looked at the world with a peculiarly racial vision, was a must (*A Long Way from Home*, 136). As a self-proclaimed spokesman for the race, McKay spoke on the organizational failings of African Americans to Leon Trotsky, the Commissar of Army and Naval Affairs, who confided that they were a "backward" race, required "uplift," and neglected the benefits of the "labor movement" (161). Though not inclined to echo Trotsky's words, McKay admitted that, in contrast to the radical bloc, African Americans did lack the proper vision, infrastructure, and goals key to the aggregation of political resources (as opposed to the segregation of its racial community). Political aggregation was needed to build an effective platform for radical agitation.[26]

The lack of political aggregation, in McKay's opinion, was partly to blame for the failure of leadership within African American communities. At the root of this problem was a social, economic, cultural, and intellectual chasm between many African American communities and their intelligentsia during the Harlem Renaissance. In 1916, this gulf yawned wider when McKay sent some of his poems to William Stanley Braithwaite, the esteemed African American author and anthologist of poetry. Commendable aesthetically but lamentable for featuring literary markers betraying McKay's racial and political identities, the poems irked Braithwaite, who desired to write literature that could veil his African ancestry and transcend the racial realism of African American literature. McKay refused to practice this "conservative" approach to literature for a few reasons. First, he viewed his poetry as "too subjective, personal, and tell-tale." Most appealing were the radical periodicals in the United States and abroad that already appreciated his "eclectic approach to literature" and his "unorthodox idea of life," both qualities interweaving his identifications with race, politics, intellectualism, and internationalism (28). Second, as his dedication to travel showed, lived experience authenticated and enlivened the literary imagination in ways that reading could not.[27] Finally, as mentioned earlier, McKay enjoyed the privileges of being a de facto political representative of his race.

In the July 1919 issue of the *Liberator*, McKay, despite and because of Braithwaite's reservations about the racial presence in his work, published what turned out to be the most celebrated poem of his career, "If We Must Die":

If we must die, let it not be like hogs
Hunted and penned in an inglorious spot,
While round us bark the mad and hungry dogs.
Making their mock at our accursed lot.
If we must die, Oh let us nobly die,
So that our precious blood may not be shed
In vain; then even the monsters we defy
Shall be constrained to honor us though dead!
Oh, kinsmen! we must meet the common foe!
Though far outnumbered let us show us brave,
And for their thousand blows deal one death-blow!
What though before us lies the open grave?
Like men we'll face the murderous cowardly pack,
Pressed to the wall, dying, but fighting back!

The poem alludes to several sources that attest to its literariness, such as the English sonnet form (a rhyme scheme of *abab cdcd efef gg*) as well as a phrase, "if we must die," from the 1604 play *Measure for Measure* by William Shakespeare, who, incidentally, made that sonnet form famous.[28] The form enabled McKay to represent and build collective resolve. Between the second and third quatrains, between exclamation and apostrophe, the poem reaches a crescendo, while the second quatrain's final line—"Shall be constrained to honor us though dead!"—concludes that the "monsters," by imposing themselves on the speaker's "lot," have incited a community of resistance and self-pride, equivalent to a social movement. The third quatrain affirms this conclusion, but it also contends that the poem as a whole testifies to the movement's potential ideological and symbolic force, even if the movement's practical or political success, the extent to which it changes society, turns out to be relatively minor. By the way, although McKay was Jamaica-born and had a history, before and after publishing the poem, of writing racially marked poetry, "If We Must Die" indeed makes no textual reference to race.

An "explosion" from a dining-car waiter's imagination in 1919 into the print of mass media, "If We Must Die" captivated the hearts and minds of political activists around the world—regardless of race. Over and again, McKay tells this wonderful story in *A Long Way from Home* (30).[29] Overlapping the end of World War I and the cultural influx of the African diaspora into Harlem and elsewhere, the poem's birth occurred during McKay's travels on the Pennsylvania Railroad, between New York City and Pittsburgh and sometimes as far south as the Baltimore–Washington, D.C., corridor, when the hostile postwar climate convinced some of his co-workers to arm themselves for protection. It evolved from a tension between the necessity of daily work and the desire for leisure. In large part, the global acclaim resulted from the way that the poem tapped the racial, class, and political anxieties of the era. Early on in his career, McKay refused to reveal to his railroad co-workers that he was a "scribbler," had literary ambitions, and was in the workforce but not of it. Daily work distracted him from his literary goals, but he still found a way to dream: "I had a desire to be away from my [railroad] fellows and off by myself, even if it were in a crowd. My mind was full of the rendezvous with that editor in New York" (12). Even when arrested on suspicion of dodging the World War I draft and then crammed in "an old-fashioned fetid hole" of a jail cell, McKay eyed his literary future: "I tried to overcome the stench by breathing through my mind all the fragrant verse I could find in the range of my memory" (12).

The genesis of "If We Must Die" has both ideological and practical meaning. McKay clung to his pen in a state of inspiration, anxiety, trepidation, and unrest. But in contrast to his habit of keeping his literary work a secret from his co-workers, he was willing to read the poem to them without fear of social recrimination. The poem strengthened his bond with the crew, yet the fact that he could write verse between the periods of work indicated the conflict between literary and manual kinds of labor. Whereas the former, to some degree, required leisure time, the latter, including jobs such as being a porter, fireman, waiter, bar boy, and houseman, hamstrung it. Daily responsibilities robbed McKay of the opportunities for leisure that would have been available in the life of a literary professional.[30] The urgency of his profession correlated with the urgency of his politics.

In the bickering between Frank Harris and Max Eastman, the editors of *Pearson's* and the *Liberator,* Eastman won the right to publish "If We Must Die," and afterward the poem appeared in countless local and international venues. Far and wide, the poem was being appropriated, even by Winston Churchill, who referred to it in a speech encouraging British troops during World War II.[31] The excitement generated by the poem affirmed McKay's political internationalism, especially during his time in Soviet Russia from September 1922 to October 1923. In the wake of meeting with Trotsky to discuss communism and the Negro Problem, McKay attended a student celebration of the Red Army in Moscow and was called to the main stage, whereupon, in response to "someone [who] demanded a poem," he recited "If We Must Die." Immediately, he was transformed into "a rare instrument and electrified by *the great current running through the world,* and the poem popped out of [him] like [a] ball of light and blazed" (162; italics mine).

The synergy between the audience and McKay, as he recited "If We Must Die," brings into stark relief the relationship between poetics, ideology, and history. First, the figurative language of political enlightenment captures how a social setting could decide the perceived aesthetic value of a literary text. Second, as much as the travels of McKay indicated his cultural and political affinities, his transnational mobility resulted from his capitalizing on his stature as a political man who gendered the politics of race and class as male, evident in the speaker of "If We Must Die" hoping that, "like men," he and the audience will engage in the proverbial bouts of masculine violent resistance.[32] Finally, this event occurred at a special stage in the historical development of Russian society, when, according to Kate A. Baldwin, a literary scholar, its "thinkers used culture as a means of fomenting change." McKay was sensitive to this ideology of cultural politics and lauded nineteenth-century Russian authors such as Anton Chekhov, Fyodor Dostoyevsky, Nikolai Gogol, Leo Tolstoy, and Ivan Turgenev: he not only "intuited . . . an affinity between Russian literature's relationship to European cultural margins and his own but . . . [also] believed this affinity had everything to do with the political potential of black art, of black culture's ability to do the work of 'social engineering.'"[33] Russian cultural politics likely preconditioned the audience's demand that McKay read a poem, and the resulting synergy that made him "the great current running through the world." It also likely stimulated his public desire to reciprocate the gesture.[34]

Unsurprisingly, McKay was sensitive to Frank Harris's accusation that he was "a bloody traitor to [his] race" (81) for following the advice of his British publisher, Grant Richards, to excise "If We Must Die" (despite its explicit absence of a racial marker) from the London edition of *Spring in New Hampshire* (1920). Performing the sort of racial muting that Braithwaite would have admired, McKay published a volume of poetry that veered away from the earlier vernacular poems of *Songs of Jamaica* and *Constab Ballads,* both published in 1912. If the London volume of *Spring in New Hampshire* identified McKay with traditional Victorian poetry in formal English, the American edition of *Spring in New Hampshire*—eventually renamed *Harlem Shadows* (1922), which features "If We Must Die"—emerged from his struggle with critical and commercial forces that briefly prevented him from being "a man [who] is faithful to his own individuality" (82).

The disagreement with Braithwaite was a symptom of McKay's broader skepticism of the political background and motives of the African American intelligentsia. Similar to the way that he believed Braithwaite was conservative, he sensed that the officials of the National Association for the Advancement of Colored People comprised "some of the more conservative Negro leaders" (89). Braithwaite's conservatism rejected the kind of racial polemics possible in radical discourse. Du Bois's conservatism, though differing from Braithwaite's because it belonged to a polemical mind, still translated into an icy self-centeredness and snobbery reflecting his quirks of personality as much as a cultural elitism that McKay could hardly bear. For this reason, McKay was never comfortable among members of the African American intelligentsia: "I happen not to be of it" but only in it (93). Beyond rubbing him the wrong way in social circles, the "damnable uniform" of African American bourgeois assimilationism (93), or "the borrowed robes of hypocritical white respectability" (176), stood in sharp contrast to the quotidian hardship that he endured when he first arrived in the United States and worked in menial jobs.

McKay reserved his harshest criticism of the African American intelligentsia for Locke. Upon meeting Locke for the first time in Paris, around 1929, McKay learned why people deemed the dean of the Harlem Renaissance as "the most refined Negro in America" (240). Yet Locke's "rococo" personal and writing styles did not impress McKay nearly as much as the hypocrisy of his deanship (240). Prefiguring Wright's "Blueprint for Negro Writing" (1937), which criticizes the Harlem Renaissance, McKay suggested that an elitist graduate of Harvard and Oxford, such as Locke, could not claim the (class) authenticity and (racial) authority that the movement required of an African American leader. Reservations grew even more when Locke, in the landmark book of the Harlem Renaissance, *The New Negro* (1925), retitled McKay's incendiary poem "The White House" as "White Houses" in order to mitigate the potential confusion between the metaphor of "the vast modern edifice of American Industry from which Negroes were effectively barred as a group" (240) and the more controversial metaphor of the White House in Washington, D.C.[35] Locke's fretting over the conflict between polemical African American literature and the interracial diplomacy of the Harlem Renaissance was not far from Braithwaite's. Both men hinted that African American literature should avoid alienating readers and aspire toward universal appeal across the color line. Locke's "artistic outlook," though a progressive revision of racial representation in art, was too "reactionary" to suit McKay's taste, much less to lead to a rebirth of African American culture (241).

McKay's criticism did not go unnoticed by Locke himself, as it did not go unnoticed by several friends and acquaintances critical of the author's candor in *A Long Way from Home*. They questioned McKay's retreat from the responsibility of racial leadership expected of successful African American writers.[36] When McKay returned to Harlem in 1921 as an international celebrity, his loss of "the rare feeling of vagabond feeding upon secret music singing" confirmed his disenchantment with politics (93). Hubert Harrison, an African American socialist and close friend, urged him to take an active role in domestic racial uplift. He "owed it to [his] race," Harrison said (93). Ever philosophical, McKay countered with ambivalence: "I have a poet's right to imagine a great modern Negro leader. At least I would like to celebrate him in a monument of verse. For I have nothing to give but my singing" (270). By restricting the meaning of African American leadership to poetic terms, though, he resisted implementing such philosophical ideas in official cultural or political capacities. Thus, his ambivalence strained his already fragile relationship with the Harlem Renaissance intelligentsia. Many of them, following the lead of Du Bois, who claimed famously that he needed to take a bath after reading *Home to Harlem,* resented the novel's unflattering portrayal of misbehavior, promiscuity, and improprieties of Harlemites. McKay's vagabond spirit was also a problem. Toward the end of McKay's decade abroad (early 1930s), James Weldon Johnson wrote him a letter, requesting his return to the United States so that he could support the Harlem Renaissance. And, a few years later, Locke interpreted McKay's self-described truancy as racial delinquency.

Despite the concerns, McKay remained committed to travel. He regarded himself a bona fide "internationalist," not simply an African American (231). While his literary and political celebrity hinged on this racial identity, some strangers viewed him in a different prism. In Russia, a British woman bonded with McKay because he was "born a British subject and had lived in London" for an extended period (167). Later, during his tour of Morocco in the late 1920s, the British consulate "accosted" McKay and inquired whether he was an "American." McKay replied, "I said I was born in the West Indies and lived in the United States and that I was an American, even though I was a British subject, but I preferred to think of myself as an internationalist" (231). Internationalism enabled him to overcome the geographic splintering of his identities and to interact with people and cultures in different lands. *A Long Way from Home* documents McKay's cosmopolitan attempts at being at home in the world, even as the degrees of separation between him and his native homes increased.

Global "Jim Crowism": Langston Hughes's I Wonder as I Wander

Poetry was for Hughes, as it was for McKay, a passport to financial solvency and the far reaches of the United States and the rest of the world. As Hughes puts it in *I Wonder as I Wander,* which first talks about his poetry readings throughout the South, "On I went, driving down the road, deeper and deeper into Dixie with poetry as a passport. That fall and winter I covered every state in the South."[37] Similarly, when he traveled toward the West Coast, his focus remained, and his reputation as a traveling poet crystallized in the public eye: "In Los Angeles, Loren Miller [a dear friend] introduced me to the audience as '[t]he first Negro poet in America to span the continent, coast to coast, with his poetry!'" (63). Reciting poetry was key to Hughes's establishing of himself as a serious artist who desired literary professionalism and prestige and who had a serious message for the world.

The profession, Hughes felt, could be broken down into two groups. The first comprised those who wanted "to write for the pulps, or turn out fake 'true' stories to sell under anonymous names as Wallace Thurman did," or those who wanted to "bat out slick non-Negro short stories in competition with a thousand other commercial writers trying to make the *Saturday Evening Post*" (5). In his first autobiography, *The Big Sea,* Hughes had already described the pseudonymous literary practices of his African American contemporary Wallace Thurman and the commercial viability of literature that avoided the conventional portrayals of African Americans. In contrast, the next autobiography, *I Wonder as I Wander,* plays up Hughes's distaste for this marketable brand of literature and affirms that he wanted to belong to a second literary group, which he defined this way: "I wanted to write seriously and as well as I knew how about the Negro people, and make *that* kind of writing earn for me a living" (5). Racial realism was capable of earning cultural prestige by imagining a primarily African American readership and stimulating, even mobilizing, African Americans. The first two sections of *I Wonder as I Wander,* "In Search of Sun" and "Poetry to the People," explain this idea.

Traveling through the U.S. South, though initially designed to earn Hughes money and commercial esteem, ends up exposing him to the deeper issue of how literary expression could correlate with racial-political action and how literature could influence the emotional, spiritual, intellectual, and even material well-being of African Americans. Mary McLeod Bethune, a prominent African American figure in American politics and higher education, encouraged Hughes, "[Y]ou must go all over the South with your poems. People need poetry" (41). Hughes followed suit; in his words, "I determined to find [whether I was in the appropriate profession] by taking poetry, *my* poetry, to *my* people. After all, I wrote about Negroes, and primarily *for* Negroes. Would they have me? Did they want me?" (41–42). Yes and yes. The presidents, administrators, teachers, and students of historically black colleges expressed great interest in Hughes. As he visited these institutions, he came face to face with, because he helped to incite, both the exercise and the censorship of African American student protest against "Jim Crowism" and Its social and political manifestations (44). Just as McKay wrote "If We Must Die" amid the turbulence of 1919, Hughes wrote or recited "Christ in Alabama," "The Negro Mother," "Cross," "I, Too, Sing America," and poems about the so-called Scottsboro Boys for African American readers hoping to come to grips with this travesty in Alabama.[38]

Hughes's understanding of Jim Crowism in the U.S. South informed the language he needed to interpret the social, class, or racial inequalities in countries located outside the United States, such as Cuba, which he first visited in 1930. In Cuba, Hughes noticed that, although darker-skinned individuals sometimes served in high political positions customarily reserved or occupied by the lighter-skinned society, Cuban color discrimination paralleled American color discrimination. The country hewed to a "triple color line," whereby civic privileges increased in proportion to the lightness of skin color (10). While experiencing an unspoken and general Cuban governmental resistance to African American travelers,[39] Hughes realized that North Americans visiting this country reinforced the native color line. Once, Hughes confronted the white manager of a beach whose policy included denying entrance to African Americans and complained, "Do you mean to tell me that you're drawing the color line on a *Cuban* beach against *American* citizens—and you're an American yourself?" (12). The fact that Hughes could still suffer a Jim Crow color line was just as appalling as the hypocrisy of American cultural nationalism that attempted to inscribe it. Discrimination of this kind motivated Hughes's political ambitions as a poet and strengthened his bond to Cuban political writers, including Nicolás Guillén and Gustavo Urrutia.

On other occasions in *I Wonder as I Wander,* Hughes analyzes the indigenous political history of color discrimination in foreign nations, but in historical comparison to Jim Crow in the United States. While in Haiti, Hughes recognized an intraracial color line between the light-skinned "mulattoes" and the dark-skinned "blacks," which correlated with class discrimination between the privileged and the menial working classes. In his words, "I was reminded strongly of my years in Washington [in the mid-1920s] where Negro society, too, was stratified—the government workers, college professors and schoolteachers considering themselves much better than the usually darker (although not always poorer) people who work with their hands" (25). In Hughes's eyes, a regrettable irony emerged when the color and class forms of discrimination in contemporary Haiti were seen against the contrasting historical backdrop of the political unity among the Haitian slaves that he studied.[40]

International Jim Crowism especially came to light during Hughes's travels in 1932 and 1933, through Soviet Central Asia, where he consistently juxtaposed the color and caste prejudice in these countries alongside that which he came across in his previous tour of the U.S. South.[41] After the debacle surrounding his stint as a writer for a Soviet-sponsored film crew, which I shall discuss in a moment, Hughes decided to tour the republic of Turkmenistan (also known as Turkmenia), "where the majority of the [Soviet] colored citizens lived," to start writing his travelogue and diary, with an eye toward publishing essays for the Russian newspaper *Izvestia* (102).[42] Bordered by what are now Afghanistan, Iran, Uzbekistan, and Kazakhstan, Turkmenistan included a nomadic population that emerged in 1925 as an autonomous republic, in the wake of the Bolshevik (or what Hughes called "October") Revolution that transpired across the Soviet Union eight years earlier. The revolution essentially transformed Central Asia from Soviet colonies into more modernized countries under working-class, if not Marxist-communist, leadership. Hughes's goal was to study Soviet Central Asia ideologically, with "*Negro* eyes": his own and those of the indigenous people, who were historically downtrodden and "colored" (116).

In this statement, what precisely does Hughes mean by "colored"? The word, which he uses interchangeably with "Negro" in *I Wonder as I Wander,* belonged to his American vocabulary of Jim Crow and refers to the darker-skinned societies of Soviet Central Asia. Upon encountering "a young Negro" in Tashkent, the capital of Uzbekistan, Hughes quips in his memoir, "Having since been around the world, I have learned that there is at least *one* Negro everywhere" (104). More than simply counting on each hand the number of dark-skinned individuals he came across, Hughes invested in the cultural and political meaning of color and racial difference. Arthur Koestler, a proletarian Jewish writing buddy whom Hughes met in Ashkabad, the capital of Turkmenistan, believed that this republic "was simply a *primitive* land moving into twentieth-century civilization"; in contrast, Hughes characterized the country as a "*colored* land moving into orbits hitherto reserved for whites," a land with its own society that was denied the civic rights it deserved (116). The differences in the extent to which Koestler and Hughes sympathized with the degenerate conditions of the colored groups exposed their antonymic racial experiences in the United States. On several occasions, "Jim Crow" was the only term that captured Hughes's intimate knowledge of, and repugnance at, the squalor of these conditions. Unlike Koestler, who had not endured these racist circumstances and who felt compelled, at times, to blame the colored Soviet Asians for their own lot, Hughes indicted the larger cultural and political systems of this region, such as those of Turkmenistan and Uzbekistan, for their complicity in maintaining the status quo.[43]

Yet Hughes did see progress. *I Wonder as I Wander* tells us that Hughes met with Tajaiv, a sixteen- or seventeen-year-old boy who gave him a tour of a dam in Uzbekistan, and both proceeded to travel further by streetcar. When both sat down inside it, Hughes mused on the societal advances made in Soviet Central Asia, as opposed to those made or avoided in the United States:

> Ten years before, a brown young Uzbek like Tajaiv would have had to ride in the back of the streetcars in Tashkent, for previous to the revolution in Asia there had been Jim Crow streetcars in Uzbekistan. The old partitions that once separated natives from Europeans, colored from white, were still there when I arrived—I saw them. But now anyone sat anywhere in the Tashkent trams. In ten short years, Jim Crow was gone on trams, trains, or anywhere else in Central Asia. Russians and Uzbeks, Ukranians and Tartars, Europeans and natives, white or colored, all went to the same schools, sat on the same benches, ate in the same co-operatives, worked in the same shops or factories, and fussed and fumed at the same problems. Gains and defeats were shared alike. In Tashkent, whenever I got on a streetcar and saw the old partitions, I could not help but remember Atlanta, Birmingham and Houston in my own country where, when I got on a tram or a bus or a train, I had to sit in the *colored section*. The natives of Tashkent, about my own shade of brown, once had to sit in a *colored* section, too. But not anymore. (172)

In vivid detail, the passage illustrates that the spatial "partitions" inside the Tashkent trams represented the transnational extension of the color line from the U.S. South through Soviet Central Asia. *I Wonder as I Wander* captures what literary scholar Brent Hayes Edwards would call a "modern expression," albeit in the relatively innocuous form of an autobiography, that exposes the cleavages (or the simultaneous connection and disconnection) in "the often uneasy encounters of people of African descent with each other."[44] As correct as this claim has turned out to be across history, with regard to the global movement, mass disenfranchisement, and political formation of the African diaspora, we must broaden it to make comparable the intranational disenfranchisement of U.S. Southern African Americans and the imperial disenfranchisement of the Tashkent citizens.[45] These two regions, although racializing darker-skinned people in different ways, share an imperialist system that degrades and segregates them in public spaces, a similarity that provoked Hughes to examine their shared imperialist conditions alongside what was at stake in the political attempts to stamp out material inequalities based on color and racial difference. In *I Wonder as I Wander,* the comparative reading of race in the United States and Soviet Central Asia frames Hughes's story about the parallels between America's Jim Crow color line and certain cultural and political forms of discrimination in the Soviet Union.

Hughes's autobiographical devotion to telling this story about the fundamental relationship between culture and politics, though, was not limited to *I Wonder as I Wander.* Hughes was well aware of the political Left, even its racial connotations, but the heightened presence of political discourse in this autobiography does not make it a conventional progression in rhetorical and literary experience from its prequel, *The Big Sea.* Biographer Arnold Rampersad has stated that Hughes's discussion of his painful breakup with his patron, Charlotte Mason, serves as narrative closure for his first autobiography and enables the second autobiography to open with a rationale for his trip to Haiti.[46] The breakup "suggests strongly," according to Rampersad, "that it was the principal cause of Hughes's most radical phase of socialism, in 1931–33." Otherwise, in *The Big Sea,* "Hughes's leftist involvements have vanished without a trace," except for a poem, not even "radical" in "sentiment," that criticizes the opening of a hotel as the bastion of the rich and as disrespectful toward the lower-classes struggling during the Great Depression.[47] What is more, Hughes reserves much of this first autobiography for talking about his strained relationship with his father in Mexico and about the rise and fall and the celebrities and patronage of the Harlem Renaissance. Yet *The Big Sea* tells us more than the biographical themes. An adolescent Hughes appeared cognizant that people embraced socialism as a means toward political unity; that this radical doctrine enjoyed international valences and contradicted the capitalism and nationalism of his own country; and that African Americans had to choose between, on the one hand, a racist subjugation in American cultural and economic nationalism and, on the other, an internationally influential form of socialism that promised to rescue them from it. Whereas his first autobiography only skims these ideas, *I Wonder as I Wander* plumbs them for their deeper meanings, such as the pros and cons of political radicalism and how they bear on his personal life, on his artistry, and on the material impact of aesthetic culture.[48]

When Koestler asks Hughes why he chose not to join the Communist Party, the poet explains his decision in *I Wonder as I Wander* with remarkable insight: "I did not believe political directives could be successfully applied to creative writing. They might well apply to the preparation of tracts and pamphlets, yes, but not to poetry or fiction, which to be valid, I felt, had to express as truthfully as possible the *individual* emotions and reactions of the writer, rather than mass directives issued to achieve practical and often temporary politics" (122). McKay, in *A Long Way from Home,* shares this romantic vision of an apolitical literature upon rejecting the proposition that there is such a thing as "a proletarian, or a bourgeois, or any special literature or art" (111). Yet, just as McKay, in reality, could not detach politics from aesthetics, Hughes's words ("I did not believe political directives could be successfully applied to creative writing") suggest he was negotiating what it meant for literature to serve an established political program. That negotiation did not prevent him from conducting his own individual (as opposed to program-related) political activities during his tour of the U.S. South, where he was performing his more polemical poems. McCarthyism's censorship of Hughes and other cultural celebrities in the United States does happen to explain, from our standpoint, the reticence of *I Wonder as I Wander* on the issue of the Communist Party.

Hughes did use his experiences, however, to speculate on how cultural work could serve a political cause. In 1932, he served as a writer for a "Negro motion-picture group" that traveled from Harlem to the Soviet Union to make a communist-inflected film, entitled *Black and White,* about the cross-racial unionization of laborers in Alabama, against the wishes of white Southern bosses and Northern investors (*I Wonder as I Wander,* 65). Hughes seized the opportunity. After all, Hollywood remained too reluctant to hire more African Americans as movie writers, and the Soviet Union was a country more hospitable to African Americans at a time when racial persecution in the Scottsboro case alarmed him. Hughes sympathized with this international group and looked forward to working on the film, until he realized that the script was written by "a famous Russian writer *who has never been in America*" and who probably had not read any books about Negroes, since "only a very few books about contemporary Negro life in our country had been translated into Russian" (76). Hughes believed that the script was an unrealistic story, despite the Comintern's approval of it as politically valuable and artistically appropriate.

In the film, some portrayals of cross-racial social and labor cooperation were too implausible, however utopian, to justify the political storyline. The fantastic images of white aristocrats and black girls dancing casually, or of white Northern workers traveling to the South and rescuing rich and poor African Americans alike from their violent conflicts with white Southern workers, were either too inconsistent with the history of American racial politics or too optimistic for the film's genres of social and political realism. Working on this film exposed Hughes to the degree to which the communist dreams of cross-racial class solidarity pressured and sometimes undermined what he felt to be art's obligation to represent or address reality.

Hughes's work on the film, similar to McKay's writing of poetry while traveling the world, enabled connections to oppressed societies by way of the ideological and practical bonds of political resistance. At the same time, both men distinguished themselves—or were distinguished by the societies they visited—as a privileged, "mobilized class." To borrow the words of John Armstrong, a political scientist, the class did not have "a general status advantage" but did "enjoy[] many material and cultural advantages compared to other groups in the multiethnic polity."[49] The contradiction typifies the relationship of McKay and Hughes to "minority" societies and cultures around the world, a dynamic that seeped into their autobiographical discourses and informed their cultural definitions and expressions of racial politics. The ambivalent politics of autobiographical form recalls a study by Seth Moglen, a literary scholar, on how aesthetic form may embody an author's awareness of and position in larger social and institutional structures of power relations. The poetic forms of modernism that Hughes adopted between the wars are "*politically significant*," in that they "may be uniquely capable of representing—and thereby enabling us to resist—the global economic and social order that has produced them."[50] Hughes—and McKay, I would add—were just as attentive to the formal experimentation that preoccupied their "high modernist" counterparts (T. S. Eliot, Ezra Pound, and the like) as they were to the exigency of geopolitical history in creative writing.

Pointing out the rhetorical and thematic similarities of McKay's and Hughes's autobiographies should not brush over one crucial difference. In *A Long Way from Home*, McKay mentions the term "color line" only twice (in the final chapter of the autobiography) and talks about race relations in the

United States (265, 269). In contrast, *I Wonder as I Wander* mentions that term close to a dozen times, with reference to metaphorical color lines that run across the world, from the U.S. South through Latin America, Soviet territory, Asia, and Europe—color lines that bend and blur according to the political histories of regions and to global narratives of imperialism. Color lines, in this respect, separate not just races but also ethnic minorities from majorities, resulting in an unfair and perpetual caste system not unlike what Hughes had witnessed and experienced firsthand in Jim Crow America. More so than McKay's, Hughes's observance of racial discrimination abroad, and his speculation on the political means of vanquishing it in foreign countries, ended up clarifying his own perspective on race relations in the United States while strengthening his own political resolve to make these relations more equitable.

The Geopolitics of African American Literature

McKay's and Hughes's autobiographies about their global travels illustrate that the politics of African American literature may include both national and transnational frames of reference. Cultural theorists Françoise Lionnet and Shu-Mei Shih have stated that "the transnational designates spaces and practices acted upon by border-crossing agents, be they dominant or marginal." The transnational also marks a "space of exchange and participation wherever processes of hybridization occur and where it is still possible for cultures to be produced and performed without necessary mediation by the center."[51] Literary scholar Wai Chee Dimock states that the tradition of American literature, when read in relation to the transnationalism of authorship or textual representations, becomes a "complex tangle of relations," "a crisscrossing set of pathways, open-ended and ever multiplying, weaving in and out of other geographies, other languages and cultures" across the planet.[52] McKay and Hughes embody transnational figures, and their autobiographies, *A Long Way from Home* and *I Wonder as I Wander*, exemplify transnational literature.

In this chapter, I have illuminated the political intricacies of transnationalism in the autobiographies of McKay and Hughes, whose stories on social disenfranchisement at home and abroad coordinate what theorists of "minority transnationalism" have called the discourses of "horizontal" and "vertical contingency." The autobiographies demand a way of reading that moves beyond the margin-center dyad to a more multinodal cartography. Again in the words of Lionnet and Shih, we must "examine the relationships among different margins," acknowledging that "[n]ot all minorities are minoritized by the same mechanisms in different places; there is no universal minority position as such."[53] Ali Behdad, a fellow theorist, has added that a paradigm of minority transnationalism must "account for the complex ways in which [minorities] have been positioned in relation to the 'white majority,'" possibly connoting "the 'vertical contingencies' of the 'minor' text," or "both the historical condition and the cultural context that define its subject as well as its reception."[54] My interpretation of the "minority transnationalism" of the autobiographies of McKay and Hughes has required a critical sensitivity to the ambivalences and ironies of their global politics. Proving their vertical contingency, the authors embodied certain ideologies of empire and nationalism, as a result of their residence and acculturation in the United States, even as they politically resisted these ideologies when they wrote literature. The authors believed that the American racial order was peculiar, even though this system enabled them, ironically, to interpret the racial orders of other countries and to experience a horizontally contingent mode of minority existence.

Even so, A Long Way from Home and I Wonder as I Wander are excellent case studies for theories of the autobiography. As literary historian William Andrews puts it, autobiography affirms the ideological and cultural condition that "the personal experience be important, that it offer an opportunity for [one to have] a sincere relation with someone else," and that "one must take one's own life (or some major portion of it) seriously enough to find in it a significance that makes reconstructing that life valuable to another."[55] McKay and Hughes wrote their autobiographies to assert the values of their lives—or the values of their records of them—by narrating the contingencies of their experiences with other minority groups at home and abroad, as well as by showing how they enhanced their own understandings of political literature through these experiences. Hughes and McKay came to see how African Americans are racialized and their literary expressions made to become geopolitical. Their books capture what David Chioni Moore, a literary scholar, appropriately calls (though with regard to Hughes only) a fascinating articulation of (American) "local color" to "global color," the provincial to the planet—a kind of "Afro-planetary vision."[56] In retrospect, McKay's and Hughes's common discourses on the global color line stemmed from their experiences as activists against the imperial exploits of racism and capitalism. That color line also generated a special language to historicize and measure the ability of literature to do political work, to ameliorate race and class relations, and to improve society. Their radical critiques of the role capitalism played in the standard subjugation of darker-skinned people across the world—the idea that the link between racial and class exploitation is not coincidental but causal—underwrote their autobiographical imagination of a global color line.

Finally, I cannot overstate the perfect collaboration of aesthetics and politics enabled by "If We Must Die." McKay's reading of the poem achieves what theater scholar Jill Dolan has called "the social potential of utopian performatives" and "participatory" roles: "utopian performatives let audiences experience a processual, momentary feeling of affinity, in which spectators experience themselves as part of a congenial public constituted by the performance's address." At these moments "spectators can be rallied to hope for the possibility of realizing improved social relations," and, to the logical extreme, they can be rallied to action.[57] In this sense, "If We Must Die" recalls *What Is the Third Estate?*—a remarkable pamphlet of antiaristocratic propaganda that I am compelled to summarize briefly here. Published in 1789 by Emmanuel-Joseph Sieyes, the pamphlet persuaded the common people of France, known as the Third Estate, to resist their government of noblemen, the Second Estate. Political historian William H. Sewell Jr. states that this pamphlet distinguished itself among the thousands that appeared just prior to the French Revolution. What makes it an "extraordinary text" is "its scintillating style, its exceptionally clear posing of the issues, and its radical conclusion [that] won it immediate acclaim"; its appearance in three editions; its "distribut[ion] and debate[]" by various political clubs and committees that had sprung up in the heated atmosphere" of the Revolution; and its "focusing [of] the political and constitutional debate that was raging" at the time "on the question of aristocratic privilege." *What Is the Third Estate?* was nothing less than a cultural phenomenon and a political flashpoint, "a case of textual determinism, in which the arguments set forth by a political intellectual structured the course of political events." When the representatives of the Third Estate followed the course of action recommended in the pamphlet and in other writings by Sieyes, the veracity and impact of the document's revolutionary ideas were confirmed. Connecting the rhetorical text and political context of Sieyes's pamphlet demonstrates the recent academic rise of "revolutionary historiography," or a political historiography of "the language and conceptual vocabulary of the [French] revolutionaries," of which Sewell is a part.[58]

Similarly, "If We Must Die" became nothing less than a cultural phenomenon and a political flashpoint for how African American authors have personally participated in, or wrote literature that was used by, a major political movement, which, in turn, capitalized on the influences of language and literature to unite the formal and informal contexts of political action. Brent Hayes Edwards rightly admonishes that, while scholarship should "strive[] to attend to the complexity of such a relationship" between literature and what writer and theorist Sylvia Wynter has called the "condition of possibility of the emergence of a doctrine," it should not conceive of "the literary to be simply propaganda or program—that is, a kind of cauldron for 'real' political praxis, socialist struggle, and direct action."[59] I heed this caution while arguing that the transformative potential of "If We Must Die" increases in direct proportion to its ideological suppleness, not necessarily in direct proportion to its "textual determinism" of political relations, such as that achieved by *What Is the Third Estate?* in 1789.

Still, is there an example in African American history of the literary determinism of racial politics, or the way that literature could directly influence race relations in American society? I believe that there is, and I pursue it in the next chapter, in which I aim to show that a very recent court case, though not as instantly consumable and "explosive" as a poem or a pamphlet, turned out to be as powerful in the realms of culture, politics, law, and jurisprudence.

5

Copyright Law, Free Speech, and the Transformative Value of African American Literature

Spanning three months, from March to May 2001, *SunTrust Bank v. Houghton Mifflin Company* encourages a fundamental scholarly reconnection of copyright law and African American literature. In early 2001, the Stephens Mitchell Trust was mortified to learn that Houghton Mifflin was planning to release a parody of *Gone with the Wind* (1936), Margaret Mitchell's bestselling and Pulitzer Prize–winning novel. As the exclusive copyright owner of Mitchell's novel, the Trust authorizes its publication and circulation as well as the creation and marketing of its derivatives, which have included a 1939 film adaptation, a 1976 television series, a couple literary sequels in the past two decades, and memorabilia.[1] But the Trust did not authorize Alice Randall's parodic novel, *The Wind Done Gone*, slated for 2001. By this point, Randall was a notable African American writer who had graduated from Harvard University with a baccalaureate degree in English literature and who had then achieved some fame as a country songwriter in Nashville, Tennessee. Nonetheless, she was neither yet in the canon of American writers nor remotely in Mitchell's class of bestselling writers. *The Wind Done Gone* was also a first novel undeniably capitalizing on the cultural cachet of *Gone with the Wind*, even while demonstrating the literary turn in Randall's own career. Alleging Randall's and Houghton Mifflin's illegal exploitation of its signature product, the Trust hired legal representation from Frankfurt Garbus Kurnit Klein and Selz, P.C., and sent a letter to Houghton Mifflin, threatening litigation and a fine of ten million dollars if the publisher failed to cease and desist from the promotion, release, and distribution of *The Wind Done Gone*. Houghton Mifflin refused. The ensuing conflict climaxed with the injunction handed down in the District Court for the Northern District of Georgia against the release of *The Wind Done Gone*, eclipsed shortly afterward by the United States Court of Appeals for the Eleventh Circuit's vacating that ruling.

The legal contest between the Trust and the publisher turns out to be as fascinating as the novels themselves. *The Wind Done Gone* tells the story of *Gone with the Wind* in the dialect and from the perspective of Cynara. Representing the imagined child of Mammy, the head African American house servant in Mitchell's novel, Cynara alleges two remarkable stories. First, she is the half sister of Scarlett O'Hara, the heroine of *Gone with the Wind* and renamed Other in *The Wind Done Gone*, due to an adulterous relationship between Scarlett's father and Mammy. Second, Scarlett herself is partially African American, the descendant of a Haiti-born great-great-grandmother. As a whole, the novel is Randall's powerful rejoinder to the tragedy of racial and sexual exploitation that has often befallen the racially mixed figure of nineteenth-century American literature. Cynara's brief marriage to and eventual rejection of a manipulative "R." (who is equivalent to Rhett Butler in Mitchell's novel), her subsequent marriage to an attractive African American congressman, and the birth of their child—all of these circumstances rescue her from the historical curse of the "tragic mulatta."[2]

Realizing the full political impact of *The Wind Done Gone*'s parody of *Gone with the Wind*, I argue, is impossible without a thoroughgoing analysis of the case it inspired, *SunTrust v. Houghton*. In only a few instances has literary scholarship been as detailed as legal scholarship on the case, sorting through the approximately one thousand pages of its court documents. The literary scholarship has also rarely gone further than restating the core arguments and analyzing the declarations of such African American luminaries as Toni Morrison, Henry Louis Gates Jr., and Randall herself in the district court case. Less attention has been paid to the mundane but still informative allegations, rebuttals, motions, affidavits, memoranda, oral arguments, and appeals of the plaintiff and defendant, not to mention the rulings by the district court judge, Charles A. Pannell Jr., and by the court of appeals that had vacated the district ruling.[3] Conversely, legal scholarship, though having already examined the details of the case, has not yet attended to the political meaning of *The Wind Done Gone* in African American literary history.[4] The parallel efforts of literary and legal studies to examine the novel have understated the political meaning of copyright law in African American literary studies.

The Wind Done Gone should have a more central place in our discussions of "remembering the past" and "writing the future" of African Americans (to pun on the titles of two recent books).[5] The racial politics of law and literature alike demand it. Put together, the previous literary and legal studies leave a crucial question unanswered: What role has law played in determining the political value of African American literature? This chapter provides one answer, describing the relationship between copyright law, free speech, and the "transformative" potential of African American literature as a story about how racial representation in this literature must strike a balance between heeding copyright laws and taking advantage of its status as free speech both protected by the First Amendment and perseverant in changing the attitudes of readers. Parody lies at the heart of my close readings of *Gone with the Wind, The Wind Done Gone,* and the documents of *SunTrust v. Houghton.* In the shorthand definition of Darryl Dickson-Carr, a literary scholar, parody allows African American authors to support or "scrutinize different political positions in African American communities."[6] The stakes of *SunTrust Bank v. Houghton* hinged on the issue of Randall's humane redemption of the African American characters in *Gone with the Wind,* an issue that the plaintiff argued and that most literary scholars have concluded is the most salient and historical "political position" of an African American author.

I discovered, though, that the stakes also turned on the actual claims, made by both the plaintiff and the district court judge, that Randall should not have literally "killed" Scarlett, a twist in *The Wind Done Gone* that coincides with the literary contamination of Scarlett's racial genealogy, in effect killing off the Southern belle's symbolic whiteness and probably drawing the Trust's ire. A subordinate point about the racial history of copyright law is pertinent here: white supremacist ideology had likely fueled the use of copyright law against Randall and Houghton Mifflin, in much the same way that it had conspired against African American politics about half a century earlier, in the 1853 case *Stowe v. Thomas,* featuring Harriet Beecher Stowe's accusation of copyright infringement against a German translation of her 1852 novel, *Uncle Tom's Cabin.* In *SunTrust Bank v. Houghton,* the decision of the court of appeals to vacate the district court ruling focuses not so much on the inspiration of Judge Pannell's ruling (the death of Scarlett) as on its jurisprudential cost (the unconstitutional application of preliminary injunctions) and, secondarily, its poor judgment (on the political role of African American literature in revising history). Yet, all the while, the appellate court's awareness of the historical persistence of racism is palpable.

Evidently, this chapter arrives at a pessimistic moment in our history, when more and more litigation has been using copyright law to attack literary derivatives on the ground of racial politics, culminating, in 2001, with *SunTrust v. Houghton.* But the appellate court's ruling in this case offers a glimmer of hope, marking the potential revision of the jurisprudence of copyright law; affirming, by way of the law, the literary determinism of political relations; and underscoring the ability of African American literature to transform society in profound ways. On the one hand, I agree with the claim of Linda Hutcheon, an expert on parody, that "parody's challenge to the very idea of [literature's] ownership" of its own textual property is under pressure in "our current litigious world." The legal pressure is a symptom of the "close historical connection between political censorship and the denigration of parody" as copyright infringement.[7] On the other hand, as authors of literary parody have contested the accusation of copyright infringement by asserting their own right to political speech, they have helped to combat the legal affront to literary freedom. The political action of literary art and artists is the byproduct of a dialectical exchange between the creative prohibition and the legal resistance occasioned by copyright law.[8] Put another way, even though *The Wind Done Gone* is itself not a novelistic parable of copyright law, *SunTrust v. Houghton* has led to a canonical redefinition of political parody, a jurisprudential reconsideration of preliminary injunctions, and a general understanding of how laws uphold political rights.[9]

The Racial Politics of Copyright Law

To talk about the racial politics of copyright law is not to rehash, at length, "the trials of law and literature." In a 2009 essay with that phrase as its title, Jennifer Travis has already described the conundrum that she and other literary and legal scholars have faced in their attempts to be interdisciplinary, such as how to make the field of law and literature at once significant and humane, socially powerful and intellectually flexible. In the process, we have come across such terminological permutations as "law in literature," "law as literature," and "law on literature."[10] "Law in literature" examines literature for its portrayals of law, its imagination of the norms of legal society and culture, its meditation on jurisprudence, or its rhetorical indictment of legal injustice. "Law as literature" reads legal texts, including contracts, statutes, constitutions, and judicial opinions, for their literary forms and themes. "Law on literature" interprets the way that law regulates literature, including the legal definitions and repercussions of literary authorship, creativity, obscenity, defamation, censorship, and property. The limitations of these approaches have been widely noted. In one example, William E. Moddelmog has stated that the law-*in*-literature approach tends to reach "a conclusion about law's hegemonic control over literary production, or an overly romantic conception of literary resistance to authority." At the same time, the law-*as*-literature approach tends to exaggerate the "explanatory force" of literature in legal studies. Neither approach enables us to explain how "literature might operate to help construct, and thus revise, legal formulations."[11] Less controversial than the interdisciplinary relevance of law and literature, returning to Travis, is the "historical evidence that such a relationship did exist."[12]

Yet, how evident has the impact of literature been *on* the law? In terms of methodology, how do we measure the legal value of literature? *SunTrust v. Houghton* is one example of how case law has enabled such an assessment. The debates arising among the literary texts, authors, and publishers in the case have served as precedent for present-day litigants, lawyers, and judges and as a topic of great interest for both literary and legal scholars. The default legal salience that *The Wind Done Gone* has accrued does not perfectly account for its *political* stakes, but it does launch us in the right direction, toward understanding the historical incompatibility between intellectual property law and African American cultural expression.

Intellectual property law, as many of us already know, traces to Article I, Section 8, of the United States Constitution. The "Powers of Congress" include the ability to "promote the Progress of Science and useful Arts, by securing for limited Times to Authors and Inventors the exclusive Right to their respective Writings and Discoveries."[13] The intellectual property law most relevant to cultural expression is copyright, which pertains to original expressions of art, as opposed to trademarks and patents, which pertain respectively to commercial business practices and to inventions. Since the nineteenth century, U.S. copyright law has emphasized the Romantic reflection of literary genius in intellectual individualism and has deemed original expression worthy of privatization and legal protection.[14] As legal historian Olufunmilayo B. Arewa notes, "it is a fundamental assumption of current copyright law that originality is implicitly mandated by the Constitution's references to 'authors' and their 'writings.'" "Originality," she goes on to say, "thus serves as a minimum threshold for copyrightability."[15] Literary parody has developed a problematic relationship to copyright; the premise of originality in the latter clashes with the premise of imitation in the former. Parody is "characterized by ironic inversion, not always at the expense of the parodied text." Irony assists in the parodic incorporation of the forms, themes, characters, or plot devices (or all of the above) of another literary text. Irony helps establish the connections "not only between meanings (said, unsaid) but between people (ironists, interpreters, targets)." And irony delineates "discursive communities [that] are constituted by shared concepts of the norms of communication" and by "sharing an ideology," although Linda

Hutcheon, in all of these quotations, downplays the notion that ideologies "necessarily define or guarantee the formation of a discursive community."[16]

Two caveats regarding African American culture are worth noting here. First, legal scholar Russ Versteeg states that only "some minimal degree of creativity" barely rising "above the level of the trivial" is needed to qualify as originality.[17] Put another way, the legal bar set for originality is not as high as that suggested by the Romantic conception of genius. The balance of my argument rebuts this suggestion. Wherever African American cultural expressions have been concerned, the standard for originality has actually been set rather high, resulting in a double standard that devalues the parodies of these cultural expressions as merely imitative and aesthetically inferior, while both treating the originality of the parodied targets as sacrosanct and failing to acknowledge the complicity of these very targets in a longstanding tradition of literary imitation. Second, we must take issue with Hutcheon's disclaimer and insist that, historically, "discursive communities" have emerged and crystallized along ideological lines whenever the copyrightability of African American cultural expression was in question or, more generally, whenever the issue of "race" underwent legal inspection.

In an introduction to a series of legal studies on "the social construction and reproduction of 'race,'" E. Nathaniel Gates affirms this point. By "the beginning of the twentieth century," he states, "the various naturalist theories developed in the preceding decades had been fully transformed into legal rules, thus institutionalizing, at the level of state power, the constricting relationships already slowly built up in practice. With the onset of the modern era, 'race' had become a fundamental legal category, taking its place alongside such other elements of individual identity as gender and nationality."[18] The title of this series, "Critical Race Theory," represents the intellectual field that lawyers and legal scholars began in the 1970s to codify the correlation of race, racism, and power both in the long history of American law and in the arguable rollback of African American civil rights in the late twentieth century. Put bluntly by Cornel West, the field pinpoints and challenges "the historical centrality and complicity of law in upholding white supremacy."[19] The field of Critical Race Theory has shown that the ideologies of race and racism have formed, and continue to form, discursive (and sometimes exclusively racial) communities divided over the history and persistence of white supremacy in the United States. The principles and authority of Critical Race Theory have proven crucial to limning the tension between copyright law and African American cultural expression. Legal scholars such as Richard Schur and Olufunmilayo B. Arewa and literary scholars such as Lovalerie

King and Paul K. Saint-Amour, to name a few, have best talked about the contradiction between copyright and the sampling or borrowing of melodies, harmonies, and rhythms characteristic of hip-hop music, an exemplary centerpiece of African American cultural expression.[20]

To sharpen an earlier point, African American literary parody has alternately supported and scrutinized the ideological and discursive formation of racial-political communities, especially those of African Americans. If parody, such as that used within satire, can, in Dickson-Carr's words, "fascinate, infuriate, and delight us to the extent that it transgresses boundaries of taste, propriety, decorum, and the current ideological status quo," the genre does so because it actually participates in drawing these aesthetic and moral boundaries, even as it critiques them.[21] The boundaries vivified and violated by African American literary parody, such as those defining realistic or stereotypical representations of race, have historically been concentric— they have a common ideological and discursive center—with those forged by African American political communities.[22] The concentricity allows me to hypothesize here that a historical, ongoing, and strategic equivalency has long existed between African American literary parody and African American politics. For this reason, the copyrightability of African American cultural expressions has been precarious. The accusations that these expressions have been borrowing or, more harshly, stealing from progenitors have likewise been political, a consequence of the subtle legal demonstrations of white-supremacist ideology. The legal *use* of parodies by African Americans, then, required sophisticated defense against such accusations, almost implying that the political claims of the parodies themselves cannot survive on their own in the public sphere.

The Wind Done Gone attacks white supremacy by operating through the parodic borrowing of information from *Gone with the Wind*. In the district court phase of *SunTrust v. Houghton*, Henry Louis Gates Jr., as the author of the groundbreaking 1987 book *The Signifying Monkey: A Theory of African-American Literary Criticism*, served as an expert on African American parody and testified on behalf of Houghton Mifflin about its political significance: "Parody is at the heart of African American expression, because it is a creative mechanism for the exercise of political speech, sentiment, and commentary on the part of people who feel themselves oppressed or maligned and wish to protest that condition of oppression and misrepresentation."[23] Gates's words, while intuitively correct and repeated by countless scholars of African American literature, still require legal qualification. How does racial representation—such as the strategy of portraying a race in a way that revises previous portrayals—undergo assessment by copyright law? How does this revision, then, become an index of the political value of African American literature? Describing *The Wind Done Gone* as "political" requires more than simply imbuing literary revisionism, vis-à-vis parody, with the aspiration to overcome the white-supremacist legacy of Mitchell's *Gone with the Wind*. It also requires attention to the legal interpretations and consequences, according to copyright law, of racial claims to cultural and political power.

Perhaps the best touchstone for understanding this issue is the 1853 case *Stowe v. Thomas,* mentioned earlier. In this case, Stowe filed a lawsuit against F. W. Thomas, a Philadelphia-based publisher of *Die Freie Presse,* which circulated an unauthorized German translation of *Uncle Tom's Cabin.* The lawsuit was a historical turning point. No previous American author was more insistent, at least in a court setting, than Stowe on securing and expanding the proprietary rights of authors. As Melissa J. Homestead, a historian of literary copyright, puts it, "no other author seems to have had the cause, desire, and means to pursue a similar claim before the U.S. Congress amended the copyright statute in 1870 to give copyright owners the right to control translations of their works."[24] Translation has been one of the many "derivatives" from original expressions that U.S. copyright law recognizes. The definition and copyright of derivatives have been important flashpoints for the tension between, on the one hand, the proprietary rights of authors and, on the other, the intellectual, creative rights of those who sought to derive their own expressions from the works of these authors.[25]

Equally important, the centrality of race to the cultural and political character of *Stowe v. Thomas* belies the legal neutrality pretended by Robert Grier, the judge presiding over the case. Judge Grier was a proponent of the Fugitive Slave Law, whose enactments in 1793 and 1850 ordered the return of escaped slaves to their masters. His ruling in favor of Thomas's translation indicates his ideological resistance to the antislavery praxis affirmed by *Uncle Tom's Cabin* and rejected by the Fugitive Slave Law. For Judge Grier, the two protagonists in Stowe's novel, Uncle Tom and Topsy, "are as much publici juris as Don Quixote and Sancho Panza," the protagonists of Miguel de Cervantes Saavedra's classic 1602 novel, *Don Quixote.* "All her conceptions and inventions may be used and abused by imitators, play-rights and poet-asters," and all her "absolute dominion and property in the creations of her genius and imagination have been voluntarily relinquished." The German translation turns out to be merely a copy of the "thoughts or conceptions" of *Uncle Tom's Cabin,* not the "concrete form" and "language" of the novel, which Judge Grier defines as "literary property."[26]

Racial bias emerges from Judge Grier's rhetorical attempt to have it both ways. He argues that, upon the release of *Uncle Tom's Cabin,* the "conceptions and inventions" and the "absolute dominion and property" intrinsic to the novel are automatically beyond Stowe's control, part of the public domain, and fair game for any kind of creative cooptation. At the same time, the fact that the German translation, in his view, refuses to alter the core "thoughts or conceptions" of the novel, as opposed to the language "clothing" them, exonerates it from an accusation of copyright infringement. In his decision, Grier succeeds in opening the door for literary derivatives to revise and disfranchise *both* the ideas and the expression of *Uncle Tom's Cabin* of their potential political contributions to the antislavery movement. Homestead's research on the context, claims, counterclaims, and ruling of *Stowe v. Thomas* shows that the case's debate over literary property reprised a political war between the contemporaneous efforts either to sustain or to restrain abolitionism. The case also supports the scholarly contentions of Lovalerie King and Stephen M. Best that law has generally mediated the relationship between race and property, that copyright law has likewise mediated the more specific relationship between racial representation and literary property, and that judges and lawyers have colluded in maintaining white supremacy.[27]

Stowe v. Thomas lays the groundwork for two ironies and one hypothesis that return us to *SunTrust v. Houghton.* First, while some African American writers (such as Frederick Douglass) embraced *Uncle Tom's Cabin* as a perfect antidote to slavery, others (such as Martin Delany) came to the conclusion that the novel was complicit in perpetuating caricatures of slaves and was not as progressive as Stowe's antislavery contemporaries thought.[28] Judge Grier's ruling in *Stowe v. Thomas,* according to Richard Schur, "in effect licensed the subsequent efforts of African American writers and intellectuals to 'rewrite' or 'write over' Stowe's characterization of Uncle Tom."[29] By this logic, *Stowe v. Thomas* paved the way for *The Wind Done Gone,* even though the ruling was intended, ironically, to permit certain kinds of writing that were presumably *contrary* to the political interests of African Americans. Second, and even more interestingly, the case arguably paved the way for the target of Randall's parody, Mitchell's *Gone with the Wind.* In a July 22, 1938, letter to a fan in Germany (of all places, in light of the 1853 case), Mitchell states, "It makes me very happy to know that *Gone with the Wind* is helping refute the impression of the South which people abroad gained from Mrs. Stowe's book."[30] What Stowe, Mitchell, and Randall have in common is that literature supported the representative attempts of authors to revise and overcome oppressive histories: in the case of Stowe, this history is one of slavery; for Mitchell, it is

Stowe's portrayal of the South; and for Randall, it is Mitchell's portrayal of African Americans (and whites) within the South.

The revisionism at the heart of literary representation—here, in the double sense of delegating authority to writers and portraying their ideas in their writings—has consistently been racial in focus. Copyright law has over time come to monitor, enforce, or reject the political meaning of racial representation through its authority over the range and meaning of derivatives. Paul K. Saint-Amour has theorized that "effective mourning, particularly the kind devoted to the working-through of the 'terrible knowledge' of communal trauma, is necessarily a public discourse and thus a form of expression important enough to the health of the democracy that it should not be infringed by excessive, private intellectual property regimes." Over the past century, the increasing privatization of literary property through what Saint-Amour calls "copyright-creep," the statutory or case-law expansions of copyright and the proportional restriction of the public domain, has come to impinge on cultural derivatives in two major ways: first, on their legal opportunities to attain publication and, second, on their creative opportunities to contribute to collective therapy and political progress.[31]

In the textual relationship between *Gone with the Wind* and *The Wind Done Gone,* what provoked the Trust, its counsel, and even Judge Pannell leading up to and during *SunTrust v. Houghton*? The common reading of the case is that the racism of Mitchell's African American caricatures and Randall's revision of them into more human terms were the primary issues at stake. The nature and legacy of *Gone with the Wind* support this reading. In the novel, African Americans come across (if I may reluctantly summarize the novel's 420,000 words) as animalistic, savage, and straight out of African jungles; as grotesque, malodorous, stupid, backward, childlike, and listless; as niggerish, insolent, and unscrupulous. Unsurprisingly, a long tradition of African American literature and scholarship has condemned Mitchell's novel.[32] In *The Wind Done Gone,* Randall contributes to this tradition by reimagining the African American (and white) characters of *Gone with the Wind* in cameo roles, but with different names: Mammy, Scarlett's nurse in Mitchell's novel, returns as Mammy or Pallas; Pork, the butler of Scarlett's father, Gerald, as Garlic; Dilcey, Pork's wife, as Mrs. Garlic; and Prissy, Dilcey's daughter, as Miss Priss.[33] More than that, Randall's reimagination not only highlights the degree to which Mitchell has dehumanized her own African American characters but also redeems the emotional, psychological, and spiritual depth of their humanity.[34] At the same time, the roles of these characters remain intact, with the help of Randall's subtle revisions to the literary and historical trademarks of *Gone with the Wind* (such as turning Tara into Tata and Twelve Oaks Plantation into Twelve Slaves as Strong as Trees), and with the help of her faithful alignment of the Civil War and postbellum American history with the temporality of Mitchell's novel.

Understandably, recent scholars have reached a consensus that the parody of *The Wind Done Gone* has mostly to do with Randall's empowerment of the denigrated African American characters in *Gone with the Wind*. Thomas F. Haddox, a literary scholar, states that Randall's novel "tries, very precisely, to make 'what happened not have happened' through a parodic repetition of 'history' that places slaves rather than masters at center stage" and through the construction of "an alternate history in which slaves have been in charge all along, pulling the strings of their clueless white masters." Patricia Yaeger, another scholar, agrees: "Randall shifts Mitchell's black characters from background to foreground; the white family members become puppets of the black agents who really run the plantation."[35] African American characters, in any case, come to demonstrate the human agency that Mitchell denies. The defense team of Houghton Mifflin, as I shall explain later, employed this line of argument to validate the parodic-cum-political importance of *The Wind Done Gone*.

Evidence from the case, however, suggests that Randall's ironic redemption of Mitchell's African American characters *did not* prompt the Trust to file the protest in court. Rather, it was Randall's literal and figurative attack on Scarlett. Whereas Mitchell's novel and its cultural derivatives maintain the unquestionable and absolute racial whiteness of Scarlett, in spite and because of her Irish "blood," Randall's novel alleges that Scarlett is biracial. (In the meantime, Randall depicts Scarlett's contraction of smallpox, her inebriated stare at her blemished beauty in the mirror, and her falling down the steps toward death [96].) If we focus on the ironic ways that Randall targets the white myths, not just the African American stereotypes, of *Gone with the Wind*, we would achieve a couple of worthwhile goals, I believe. We would highlight the historical identity of biology and culture in contemporary public discourses on race, an analysis neglected in our preoccupation with the African American characters of Mitchell's and Randall's novels. Plus, we would see that the rhetoric of the plaintiff and Judge Pannell in *SunTrust v. Houghton* converged on the literal and symbolic death of Scarlett.

"Tara Was Her Fate": Margaret Mitchell's Gone with the Wind

Left understated in the 2001 case is the original interplay of biology and culture in *Gone with the Wind*. As we all know, the historical romance begins in 1861, when the regional, ideological, and political conflict over slavery is at a climax and when America is plummeting into a divisive civil war. Recording this turmoil while following the complex life of Scarlett, a sensational Southern heroine, before, during, and after the Civil War, the novel contrasts the ancestries and behavioral styles of her parents, Gerald and Ellen (Robillard) O'Hara. The heroine's courage and ambition to restore Tara to its pre–Civil War glory evolve over the course of her traumatic wartime experiences, but these traits are also predestined.

Scarlett's fearless and assertive disposition comes from her father's Irish background. Gerald's identity crystallizes when he immigrates to America in his early twenties, after having left the brewing conflict between his family of O'Haras, then living in Ireland, and the British government, which suspects that the family, along with other culpable Irish citizens, has been planning a social revolution. Since Gerald's undersized build disqualifies him from joining the rebellion, he embraces the ethos that "little people must be hardy to survive among the large ones" and embarks on a voyage to the American South, where his notoriously "brisk and restless vitality" in securing land and commanding slaves overshadows the cultural inelegance that would become his trait among the local gentry.[36] Here, Gerald attributes to his Irish ancestry the desire for and defense of land ownership: "to anyone with a drop of Irish blood in them the land they live on is like their mother." He says directly to Scarlett that, despite her youth, "'Twill come to you, this love of land. There's no getting away from it, if you're Irish" (39).

In contrast to Gerald's brusqueness, Ellen's refinement also influences Scarlett. Several issues regarding Ellen's upbringing coalesce to inform her "efficient and unruffled" mannerism, despite "the daily emergencies of Gerald's turbulent household" (42). The issues include Ellen's French ancestry, her aristocratic birthplace on the Georgia coast, her early exposure to a social life by no means as troubled as Gerald's, and her mysterious solemnity (42).[37] Yet, after Gerald's courtship, Ellen's resentment toward her family for allegedly driving away her prior true love interest—Philippe Robillard, a murdered cousin—prompts her to marry him at the young age of fifteen, against her father's wish. (Presumably, this decision would have opposed the wish of Ellen's mother had she still been alive at the time.) Ellen then moves away from that "graceful dwelling" of French colonial architecture, from "the entire civilization that was behind the building of it, and she found herself in a world that was as strange and different as if she had crossed a continent," a world called Tara (58). Located in northern Georgia, where Ellen and Gerald have constructed a magnificent home, Tara represents the clash of their personal cultures and memories but also where Scarlett and her two younger sisters, Suellen and Carreen, are born and reared and where she returns after the Civil War to take psychological, emotional, and spiritual refuge.

Emergent from this thematic interweaving of Ellen's and Gerald's personal histories, the biological and cultural ontology of Scarlett recurs throughout *Gone with the Wind* as the metaphor of blood. Literary scholar Eliza Russi Lowen McGraw states that the "text's preoccupation with Scarlett's Irish blood reflects the genealogical concern of her society as well as a contemporary belief in the predominance of stereotypical ethnic characteristics."[38] In Scarlett's teenage years, her vanity and obstinacy translate "the easily stirred passions of her Irish father and nothing except the thinnest veneer of her mother's unselfish and forbearing nature" (*GWTW,* 62). Although these aspects of her personality are behavioral markers, Mitchell highlights their inherent biological nature: in Scarlett's "bosom," there "frequently raged . . . the blood of a soft-voiced, overbred Coast aristocrat mingled with the shrewd, earthy blood of an Irish peasant" (89).

During Scarlett's greatest bouts of fury, her father's blood coursing through her body overwhelms her mother's blood. When Ashley Wilkes, the heir to Twelve Oaks plantation, with whom she has long been infatuated, declares his intention to marry his cousin, Melanie Hamilton, Scarlett's "rage broke, the same rage that drove Gerald to murder [a man in Ireland] and other Irish ancestors to misdeeds that cost them their necks. There was nothing in her now of the well-bred Robillards who could bear with white silence anything the world might cast" (120). Mitchell's identification of blood with behavior explains Scarlett's jealousy, which evolves into respect for Melanie, who, later in the novel, remains devoted to Ashley and demonstrates maternal fortitude during the Union army's invasion of Tara.

Blood also explains Scarlett's desire to renovate Tara. By nineteen she is a widow who, with a small child, has braved the road back to Tara amid the war raging about her. During this time, Scarlett grows sophisticated and profound enough to realize that the revolutionary and imperial legacies of her father and mother predestine her for leadership. Contrary to patriarchal norm, she has become the head of her family—superseding even her own second husband, Frank Kennedy—as a clever businesswoman and vocal leader. The following passage represents this narrative turning point, when

Scarlet begins life at Tara near the end of the Civil War, without the stability of patriarchal family and genteel Southern society to which she has been accustomed. Her mother has been stricken by death; her father, senility; her sisters, illness; and everyone else in her social circle, fatigue. Contradicting the conventional portraiture of her as a "belle," Scarlett grabs the helm:

> Of a sudden, the oft-told family tales to which she had listened since babyhood, listened half-bored, impatient and but partly comprehending, were crystal clear. Gerald, penniless, had raised Tara; Ellen had risen above some mysterious sorrow; Grandfather Robillard, surviving the wreck of Napoleon's throne, had founded his fortunes anew on the fertile Georgia coast; Great-grandfather Prudhomme had carved a small kingdom out of the dark jungles of Haiti, lost it, and lived to see his name honored in Savannah. There were the Scarletts who had fought with the Irish Volunteers for a free Ireland and been hanged for their pains and the O'Haras who died at the Boyne, battling to the end for what was theirs.
>
> All had suffered crushing misfortunes and had not been crushed. They had not been broken by the crash of empires, the machetes of revolting slaves, war, rebellion, proscription, confiscation. Malign fate had broken their necks, perhaps, but never their hearts. They had not whined, they had fought. And when they died, they died spent but unquenched. All of those shadowy folks whose blood flowed in her veins seemed to move quietly in the moonlit room. And Scarlett was not surprised to see them, these kinsmen who had taken the worst that fate could send and hammer it into the best. *Tara was her fate, her fight, and she must conquer it.* (414; italics mine)

Absolute in the exclusion of African ancestry, the racial genealogy of Anglo-Irish and Anglo-French ancestries predestines Scarlett for cultural grit and for expressing entitled condescension toward "white trash" (68, 74). Here, I deviate from two recent scholarly opinions. First, if we assume that whiteness means sexual and cultural conservatism, Scarlett is counternormative. Diane Roberts has argued that Scarlett is more "red" or "scarlet" in her "potential for transgression," in "her femaleness, her physicality, her sexuality," and less "white" in her inability to demonstrate the Southern "decorum she has been taught," explaining her gravitation toward Rhett, "a man who also struggles with white decorum."[39] Second, if we assume that Mitchell's imagination of Rhett comprises the anxieties and fantasies about African Americans and Arabs circulating during her life, then, at least where this protagonist is concerned, racial whiteness is symbolically hybrid, alleging the tropes of dark and evil alongside those of light and good.[40] Yet such hybrid notions of whiteness, I would counter, are not the mythical aspects of whiteness that have persisted in the public imagination of *Gone with the Wind*. Nor are they ones that governed the discourse of *SunTrust v. Houghton*. Rather, the more popular notion of whiteness implies a racial supremacy in contrast to the alleged racial inferiority of African ancestry, harnessed in the metaphor of blood. The alleged racial superiority of Scarlett in *Gone with the Wind* reflects the segregation of her blood and behavior from those of African Americans. By the same token, Scarlett's association of Irishness with privilege runs counter to the tendency of nineteenth-century American society to lump and denigrate Irish and African American citizens together as lower class.[41] Mitchell's elimination of the racial intermixture of blood protects the integrity of Scarlett's whiteness, supported by the generations and millions of consumers of the novel *Gone with the Wind* and its derivative works that have helped to elevate that integrity to the mythic proportion of purity.[42]

"Every Woman I Ever Knew Was a Nigger": Alice Randall's The Wind Done Gone

Fueling the parodic force of *The Wind Done Gone* is Alice Randall's fancy that Scarlett is not racially pure, or that *Gone with the Wind* is as much a story of "miscegenation" as it is a story of the South. Written as a diary and also set during the Civil War and its aftermath, *The Wind Done Gone* begins the critique with its own title, whose words ("the wind done gone") play on those of the speaker of Ernest Dowson's 1896 poem "Non Sum Qualis Eram Bonae sub Regno Cinarae." Haunted by "an old passion" named Cynara, the speaker utters the phrase "gone with the wind," the title of Mitchell's novel: "I have forgot much, Cynara! gone with the wind, / Flung roses, roses riotously with the throng."[43] The speaker explains his "fashion" of loyalty to Cynara, including, ironically, his carnal affair with another woman. Out of that line, Mitchell crafts her own, describing Scarlett's wonderment upon returning to Tara after the Union army's successful invasion of the South during the Civil War: "Was Tara still standing? Or was Tara also gone with the wind which had swept through Georgia?" (*GWTW*, 390). Randall's portrayal of Cynara in *The Wind Done Gone* at once gestures to the triangular sexual relations in Dowson's poem, while beginning to expose the historical fact of miscegenation repressed in *Gone with the Wind*.

Several storylines in *The Wind Done Gone* confirm that it is a parody of *Gone with the Wind*.[44] One explanation for Randall's success as a parodist is that she ties up the narrative ends that Mitchell has left loose. The loose ends include places that discount or understate information, a possible result of Mitchell's intent on making the narration economical in presenting information or cutting out scenes for the sake of narrative exposition. Exploiting these silences, Randall's novel speculates on what the world of *Gone with the Wind* would look like if race plays a more visible role in how the white characters perceive and interact with one another, how they view their own identities, and how we, as readers, perceive and understand them. In a sex scene between Cynara and R.—to repeat, equivalent to Rhett, Scarlett's temperamental third husband in *Gone with the Wind*—the mistress moans, "[T]his is what we loved, him teaching me, and me touching him. It was good for us, that. Good and gone, like the wind done gone."[45] R. is also equivalent to the speaker of Dawson's poem, and Scarlett, equivalent to "Other," is the woman the speaker is kissing. By the end of Randall's novel, the phrase "the wind done gone" returns to signal that Cynara now celebrates what Other despises: the Union army's signal of progress for African Americans and the nation as a whole. Giving birth to and loving "a little black baby" enable Cynara to overcome the racial self-hate instilled by her tension with Other.

Obviously, Randall is treading into the thematic territory of miscegenation. In addition to Scarlett's death, the Trust forbade miscegenation in the sequels to *Gone with the Wind*. A contract prepared by the Trust and signed by Emma Tennant, a British novelist, for the writing of a sequel stipulated that Tennant needed, in the words of one investigative journalist, to "retain Ms. Mitchell's tone, vision and characters. It also forbade Ms. Tennant from including 'acts or references to incest, miscegenation, or sex between two people of the same sex.'"[46] Unfortunately for the Trust, *The Wind Done Gone* fills the original world of *Gone with the Wind* with the social, cultural, and biological miscegenation between the races.

Randall suggests that African Americans are crucial to the social bonds appearing in *Gone with the Wind*. Since Garlic introduces Mammy to Planter, and since Cynara, R., and Other have a fraught relationship, the readers of *The Wind Done Gone*, many of whom might already have read *Gone with the Wind*, must rethink Mitchell's novel in relation to the plausibility of Randall's ironic claims that Other descends from Africa and that this possibility poses serious problems for the longstanding myth of her whiteness. Other's psychological and cultural attitude comes from Mammy's influence, whereas Scarlett's is attributable to an inborn and inbred amalgam of her gritty father and refined mother. In Mitchell's novel, when Scarlett returns to Tara after the Civil War, "the oft-told family tales to which she had listened since babyhood, listened half-bored, impatient and but partly comprehending, were crystal clear. . . . Tara was her fate, her fight, and she must conquer it" (*GWTW*, 414). In Randall's novel, Cynara reflects on this myth: "I wonder what [Other] would feel now if she knew, if I told her, if she ever come to understand that Mammy used her, used her to torment white men. Other was Mammy's revenge on a world of white men who would not marry her dark self and who had not loved her Lady. Did Other see how she had been weaned to pick up hearts and trained to dash them down, both with casual ease? Who convinced her to conquer?" (*TWDG*, 54). Other's anxious approach to white men is a byproduct of Mammy's attitude toward the racism and sexism of these men, even as Other participates in the exercise of these doctrines as part of her accumulation of social and material privilege.

The plausibility of Other's embodiment of Mammy's traits, and her expression of them in her own peculiar way, is questionable. Vilified as a woman closer to Other than to Cynara, Mammy allows the sale of her own daughter on the auction block (31). Cynara's reflections, nonetheless, urge us to think about the cultural and ideological influence of African American slaves over the disposition of their white masters. Cynara affirms this viewpoint when she states that "[t]here was always something African about Planter, and Garlic was it," and that "[e]ven Planter's love of the land had something African in it, . . . [as] [b]lack people are ancestor worshippers" (63). The desire of whites to uphold their own privilege, *The Wind Done Gone* suggests, does not necessarily contradict the extent to which African American society and culture may have shaped their worldviews.[47]

Randall further complicates our literary memory of Scarlett's whiteness by redrawing her genealogical portrait. In one section of *The Wind Done Gone*, we come across the letters exchanged between Lady and Cousin (Ellen and Philippe), her initial love interest (prior to Gerald), before he is mysteriously murdered in a New Orleans barroom brawl. *Gone with the Wind* tells us that "a package containing a miniature of Ellen, which she flung to the floor with a cry, four letters in her own handwriting to Philippe Robillard, and a brief letter from a New Orleans priest" arrived to announce her cousin's death (57). Based on the established literary fact that Ellen and Philippe wrote to one another, Randall imagines a scene in which R. meets with Cynara and hands her the "love letters" that "Lady had written to Cousin and the letters he had written to her," all of which Lady once hands to Mammy, who then transfers them to Garlic, who then passes them on to R. (*TWDG*, 119, 127).

Writing into the narrative interstices of *Gone with the Wind*, Randall urges us to recast our literary memory of Ellen's family history, which Mitchell has restricted to French ancestry, in order to account for African ancestry. Lady admonishes Cousin that they cannot marry. As her disapproving mother puts it, "the curse of Haiti is upon us" (122). The mother is referring to the French colony, Saint-Domingue, that becomes Haiti while she and her husband, "a soldier of Napoleon," flee the country in 1791, the actual first year of an African slave rebellion there (*GWTW*, 42). In response to Cousin's confusion over the relevance of Haiti to their premarital challenge, Lady discloses that their great-grandmother "was a Negresse" (*TWDG*, 124)—hence the introduction of the possibility that Other herself is not exclusively white but a descendant of the great-great-grandmother, a Haiti-born "Negresse." Inevitably, this newfound racial genealogy renders essential Other's racial "blackness," positing the one-drop rule for what constitutes her ancestral "Negresse," while deconstructing the cultural and biological genealogy of whiteness.

The tension between Other and Cynara turns on Cynara's profane allegation of Other's African ancestry: "She was just a nigger" (133). The epithet captures the tangle of anxiety and trauma elicited from Mammy's favoritism of Other, while anticipating Cousin's reasoned response, in a letter, to Lady's confession of the African ancestry:

> I am surprised you put those words to paper. I am proud of you, very proud, and I should like to marry you. . . . Of course Mammy knows. They've seen all manner of white-looking nigger children. What farce this is. It's a pity Molière didn't live in this city and this part of the country. Instead of writing the Imaginary Invalid, he could have written the . . . what would we call ourselves? Niggers Who Knew Not? Can you be a Negro if you don't know you're a Negro? I would have said a nigger knows he's a nigger. Always. Absolutely. But what if he doesn't? So . . . we are each to pour a little more milk in the coffee and not tell. We were the ones who were not supposed ever to know—the first to be white not black with a secret. See how well our love serves us. If we had not fallen in love, we might never have discovered our darkness. (125)

The issue that arises from Cousin's soliloquy is not simply whether the O'Haras are "black" or "white" but whether one's own racial self-knowledge, or the information one knows about one's own racial background, determines one's racial identity. "Other never knew" the depth of her African ancestry, according to Cynara, mainly because her mother succeeded in withholding that information from her (127). The limitation of Other's racial self-knowledge to the Anglo-Irish and Anglo-French histories of her family predetermines her identification with white Southern aristocracy, while perpetuating the myth of her racial purity. Randall downplays the unfortunate story of how Other's racial self-misconception gives her a false sense of social and cultural superiority to Cynara and other African Americans, almost replacing it with the redemptive story of the sympathy for racial difference shared by Lady and Cousin. Aside from Cousin's will to marry Lady, regardless of her African ancestry, Ellen appreciates the color of Cynara's skin, implicitly disagreeing with the latter's simultaneous desire for whiteness and disdain for blackness. For Cynara, Lady "made a list of everything that was brown and beautiful in the world," especially the fruits and vegetation of nature (136). Lady's attempt to redeem dark skin color does not go far enough to console Cynara, who comforts herself by arriving at her own hypothesis on the racial symptom of Other and the like: "[A]ll women are niggers. For sure, *every woman I ever knew was a nigger*—whether she knew it or not" (177; italics mine).

In other words, all women—all of humankind, for that matter—capable of claiming Anglo-Saxon ancestry could just as legitimately be traced to African ancestry. The technologies and discourses of historical knowledge delimit, if not restrict, any human claim to racial homology. Conversely, the more information one can access and know about one's own racial history, the more logically one can identify with or reject a certain racial group. The absence of such information, or the willful ignorance of it, may help make sense of this kind of conduct, but it also renders racial identity, or racial self-knowledge, provisional. In *The Wind Done Gone*, Randall suggests that, just as the information presented by *Gone with the Wind* is fair game for revision, so is the history or genealogy of race. Scarlett may be white simply because Mitchell says so, but that fact does not mean another author, such as Randall, cannot come along and tell an ironic story in which no race, neither whiteness nor blackness, is pure and fixed.

The death of Other, finally, marks Cynara's independence from the tragic mulatta figure and *The Wind Done Gone*'s independence from parody's imitative impulse. Contrary to the viewpoint that Randall's novel revolves entirely around the details of Mitchell's, I venture that beginning especially with Other's death in chapter 47 (out of 114, not including the postscript), or after about 45 percent of the text, *The Wind Done Gone* makes a dramatic turn toward imagining the protagonist and African American political life beyond the white-supremacist logic of race and historical romance in *Gone with the Wind.* Shortly after the death, Cynara is unexpectedly invited to the Washington, D.C., home of Frederick Douglass, the African American former slave who was once the leading abolitionist before and during the Civil War and who turned out to be, in this temporal period of the novel, the leading author, political activist, and statesman in the postwar era, certainly until the coincidence of his death and the phenomenal rise of Booker T. Washington in 1895. The broken home and spirit that have been the hallmarks of Cynara's identity circumscribe both her continued longing for R., who is heart-stricken and has gone to bury Other, and her initial hesitation to accept the invitation and attend without him: "I'm not sure if I should go" (96). In due time, she decides to take the risk, her own voice rising and strengthening: "I want to go to Mr. Frederick Douglass's house and I wouldn't be sorry to go without R. if I could go in propriety. I like moving among these Capital City Negroes" (104). Accepting the invitation and entering an elite circle of African American society—in the Baltimore–Washington, D.C., corridor no less, a far cry from her more familiar dominion of Atlanta—signal the commencement of her self-esteem, despite the Southern nightmares that continue to haunt her.

At the party, Cynara's experience of talking with Douglass himself is less important than their communion in the same progressive African American society. She states, "We, Frederick Douglass and I, barely exchanged three sentences, but he looked at me as [three women from Fisk University] sang ["Soon I Will Be Done with the Troubles of the World"], and I could see that he liked what he saw" (108). Douglass's tacit approval of Cynara's attendance, coupled with her realization that the party is "the kind of event to which [she is] not frequently invited," because "[m]ulatto mistresses of Confederate aristocrats have little standing in Negro society," permits her into what she calls "a kind of Negro open house," or what I would call an African American community that has attained power in the informal and formal realms of culture and politics (108–9). As I have mentioned earlier, in chapters 2 and 3, Cynara's experience has been the story of Reconstruction in the late 1860s and early 1870s, when constitutional amendments, economic growth, increased political representation, and the rise of literacy among African Americans across the nation bolstered and protected their claims to civil rights. Racial uplift simultaneously clashed with the ideologies and practices of white supremacy in the postbellum nineteenth century. Randall telescopes these issues of Reconstruction—the issues of conflict along lines of race, class, politics, and generation but also the issues of African American resilience and success in the face of conflict—in the second half of her novel.

A history dreaded and neglected in *Gone with the Wind,* the era of Reconstruction emerges in Randall's union of Cynara and an African American congressman at Douglass's party. The congressman is the human trope of Reconstruction, which saw an unprecedented number of African Americans elected to Congress and enjoying political clout.[48] Accorded the deference of even someone as stately as Douglass, the congressman is the one who explains to Cynara the importance of African American agency, applicable as well to her own symbolic flight from the tragic mulatta. As the Fisk University women croon "Go Down, Moses," a Negro spiritual which causes Cynara to be "amazed by their performance—the haunting combination of the raw and the refined," the congressman admonishes, "Be not amazed. . . . We see it daily. We are the chosen ones, the ones who sometimes snatch victory from the jaws of tragedy. . . . Until [tragedy] is transformed by our own energy, our own muscle, our own brain, every second of our very existence on these shores is tragic" (109–10). The political challenges of this congressman and the personal challenges of Cynara turn out to be as striking in their thematic parallelism as they are in their practical intersection, resulting in the demise of her relationship with R. (152–53).

Randall's coordination of the dismantling of Scarlett's genealogical whiteness with the definition of African American political identity is significant. In the first instance, *The Wind Done Gone* becomes a parody by borrowing fundamental information from *Gone with the Wind* primarily to critique Mitchell's perpetuation of racial stereotypes and historical misrepresentation. In the second instance, Randall's novel transcends, in innovative ways, the world of Mitchell's novel to attend to African American political history. The death of Scarlett is a flashpoint for analyzing racial mythology but also for examining the strategic turn within parody from imitation to originality. Admittedly, this inference tempers my intervention (stated at the outset of this chapter) into the preoccupation of scholars with the African American characters of *Gone with the Wind.* At this point, I am prepared to say, more precisely, that Randall's genealogical critique of whiteness best reveals parody's revision of original expression, while her thematic deepening of blackness reveals equally well the genre's transcendence of it.

"Killing Off Ms. Scarlett": The District Court

When *SunTrust v. Houghton* appeared in district court, on the docket of Judge Charles A. Pannell Jr., his goal was not to make a finding of the guilt or innocence of Houghton Mifflin. Rather, the goal was to determine whether he should enjoin the publication of *The Wind Done Gone* prior to and during the district trial by jury (if he deemed it should go that far), at the end of which the court would entrust the selected jurors to make the finding. For weeks, Judge Pannell encountered a host of evidence. SunTrust Bank submitted detailed charts, each arranged by quotations and page numbers, summarizing the plots of Randall's and Mitchell's novels and alleging instances in which plagiarism may have occurred. Aside from the letter sent to Houghton Mifflin threatening a lawsuit, the plaintiff entered the official paperwork housed at the Library of Congress on the Stephen Mitchell Trust's registration and renewal of the copyright for Mitchell's *Gone with the Wind* and its derivative works. Also submitting sworn declarations and relevant evidentiary documents, the supporters of the plaintiff's motion included the lawyers and legal counsel associated with or invited by the plaintiff, in addition to the members of the committee established to oversee the Trust. Experts on literature and book publishing—including literary professors, specialists in literary copyright law, executive editors of publishing houses, creative writers, literary critics, and even the president of a philanthropic foundation—also provided supporting statements.

Houghton Mifflin mounted a comparably strong defense. Securing and presenting its own host of remarkable documents and experts, the publisher argued that the transformative potential of *The Wind Done Gone* must not be suppressed. The company submitted the declarations and curricula vitae of literary professors; an affidavit containing evidence of numerous parodies of *Gone with the Wind* already circulating in the American consumer market; charts itemizing the racist language and African American caricatures in Mitchell's novel; and statements by Randall herself, by senior editors and executive administrative officers at Houghton Mifflin and other entertainment companies, by literary and cultural luminaries, and by national organizations submitting amici curiae, all in favor of publishing *The Wind Done Gone* without delay.

A consistent theme for the defense was that "parody" properly describes the ironic relationship of *The Wind Done Gone* to *Gone with the Wind*. Randall herself uses broader language to justify this relationship. "If I had made only one or a few allusions," she states in her submitted declaration, "my literary critique would have been lost."[49] Despite her intent, she conformed it to the legal contingency of parody, which happens to enjoy special political status and favorable treatment in precedent court cases involving the First Amendment. Next, the defense countered the plagiarism accusation in a couple of ways. First, the originality of *The Wind Done Gone* contradicts the claim that Randall copied *Gone with the Wind* verbatim. Second, even if there were some amount of copying, the doctrine of "fair use" approved the political license of copying. For the criticism of parody to resonate, the original target of ridicule must, after all, be relatively discernible within it. A lawyer for the defense, during a preliminary injunction hearing held on April 18, 2001, in district court, underscored this point by lifting almost verbatim (and, coincidentally, without any attribution) a sentence in the declaration Henry Louis Gates Jr. had previously submitted to the district court: "Parody is a creative mechanism for the exercise of political speech and commentary on the part of people who feel themselves oppressed."[50] To be clear, pace the defense lawyer's logical leap, parody is not automatically for the oppressed, though the irony inherent to parody does indicate an awareness of the power relations among the literary ironist, the target of irony, and the reader. Still, parody does enjoy constitutional protection, in addition to its fair-use protection: it demands that U.S. courts of law honor literature, among other cultural media, as a political demonstration of free and critical speech and thus as a legal exercise of First Amendment rights.

The best precedent language for this argument, to which both the plaintiff and the defense referred, appears in the United States Supreme Court's 1994 ruling in *Campbell v. Acuff-Rose Music, Inc.* In this case, Justice David H. Souter, in writing for the unanimous majority, opined that "Ugly Woman," a 1989 song that its writer, the rap group 2 Live Crew, calls a parody of Roy Orbison's famous 1964 rock-'n'-roll song "Oh, Pretty Woman," is entitled to fair-use protection:

> The more transformative the new work, the less will be the significance of other factors . . . that may weigh against a finding of fair use. The heart of any parodist's claim to quote from existing material is the use of some elements of a prior author's composition to create a new one that, at least in part, comments on that author's work. . . . [P]arody has an obvious claim to transformative value. . . . Like less ostensibly humorous forms of criticism, *it can provide social benefit,* by shedding light on an earlier work, and, in the process, creating a new one. We thus line up with the courts that have held that parody, like other comment or criticism, may claim fair use.[51]

Justice Souter states that the "fair use of a copyrighted work" is permissible "for purposes such as criticism [or] comment." Whether the parody "is in good taste or bad does not and should not matter for fair use." Most important is the "transformative value."[52]

The Supreme Court precedent was not enough to sway Judge Pannell in the defense's favor. Referring to this and to an additional set of legal precedents, the plaintiff persuaded him to believe that literary trusts should "control the characters" in cultural expression, especially if "the characters are well enough clearly defined that they can sustain sequels."[53] The fifteen characters that appear in both Mitchell's and Randall's novels, according to one lawyer for the plaintiff, "have an extraordinary amount of definition and detail which brings them alive."[54] Institutions such as the Trust, a "copyright holder," have "the exclusive right to authorize derivative works [such as sequels] . . . [and] control the fate of [the] characters, to determine how these characters will be used."[55]

Spinning this thread of reasoning into the fabric of its complaint, Sun-Trust Bank objected to Randall's imagination in *The Wind Done Gone* of the death of Scarlett—who, at the end of *Gone with the Wind,* is actually still alive. Randall's literary murder of Scarlett means, in the plaintiff's words, that "the ability of the Trust to authorize future sequels will be compromised, even maybe precluded because the character is no longer alive."[56] (Evidence shows that the words ring with hypocrisy. Mammy is killed at the outset of the *authorized* 1991 sequel to *Gone with the Wind,* Alexandra Ripley's *Scarlett.* The Trust, also listed as the copyright holder of this novel, was not opposed to killing off an African American character.) During oral arguments, even Judge Pannell seemed irked by Scarlett's death: "I guess what really troubles me is *killing off Ms. Scarlett.*"[57] (The myth of her persona is evident, since here she should have been called "Ms. O'Hara.")

Two days after the preliminary injunction hearing, on April 20, 2001, Judge Pannell issued the awaited order in support of the plaintiff, SunTrust Bank. The "defendant's publication and sale of *The Wind Done Gone,*" he announced in a written statement, "will infringe the plaintiff's copyright interests as protected under the copyright laws. Accordingly, the court hereby GRANTS the plaintiff's motion for a preliminary injunction, . . . [and] the defendant is hereby PRELIMINARILY ENJOINED from further production, display, distribution, advertising, sale, or offer for sale of the book."[58] His review of both *Gone with the Wind* and *The Wind Done Gone* concluded that a "substantial similarity" of copyrightable features—such as the "characters, character traits, scenes, settings, physical descriptions, and plot"—exists between the two novels. More to the point, Randall "takes" these literary elements "directly" from Mitchell's novel.[59]

Contrary to the claim of the defendant, Houghton Mifflin, the parodic intent and evidence in *The Wind Done Gone* also do not contradict the plaintiff's allegation that it is a sequel to *Gone with the Wind.* Randall's novel is just as much a commercial product as it is a political product, and this hybridity lent credence to the plaintiff's argument that this novel could compete in and partially usurp the market reserved for the derivative works (or sequels) of Mitchell's novel. Judge Pannell asserted that the plaintiff, not Randall, would suffer the greatest harm if the court failed to grant the request for a preliminary injunction against the release of *The Wind Done Gone*. The district court favored copyright protection over what the defense claimed to be the public interest in the novel.

"Sufficient Comment and Criticism": The Court of Appeals

Unlike the debate and the evidence presented at the district court stage of *SunTrust v. Houghton,* the topic and nature of the exchanges narrowed at the appellate stage, where the presiding judges of the United States Court of Appeals for the Eleventh Circuit (Judges Stanley F. Birch Jr., Stanley Marcus, and Huntington Wood Jr., from the Seventh Circuit sitting by designation) concentrated on whether Judge Pannell abused his discretion in privileging the copyright-infringement protection of a primary artistic work over the First Amendment protection of a secondary artist who sought to transform this work in the service of a "political" statement.

A few days after Judge Pannell's ruling, Houghton Mifflin filed a motion for an expedited review of the principles of this ruling in the court of appeals. Houghton Mifflin contended that it held the right to do so, based on four prerequisites: its appeal would prevail, based on the merits of its argument; it would suffer irreparable harm, unless the appellate court overturns Judge Pannell's ruling; others likewise would suffer comparable harm; and the public interest in the case and its ramifications were outstanding. Houghton Mifflin claimed that if the injunction were not vacated or stayed by the middle of May 2001, then the harm to Randall and Houghton Mifflin would be too great to overcome. Reiterating the same points it raised in district court, Houghton Mifflin stressed that Judge Pannell exaggerated the amount of *The Wind Done Gone*'s textual appropriation of *Gone with the Wind,* while underestimating the parodic and critical nature of each allusion in Randall's novel to Mitchell's novel. The political entitlement of literary appropriation and allusion to constitutional protection in copyright law was not dismissible. Of course, SunTrust Bank responded in detail to these challenges. Like Houghton Mifflin, it also recounted the key claims of its district court argument, including the claim that *The Wind Done Gone,* as a novel that partially continues where *Gone with the Wind* leaves off, would unfairly occupy the market of literary sequels authorized by the Stephens Mitchell Trust and would cause irreparable harm.[60]

On May 17, 2001, the appellate court, to strengthen its evaluation of the district court's opinion, directed the opposing parties and their amici curiae (or "friends of the court") to submit briefs on the "jurisprudential principles" in the case *Cable News Network v. Video Monitoring Services* (*CNN v. VMS*).[61] In 1991, this same court of appeals (though with Stanley F. Birch Jr. and two different judges) overruled a preliminary injunction, levied at the district level, prohibiting VMS from recording and redistributing CNN's broadcasts. Paul A. Stewart, a scholar of intellectual property law, states that this appellate court argued that the district court "had no authority to issue an injunction extending beyond the specific copyrighted work that the defendant had copied."[62] Eventually, it remanded the case to the district court, ordering a rehearing; the district court turned the preliminary injunction into a permanent one; and, a year later, the appellate court ironically refused to question the validity of this change and dismissed VMS's second appeal. Perhaps since this court of appeals, in 1992, never issued a ruling on the permanent injunction, the 2001 court sought to revisit the case (though not to treat it as a binding precedent) and to apply it to the district-court-imposed injunction in *SunTrust v. Houghton*.

Of course, the briefs supporting SunTrust Bank and Houghton Mifflin opposed each other. The former described the relationship between the Copyright Act's establishment of the "idea/expression dichotomy," or the distinction between the copyrightability of ideas (which is false, because they are free) and of expression (which the act upholds).[63] In SunTrust Bank's response to the appellate court's notice, the company further stated that the "jurisprudential principle" of *CNN v. VMS* teaches us that an "overbroad injunction, one which prohibits the dissemination of future, uncopyrighted speech, does not strike that balance properly"—that is, the balance between "the protection of original works under the Copyright Act and the free flow of information under the First Amendment."[64] The injunction against the release of *The Wind Done Gone* was not overbroad because the district court's decision focuses on the novel alone, not on the other critical statements that Randall, Houghton Mifflin, or others may want to make in conformance with the Copyright Act. In this respect, Judge Pannell's ruling sustained the First Amendment protection to which these parties are entitled, while recognizing the copyright protection to which the Trust is entitled. A balance had been struck, SunTrust Bank concluded.

Houghton Mifflin's supporters, whose briefs outnumbered those on record for SunTrust Bank,[65] also remarked on the applicability of *CNN v. VMS* and highlighted the imbalance between the protections of copyright and the First Amendment, but their reading of the case led them to the opposite conclusion. The position taken by SunTrust Bank—that the injunction was not overbroad, because it presumably focused on the novel's expression alone, not on its ideas—fails to realize that the district court's discretion discounted the regulatory need of the Copyright Clause to encourage the free, political speech granted by the First Amendment. The scope of copyright ownership is a monopoly but is still limited enough to allow the intellectual flow of ideas prerequisite to public education and political debate. Any litigation of copyright ownership that in effect precludes this intellectual flow exemplifies an act of "over-reaching."[66] Political opinion and discussion deserve the greatest degree of privilege and protection. In this regard, Judge Pannell, by mitigating this degree in his ruling for SunTrust Bank, had instituted a relative imbalance between the Copyright Clause and the First Amendment.

One important amicus curiae brief is worth mentioning here. Submitted by the Pen American Center, American Booksellers Foundation for Freedom of Expression, Freedom to Read Foundation, Washington Lawyers' for the Arts, the First Amendment Project, and the National Coalition against Censorship, the brief appears to side with Houghton Mifflin, given the united front of its authors in the literary, literacy, civil rights, and publishing industries and given its recommendation that *The Wind Done Gone* be released. Certain parts of the brief are quite nuanced, including a subtle critique of Houghton Mifflin itself. The brief implies that the ongoing legal debate over whether *The Wind Done Gone* is entitled to protection from the Constitution's First Amendment has gotten too bogged down in terminological details of what exactly is a "parody." More important is reaching a proper measurement of the political value of Randall's novel, a value that enhances the constitutionality of the literary genre: "[T]he question here is not whether the work at issue can be unequivocally called a parody. This important case cannot be decided by labels. . . . The real issue is whether the book contains *sufficient comment and criticism* to be entitled to the added protection against an injunction required by the Supreme Court. On that issue, there can be no doubt."[67]

In line with this reasoning, and mindful of the parties' responses to the court's jurisprudential question on *CNN v. VMS*, the United States Court of Appeals for the Eleventh Circuit published on May 25, 2001, a brief synopsis of its decision. Ruling in favor of Houghton Mifflin, the appellate court concluded that the district court failed to honor the constitutional protection of parody. It vacated Judge Pannell's decision and remanded the case to his court. The district court's "entry of a preliminary injunction in this copyright case," the appellate court announced, "was an abuse of discretion in that it represents an unlawful prior restraint in violation of the First Amendment." The discretion was abusive insofar as it was "unbridled" and too "extraordinary" and "drastic" for the case at hand.[68]

More relevant to our purpose, the court, then, released a more detailed, sweeping discussion of its rationale for the decision regarding the political value of African American literature. The judicial protection of free speech is required, the court stressed, even when a second artistic work's parodic borrowing from a first work exceeds the boundaries of fair use. (This borrowing must stop short of piracy, however.) The court also decoupled two often conflated concepts: the ownership of a work, which represents ideas and information; and the ownership of that work's copyright, which pertains to the expression of ideas and information.[69] In doing so, the court reminded all that copyright law does not intend to shield an artistic work from the criticism of its ideas and information, which subsequent artists should always be permitted, under the protection of fair use, to incorporate for the sake of education and debate. In remanding the case to the district court, the appellate court stipulated that "a viable fair use defense is available" and that Judge Pannell's "issuance of the injunction was at odds with the shared principles of the First Amendment and the copyright law, acting as a prior restraint on speech because the public had not had access to Randall's ideas or viewpoint in the form of expression that she chose."[70] The appellate court is not concerned with the impetus of Judge Pannell's ruling—such as the literal or symbolic killing of Scarlett, as I have shown—but, rather, the jurisprudential meanings of it, such as the illegal blunting of African American literature's political impact.

On this latter point, even as the appellate court advances the Supreme Court's 1994 logic, in *Campbell v. Acuff-Rose Music,* on the constitutional value of parody, it recognizes the limitations that the legal application of parody, its definition as comedy or ridicule, has imposed on political discourse. Ironically, Houghton Mifflin, which, in the end, benefited from the parody defense, is culpable for perpetuating these limitations:

> The Supreme Court's definition of parody in *Campbell* . . . is somewhat vague. On the one hand, the Court suggests that the aim of parody is "comic effect or ridicule," but it then proceeds to discuss parody more expansively in terms of its "commentary" on the original. . . . In light of the admonition in *Campbell* that courts should not judge the quality of

the work or the success of the attempted humor in discerning its parodic character, we choose to take the broader view. For purposes of our fair-use analysis, we will treat a work as a parody if its aim is to comment on or criticize a prior work by appropriating elements of the original in creating a new, artistic, as opposed to scholarly or journalistic, work. Under this definition, the parodic character of *TWDG* is clear. *TWDG* is not a general commentary upon the Civil War–era American South, but a specific criticism of and rejoinder to the depiction of slavery and the relationships between blacks and whites in *GWTW*.[71]

Upon the publication of the appellate court's initial synopsis of its ruling, SunTrust Bank filed an emergency petition. It requested a rehearing en banc (with the entire twelve judges of the United States Court of Appeals for the Eleventh Circuit, not merely Judges Birch, Marcus, and Wood) to reassert its position in the case while rejecting the appellate court's conclusion. Houghton Mifflin accepted the appellate court's invitation to respond and provided a brief reasserting its own positions as well as supporting the conclusion. The unanimity of the three judges in the appellate court provided them the ample leverage needed to deny SunTrust Bank's request. The decision portended the improbability that the Supreme Court of the United States would even hear the case, much less vacate the court of appeals' ruling, given that the Supreme Court itself already ruled recently and unanimously for 2 Live Crew in *Campbell v. Acuff-Rose Music, Inc.*[72] SunTrust Bank, realizing its sealed fate, settled out of court with Houghton Mifflin, bringing the 2001 case to a close.[73]

"Who Controls How History Is Imagined?": Free Speech and the Transformative Value of African American Literature

The appellate decision dealt a serious blow to the plaintiff of *SunTrust v. Houghton* for two major reasons. First, its vacating of the lower court's ruling meant that Houghton Mifflin had license to publish *The Wind Done Gone*. The release would have rendered moot an intention of the initial lawsuit: to enjoin the circulation of the novel. Once that happens, given that Houghton Mifflin had already advertised the novel's release on June 7, 2001, SunTrust Bank's alleged harm would already have been done in the public sphere, even if the trial by jury had handed the plaintiff moral and practical victories that mandated a monetary award and the destruction of all copies of Randall's novel within Houghton Mifflin's reach. Second, as suggested earlier, SunTrust

Bank faced what seemed to be an arduous uphill battle in achieving victory in the appellate court or the U.S. Supreme Court. Hence, the settlement between SunTrust Bank and Houghton Mifflin made sense. The appellate ruling encouraged the settlement, which occurred in the interim period between when the case was returned from the appellate court and when it would have been reconsidered by the district court.[74]

The court of appeals accepted Houghton Mifflin's district court defense of the political salience of a historical novel. As Thomas F. Haddox, a literary scholar, notes, Randall's self-described role as "revisionist historian" blurred the line between history and fiction, correcting the version of Southern history in *Gone with the Wind*.[75] Since copyright protection explicitly covers only the expression of ideas, not the ideas themselves, the plaintiff's complaint rested on an erroneous argument for the copyrightability of the historical ideas and facts of *Gone with the Wind,* such as those related to the antebellum, wartime, and Reconstruction eras of the South. The plaintiff's division of literature from history, as opposed to Randall's merging of them, was a disingenuous attempt to have it both ways: to claim the copyright ownership of both Mitchell's literary world and the mid-nineteenth-century historical world to which it refers. SunTrust Bank's allegations of Houghton Mifflin's copyright infringement obscured the fact that *Gone with the Wind* is as much a derivative work of historiographical reconstruction as it is an original work of literary construction, that history and literature are almost always tightly wedded, and that history is fair game for literary criticism.

For Houghton Mifflin, then, the "transformative" value of *The Wind Done Gone*—to borrow the term of the Supreme Court in *Campbell v. Acuff-Rose Music, Inc.*—comes from its attack on both the literary and the historical qualities of *Gone with the Wind.* As I have stated earlier, the actual death of Other signals the transformative effect of Randall's novel, turning the tables on the mythic cultural and commercial status of Mitchell's novel and undermining SunTrust Bank's attempt, in the 2001 case, to "control" history. As Toni Morrison, in support of Houghton Mifflin, put it in her declaration to the district court,

> The real point of the request to enjoin, the question that seems to me to underlie the debate is *"Who controls how history is imagined?"* "Who gets to say what slavery was like for the slaves?" The implication of the claims suggests a kind of "ownership" of its slaves unto all future generations and keeps in place the racial structures *Gone with the Wind* describes, depends upon, and about which a war was fought.[76]

Taking Morrison's idea to its logical extreme, the plaintiff's claim that a substantial similarity exists between Mitchell's and Randall's novels served the Trust's desire to uphold the fundamental distinction it sought to maintain in its contract with Donald McCaig for his 2007 novel, *Rhett Butler's People,* the second sequel to *Gone with the Wind:* "[N]either Scarlett O'Hara nor Rhett Butler may die, thus preserving the expectations of an avid reading public, as well as the Mitchell Trusts' ability to authorize sequels in the future."[77] As troubling as Scarlett's actual death in *The Wind Done Gone* may have been for the Trust, the symbolic death of her character—her racial death as a purely white woman, not just her narrative death as a literary character—turns out to be equally, if not more, troubling, so troubling that here, too, the Trust has sought to prevent such death in contracts with derivative authors. The references made by the plaintiff and Judge Pannell to the life and death of Scarlett suggest a common anxiety over Randall's usurping of that character's meanings. The case effectively pitted copyright law against the free speech of racial representation in African American literature.

Although the parody argument helped Houghton Mifflin succeed in the case, I still claim that it *did not go far enough* in elucidating the transformative potential of *The Wind Done Gone.* An opportunity was missed to resolve the historical conflict between copyright law and the First Amendment. Jed Rubenfeld—a professor of law at Yale University who served as counsel to Alice Randall in *SunTrust v. Houghton* and who has recently published an excellent article on the constitutionality of copyright—is correct that the "confrontation between copyright law and the First Amendment" was "invisible" for the district court, which "saw no First Amendment difficulty at all." In contrast, "the appellate court saw the difficulty, but decided the case within the confines of copyright doctrine, rather than meeting the conflict head on." In case law, such "tensions" include the tendency of plaintiffs and judges to prioritize copyright over free-speech entitlements. In legal scholarship, in Rubenfeld's view, there has been a simultaneous neglect of the First Amendment within copyright law.[78]

Rubenfeld in his scholarly work has put copyright law and, for that matter, copyright scholarship "on trial." Fighting for "the freedom of expression," he seeks a legal paradigm that resolves the main tension between copyright law and the First Amendment, in addition to the corollary tension between copyright and creative expression, which I have already described at the outset of this chapter, on the racial politics of copyright law. From Rubenfeld's perspective, the appellate review of *SunTrust v. Houghton* did not question as much as it should have the fact that "'parodic' and 'critical' treatments of copyright material are highly favored," if not *too* highly favored, in definitions of fair use.[79] Consequently, the narrow conception of fair use, he goes on to say, is equated with the broad conception of free speech, when, in fact, the former includes only criticism, while the latter includes this and everything else. The constitutionality of copyright law, then, deserves further scrutiny, especially when its fair-use directive, however permissible it may have been for artists, impinges on the creative freedom of derivative works.

The parody argument indeed exploits the loophole that the First Amendment affords in copyright law. Prior to the case, Houghton Mifflin's initial catalogue description of *The Wind Done Gone,* entered by the plaintiff as legitimate evidence, *does not explicitly call the novel a parody.* Instead, *The Wind Done Gone* was merely subtitled "a novel" and portrayed as "a brilliant rejoinder"; "an inspired act of literary invention"; "the story that has been missing from the work that more than any other has defined our image of the antebellum South"; "[a]lluding to events in *Gone with the Wind* but ingeniously and ironically transforming them"; "an exquisitely written, emotionally complex story"; "[a] passionate love story"; "a wrenching portrait"; "a book that gives voice to those whom history has silenced"; "a[n] elegant literary achievement of significant political force"; and "a novel whose time has finally come."[80] Randall's novel comes across as a serious, multilayered, and, at best, ironic critique of Mitchell's novel—which, perhaps, could have been the connotations of parody all along. An argument still could be made that Houghton Mifflin's defense was an opportunistic exploitation of the constitutional loophole of parody. I cannot help but agree, in this regard, with the lawyers of SunTrust Bank who wondered aloud whether Randall and Houghton Mifflin deserved the degree of legal protection they sought, "simply by claiming—by shouting parody in a crowded literary marketplace." On another occasion, the plaintiff quoted from U.S. Supreme Court Justice Anthony M. Kennedy, who, in a concurring opinion in *Campbell,* admonishes that "as future courts apply our fair use analysis, they must take care that not just any commercial takeoff is rationalized *post hoc* as a parody."[81] If focused on exclusively, parody could distract one from realizing some of the broader issues of constitutional philosophy at stake in the case.[82]

That said, I do not go as far as Rubenfeld does in concentrating on the philosophical shortcomings of *SunTrust v. Houghton* and in dismissing politics from legal consideration. Rubenfeld believes that "First Amendment scholarship," such as that of its pioneer, Alexander Meiklejohn, "paints art too politically," such as when it ascribes literature to the "many forms of thought and expression . . . from which the voter derives the knowledge, intelligence, [and] sensitivity to human values." This "art in the ballot booth" exaggerates the political potential of art. Rubenfeld's dismissal of a political category for art affirms a dichotomy between the political sphere and the artistic sphere, when both, historically, have been imbricated. The "democracy-based account of the First Amendment," he states, "cannot apply to art without falsely politicizing it." But, in light of the evidence presented in this chapter, the basis for that statement is not clear. Finally, Rubenfeld's conception of the First Amendment as protecting the "freedom of imagination" seeks to indict the traditional privileging of so-called high art over low art, a hierarchy that constrains the semantics and limits the protection of "freedom of expression."[83] Yet this non sequitur draws too many typological distinctions between the imagination, on the one hand, and its expression, "projection," "exercise," "communication," and "misrepresentation," on the other.[84]

Allow me, here, to expound on this last critique. The terminological inconsistency of legal scholarship on literature has occurred in the past, regarding the distinctions of the "nonrepresentational" from the representational natures of art.[85] What this language fails to realize is that any line drawn between representation and, say, "nonrepresentation" or "misrepresentation" is bound to be arbitrary, subjective, and hermetic and to boast a claim to absolute truth, when such a line is always contestable. "Representations of the world in written discourse," as Louise A. Montrose, a literary scholar, reminds us, "participate in the construction of the world: they are engaged in shaping the modalities of social reality and in accommodating their writers, performers, readers, and audiences to multiple and shifting subject positions within the world that they themselves constitute and inhabit."[86] Written representations, such as literature, are as "engaged" with the social world as they are with the legal and political worlds. Measuring the social value of literature requires a flexible understanding of the way representations work in both legal and political senses, among others. Social value requires thinking about representation as accommodating, not dividing, the imagination and its various media of cultural expression, its popular consumption, and its repercussions in law and society.

Saying, then, that *SunTrust v. Houghton* has benefitted only Randall, Houghton Mifflin, and the readers of *The Wind Done Gone*—or has also benefited only writers, publishers, and readers facing similar legal situations—would reduce the case's legal and political impact. The case has already served as legal precedent to district court cases *outside* of copyright law, involving various motions by plaintiffs for preliminary and permanent injunctions. In 2003, one case featured a securities dealer's motion (which was denied) to enjoin its clients from arbitrating monetary compensation for underachieving investments. In that year, another case addressed a publisher's motion (also denied) to enjoin street vendors from selling its newspapers to car drivers and passengers at roadway intersections. One year later, yet another case (and yet another denial) concerned an investment firm's motion to enjoin a broker and fellow investors from arbitrating a recovery of monetary losses from poorly performing stocks. But in 2003, a church's motion was granted to enjoin its county's prohibition of its Christmas display, "Jesus Is the Reason for the Season," in a public park.[87] Evidently, in the cases of the rejected motions, the district court has consistently prevented corporations from restricting the rights of litigious individuals or groups aiming to seek, maintain, or recover financial livelihood. In the case of the granted motion, the court has upheld an organization's right, protected by the First Amendment, to freedom of expression and religion. Thanks to *SunTrust v. Houghton,* which has helped to clarify the political power of racial representation in relation to copyright law and literary history, a new precedent has emerged to help defend free speech and cultural expression in circumstances beyond these terms, too.

6

The Political Audacity of
Barack Obama's Literature

Barack Obama recalls in his 1995 memoir, *Dreams from My Father,* the period between 1985 and 1988 when he was director of the Developing Communities Project (DCP), a community organization serving poor African Americans on Chicago's South Side. He formed "an uneasy alliance" with Rafiq al-Shabazz, one of the area's "self-professed nationalists," to institute a job-training center in the city.[1] In due time, Obama and others within the DCP began to express reservations over Rafiq's vitriol. The nationalist "would interrupt the discussion with [DCP leaders] with long lectures about secret machinations afoot, and all the black people willing to sell their people down the river, . . . the veins in his neck straining, . . . as if he were an epileptic in the midst of a seizure" (196). Obama's disparagement of Rafiq's style implies a contrast between the two men: one is intellectually cool, the other emotionally hot. More important, this scene sets up another, thereafter, in which the two debate the merits of "black nationalism," or what the scholar Michael Eric Dyson defines as "a response of racial solidarity" among African Americans to what they believe to be "the divisive practices of white supremacist nationalism" within the United States.[2]

By the late 1980s, Obama had already encountered black nationalism, such as in *The Autobiography of Malcolm X,* published in 1964 and co-written by the Nation of Islam's former leader Malcolm X and the journalist Alex Haley. In the late 1970s, as a student in Punahou School, a private high school in Honolulu, Hawaii, Obama read the book closely (and privately, in lieu of his assigned homework) and learned about race and racism. Over time, life experience distilled Obama's memory of the book and encouraged him to test black nationalism's viability. "Ever since the first time I'd picked up Malcolm X's autobiography," Obama states in the memoir, as he reflects on Rafiq, "I had tried to untangle the twin strands of black nationalism, arguing that nationalism's affirming message—of solidarity and self-reliance, discipline and communal responsibility—need not depend on hatred of whites any more than it depended on white munificence" (197–98). The expression of black nationalism as antiwhite vengeance, in other words, impaired any political vision of interracial reconciliation and undermined the country's democratic, cross-racial "capacity for change" (198).

Obama's reflection on Rafiq ends with a distinction of political action as "inside" or "outside" history. Being inside history affirms the "progression" of human development, whereas being outside denies it. The former attends to the complexity of human identity, whereas the latter clings to the myths that ignore it:

> For when the nationalist spoke of a reawakening of values as the only solution to black poverty, he was expressing an implicit, if not explicit, criticism to black listeners: that we did not have to live as we did. And while there were those who could take such an unadorned message and use it to hew out a new life for themselves—those with the stolid dispositions that Booker T. Washington had once demanded from his followers—in the ears of many blacks such talk smacked of the explanations that whites had always offered for black poverty: that we continued to suffer from, if not genetic inferiority, then cultural weakness. It was a message that ignored causality or fault, a message outside history, without a script or plot that might insist on progression. (198)

Obama is contrasting two kinds of African American politics. There is a cohort of manipulative leaders of black nationalism, such as Rafiq and "stolid" followers, who accept the myth that antiwhite hatred is prerequisite to African American political unity. There is also a more skeptical group, including Obama, that indicts not only this myth but another myth, ironically shared by both black nationalists and white racists, that African Americans suffer from "genetic inferiority" and "cultural weakness." For Obama, the racial myths spewed by Rafiq indicate not a progression in African American political ideology but a regression.

Coincidentally, in the same year that *Dreams from My Father* first appeared, Dyson, quoted earlier, published *Making Malcolm: The Myth and Meaning of Malcolm X*, sharing Obama's interest in counteracting the myths of the assassinated leader. *Making Malcolm* culminates with an analysis of *Malcolm X,* the biographical film directed by Spike Lee, released in November 1992, and crucial to what was then a resurgence of public interest in Malcolm X. Dyson brings critical sophistication to the public conversation when he notes that Lee's "impressive" film wades through the thicket of "myth and romance" enclosing Malcolm X. Born from the "contemporary revival of black nationalism," the myths have "focused renewed attention" on Malcolm X and increased his value in popular culture, such as clothes, posters, and rap music. Dyson goes on to say that the lack of "intellectual attention" Malcolm X has received—far less than the kind paid to Martin Luther King Jr.—has allowed "myth and caricature" to reduce the Nation of Islam's former leader to four simplistic stereotypes: "hero and saint," "public moralist," "victim and vehicle of psychohistorical forces," and "revolutionary figure judged by his career trajectory from nationalist to socialist." Dyson closes with the simple but elusive question, "Whose Malcolm is it?"[3]

In *Dreams from My Father,* we see how "it" becomes Obama's. He reveals how present-day versions of black nationalism have discounted Malcolm X's philosophical shifts on the subjects of race, culture, politics, and nation. Common lay and even scholarly perceptions anchor black nationalism to Malcolm X's early doctrine. Melanye T. Price, a political scientist, identifies the protocols, within African American communities, as institutional "self-determination"; economic, political, and intellectual "self-sustenance"; psychological resistance to white-supremacist or antiblack racist thought; and, to a lesser degree, since it is outside the national setting, global or Pan-African unity against racial oppression.[4] As enabling as black nationalism may have been for Malcolm X and his followers, Obama saw it as disabling, especially when severed from the evidence of Malcolm X's own ideological evolution from this doctrine toward one of interracial reconciliation. How did Obama's own creative writing build on the accomplishments of the Black Power and Civil Rights Movements—movements that overlapped in the early 1960s, alongside Malcolm X's own ascent to political prominence—while transcending their political terms and anticipating the possibility of racial reconciliation in America?

By reclaiming the histories of African American literature and politics, Obama suggests that *The Autobiography of Malcolm X* is not the Islamic urtext of black nationalism but a more complex, nuanced, and universal story of human change than what readers might expect. Malcolm X's is the story of how one person unmoors himself from religious and political monomania and charts a new path through life, all the while guided by an interior moral compass. This bildungsroman anticipates Obama's own in his memoir, in which he appreciates the 1960s as a formative period of racial awakening and civil rights but also criticizes it as a decade whose myths must be overturned.

In fairness, I should admit here that Obama replaces one myth with another: early Malcolm X, the black nationalist, with late Malcolm X, the racial reconciler. Obama creates and tells as many cherished stories as those he refuses to inherit. Nonetheless, as only the third African American (after Republican Edward Brooke of Massachusetts and Democrat Carol Moseley Braun of Illinois) to serve in the United States Senate since Reconstruction, and as the first such person to become president of the United States, Barack Obama is the most politically successful and socially significant writer to "represent the race" in the realms of both formal and informal, or governmental and cultural, politics. And I should also admit that, of all the chapters in this book, this one has posed the most problems. Scholars will have to write lengthy books to account for the numerous opinions and information circulated by the pundits and the twenty-four-hour news cycles since the release of Obama's memoir in 1995—opinions and information born and archived on the Internet, played and replayed on television, and printed and rehashed in newspapers and magazines. In this chapter, my study of Obama is as modest as this book's political history of African American literature: I am focusing on the most salient moments when literature and politics combined to gauge and sometimes transform the attitudes of American society. The publication of Obama's *Dreams from My Father,* along with that of his 2006 and 2008 books, *The Audacity of Hope: Thoughts on Reclaiming the American Dream* and *Change We Can Believe In: Barack Obama's Plan to Renew America's Promise,* represent these moments in our recent era.

Given that the primary text of this chapter is *Dreams from My Father,* one of my temptations had been to wrap literary analysis only in biographical clothing, depending as much on the evidence of Obama's strategies of racial representation as on the harmonies and discrepancies between narrative temporality inside the memoir and historical data outside it, between the rhetoric of Obama's political philosophy and the facts of his political life. But the best and most comprehensive biography of Obama's life prior to his presidency, David Remnick's *The Bridge: The Life and Rise of Barack Obama* (2010), has already accounted for these harmonies and discrepancies. Fortunately, then, my study can focus less on whom Rafiq, among others, represents in Obama's real life—data that already exist and have been confirmed—than on whom this character represents in the political life of African American literary history.[5]

In this chapter, I have also eliminated certain popular topics of literary and political analysis that my research has countlessly come across, mostly in the mainstream media but not so much in scholarship, which, as of this writing (in 2010), has not yet published many literary studies of Obama in the conventional academic outlets. (Aside from lectures, panels, and roundtables in academia, the publication of scholarship tends to move at a slower pace than publication in the mainstream media.) The popular topics include the biographies of Obama's immediate and extended family; the records of his life at his alma maters, Occidental College, Columbia University, and Harvard Law School; his legislative successes and failures as an elected official; the literary clues to his style of governance; the complete "Obama canon" of literature that he has cited in his writings, interviews, and speeches; the eloquence of his speeches; the elegance of his oration; and his stature in a tradition of political memoirs written by former presidents and presidential hopefuls.[6] I do my best not to pass judgment on Obama's policies, for such partisanship is neither the intent of this chapter nor necessary to prove the importance of literary works, both those he has written and those he has read, to his political worldview and success. I analyze the writings by Obama that address the main issue of my book, about the historical relationship between literature and politics, and the main issue of this chapter, about the way he consummated this relationship in his recent lives as a writer and a public official.

I proceed with the assumption that Obama's writings are well known. As of May 2008, more than three million copies of his books were in print, and certainly more have circulated since his election to the presidency.[7] Yet I also assume that the readers' recollections of the books, as in the case of most literature, may be uneven; and the writings may not have been read closely, if at all. Even if these first two assumptions are false, the writings may not have been read "critically," with an eye toward making "the connections between the progress of human lives and their verbal representations." This is the high standard that Marjorie Perloff, a prominent literary scholar, reaffirms in the enlightening speech she delivered at the 2008 Modern Language Association conference, "The Audacity of Literary Studies."[8] Despite the extraneous and overwhelming noise of information surrounding Obama, this is the high standard I hope to meet in this chapter.

Critics and scholars generally agree that *Dreams from My Father* is a fine piece of writing. Biographer Arnold Rampersad remarks that the "book is so literary, . . . so full of clever tricks—inventions for literary effect—that I was taken aback, even astonished. But make no mistake, these are simply the tricks that art trades in, and out of these tricks is supposed to come our realization of truth."[9] The literary quality of Obama's memoir has much to do with the range and depth of his attention to literature across his life. We know now that Obama wrote artistic literature in a private journal, published examples of it in campus literary magazines in high school and college, took academic courses on it, informally read a lot of it in his spare time, and even assigned it in the law courses he taught. *Dreams from My Father,* as his first book, effectively drew on his deep literary experiences.[10] Unfortunately, the second and third books, *The Audacity of Hope* and *Change We Can Believe In,* sacrifice literariness for political exigency, according to the consensus of reviewers. As one senior magazine editor, Andrew Ferguson, puts it, this "is the work of a professional politician under the careful watch of his advisers," so predictably "boilerplate" that "we have lost a writer and gained another politician. It's not a fair trade."[11] One can easily imagine the reviews of *Change We Can Believe In,* which, as a collection of policy essays alongside campaign stump speeches, is even less a work of literature qua literature. The treatment of all three *popular* books as fair game in an academic mode of analysis often reserved for *rarified* books, despite their evident differences in literary quality, has turned out to be as difficult for me as overcoming the discrepancies in analytical style and deliberation between the mainstream media and literary academia.

Guiding my analysis is the theme, mentioned earlier, of being "inside" or "outside" history—again, what Obama calls being with or without "a script or plot that might insist on progression." Obama borrows the very words of Ralph Ellison's 1952 novel, *Invisible Man,* to talk about how examples of rage could threaten to foreclose a new brand of politics that uses race to unite, not divide, American society. Academic scholars have long discussed this Ellisonian notion of being inside or outside African American history, but they have neglected the hallmark African American political despair and isolationism that Ellison, to Obama's disappointment, reaffirms in the novel. Even as Obama reiterates the desire of the main character midway through *Invisible Man* to control rage, he questions that character's despondence and vengeance over America's political failures. Ironically, only by clinging to this dual perspective was Obama able to temper the unrealistic expectations for a postracial world, while assuaging fears that race and racism would be too difficult for him to overcome in his campaign for the forty-fourth presidency of the United States.

"A Prisoner of Fate": Race, Genealogy, Myth, Literature

Dreams from My Father belongs to the geopolitical genre of African American autobiography, which I have already examined in chapter 4, in reference to Claude McKay and Langston Hughes. Born in Honolulu, Hawaii, on August 4, 1961, Obama wrote a transnational bildungsroman, divided into three broad sections of genealogy and geography, in which autobiographical temporality usually, but not always, hews to historical chronology. The first section (of six chapters), called "Origins," spans the first twenty or so years of Obama's life, when he lives in Hawaii with his white maternal grandparents (Stanley and Madelyn Dunham), attends Occidental College in Los Angeles, and then transfers to Columbia University in Harlem. The next section (chapters 7 to 14), "Chicago," covers a three-year period in his mid- to late twenties as a Chicago community organizer. The final section (of five chapters), "Kenya," deals with the brief period just before his entrance, at the age of twenty-seven, to Harvard Law School, when he retraces the steps of his father, Barack Obama Sr., and unites with relatives in Kenya. Obama's travels, according to the memoir, are both physical and metaphysical, stimulating his flashbacks of family, acquaintances, and social myths. As the scholar Brent Hayes Edwards has noted, the "process," not only the "physical location," of international experience reveals the extent to which the African diaspora has suffered alienation in the world.[12] Obama portrays alienation as both the genealogical omen of Kenyan paternity and the socioeconomic omen of African American history.

A series of identities—one biracial, another African American, and another African diasporan—that Obama calls his own bespeak the notoriety of racial discrimination and interracial contact in American history. The memoir states that he had encountered racist or prejudicial myths about African Americans on television, on radio, in movies, in music, in department stores, in the most casual social and cultural situations, and in the political media. His obliviousness as a child to the sharp difference in skin color between his Kenyan father and Kansan mother had given way to his "need[ing] a race" for personal stability, for straightening out the stories of his father and family, even for learning something as minuscule as the tribal etymology of his inherited first name (27). By the time he traveled to Kenya, Obama had come to feel more stable in his biracial ancestry, even though his mixed heritage continued to confuse onlookers. In the introduction to the memoir, written not long after his return, Obama still laments, "[P]eople who don't know me well, black or white, discover my background" and begin "the split-second adjustments, . . . the searching of my eyes for some telltale sign. They no longer know who I am. Privately, they guess at my troubled heart, I suppose—the mixed blood, the divided soul, the ghostly image of the tragic mulatto trapped between two worlds" (xv).

Obviously, Obama's attention to his absent father, a person who visited him only once, when he was ten and living in Hawaii, is a key theme in the memoir. *Dreams from My Father* could also have been "Dreams *of* My

Father." The preposition "of" signifies the author's reading or imagination of his father. At once involuntary yet hopeful, the mental images led him on a "journey" spiritual as well as genealogical and geographical, as he tried to identify with a father. The journey was also racial, as he tried to identify with Africa and its diaspora in the United States. Although the title has the preposition "from," implying Obama (Jr.)'s inheritance of dreams, he was as skeptical of their meanings as he was beholden to their political calling. The memoir tells us that Obama wondered whether his own ideological eyes belonged to his father, a man too flawed to share the "attributes" of leadership that came to characterize African and African American icons such as Martin Luther King Jr., Malcolm X, W. E. B. Du Bois, and Nelson Mandela (220). Once a senior economist of Kenya, Obama Sr.'s several political and personal troubles included offending his socialist government, bearing the scorn of its prime minister, and suffering a blacklisted status. Obama Sr. was also legendary within the Obama family, after having multiple wives and repeatedly abandoning them and their children, including Obama (Jr.) himself in 1963, while descending into alcoholism, poverty, and, in 1982, a tragic death in an automobile accident.

Obama's notion of inheriting and playing out his father's dreams fueled his anxieties over whether he was predestined for certain personal and political challenges. Like "the Old Man," was he "living out a preordained script, as if [he] were following him into error, a captive to his [father's] tragedy" of making multiple "mistakes" for which he had to atone, unfairly or not (227)? After a long period of reluctance, between spending a few years in Chicago as a community organizer and entering Harvard University Law School in 1988, Obama traveled to Kenya to retrace his father's steps, as part of his investigation into the stories behind the mistakes. The "personal, interior journey" called *Dreams from My Father*, moreover, remains Obama's public journey to confront, face to face, the fears and desires of an American public trying to understand his complex identity. It is also a journey to counteract the possibility of biographical predestination, in which his father's past might predict Barack's present and future experiences.

The theme of predestination is central to *Dreams from My Father*, emphasized in the depiction of Obama's time as a fledgling community organizer. The memoir informs us that he grappled with whether fellow African American officials working within as well as for the betterment of African American communities "felt as trapped as those [they] served, an inheritor of sad history, part of a closed system with few moving parts, a system that was losing heat every day, dropping into low-level stasis": "I wondered whether

[they], too, felt *a prisoner of fate*" (231; italics mine). Whether those "served" were truly "trapped" is questionable. If anything, they may have been trapped as much within public assumptions of their distress (Obama's assumptions included) as within their environmental conditions. That said, the sentences, coupled with his deliberation over his father's mistakes, mark Obama's analysis of the way race has historically connoted an almost automatic pattern of deeds and misdeeds, action and inaction, in American social relations. Over and again in the memoir, he paraphrases an existential question: "Where do I belong?" The question undergoes a permutation in which Obama speculates on how any member of his family, of his private social circle, or of society in general could achieve a sense of belonging without considering whether this identity was predetermined, a byproduct of history insuppressibly and forever manifest (115, 118).

In *Dreams from My Father,* the themes of history and historiography, stories and storytelling, even selected myths and mythmaking, are crucial to our understanding of how Obama interpreted the ongoing life of the past in the present, to the role of family genealogy in racial self-discovery. He portrays himself as paying keen attention to upholding the transmission of stories, whether through oral tradition or in print, and to discerning fact from fiction. For many years, he had doubted Stanley Dunham's repeated story of Obama Sr.'s upbraiding of a racist white stranger at a bar in Hawaii (where Obama Sr. attended college and, upon his departure, left behind his son, Obama Jr., who was just born in Honolulu). But when Obama Sr.'s college classmate contacted Obama Jr. and repeated the same story, the stranger turned out to share Stanley's "note of disbelief—and hope" in the storytelling, an intonation of the story's status as not exclusively myth or truth but a little bit of both (11). The distinction of myth from truth is the challenge of genealogy and historiography, or the challenge of studying and writing ancestral history. One must communicate the miracles of a generation while presenting the full and verifiable facts supporting or discrediting them. *Dreams from My Father* is certainly Obama's own "story of race and inheritance," as the book's subtitle succinctly puts it, but it is also his preoccupation, shared with fellow African American writers across time, with methodology: specifically, with the genealogical and historiographical stakes in writing and rewriting myths, not just with the truth or fallacy of myths.

Reading and writing literature brought Obama closer to realizing these stakes. Poets and poetry had long guided his racial outlook. While a Punahou student, he read poetry and tried to write his own. At one time he penned verses for the school's literary magazine; at another he appreciated the "blunt poetry" of *The Autobiography of Malcolm X* (86).[13] Stanley, his white maternal grandfather, had been an occasional poet and had become best friends with an experienced African American poet, Frank Marshall Davis, whom Obama closely observed and whose words guided him during his move from Punahou School to Occidental College in 1979 (17, 89, 97). Next, Obama's "careful" choice of "performance poets," alongside the "more politically active black students," eased his turn to politics at Occidental (100). Two years later, when he transferred from there to Columbia University, he majored in political science but continued to work on his literary writing, "keeping a journal of daily reflections and very bad poetry," an outlet when he "stopped getting high," started an athletic regimen, concentrated more on his academic studies, and "began to grasp the almost mathematical precision with which America's race and class problem joined" (120–21). Nonetheless, Obama's affinity for literature inspired what he calls, in *Dreams from My Father*, "a record of a personal, interior journey—a boy's search for his father, and through that search a workable meaning for his life as a black American" (xvi).

Obama's relationship to Frank Marshall Davis deserves further discussion. Obama was a youth in Hawaii when they first met, when Frank was about eighty years old. During the Great Depression of the 1930s, Frank was involved in the Chicago branch of the Federal Writers' Project, a federally funded, "New Deal" program designed to advance the arts despite the economic downturn. In the program, Frank rubbed elbows with the likes of Margaret Walker and Richard Wright, famous African American authors of the "Chicago Renaissance" of the late 1930s and 1940s, and in this period he published such books as *Black Man's Verse* (1935), *I Am the American Negro* (1937), and *Through Sepia Eyes* (1938), all with Chicago-based Black Cat Press. By the time he encountered Obama in Hawaii, Frank had settled there for the twilight of his life and had become good friends with Obama's grandfather Stanley, who introduced Frank's poems to Obama. At some point, Frank performed poetry before Obama and others. Together, Stanley and Frank had helped to expose Obama to certain representations of African American experiences—perhaps those of Chicago, where, coincidentally, Obama had already visited (at the age of eleven) and where, later on, he happened to be following local politics during his training as a community organizer.

Eventually, the more Obama realized the frustration of African Americans with racial prejudice and discrimination, the more compelled he was to go to the library and borrow the books that talk about this subject. Privately, with the mind of a bookshelf scholar inside a teenager's body, he gathered the writings of famous African American authors who reached their prime in Frank's generation (including Wright, James Baldwin, and Ralph Ellison) and of those who reached their primes before and after it (including W. E. B. Du Bois and Langston Hughes, on the one hand, and Malcolm X, on the other).[14] Obama hoped that these authors would "corroborate this nightmare vision" of racial prejudice and discrimination. With the literature, he writes, "I would sit and wrestle with words, locked in suddenly desperate argument, trying to reconcile the world as I'd found it with the terms of my birth" (85).

Obama attributed his growing racial sophistication not solely to African American writers but to white writers as well. At Occidental College, when Marcus, one of the "more politically active black students," introduced him to Regina, they all discussed *Heart of Darkness,* the classic 1902 novella by Poland-born Joseph Conrad (100). Marcus jokes, "I'm trying to tell Brother Barack here about this racist tract he's reading." Obama grabbed the book from Marcus, who was holding it aloft, and thrust it into his backpack. Obama then shielded his literary taste from ridicule: "Actually, he's right. . . . It is a racist book. The way Conrad sees it, Africa's the cesspool of the world, black folks are savages, and any contact with them breeds infection." Aside from the fact that the book was part of a school assignment and that he had little choice but to read it, Obama was insistent: "[T]he book teaches me things. . . . About white people, I mean. See, the book's not really about Africa. Or black people. It's about the man who wrote it. The European. The American. A particular way of looking at the world. If you can keep your distance, it's all there, in what's said and what's left unsaid. So I read the book to help me understand just what it is that makes white people so afraid. Their demons. The way ideas get twisted around. It helps me understand how people learn to hate" (102–3). This scene shows Obama's broadening awareness of race and his attempt to understand racial prejudices generally as people encountered and drew conclusions about him. Literature turned out to be an active part of his intellectual growth and, eventually, his political action.

"Some Hope of Eventual Reconciliation": Re-presenting Malcolm X

The fact that Obama likened political action to poetry makes perfect sense. *Dreams from My Father* states that his growing pains as a community organizer in Chicago, where he moved in 1985, partially came from the tension he negotiated between poetic abstraction and political pragmatism. Once, he submitted "a third-week report" on his community-organizing activities to Marty Kaufman, the man who hired Obama a little over one year after his graduation from Columbia in 1983—more precisely, right after the period when Obama worked for one year at an international corporation and then for another three months as an organizer of student volunteers at Harlem's City College. Marty read the report and provided encouragement but had to remark on its fledgling nature: "Yeah, not bad. You're starting to listen. But it's still too abstract, . . . like you're taking a survey or something. If you want to organize people, you need to steer away from the peripheral stuff and go towards people's centers. The stuff that makes them tick. Otherwise, you'll never form the relationships you need to get them involved" (158). Obama questioned the potentially "manipulative" objectives of this approach. Marty "sighed": "I'm not a poet, Barack. I'm an organizer" (159). The criticism at first confused Obama: "I still had no idea how I might translate what I was hearing into action" (159). Yet, in due time, while conceding that he had a lot to learn, Obama reached a fundamental conclusion: that imagining community organizing as poetry was prerequisite to realizing that "[s]tories full of terror and wonder, studded with events that still haunted or inspired," could help explain the lives of communities (190). Marty "was wrong, though, in characterizing the work. There was poetry as well—a luminous world always present beneath the surface, a world that people might offer up as a gift to me, if I only remembered to ask" (190–91). In a pragmatic way, poetry captured "the struggle to align word and action, our heartfelt desires with a workable plan" (204).

One African American writer whom Obama read in Hawaii and who helped him grasp this struggle is Malcolm X, whose autobiography "seemed to offer something different" (86). Obama was attracted not to the early version of Malcolm X found in chapters 1 through 9 of *The Autobiography of Malcolm X*—where we encounter Malcolm Little, born in Nebraska, reared in Michigan, and living in Boston and Harlem under the combined duress of racial violence, familial instability, social impropriety, and criminal temptation. Instead, Obama was attracted to Malcolm X's "repeated acts of self creation" that began in chapter 10, when Malcolm had been sentenced to ten years in a Norfolk, Massachusetts, prison for possessing stolen valuables and illegal firearms. There, he underwent an awakening. He regretted his former life as a burglar and drug addict, although his resentment built toward the whites he faced during this period. A fellow inmate introduced him to the philosophical tenets of Islam, to the Nation of Islam, and to the teachings of the organization's founding leader, Elijah Muhammad. Inspired to argue that Judeo-Christian and Western paradigms of education have unfairly privileged Anglo-Saxon history, Malcolm committed to reading all kinds of literature, such as the Holy Bible, the dictionary, and even the writings of William Shakespeare, to realize and critique their hegemonic historiographies that, broadly put, privilege white over African American political interests. Malcolm's gravitation toward the teachings of the Nation of Islam within prison, and toward the organization upon his parole, bespoke his commitment to forging within political praxis a transcendent form of knowledge that aimed to convert those "brainwashed" African American opponents of black nationalism. In the autobiography, after providing a brief biography of Elijah Muhammad, Malcolm (now with the "X" to replace his surname of allegedly white inheritance) recalls the kind of vitriolic speech of racial uplift he regularly delivered on behalf of the Nation of Islam, the "uncompromising words, uttered anywhere, without hesitation or fear," criticizing the "ignorant" non-Islamic African Americans: "*That devil white man does not want the Honorable Elijah Muhammad stirring awake the sleeping giant of you and me, and all of our ignorant, brainwashed kind here in the white man's heaven and the black man's hell here in the wilderness of North America.*"[15]

Over time, Malcolm X changes. He discerned the flaws and limits of Elijah Muhammad's political organization. In 1964, during his trip to the Muslim holy city of Mecca, he began to soften his antagonistic stance toward whites, even believing in the possibility of a relatively peaceful, color-blind brotherhood with them. In preparing to write letters to his family and acquaintances back in the United States, he realized that the "*color-blindness* of the Muslim world's religious society and the *color-blindness* of the Muslim world's human society: these two influences had each day been making a greater impact, and an increasing persuasion against my previous way of thinking" (339). By the time he returned home and resumed his political activities, he had changed his name to El-Hajj Malik El-Shabazz and divorced from the Nation of Islam. The promise of a color-blind brotherhood intrigued him, but his conclusion persisted that whites must repent for their historical and ongoing sins of racism. For that reason, he still hedged against wholeheartedly embracing interracial cooperation as an alternative political strategy for African Americans.[16]

To be clear, *Dreams from My Father* reveals no evidence that Obama shared Malcolm X's devotion to Islam. In the memoir, pre-Mecca Malcolm X does represent, though, the specter of black nationalism that Obama had to vanquish as both political author and literary subject. Conceivably, Malcolm X struck Obama's curiosity because, as mentioned earlier, the writing of *Dreams from My Father* and its publication in 1995 coincided historically with the circulation of Spike Lee's 1992 movie *Malcolm X* in the popular and academic imaginations. Another conceivable reason for Malcolm X's centrality is that the date of his assassination (February 21, 1965) and the modern resurgence of black nationalism (between 1965 and 1973) known as the Black Power Movement, fit within the temporality of Obama's memoir, as does the Black Arts Movement, the artistic branch of the Black Power Movement, featuring African American authors ranging from Amiri Baraka and Haki R. Madhubuti to Nikki Giovanni and Ntozake Shange, which likewise sought to channel the political doctrine of black nationalism.[17]

On the autobiographical surface, Obama seems too young and disconnected to be affected by this milieu. We see that he was a child during the era, not a child of it. In 1965, the year of Malcolm X's assassination, Obama was three years old (and turning four on August 4) and living in Oahu, Hawaii, with his mother, Ann Dunham, who had just divorced a year earlier from Obama Sr. In 1973, when black nationalism was declining, Obama was twelve. He was only two years removed from having lived and studied in Jakarta, Indonesia, for four years under the guardianship of his mother and stepfather, Lolo Soetoro, an Indonesian oil consultant. Now, he was enrolled in Hawaii's Punahou School. At this temporal moment in the memoir, the cultural and political repercussions of black nationalism seem to be subtly affecting Obama as a teenager—a coincidence, given that Malcolm X was also probably on his mind in the early 1990s while he was drafting the following scene in *Dreams from My Father*: in New York, Obama was watching "a new play by a black playwright, . . . a very angry play, but very funny," in "[t]ypical black American humor," but along with a white woman whom he once "loved" and who complained that blacks were "so angry all the time" (210–12). Later, in Chicago, he watched Ntozake Shange's play, first produced in 1975, *For Colored Girls Who Have Considered Suicide When the Rainbow Is Enuf*, with Ruby Styles, an African American single mother and office manager from Chicago's North Side who empathized with the play's indignation at racial injustice (204–6). The different reactions of Obama's companions reaffirm in the memoir that black theater, a founding genre of the Black Arts Movement, was a remarkable medium for the African American expressions of sorrow and rage that could be racially divisive.

The memoir also tells us that the story of Malcolm X was equally palpable. *The Autobiography of Malcolm X* was still fresh on Obama's mind when he played a basketball game at a local gymnasium with Ray, a friend who was also one of the few African American students at Punahou School. Afterward, they "strike up a conversation" at the gymnasium with Malik, who "was a follower of the Nation of Islam but . . . since Malcolm had died and he had moved to Hawaii he no longer went to mosque or political meetings, although he still sought comfort in solitary prayer" (87). Before long, a couple eavesdropping men interrupted the conversation with crude racist, xenophobic, and sexual jokes about Muslims who pilgrimage to Mecca. Ray laughed (as did Malik), prompting Obama to rebuke his friend: "What are you laughing at? . . . You've never read Malcolm. You don't even know what he says." Upon grabbing the basketball from Obama and heading to a basketball hoop, Ray replied, "I don't need no books to tell me how to be black" (87). In one motion, as quickly as he snatched the ball, Ray snatched Obama's fraternal claim to authentic "blackness" (and masculinity) among the basketball players. Ray deferred not to the well-informed, intellectual approach to blackness that Obama had mostly embraced to understand his biracial heritage. Rather, Ray preferred the intuitive, almost macho, approach inculcated from his life in Los Angeles prior to moving to Hawaii (as a result of his father's army transfer). Although the presence of other basketball players in this sports environment may have influenced Ray's behavior, his critique in Hawaii was consistent with Marty's in Chicago: that Obama is too abstract, too cerebral, to connect with blackness.

Yet Obama's early impressions of *The Autobiography of Malcolm X* suggest that abstraction deepened his connection to blackness. The appeal of the middle to latter stages of Malcolm X's political development show that the parallel focus of Ray and Marty on the inauthenticity of abstraction played to the myths of race, culture, politics, and intellectual elitism that Obama planned to overcome:

[T]he blunt poetry of [Malcolm X's] words, his unadorned insistence on respect, promised a new and uncompromising order, martial in its discipline, forged through sheer force of will. All the other stuff, the talk of blue-eyed devils and apocalypse, was incidental to that program, I decided, religious baggage that Malcolm himself seemed to have safely abandoned toward the end of his life. . . . And, too: If Malcolm's discovery toward the end of his life, that some whites might live beside him as brothers in Islam, seemed to offer *some hope of eventual reconciliation,* that hope appeared in a distant future, in a far-off land. In the meantime, I looked to see where the people would come from who were willing to work toward this future and populate this new world. (86; italics mine)

The notions that Malcolm X discarded the "religious baggage" of black nationalism by the time of his death and that he believed "some whites might live beside him as brothers in Islam" instilled in Obama "some hope of eventual reconciliation" in race relations, while guiding his cultural and political readings of African American history. Short of achieving an interracial coalition of activists, the reconciliatory ethos of late Malcolm X brought Obama as close as possible to Martin Luther King Jr.'s principles of the Civil Rights Movement, with an appreciation for the continued development of racial representation in African American intellectual culture and politics alike.[18]

"What Is Your Pahst and Where Are You Going?": Re-presenting Ralph Ellison

We cannot skim past the language Obama uses in *Dreams from My Father* to rescue Malcolm X from the mythical grip of black nationalism. To repeat, Obama argues that this ideology exists "outside history, without a script or plot that might insist on progression" (198)—the sort of language that appears in Ralph Ellison's *Invisible Man*. In this novel, the protagonist (let us call him the Invisible Man) has just lost the trust of a wealthy white trustee and the obsequious African American president of the Southern college he is attending, because he has taken the trustee not only around campus (where he is supposed to go) but also around the countryside (where he is not supposed to go and where they run into a host of problems, including an African American sharecropper whose evident incest disturbed the trustee). Suspended from the college, the Invisible Man leaves the South and arrives in Harlem, where, upon seeing people gather around and protest yet another eviction of an African American resident, something inside prompts him, almost against his will, to deliver a memorable speech to the crowd. He advises them to suppress their urge to riot and attack the white evictors. Instead, they must remain "law-abiding" and "slow-to-anger," to organize wisely behind a leader, which, at this moment, he is starting to exemplify.[19] Soon enough, the crowd heeds his advice and helps to return the furniture to the residence, but then racially prejudiced policemen arrive to break up the scene and end up reinciting the crowd. As the Invisible Man runs away, Brother Jack, a white member of a political organization called the Brotherhood, catches up to him, compliments his demonstrated leadership, and invites him to the Brotherhood. Over the course of their conversation, the Invisible Man refers to both Booker T. Washington and the

"Founder," presumably the even greater predecessor who had founded the Invisible Man's own college, and remarks, "the Founder came before him and did practically everything Booker T. Washington did and a lot more. And more people believed in him. You hear a lot of arguments about Booker T. Washington, but few would argue about the Founder." Brother Jack replies, "No, but perhaps that is because the Founder lies outside history, while Washington is still a living force. The *new* Washington," to wit, the Invisible Man, "shall work for the poor" (306). Part of the Invisible Man's conundrum, then, is to figure out his place in political history—precisely, whether he will be "inside history," a reincarnation of Washington but with a new focus on class, or "outside history," a legend or tale that continues to survive in static form, regardless of new facts or events.[20]

A host of scholars have explored Ellison's distinction of "inside" from "outside" history. Most recently, Jim Neighbors has noted that Ellison explores "the question of what makes up history, which is really a question of *whose* history, which is itself a question of who is *naming* history," and which is a question of how a competing "array of historiographies" can also bespeak a competing array of political ideologies.[21] Paul Allen Anderson has pointed out that the will of one black nationalist character, whom I shall describe later, to "plunge outside history" results in his "alienation from American life."[22] And H. William Rice takes the notion of "inside history" to mean that, from a metaliterary standpoint, *Invisible Man* itself shows the degree to which literature can be ensconced within history, capturing its vicissitudes or even prognosticating its current course into the future.[23] After all, Ellison himself says in 1982, in his thirty-year-anniversary introduction to *Invisible Man*, "while fiction is but a form of symbolic action, a mere game of 'as if,' therein lies its true function and its potential for effecting change. For at its most serious, just as is true of politics at its best, it is a thrust toward a human ideal."[24] Being inside history is incumbent on all literary writers, despite the potential limitations of literature alone to transform society.[25]

Yet, what about the tragedy of Ellison's novelistic vision? The vision correlates, on the one hand, the political pessimism of being inside history with the facts of history and, on the other, the political optimism of being outside it with the illusions of myth. In this regard, Obama's memoir holds Ellison accountable by arguing the converse: that optimists can be inside history, too, if they are willing, socially and politically, to collaborate with and share the hope of others. Specifically, Obama's political theory of empathy disagrees with the rejection of community in *Invisible Man*, even as he shares Ellison's language of political history. To repeat an earlier point, Obama once admitted that neither *Invisible Man* nor, for that matter, the literature of Baldwin, Hughes, Wright, and Du Bois could rescue him from the "nightmare" of racism. Each work tells more or less the same story, "the same anguish, the same doubt; a self-contempt that neither irony nor intellect seemed able to deflect." All of them, he went on to say, are "in the same weary flight, all of them exhausted, bitter men, the devil at their heels" (*Dreams from My Father,* 85–86). Aside from Ellison, all of these authors had, over their careers, grown disappointed with the unfulfilled promise of racial progress in America; Baldwin, Wright, and Du Bois recoiled from the country and moved abroad as expatriates, rarely returning to their native homes, and Hughes spent extended time abroad considering expatriation. Ellison did not take expatriation as seriously, but *Invisible Man* nonetheless begins and ends with the same fact: the narrator, equally disappointed and befuddled by racial politics in America, prefers to live below Harlem's streets, as a recluse.

The lives of these African American authors and the imagined lives in their literary writings contradict the sovereign theme, in *Dreams from My Father,* that Obama sought to attach himself to communities as an older man. David Samuels, a nonfiction author, touches on this idea in what is, so far, the most probing study of Obama's life and writings in relation to *Invisible Man.* Contrary to Ellison's modernist tendency to show how "personal identity trumps allegiance to the group," Obama's memoir "does not end with the expected discovery that we are all radically alone in the world, but rather with the discovery that he is a member of a strong and loving black African family—even if the father he identified with as a child is a myth created by guilty white liberals." Samuels's underlying argument that, in the memoir, Obama "believes in the old-fashioned, unabashedly romantic, and, in the end, quite weird idea of racial authenticity that Ellison rejected" leads to two claims. First, Samuels suggests that Obama, within his heart, privileges his black African ancestry over his white American ancestry, along with the racial purity over the biracial mixture of his ancestry. Second, and by implication, Obama's political success could be attributed to his exploitation of the guilt of present-day whites over their unintended complicity in racism and over the potential historical complicity of their ancestors in it. Obama should be more "honest" (if disagreeable) "about who he is and what he believes."[26] These two claims are problematic and rebuttable. The first perpetuates the belief, to be addressed in the next section on Obama's relationship to his former church pastor, that he embodies political anger, even though his literary and political accomplishments refute this perception.[27] The second misreads Obama's appeal to whites, who, like African Americans, have been drawn to his mantras of political hope and racial reconciliation—mantras that, contrary to Samuels's term "guilty white liberals," refuses to obsess over the need of whites to repent for historical crimes. As a community organizer, Obama anticipated and participated in the kind of social change that promoted mutual understanding across racial lines.

Indirectly, Obama's memoir indicts the hopelessness and isolationism conveyed by Ellison and the African American writers of his generation. If we accept the scholarly skepticism that *Invisible Man* cannot be, to quote Neighbors again, "coherently converted into grounds for ethical action, or objective historiography," then we must also hypothesize that the novel forecloses Obama's mantras of hope and reconciliation.[28] In Chicago, community organizing enabled Obama's identification with a struggling African American constituency in need of more resources: "Through organizing, through shared sacrifice, membership had been earned. And because membership was earned—because this community I imagined was still in the making, built on the promise that the larger American community, black, white, and brown, could somehow redefine itself—I believed that it might, over time, admit the uniqueness of my own life" (*Dreams from My Father,* 135). Stories and storytelling, in his view, also were precious to the formation of political identities, in that "the language, the humor, the stories of ordinary people were the stuff out of which families, communities, economies would have to be built" (195). He proceeded to comprehend the expressions of hatred by members of the African American community both toward each other and toward other communities. In both of these personal examples, African American struggles and expressions of anger were for Obama either points of entry toward or points of exit from an argument for the commonness of American experience. Despite the thematic contradictions between *Invisible Man* and *Dreams from My Father,* Obama in his autobiography, just like the Invisible Man in Ellison's novel, represents the valiant historiographical attempt to understand the past articulations of rage in black nationalism (or political resistance, more broadly) and to negotiate their present recurrences. Obama eyes racial reconciliation on behalf of social change, likely with an awareness of the Marxist pitfall of racial reconciliation, as shown in *Invisible Man,* that class might trump race to such a degree that the causes and effects of racism are ignored.

The Invisible Man oscillates between two extreme forms of political leadership—liberal integrationism and black nationalism—as he decides between the political strategies of class and race. The portrayal of Booker T. Washington in Ellison's novel is consistent with the historical portrait of

Washington as an African American who had accommodated white political interests so blatantly that his programs for interracial reconciliation may have impeded the political progress of African Americans toward civic equality. For the Brotherhood, a Washingtonian African American is more likely to follow their Marxist agenda, which politicizes everyone's socio-economic "dispossession" rather than the racism faced by African Americans alone (*Invisible Man*, 385). Likewise, the novel's portrayal of Ras the Exhorter (who, in a fit of political rage, becomes Ras the Destroyer), a West Indian, is consistent with the historical portrait of Marcus Garvey, a Jamaican-born black nationalist, even though Ellison has stated that Garvey was not consciously on his mind when he sketched the character (485).[29] In this respect, Ras also stands outside history. In the words of Clifton, an African American member of the Brotherhood who speculates on the West Indian's antagonism, "I suppose sometimes a man *has* to plunge outside history. . . . Plunge outside, turn his back . . . Otherwise he might kill somebody, go nuts" (377). Antithetical to Washington, Ras has attacked white political interests so blatantly, with no program of interracial reconciliation, that, ironically, *like* Washington, he also may impede the political progress of African Americans. But Ras attacks African Americans, not only whites, who have expressed the spirit of racial reconciliation, including Clifton and the Invisible Man in their earlier ideological stages. When the Invisible Man declares that all men, including African Americans, "need allies to win" and should "want a brotherly world," Ras retorts in staccato patois: "Don't be stupid, mahn. They *white*, they don't have to be allies with no black people. They get what they wahnt, they turn against you. Where's your black intelligence?" Most relevant, Ras asks the two African American men of the Brotherhood, "*What is your pahst and where are you going? . . . Nowhere!*" (375; italics mine). The irony of the Invisible Man's dilemma is that his "pahst" is predetermining his destiny. He cannot know where he is going until he knows where he is coming from.

By the novel's end, the Invisible Man has come to learn the calamity of existing outside history. Clifton has dropped out of the Brotherhood and, in the process, moved away from a political historiography premised on Washingtonian analogies. Instead, he has chosen the more controversial mythology in conducting "Sambo" puppet shows, representing the race as the "Old Negro," minstrel type. (This distinction assumes that one does not characterize Washington as a political embodiment of the minstrel caricature, à la the obsequious, docile ingratiation toward whites of the "Uncle Tom" figure, drawn from Harriet Beecher Stowe's 1852 novel, *Uncle Tom's Cabin*.) The Invisible Man wonders, "How on earth could [Clifton] drop from the Brotherhood to this in so short a time? . . . It was as though he had chosen—how had he put it the night he fought with Ras?—to fall outside of *history*. . . . But he knew that only in the Brotherhood could we make ourselves known, could we avoid being empty Sambo dolls" (434). Put even more clearly later, he thinks, "Why should a man deliberately plunge outside of history and peddle an obscenity. . . . Why should he choose to disarm himself, give up his voice and leave the only organization offering him a chance to 'define' himself?" (438). The Invisible man reaches the conclusion that when one is outside history, myth has succeeded in controlling one's political self-definition or one's place in political progress. Being inside history, conversely, means overcoming myth and writing history for the sake of sustaining progress. Similar to Obama's *Dreams from My Father*, Ellison's *Invisible Man* features the protagonist's autonomous narration of history, as well as his own story, to define his place in the world, contrary to the exploits of myth.[30]

Rafiq is to Obama, then, as Ras is to Ellison: both characters enable the authors to confront the mythical specter of black nationalism in African American history. For Obama in his memoir, his depiction of an argument with Rafiq allows him to critique the notion that, for an African American community "already stripped of their history, a people often ill equipped to retrieve that history in any form other than what fluttered across the television screen, . . . [n]ationalism provided that history, an unambiguous morality tale that was easily communicated and easily grasped" (198). Black nationalism succeeds in reducing the complexity of African American politics to antiwhite hate and antiblack condescension. The doctrine perpetuates the myths of rage and irresponsibility in African American communities, especially among the lower-class societies whose political resources and rights have long been unfulfilled. Rafiq's simultaneous pride in but distrust of African Americans; his vocal intimidation but lack of organizational influence; his ideological but impractical and vague approaches to social change—all of these contradictions exemplify "the distance between our talk and our action," a distance that black nationalism fails to overcome (203). Obama's hope, then, is to develop a new kind of politics that closes this distance. He hopes to overcome the myths of race, culture, and politics that have worked to corrupt everyone's sensibilities. And he hopes to inspire the disaffected and disenfranchised members of the African American community to participate in progressive politics.

"A More Perfect Union":
Re-presenting the Reverend Jeremiah Wright

The Audacity of Hope fulfills *Dreams from My Father*'s promise of a new kind of politics. In this respect, the two books are more similar than different. In the prologue to *The Audacity of Hope*, Obama confesses, "I am a prisoner of my own autobiography: I can't help but view the American experience through the lens of a black man of mixed heritage, forever mindful of how generations of people who looked like me were subjugated and stigmatized, and the subtle and not so subtle ways that race and class continue to shape our lives."[31] Although autobiographical imprisonment connotes a pejorative meaning, the main point is that Obama is, for better or for worse, living history—certainly in the Ellisonian sense of history. Racial prejudice denies him the opportunity to reject the identity of "a black man," even as the increasing social tolerance of racial difference has now encouraged him to restate that identity as "mixed heritage." Core features of Obama seen in the first book resurface in the second: his restless desire for social change; his proclivity for politics; his transnational sensibility; his rhetorical emphasis on stories and storytelling, myths and mythmaking; his thematic focus on close readings of literature and language to understand the political world; and his emphasis on the role of culture in social change. The two books are perfect companion pieces.[32]

Still, the books are different in other ways. A collection of nine essays plus a prologue and an epilogue, *The Audacity of Hope* is more formally political than *Dreams from My Father*, because it outlines public policy more often than it tells his life story. Obama wrote the memoir when he was neither yet an Illinois state senator (which lasted from 1997 to 2004) nor a United States senator representing Illinois (from 2005 to 2008), when he was willing to be more revealing of his private life, more experimental in literary expression, and more radical in political opinion. He states almost this much in the preface to the memoir's second edition, which arrived in late 2004, only "a few months" after winning the Democratic nomination for Illinois's United States Senate seat; it also came only a handful of months after he had delivered, in July 2004, the rousing keynote address at the Democratic National Convention (*Dreams from My Father,* viii). As he read the memoir in its originally published form, he had "the urge to cut the book by fifty pages or so," a decision of self-censorship based both on his current editorial maturity and on the fact that "certain passages have proven to be inconvenient politically, the grist for pundit commentary and opposition research" (ix). The original

1995 introduction to the memoir also admits that, when he first conceived the book, he listed numerous potentially volatile policy issues, ranging from "civil rights litigation" to "affirmative action," that he considered tackling (xiii). But the allure of spiritual, racial, cultural, political, and genealogical self-exploration was too powerful to ignore in *Dreams from My Father*. Although this subject displaces, say, the topic of affirmative action from the memoir, Obama does attend to it in a careful way in *The Audacity of Hope*, which revolves around his first year and a half in the United States Senate.[33]

The Audacity of Hope, which Obama finished writing in summer 2006 and released in October of that year, progresses from *Dreams from My Father* also by demanding a reading of race independent of political nostalgia. In the seventh chapter, "Race," Obama suggests that a magnificent, star-studded funeral, held at a Detroit, Michigan, church for Rosa Parks, the legendary civil rights activist who died in October 2005, failed to advance our understanding of the racial (and class) problems exposed two months earlier by Hurricane Katrina. In his words, "I wondered what Rosa Parks would make of all this—whether stamps or statues could summon her spirit, or whether honoring her memory demanded something more" (*Audacity of Hope*, 230–31). The "something more" is a progressive, not regressive, vision of politics: it is attentive alike to the lessons of history, the realities of the present, and the anticipation of the future, but not obsessively so in either case.

The conceptual balance among the three contexts should temper the potential belief among those who listened to his 2004 Democratic National Convention speech—and the readers of *The Audacity of Hope*—that "we have arrived at a 'postracial politics' or that we already live in a color-blind society" (232). Racial prejudice, based on stereotypes, still exists and afflicts everyone. Obama goes on to say that "it's unrealistic to believe that these stereotypes don't have a cumulative impact on the often snap decisions" in daily life (235). The goal, then, is *not* to derive a new politics beyond race. Rather, the new politics must visit the historical and contemporary problems of racial discrimination yet behold an optimistic future in which different races can celebrate a shared, common American experience. Put another way, Obama's different uses of the word "dream" in the title of the first book ("dreams from my father") and the subtitle of the second ("thoughts on reclaiming the American dream") capture his argument that "the service of perfecting an imperfect union" has been, and should continue to be, the collective dream of the American people (362). In new ways, this argument in *The Audacity of Hope* advances the critique derived in *Dreams from My Father*: that the isolationist, hopeless, or vengeful myths of racial politics, born out of the black nationalist movements of yore, ignore the core decency of many Americans who seek to reconcile with each other, regardless of their differences, in the nation's best interest.

At the dawn of the twenty-first century, Obama suggests that the time is ripe in the United States for political empathy to overcome the antagonism of human difference. In a chapter of *The Audacity of Hope* called "Values," Obama argues that "our democracy might work a bit better if we recognized that all of us possess values that are worthy of respect," even if these values cause political disagreement (57). There are signs that increasing mutual and fundamental respect is emerging in the "cross-pollination" of social identities and beliefs, as well as in the revision of social expectations across the country (51). If juxtaposed with the history of political division in American society, then these current changes may seem ironic. If regarded as the political future of the United States, then they lay the groundwork for equal opportunity and nondiscrimination at the heart of a healthy democracy. For Obama, in "every society (and in every individual), these twin strands—the individualistic and the communal, autonomy and solidarity—are in tension, and it has been one of the blessings of America that the circumstances of our nation's birth allowed us to negotiate these tensions better than most" (55). The "tension" caused by our diversity may strain our body politic in the short term but strengthen it in the long term.

The dualistic tone present in Obama's historiography recasts social conflict as the growing pains of a promising nation. The chapter "Our Constitution" best conveys this tone in a discussion of the U.S. Constitution. Even as the Constitution continues to be used (by the U.S. Supreme Court) as a guide to our legal and civic rights, Obama recalls the racist context in which the Founding Fathers, such as Thomas Jefferson, authored the document. He does not wholly reject the "school of thought that sees the Founding Fathers only as hypocrites and the Constitution only as a betrayal of the grand ideals set forth by the Declaration of Independence" (96):

> How can I, an American with the blood of Africa coursing through my veins, choose sides in such a dispute? I can't. I love America too much, am too invested in what this country has become, too committed to its institutions, its beauty, and even its ugliness, to focus entirely on the circumstances of its birth. But neither can I brush aside the magnitude of the injustice done, or erase the ghosts of generations past, or ignore the open wound, the aching spirit, that ails this country still. (96–97)

The keyword "love" implies jurisprudential sophistication that discourages the excessive literalism of the most conservative legislators and judges who view the Constitution as a static text. Love also implies a belief in the ability of African Americans, despite the contradictions they face, to subordinate their anger or resentment to a reinvestment in the nation's founding principles of democracy. Obama can at once appreciate the revolutionary magnificence of the country's birth yet also indict the civic inequalities entrenched therewith. He can at once feel buoyed by the founding theory of egalitarianism yet also feel dismayed by its historical and ongoing practice of racism. He can at once believe that a world can exist in which race does not matter as much as it used to yet also concede that his "blood of Africa" militates against the naïveté of postracialism. Contrary to the academic notion that Obama's rise to celebrity occasions "doubts" over "blackness," "uncertainties" that "make it easier to contemplate a possible future in which the ethnoracial categories central to identity politics would be more matters of choice than ascription," let the record of his writings show that even Obama does not go so far as to expect the arrival of a truly postracial world anytime soon, even though his presidential campaign exploited the popular correlation of his election with that world's proximity.[34] Such a world is not necessary. Rather, Obama encourages the ironic building of national unity through celebrations of racial diversity, among many other kinds of diversity, in American society.

No wonder Obama embraces Abraham Lincoln, despite the fact that, a century and a half ago, he happened to harbor racist views of African Americans while confronting the issues of race, slavery, and the Civil War.[35] The sixteenth president of the United States helps the forty-fourth reconcile the contradictions of race and nation while expressing love for both. Lincoln's "presidency was guided by a practicality that would distress us today," because he never abandoned "conviction for the sake of expediency," and he maintained "within himself the balance between two contradictory ideas—that we must talk and reach for common understandings," even if our engagement with each other presumes difference of opinion (*Audacity of Hope*, 97–98). Obama has come to realize that the United States was born and reared through the theoretical and practical contradictions of democracy, in much the same way that a maturing Malcolm X experienced them over the course of his life.

On February 10, 2007, Obama declared this "practicality," or political pragmatism, of Lincoln when he announced his candidacy for president of the United States. This speech, according to magazine editor Scott Horton, turned out to be "the most impressive and effective invocation of history in the course of the '08 campaign," primarily because of the symbolism of Lincoln.[36] Obama's speech was held at the Old State Capitol in Springfield, Illinois, where Lincoln himself delivered his memorable 1858 speech "House Divided," on the threats of slavery and the Civil War to national unity. Obama's speech began the long campaign to proclaim the philosophical seeds planted in *Dreams from My Father* and cultivated in *The Audacity of Hope*. Entitled "Declaration of Candidacy" in his third and latest book, *Change We Can Believe In,* this speech appears along with six others from his presidential campaign. (Technically, the 2008 book has a foreword by Obama but is written and copyrighted by "Obama for America," which refers to Obama in the third person, such as when the organization says in the introduction, "Barack Obama believes that we can change course, and that we must. He looks to the future with optimism and hope.")[37]

The characteristic language of *The Audacity of Hope* resurfaces in "Declaration of Candidacy." Referring to the historic location of his speech, Obama states, "It was here we learned to disagree without being disagreeable—that it's possible to compromise as long as you know those principles that can never be compromised; and that so long as we're willing to listen to each other, we can assume the best in people instead of the worst." He goes on to say that the "genius of our founders is that they designed a system of government that can be changed" and that "in the face of impossible odds, people who love their country can change it" (194–96). The nationalist language of love recurs, but other language does not. Neither "African American" nor "black" appears in this speech. The word "race" appears, but not in terms of "the blood of Africa" as in *The Audacity of Hope* but in terms of the political campaign: "That's why I'm in this race" (201). At best, there are only passing references to Martin Luther King Jr. ("we heard a King's call to let justice roll down like water, and righteousness like a mighty stream") and slavery ("As Lincoln organized the forces arrayed against slavery"), but the speech does not engage race as forcefully as some recent scholars have suggested (196, 201).[38] Obviously, Obama's language defuses the political charge of race to appeal to the broadest electorate possible. His expression of nationality also marks the logical progression of his political philosophy from the realism of *Dreams from My Father* and *The Audacity of Hope* to the optimism of his presidential campaign. "Declaration of Candidacy" asserts that through "the essential decency of the American people, . . . we can build a more hopeful America" (195). Needless to say, Obama succeeded and was elected to the presidency on Election Day in November 2008 and was inaugurated on January 20 of the following year.

Perhaps more than any other racial controversy, the inflammatory remarks that the Reverend Jeremiah Wright Jr. made as pastor of Chicago's Trinity United Church of Christ (Trinity Church) challenged Obama's campaign. The content and style of Reverend Wright's speeches, especially their bombastic criticism of the United States, potentially consigned Obama to the anger that has long been associated with African American political struggles for civil rights. In response to the sensational looping of the remarks through the news media, many in the American electorate began to question Obama's true convictions. A majority of white voters polled in the wake of this incident believed that Reverend Wright and Obama shared the same views of the country.[39] Reverend Wright turns out to have played a crucial role in Obama's development, according to *Dreams from My Father,* of a spiritual language and literacy of the real world. But here, through hindsight, we also see that Reverend Wright, the real person we have come to see in the media, clashes with Reverend Wright, the memoir's literary character, the latter of which Obama restores and revises in a speech designed to stem the racial controversy.

In the "Chicago" section of *Dreams from My Father,* Obama describes a period of his community organizing, in 1987, when he was meeting with a lot of African American ministers. Some were "often . . . suspicious or evasive, uncertain as to why this Muslim—or worse yet, this Irishman, O'Bama—wanted a few minutes of their time." Others "conformed to the prototypes found in Richard Wright novels or Malcolm X speeches: sanctimonious graybeards preaching pie-in-the-sky, or slick Holy Rollers with flashy cars and a constant eye on the collection plate" (279). Eventually, when they sat down together, the ministers' preconceptions and Obama's stereotypes dissolved. What remained, aside from mutual understanding, were questions about the faith of Obama, who, at this point in the memoir, was a religious "skeptic." When encouraged to attend church, he "would shrug and play the question off": "while I believed in the sincerity I heard in their voices, I remained a reluctant skeptic, doubtful of my own motives, wary of expedient conversion, having too many quarrels with God to accept a salvation too easily won" (286–87). Several of the ministers directed him to Reverend Wright. Serving the younger ministers in the community "as a mentor of sorts, his church a model for what they themselves hoped to accomplish," Reverend Wright was widely respected, although some of the older pastors "were more cautious with their praise, impressed with the rapid growth of Trinity's congregation but somewhat scornful of its popularity among young black professionals" (280).

In October 1987, when Obama and Reverend Wright finally met each other, Reverend Wright was instantly unlike the other African American ministers. He greeted Obama by his first name, "as if [they] were old friends" (281). More appealing than the other African American ministers (not simply because Obama was a rising African American professional, too), Reverend Wright had embodied and overcome contradictions. He once joined "the Marines out of college, dabbling with liquor, Islam, and black nationalism in the sixties," enrolled in "Howard, then the University of Chicago, where he spent six years studying for a Ph.D. in the history of religion," and learned "Hebrew and Greek, read the literature of Tillich and Niebuhr and the black liberation theologians." Obama marveled at "this capacious talent of his—this ability to hold together, if not reconcile, the conflicting strains of black experience—upon which Trinity's success had ultimately been built" (282). (Along Obama's lines of thought, I would also add that the strains of "white experience," stereotyped here as academic pedigree, also coexisted in Reverend Wright's "capacious talent.") Over time, Obama learned more about Reverend Wright, about the spiritual challenges faced by Trinity's working-class and professional congregation, and about the church's ability to foster a "cultural community . . . more pliant than simple nationalism, more sustaining than [Obama's] own brand of organizing" (286). Reverend Wright's kind of leadership and the church's cultural conditions lured Obama to one of Trinity Church's Sunday services, shortly after he learned of his admission to Harvard Law School in February 1988 and shortly before his trip to Europe and then Kenya.

Obama witnessed a moving sermon and service at Trinity Church. Entitled "The Audacity of Hope," Reverend Wright's sermon so influenced Obama that he borrowed its title for his second book (*Audacity of Hope*, 356). A "meditation on the fallen world," the sermon encouraged the congregation, as it grew in excitement, to be hopeful and prayerful in spirit, despite the challenges in the world (*Dreams from My Father*, 293):

> People began to shout, to rise from their seats and clap and cry out, a forceful wind carrying the reverend's voice up into the rafters. *As I watched and listened from my seat, I began to hear all the notes from the past three years swirl about me. The courage and fear of Ruby and Will. The race pride and anger of men like Rafiq. The desire to let go, the desire to escape, the desire to give oneself up to a God that could somehow put a floor on despair.*
> And in that single note—hope!—I heard something else; at the foot of that cross, inside the thousands of churches across the city, I imagined

the stories of ordinary black people merging with the stories of David and Goliath, Moses and Pharaoh, the Christians in the lion's den, Ezekiel's field of dry bones. Those stories—of survival, and freedom, and hope— became our story, my story; the blood that had spilled was our blood, the tears our tears; until this black church, on this bright day, seemed once more a vessel carrying the story of a people into future generations and into a larger world. Our trials and triumphs became at once unique and universal, black and more than black; in chronicling our journey, the stories and songs gave us a means to reclaim memories that we didn't need to feel shame about—memories that all people might study and cherish— and with which we could start to rebuild. (294; italics mine)

In addition to the coalescence of memories of Ruby, Will, and Rafiq, this passage marks the divergence of *Dreams from My Father* from the modern (or post-slave-narrative) tradition of African American autobiography that critiques the Christian church. Frederick Douglass, W. E. B. Du Bois, and Booker T. Washington in the nineteenth century, along with Zora Neale Hurston, Richard Wright, James Baldwin, Malcolm X, and Maya Angelou in the twentieth, defined their awareness of race, politics, and African American culture by questioning, ignoring, rejecting, or ridiculing the merits of the church. In contrast, Obama's memoir foregrounds that the church had enlightened him further to the themes of racial predestination and black nationalism that had haunted him as a Chicago community organizer. The church had also provided a spiritual literacy for him to interpret real-world problems and a spiritual language for him to communicate hope in the future.[40] Obama appreciated the contradictions of the religious calling: even as it was specific to Trinity Church and the many African American churches in Chicago, its universality of spiritual conversion ignored the distinctions of race, ethnicity, region, culture, and class. Only when a boy sitting beside him became "slightly apprehensive as he handed [Obama] a pocket tissue," when the boy's "mother glanced at [him] with a faint smile before turning back to the altar," and when "as [he] thanked the boy . . . [he] felt the tears running down [his] cheeks" did Obama's own conversion become manifest (295).

Evidence states that Obama had been a faithful parishioner of Trinity Church for a couple decades, certainly since his baptism there in 1988. A series of events, though, strained his relationship to Trinity Church and to Reverend Wright, including the endless broadcasting, in early March 2008, of the incendiary sermons that the former pastor delivered there. The most notorious excerpt was, "No, no, no, not God Bless America. God damn

America!"[41] To stem the devastating flood of controversy and to salvage his reputation and his association with Trinity Church, Obama gave what the media and academics have called the "race" speech in shorthand but what is officially entitled "A More Perfect Union."[42] Delivered on March 18, 2008, at the National Constitution Center, a museum designed to celebrate the history and meaning of the U.S. Constitution, the speech reaffirms the principles of his progressive political philosophy and returns to the analytic strategies used in *Dreams from My Father* and *The Audacity of Hope* to confront and overcome the myth of black nationalism.

The speech's title excerpts the Constitution's hallowed preamble: "We the People of the United States, in Order to form a more perfect Union, establish Justice, insure domestic Tranquility, provide for the common defence, promote the general Welfare, and secure the Blessings of Liberty to ourselves and our Posterity, do ordain and establish this Constitution for the United States of America."[43] Building on this sentence, whose first two clauses open his own speech, Obama returns to the paradoxical image of the Constitution he has portrayed in the chapter "Our Constitution" in *The Audacity of Hope*: the document sanctions the enslavement of Africans and their descendants in the New World, even though its original egalitarian spirit should have instantly abolished slavery. He strikes at the contradiction between the egalitarian theories and the racist practices lived by the Founding Fathers and later indicted by Frederick Douglass: that "words on a parchment would not be enough to deliver slaves from bondage, or provide men and women of every color and creed their full rights and obligations as citizens of the United States," and that "Americans in successive generations who were willing to do their part—through protests and struggle, on the streets and in the courts, through a civil war and civil disobedience and always at great risk—to narrow that gap between the promise of our ideals and the reality of their time" (*Change We Can Believe In,* 216). Ever since, Americans (and especially African Americans) have had to resolve the longstanding tension between the written and unwritten laws of race and racism in order to fulfill the democratic and egalitarian ideals of the Constitution, despite the failings of its authors and their ideological heirs. Most recently, Obama has attributed this resolution to collective will, to a belief that "we cannot solve the challenges of our time unless we solve them together—unless we perfect our union by understanding that we may have different stories, but we hold common hopes" (216). Again, these points are not new; they appear in the chapter "Values" in *The Audacity of Hope* and in "Declaration of Candidacy," his monumental speech officially beginning his presidential campaign.

"A More Perfect Union" detours through a reiteration of his biracial ancestry, which was by the time of the speech rather well known and which helps him explain his anomalous candidacy but also the media's attempts to racialize political issues and polarize the electorate. Within this context, Obama points to one "discussion of race in this campaign that has taken a particularly divisive turn": Reverend Wright's use of "incendiary language" to "express views that have the potential to widen the racial divide" and to "denigrate both the greatness and the goodness of our nation" (218). Although in *Dreams from My Father* he does not characterize the language in this pejorative way, Obama contends in "A More Perfect Union" that Reverend Wright's "profoundly distorted view of this country" is too cynical, too emphatic on the racism and moral ills of America, rather than on the democratic promise of it (218). These comments are "not only wrong but divisive," especially at a time when Obama's campaign is trying to accentuate this very democratic promise (219). Obama hopes that Americans can come together through his presidential campaign, despite and because of their many differences. He wants them to look toward the positives of the future, not dwell on the negatives of the past.

At this point, "A More Perfect Union" takes a number of remarkable analytic, if not literary, turns. First, Obama recites the very passage from *Dreams from My Father* that I quoted earlier, except that it leaves out the lines I have italicized: "As I watched and listened from my seat, I began to hear all the notes from the past three years swirl about me. The courage and fear of Ruby and Will. The race pride and anger of men like Rafiq. The desire to let go, the desire to escape, the desire to give oneself up to a God that could somehow put a floor on despair" (*Dreams from My Father*, 294).[44] The excision is understandable. Given the nature and setting of the speech "A More Perfect Union," these sentences would have distracted the audience. They assume that one has read *Dreams from My Father* and interpreted the meaning of these three characters. Most important, Trinity Church, the site of his religious conversion and spiritual maturation, is as self-contradictory as he presumably is: "The church contains in full the kindness and cruelty, the fierce intelligence and the shocking ignorance, the struggles and successes, the love and, yes, the bitterness and bias that make up the black experience in America." Needless to say, the church is also as self-contradictory as its leader, Reverend Wright: "He contains within him the contradictions—the good and the bad—of the community that he has served diligently for so many years" (*Change We Can Believe In*, 221).

The excision from "A More Perfect Union" of the autobiographical information on Rafiq, Ruby, and Will is also ironic. In the speech, Obama reinstates the critique of black nationalism he has already waged in his memoir. After stating the now famous line that he "can no more disown" Reverend Wright than he can disown the African American community and his white grandmother, both of whom have likewise expressed their share of racial prejudice and political incorrectness, Obama argues that if he ignores the meaning of Reverend Wright, or if America ignores the challenges of race and racism, then we "would be making the same mistake that Reverend Wright made in his offending sermons about America—to simplify and stereotype and amplify the negative to the point that it distorts reality" (222). The sophistication, empathy, and optimism that Obama desires is missing in Rafiq, Ruby, Will, the Chicago community, and the memories or histories of Malcolm X, the other examples of black nationalism detailed in *Dreams from My Father,* and now in Reverend Wright. Despite the roadblock caused by the controversy, Obama seized the moment for his own presidential campaign by reaffirming the principles of democracy and hope that he had been building prior to and in the early stages of his life in political office. At the same time, it allowed him to toe the political line between realism and optimism, to temper the utopian postracialism that Obama ascribes to his "critics" and that, I would venture, includes his supporters: "I have never been so naïve as to believe that we can get beyond our racial divisions in a single election cycle, or with a single candidacy" (226).

No wonder William Faulkner is such an appropriate literary reference at one of the most important moments in "A More Perfect Union." Here, Obama is defending Reverend Wright and explaining why he is speaking out on race in the first place, while rebuking the simplistic and negative discourses that may reduce the complexity of the issues at hand. In discussing the historical role of race in our nation's imperfection, Obama states, "As William Faulkner once wrote, 'The past isn't dead and buried. In fact, it isn't even past'" (222). Gavin Stevens, a character in Faulkner's 1951 three-act play/novel, *Requiem for a Nun,* does not say this exact phrase but something like it, which deserves a brief explanation to keep it in context.

Requiem for a Nun includes many of the characters in its prequel, the 1931 novel *Sanctuary.* Gavin is a lawyer investigating the murder of his nephew's (Gowan Stevens's) infant by the nursemaid, Nancy Mannigoe, an African American former drug user and prostitute who, in court, has admitted to committing the crime on God's behalf, who consequently has been the victim of the public's racist and righteous indignation, and who has been convicted and sentenced to death. As time goes on, Gavin realizes that his nephew's wife, Temple Drake, may have been more involved in the circumstances of the murder than many people realize. *Sanctuary* tells us that Temple has a regrettably unsavory past, in which she has been promiscuous, raped by a bootlegger, imprisoned in a brothel, and a perjurer. In *Requiem for a Nun*, we learn that she has been on the verge of endangering her marriage and two children, an infant girl and an adolescent boy, by running off with that bootlegger's brother. Nancy, who also serves as Temple's confidante, realizes the gravity of this predicament and believes that killing the girl would have provided a more honorable death than a gradual death at the hands of corrupt guardians and reprehensible living conditions. When Gavin and Temple meet to talk about the investigation and he suggests to her that dishonesty seems to be marring the facts, she declares that it does not matter "whose" "lie" it is, only that the death has occurred. He responds, "Yet you invented the coincidence." She replies, "Mrs. Gowan Stevens did." He clarifies, "Temple Drake did. Mrs. Gowan Stevens is not even fighting in this class. This is Temple Drake's." When she retorts, "Temple Drake is dead," he corrects her with the famous two lines, which differ slightly from Obama's: "The past is never dead. It's not even past."[45] The point of this exchange is that Temple has been trying to proceed from her despicable persona prior to her marriage to Gowan, while Gavin is implying that she has not been able to do so. The failings of her premarital persona have ended up tainting her moral choices, sacrificing the well-being of her innocent daughter, compromising the ethics of her reformed nursemaid, exploiting the judicial legacy of racial criminalization, and impeding her path toward self-redemption.

The text and context of *Requiem for a Nun* reflect one major theme in Faulkner's oeuvre: the life of the past in the present and in the future has often been a curse, often too difficult to defeat in one blow. For Faulkner, and now for Obama in "A More Perfect Union," the history of race and racism has been like this curse: it has been not merely a record of events but a record that has shaped so many social attitudes that it persists today in forms alternately material and ideological, pragmatic and mythical, fueling an anxious political imagination of race and racism in America's future. Obama concludes the reference to Faulkner by stating, "We do not need to recite here the history of racial injustice in this country. But we do need to remind ourselves that so many of the disparities that exist in the African-American community today can be directly traced to inequalities passed on from an earlier generation that suffered under the brutal legacy of slavery and Jim Crow" (222). As "A More Perfect Union" serves, on the whole, to remind Americans of the history of race and racism, the speech also resolves the conundrum faced by the narrator of Ralph Ellison's novel *Invisible Man*: that one should always be "inside history," with an eye toward political progress in America's best interest.

If so, then in "A More Perfect Union" why does not Obama refer to Ellison, the modernist contemporary of Faulkner who also looked at the contemporary life of the past? Perhaps the answer lies in a sentence stated, ironically, by Ellison himself. In his 1963 essay "The World and the Jug," Ellison replies to the claim of Irving Howe, a cultural and social critic, that Ellison and James Baldwin, the two younger authors competing with Richard Wright for leadership in the African American literati, have both failed to produce realistic images of African American life alternative to those found in Wright's 1940 bestselling novel, *Native Son.* The violence, anxiety, anger, fear, and delusions of Bigger Thomas, the protagonist of Wright's novel, are the emotional and psychological bookmarks for his misfortunes, including criminal flight, resisting arrest, sociological court trial, and the conviction of guilt. In Howe's view, these are the qualities of an exemplary African American novel. Ellison, in refuting Howe's criticisms and their wrongheaded assumptions point by point, concludes that he has "no objections to being placed beside Richard Wright in any estimation which is based not upon the irremediable ground of our common racial identity, but upon the quality of our achievements as writers." The tendency of white critics to privilege race over quality in categorizing African American writers coincides with another tendency of theirs to restrict literary influence exclusively to relationships within racial groups. Ellison balks at both:

> But perhaps you will understand me when I say [Wright] did not influence me if I point out that while one can do nothing about choosing one's relatives, one can, as artist, choose one's "ancestors." Wright was, in this sense, a "relative"; Hemingway an "ancestor." Langston Hughes, whose work I knew in grade school and whom I knew before I knew Wright, was a "relative"; Eliot, whom I was to meet only many years later, and Malraux and Dostoievsky and Faulkner were "ancestors"—if you please or don't please![46]

For a couple reasons, this kind of statement in Ellison's day riled up proponents of authentic African American aesthetics and culture—such that the aesthetics and culture were by, for, and about African Americans. Literary scholar Kenneth W. Warren states that Ellison first refuses to take for granted "a natural lineage" binding Ellison to American authors of African descent (such as Wright and Hughes). Second, he accepts "white writers as standards and influences" (including Ernest Hemingway, André Malraux, Fyodor Dostoievsky, and Faulkner).[47]

The relative-ancestor analogy poses a problem for Obama. Ellison refuses to acknowledge that relatives could be ancestors, too, that fair-minded African American writers could choose ancestors that bear their likeness in body and style, while not disparaging society if it, unfairly or not, happened to presume this association in the first place. Yet and still, the analogy has operated silently in Obama's selections of the post-civil-rights generation over the civil-rights generation, American nationalism over black nationalism, Faulkner over Ellison, and, for that matter, Lincoln over Douglass.[48] The fact that Obama shares with Reverend Wright an African American identity does not necessarily mean that he must agree with his former pastor on how to view America. Likewise, the fact that *Invisible Man* has shaped Obama's political and historical understanding of race does not necessarily mean that he must cite Ellison to communicate it. For both Ellison and Obama, the biology of race does not automatically trump all other kinds of connection.

An event soon after "A More Perfect Union" proved this point. At the April 2008 events for the National Association for the Advancement of Colored People and for the National Press Club, Reverend Wright made another round of inflammatory statements. Darryl Pinckney, a well-known novelist and literary critic, explained the view of many observers that, ever since Obama's "Philadelphia speech enhanced his stature," it was "all the more disconcerting that in the name of defending his church a black minister committed to social gospel seemed determined to ambush the first potentially successful campaign for president by a black person."[49] Implicitly, Obama and his political advisers expressed this view, too. The following month, Obama chose to disavow Reverend Wright publicly and to withdraw his family's membership at Trinity Church. He sought to dissociate himself from any more controversies at the church, to protect its members from further harmful attention from the political media, and to ensure his presidential campaign's success. Politically, the resignation worked, while he still maintained the rhetoric of Christian faith that broadened his cross-racial appeal to the American religious electorate—a faith that was, of course, born and reared in the African American pride of Trinity Church.

Epilogue

The Politics of African American Literature after Obama

The story of my book—or, more precisely, the backstory—is the story of how my thesis has a vexed relationship to the literary scholarship of the original Black Studies era. Always mindful of the imagery in Eddie S. Glaude Jr.'s 2007 book, *In a Shade of Blue: Pragmatism and the Politics of Black America,* I have tried to "step out of the shadows" cast by this era, whose scholarly conceptions of literature, political action, and social change could perpetuate myths and promote complacency in political valuations of African American literature.[1] My introduction explicitly lays out my critiques, and the subsequent chapters historicize and implement them. Even my choices of study in each chapter, however subtle they may turn out to be, reflect my methodology. A political genealogy of early African American literature, I claim at the outset, is attributable to Thomas Jefferson, not only to a person of African descent. Frederick Douglass was prescient and powerful in the postbellum era, not just in the antebellum era, which has been overstated as his most radical, and his most effective, stage of political action. African American authors of racial uplift should be perceived as sophisticated agents of social change, not as elitists misguided in their cultural calculus of political power. Langston Hughes and Claude McKay were transnational, not merely African American, writers of racial politics. Alice Randall has interrogated racial essentialism in deconstructing Margaret Mitchell's African American caricatures. And, finally, Obama has refused to succumb to the myths of black nationalism foisted upon him. Each chapter, in some way, challenges one or more protocols of African American historiography that, in the era of Black Studies, had crystallized theories of literature and racial politics. Such theories retrofitted a multilayered teleology of Black Power, a teleology inattentive to the formal and informal distinctions of political action as well as to the broader political problems of racial authenticity, of ideological cohesion within a racial constituency, of privileging popular culture over intellectual culture, and of highlighting black nationalism instead of racial internationalism.

Inevitably, the main themes I have raised in this book recall "the crisis of the intellectual," a controversial idea most thoroughly explored by Harold Cruse in his landmark 1967 book, *The Crisis of the Negro Intellectual: A Historical Analysis of the Failure of Black Leadership*. A vocal social, cultural, and political critic, Cruse published the book during the rise of racial nationalism, when he could assail without remorse the attraction of "Negro creative intellectuals" to racial integration, a cornerstone concept of the Civil Rights Movement. In the book's fourth chapter, "Cultural Leadership and Cultural Democracy," Cruse laments that "[t]he leaders of the civil rights movement, along with all the 'civil writers,' subordinate themselves to the very cultural values of the white world that are used either to negate or deny the Negro cultural equality, and to exploit his cultural ingredients and use them against *him*." Implicitly, such words demonstrate what Cruse calls "the Negro point of view," a perspective attentive to the willing subservience, not only to the enforced exploitation, of bourgeois African Americans in commercial and corporate cultures. To be sure, that perspective is also a problem: it aggrandizes ideologies of racial authenticity, autonomy, and advocacy that sacrifice, on the altar of "Afro-American Nationalism," what has turned out to be productive political coalitions across racial groups.[2] Cruse's critiques are thus alternately provocative and egregious. Yet, despite the many failings of his logic, it was prophetic. As Hortense J. Spillers, a cultural theorist of race, notes in her 1994 reassessment of the silver anniversary of *The Crisis of the Negro Intellectual*'s publication, the commercial and corporate cultures of African American intellectualism, as seen from Cruse's vantage point in the 1960s, now take place in academic institutions of higher education, where the "crisis" remains palpable.[3]

If we use the nearly three decades separating Cruse and Spillers to coordinate a longer African American intellectual history, then we could certainly expect the suggestion not only that the "crisis" remains but also that its corollary remains as well: namely, that the political efficacy of intellectual agents *outside* intellectual enclaves can improve only once the agents and their imagined constituents collectively overcome the ideological, cultural, and economic differences and stereotypes that have long alienated these two groups from each other.[4] In this book, I have not attempted to refute this point. I grant that there are limitations to the social reach of intellectual culture—analogous to the limitations of literature in reaching those who happen to be illiterate—despite how romantically captivating and politically legitimate this culture may have been to its purveyors across the centuries. What I have attempted to do in this book, rather, is question the idea of dismissing the political possibilities and realities of intellectual culture, something that *The Crisis of the Negro Intellectual* encourages us to do in order to mitigate our misunderstanding and misappropriation of Marxism and "Afro-American Nationalism." Intellectual culture is more politically effective, elastic, and expansive than what Cruse suggests. As cultural scholar Nikhil Pal Singh puts it, such nationalism "leads [Cruse] to privilege the forms of polemical and rhetorical address, and to consistently fall back upon the narrower sense of cultural politics as a politics of identity and representation at the expense of a full analysis of the general workings of the 'cultural apparatus' vis-à-vis the larger economy, and the specific political implications of the black intellectual's location within it."[5] I have argued that "cultural politics," if an *informal* context for describing "identity and representation," have gone hand in hand but also joined flexibly with the *formal* structures of law, government, and social policy, while describing how certain African American writers had overcome the "crisis" of social detachment that had afflicted others within their intellectual circles.

Instead of looking at the "failure of black leadership," as Cruse bemoans in his 1967 subtitle, my book as a whole shows what is at stake if we derive a vocabulary attuned simultaneously to the historical complexities of African American leadership, which includes both its failures and successes, and to our new racial and political realities. As Melissa Harris-Lacewell, a scholar of African American politics, has recently noted regarding academic intellectuals who doggedly hold Obama to a race agenda,

> African-Americans are now citizens capable of running for office, holding officials accountable through democratic elections, publicly expressing divergent political preferences and, most importantly, engaging the full spectrum of American political issues, not only narrowly racial ones. The era of racial brokerage politics, when the voices of a few men stood in for the entire race, is now over. And thank goodness it is over. Black politics is growing up.[6]

Addressing the core concerns of both Cruse and Harris-Lacewell—which we should—demands striking a balance. We must acknowledge and account for how the claims of African American intellectual oligarchies to representative political action can be problematic in spirit, in organization, and in practice. But we must also remember that the qualities of intellectual life, such as the ongoing attainment of higher education (either in school or otherwise), such as improved critical reasoning, and such as enhanced rhetorical communication, have long been crucial to the democratic development of the United States, particularly to the formal and informal elections of its leadership and to the political representation of its constituents. Striking that balance has turned out to be key to grasping how today's "new black politics" operates for better and for worse, and why it has succeeded and failed. Likewise, this sort of balance helps us explain not only the political history of African American literature but also why this history is, at bottom, a contest among generations.

I would be disingenuous, then, if I did not also state here that the vexed relationship of my book to the Black Studies era finds some reflection in Obama's own relationship to that era. The Reverend Jeremiah Wright Jr. was a disciple of what was called black liberation theology, which began in the 1960s and, according to essayist Darryl Pinckney, issued a "critique of 'white theology' for its failure to address the culpability of the white man in the oppression of African Americans and for having encouraged the notion that black people were lesser beings in the eyes of God and therefore incapable of Christian witness."[7] This theological tradition informed the "black church" of the twentieth century, examined by the scholar E. Franklin Frazier as "a nation within a nation," or as a byproduct of black nationalism. The theologian Dr. Howard Thurman wrote about it; Martin Luther King Jr. read Thurman's work, was his mentee, and studied it; and James H. Cone, whose books Black Theology and Black Power (1969) and A Black Theology of Liberation (1970) are now classics of the tradition, rearticulated it. Reverend Wright adopted this line of thought to develop a "cultural nationalism in the pulpit," Pinckney goes on to say, that "involves an extreme kind of Afrocentrism" that, among other things, condemns racial "assimilation" as sinful.[8]

In Chicago's Trinity United Church of Christ, where Wright was pastor from 1972 to 2008, Obama joined a "power base" for African American communities. As I already outlined, however, Trinity Church's traces of Black Power became a political liability during Obama's presidential campaign, which emphasized racial reconciliation.[9] Obama also confronted the political permutations of Black Power as late as 2000, when he ran against incumbent Bobby Lee Rush, a former member of the militant Black Panther Party, for the United States House of Representatives for Illinois's First District. The Reverend Jesse Jackson (Sr.), another former congressman who participated in the Civil Rights Movement alongside Martin Luther King Jr., was also a harbinger of the past that Obama had to reckon with during his 2008 presidential campaign. Although decidedly critical of the militant principles of the Black Panther Party, the generation that King and his brothers and sisters in arms represented also posed challenges.[10] Obama overcame all these hurdles, but the truth was clear: Obama was a child during the modern civil rights movement—which includes both King's Civil Rights Movement of the 1950s through the early 1960s and, say, Stokely Carmichael's Black Power Movement of the late 1960s through the 1970s—but not a child of it.

If Obama's is a story of the challenge of being at once an African American and a political activist without being beholden to the Black Power and Civil Rights Movements, then it also talks about his genuine attempt to bridge the divide inevitably separating him from that generation. Likewise, even as I go against the grain of African American literary scholarship that emerged from the 1960s, 1970s, and even as late as the 1980s, I appreciate the political urgency of this era enough to write this book and will try to argue, in the balance of this epilogue, that the politics of race still matter, not just now but even after Obama's presidency.

To wage this hypothesis, I will continue to stress the main points of the foregoing chapters: the evolution of this literature in both informal and formal contexts of political action and representation; the intellectual debates, also over time, on the link between these two contexts; and the recent implications of this topic for African American historiography. For reasons I have already explained, Jefferson's use of literary criticism to wage political criticism of New World Africans in early America serves as the ideal starting point for my study, while Obama's personal connection of literature to social action in his political rise serves as an adequate end. Together, what these, and the middle chapters, suggest is that African American attainment of civil rights in the formal realms of electoral and governmental politics marks a developmental stage of African American literature. Within the claim that there exists such a political phase of African American literature *after* Obama is the assumption that electoral and governmental events will continue to deserve salience in literary historiography, that they can significantly influence the creative choices of African American writers, and that they can guide our assessment of African American literature's social impact. In this book, nowhere is this assumption more crucial (and, admittedly, convenient) than in the final chapter, on the literary life and political rise of Obama. Yet the seed had already been planted at least a century earlier in African American intellectual and political thought.

In "Of Our Spiritual Strivings," the first chapter of W. E. B. Du Bois's prescient 1903 book, *The Souls of Black Folk*, Du Bois helps codify intellectual history in such political terms. He explains the meaning of the Civil War in the 1860s alongside the 1870 ratification of the Fifteenth Amendment to the United States Constitution, which prohibited using the "race, color, or previous condition of servitude" of African American citizens to deny them the right to vote. "The ballot, which before [the African American] had looked upon as a visible sign of freedom, he now regarded as the chief means of gaining and perfecting the liberty with which war had partially endowed him. And why not? Had not votes made war and emancipated millions? Had not votes enfranchised the freedmen? Was anything impossible to a power that had done all this?" The political trope of the ballot invigorates Du Bois's subsequent rhetoric that the post-Reconstruction, or post-1876, ideal of "book-learning," which, in many areas of the South during slavery, had been outlawed, "began to replace the dream of political power."[11]

History has shown that in Du Bois's long generation, lasting from around his birth in 1868 to his death in 1963, from the dawn of African American freedom through the following century of Jim Crow segregation, "dreams" of African American empowerment did not involve strategies of substituting the political with the intellectual, implying that each context was separate, successive, or displaceable. Rather, the dreams realized that the two contexts were already imbricated in social change. In the year after Du Bois passed away, King accepted the Nobel Peace Prize "in behalf of a civil rights movement which is moving with determination and a majestic scorn for risk and danger to establish a reign of freedom and a rule of justice." In doing so, King stated that he had "the audacity to believe that peoples everywhere can have three meals a day for their bodies, education and culture for their minds, and dignity, equality and freedom for their spirits."[12] Ever reflective on the history of civil rights, King asserted that "education and culture" were as crucial to social maturity as they were to political maturity. His Nobel speech, an affirmation of love and nonviolent suasion, of African American resilience against racist brutality, rather than of antagonism and militancy, is one of the greatest celebrations of the power of an African American's intellect to shape America's political culture. The 2008 presidential election reaffirmed these words of 1964.

If we take this logic further, we could also argue that the 2008 election of an African American to the U.S. presidency—a person who, in 2009, no less, also won the Nobel Peace Prize for his diplomacy—not only calls for celebration but also, theoretically, could portend an omen. To borrow the opening words of *The Souls of Black Folk,* not only is "the problem of the Twentieth Century . . . the problem of the color line," but we can still claim that, to an extent, the "color line," or Du Bois's metaphor for "race," remains a "problem" in the twenty-first century.[13] If so, then to what extent has the *electoral success* of Obama and other African American politicians of his generation reflected a mitigation of racial problems in the United States? And where does African American literature fit into all this? As far as this book has been concerned, my circling back to the state of African American literature is central. My thesis has been that portrayals of race, or racial representations, in African American literature have been historically preoccupied with the political hurdle of race. Can this thesis apply to African American literature written in the wake of an electoral event whose political symbolism suggests that a large part of the "American people" succeeded in leaping over that hurdle?

To venture a hypothesis, I must first declare that post-Obama African American literature is not the same as postracial African American literature. The concept of "postrace" has emerged, most notably, in reference to well-educated, exciting, elected, and mostly Democratic African American officials.[14] A handful includes Cory Booker, mayor of Newark, New Jersey; Deval Patrick, governor of Massachusetts; Artur Davis, member of the U.S. House of Representatives from Alabama's Seventh District; Harold Ford Jr., former member of the U.S. House of Representatives from Tennessee's Ninth District; Michael Nutter, mayor of Philadelphia; and, of course, President Obama, who was also formerly member of the Illinois Senate from the Thirteenth District and U.S. senator from Illinois. Their dates of birth reveal that they were mere children during the modern civil rights movement, and their credentials at Ivy League institutions highlight their common ability to navigate majority-white societies while excelling in rigorous academic environments.[15] In part, this kind of profile explains the "appeal" of Booker and Obama, according to magazine writer Peter J. Boyer, that "transcends race": "Both men, reared in the post-Selma era and schooled at elite institutions, developed a political style of conciliation, rather than confrontation, which complemented their natural gifts and, as it happens, nicely served their ambitions."[16] (For Obama's presidential campaign, riding the tsunami of backlash against George W. Bush's sitting presidential administration helped, of course.)

Although not unprecedented, the rise of recent African American politicians of this postracial sort is phenomenal.[17] Key to understanding the electoral success of these "Baby Boomers," their ages ranging from forty to fifty-four, is their ability to bridge King's Civil Rights Movement and the new millennium. One reason that David Remnick titles his recent biography *The Bridge* is that Obama, its subject, represents that transgenerational "bridge." In Obama's March 4, 2007, speech at the Brown Chapel in Selma, Alabama, only one month after he announced his campaign for president, he recognized the city's legacy in the Civil Rights Movement: King spoke at the chapel himself on January 2, 1965; and two months later, police brutality attempted to halt a series of symbolic civil rights marches from Selma, eastward to Edmund Pettus Bridge, the penultimate passage to Montgomery, Alabama's state capital. Obama talked about the "Joshua generation," a biblical analogy for this movement's descendants who were overcoming the hurdles of racial prejudice and discrimination and who were closer to crossing the bridge into the "Promised Land" of full American citizenship than were the "Moses generation" of African American civil rights activists, ranging, in Obama's words, from Du Bois and Anna Julia Cooper to King and Rosa Parks, who could only at best see the Land from afar. Listeners, young and old, acclaimed Obama. In Remnick's words, his "rhetoric created a parallel between the particularities of a candidate's life and a political struggle; put forth the self-appointment of a young man to continue and develop a national movement; and delivered it all in the rhetoric of the traditional black church—the first liberated space among the slaves and still the essential black institution. In Selma, Obama evoked not Lincoln but King; he adopted the gestures, rhythms, and symbols of the prophetic voice for the purposes of electoral politics."[18] Implicitly, Obama's election would be that moment of passage, that connection of past to future, of appreciating the struggle of race, even as he personally expected to struggle leading a nation where race should not matter foremost.

In the popular imagination, then, a postracial moment pertains very much to the promise of a present and future in which race is no longer the main determinant of social relations and of the nation's democratic growth. Yet the future possibility of such racial transcendence inevitably requires a counterbalancing attempt to transcend history—the history in which the social and democratic challenges of race dominated the narratives of civil rights struggles. Fundamentally political, that history hovered, and still hovers, as a specter of intergenerational tension over the "new black politics" and over the promise of postracial politics. As journalist Matt Bai wrote in his informative essay "Is Obama the End of Black Politics?"

The generational transition that is reordering black politics didn't start this year. It has been happening, gradually and quietly, for at least a decade, as younger African-Americans, Barack Obama among them, have challenged their elders in traditionally black districts. What this year's Democratic nomination fight did was to accelerate that transition and thrust it into the open as never before, exposing and intensifying friction that was already there. For a lot of younger African-Americans, the resistance of the civil rights generation to Obama's candidacy signified the failure of their parents to come to terms, at the dusk of their lives, with the success of their own struggle—to embrace the idea that black politics might now be disappearing into American politics in the same way that the Irish and Italian machines long ago joined the political mainstream.[19]

Since the August 10, 2008, publication of Bai's essay in the *New York Times,* evidence has shown that the "generational transition" from the Civil Rights era to the new millennium did not cripple new African American politics. Obama has succeeded either in alleviating the instances of friction that had existed between his and the prior generation of African American activists and politicians or in overcoming those he could not on his way toward winning the presidency.

The electoral achievements of Obama and others, however, do not mean that intergenerational conflict is gone forever. If anything, their experiences on the campaign trail indicate how the patterns of history helped entrench such conflict in the present era. Equally remarkable as Booker's rapid ascendance as Newark's mayor is that he did so in a city that was, in the 1960s, a major hub of Black Power and Black Arts in the Northeast. In the words of Amiri Baraka, a Black Arts poet and one of its more notorious residents, Newark was a place where "[w]e were agitating furiously. . . . I had stamped 'Black Power!' across buildings around the city. We were putting out leaflets and stuff. We had to fight, we had to struggle. That was clear, because we saw ourselves as Malcolm [X]'s children."[20] In the subsequent decades, such as when Sharpe James was elected mayor in 1986, racial pride became a mantra for the history and the progress of the majority–African American city. Booker was a figure of political transition; he was trying to rise at a time when an exclusively African American constituency could become an exclusively African American electoral demographic. The historian Thomas J. Sugrue states that "Black electoral politics in the four decades between the passage of the Voting Rights Act and the beginning of Obama's presidential campaign was anything but monolithic. Some politicians were the heirs of black power, particularly those with safe seats in overwhelmingly black districts, who did not depend on white electoral support and who could use explicit race-based appeals to rouse their supporters."[21] As a representative of the new black politics, though, Booker needed two elections, a 2002 defeat and a 2006 victory, to convince longstanding Newark voters that he was not the worst that the new millennium had to offer—that he was neither an academic elitist nor unfamiliar with the working-class interests of African Americans nor illiterate in the "authentic" vernacular of local African American communities. In his run-ups to mayor, the public and whisper campaigns Booker faced, unabashedly attacking his racial and regional authenticity, encoded the very cultural and political stereotypes that have long besmirched African American intellectuals and colluded in estranging them from African American constituencies. And the cynicism of elder African American members of the Civil Rights era only compounded the equally persistent forms of racism (which can go without saying) that the African American political avant-garde has faced in recent years.

Race, then, does not perish but persists in the new African American politics. The representatives of this movement are in constant negotiation with the political history of race, even as they are trying to forge their identities in an evolving America. More precisely, they are in direct negotiation with the living civil rights activists of the Moses generation and with the memories of historic struggle in the living descendants of this generation and in the cultural and political artifacts that emerged from it. For this reason, the idea of a postracial America is misleading, not so much because race remains a problem but, rather, because the prefix "post-" implies that a current event, such as a presidential election, can turn race into a hermetically sealed historical event, into a segment of the past as irrecoverable as time itself. That is impossible. Race can always persist both during and after historical events in the realm of human ideas. To borrow again Frederick Douglass's cynical but accurate words on race after slavery's end, in his 1865 essay "The Need for Continuing Anti-slavery Work," discussed in chapter 2, race can persist as ideological phantasmagoria in the twenty-first century, even after Obama: "It has been called by a great many names, and it will call itself by yet another name; and you and I and all of us had better wait and see what new form this old monster will assume, in what new skin this old snake will come forth next."[22]

A century and a half after Douglass penned these words, now may be the time for the racial cynicism familiar in African American political history to come to an end. Of course, recent years have witnessed the rise of scholarship warning us that we cannot transcend race. Today, race still matters, to be sure. To take only two examples, the Spring 2009 issue of the journal *Du Bois Review: Social Science Research on Race,* entitled "Obama's Path," includes several essays that document the statistical results and examine the sociological implications of Obama's election to the presidency, all the while critiquing as a myth the popular notion that this event signaled an emerging era of postracial politics.[23] Unsurprisingly, one of the issue's coeditors (who also serves as the journal's coeditor), Lawrence D. Bobo, cocontributed an essay to another pathbreaking work of scholarship, a 2010 book jointly edited by Hazel Rose Markus and Paula M. L. Moya, entitled *Doing Race: 21 Essays for the 21st Century.* Addressing the "challenge" faced by today's students in "talking about race and ethnicity," the editors say that although claims abound that doing so is "unnecessary in a 'post-race'" world, the remarkable collection of essays shows that "race is a dynamic system of historically derived and institutionalized ideas and practices," as well as "an ongoing social process."[24] I would add that we cannot transcend race also because it mattered yesterday: race has not yet transcended African American political history.

I still maintain that we can transcend the longstanding political cynicism of race. Instead of committing to the idea that we are in a postracial world, that race is no longer relevant, that it is coming to an end, we should further embrace race as a concept, with one caveat: as a metaphor, race is so elastic as to allow us to think broadly about the communities among Africans and their descendants around the world but also about the increasing need for empathy to alleviate the various disconnections that hinder interpersonal relations across the African diaspora. As Brent Hayes Edwards asks at the outset of his seminal scholarly book of 2003, *The Practice of Diaspora: Literature, Translation, and the Rise of Black Internationalism,* "Is it possible to rethink the workings of 'race' in the cultures of black internationalism through a model of *décalage*?" His answer is manifold:

Any articulation of diaspora in such a model would be inherently *décalé,* or disjoined, by a host of factors. Like a table with legs of different lengths, or a tilted bookcase, diaspora can be discursively propped up (*calé*) in an artificially "even" or "balanced" state of "racial" belonging. But such props, of rhetoric, strategy, or organization, are always articulations of unity or globalism, ones that can be "mobilized" for a variety of purposes but can never be definitive: they are always prosthetic. In this sense, *décalage* is proper to the structure of a diasporic "racial" formation, and its return in the form of *disarticulation*—the points of misunderstanding, bad faith, unhappy translation—must be considered a necessary haunting.[25]

With Edwards's words as guidance, I hypothesize that the alleged desire to move away from race in postracial discourse is not entirely toward a "color-blind" society, although that may be a partial desire. This move also encourages us to overcome the cultural and political monopoly over race enjoyed by indigenes of the Black Power era (and less so by those of the Civil Rights era, which believed more readily, though not always, of course, in the democratic potential of the United States). To be clear, the possibilities of color-blind and diasporic notions of society are on the surface antonymous in their rejection and rethinking of race, respectively. Nonetheless, they share the goal of prying African American identity from the grip of the 1960s. James Edward Smethurst, a cultural historian, states in his 2005 book, *The Black Arts Movement: Literary Nationalism in the 1960s and 1970s*, that the cultural nationalism of this decade, though highly complex, reiterated "that the bedrock of black national culture was an African essence that needed to be rejoined, revitalized, or reconstructed, both in the diaspora and in an Africa deformed by colonialism."[26] Within today's reservations about race that have assumed the language of postracial desire, then, could be a profound resistance to the historical overstatement of the cynical African American politics that had crystallized in the 1960s and 1970s. The reservations could also include a desire to reassess how diaspora itself had been reduced too much and too often to the political narrative of racial unity—a narrative ingrained during these two decades. A more critical and capacious notion would appreciate diaspora as a political narrative of empathy in which race is a contestable category but, nonetheless, a useful one that can account for what is at stake when we interact with one another because of our similarities or in spite of our differences.

The promise of African American literature after Obama could be not a wish fulfillment to move away from race per se but an opportunity to plumb deeper within its metaphors, to rethink the traditional history of African American politics, and to conduct new kinds of revisionist historiography, or new rewritings of history, that recover the stories of race that had been elided as a consequence of the 1960s and 1970s. It almost goes without saying that Obama's memoir, *Dreams from My Father: A Story of Race and Inheritance*, which I analyzed in chapter 6, could have qualified for this future kind of literature had it been released for the first time a quarter of a century after its initial 1995 publication. Told across his campaign and in this book, the refrain, of course, is that he descends from a black father from Kenya and a white mother from Kansas. What makes his stories of "race and inheritance" so remarkable, however, is not that Obama is interracial in identity but that the great symbolic gulf between Kenya and Kansas is so wide that the history of American slavery, a dominant political narrative of race in America, vanishes from autobiographical view. And, ironically, this history vanishes even as Obama details, throughout his memoir, his own struggles with the ideological phantasmagoria of slavery, with its repercussions in the current forms of racial prejudice and discrimination. Time will tell what Obama will write about in his memoir after his own presidency.

A less hypothetical example, because it actually appeared in more recent years, is the novel Toni Morrison published in the year Obama was elected president, *A Mercy*. A companion piece to her 1987 novel, *Beloved,* which, along with the other "neo-slave" novels of that decade, reminded us of the living curse of slavery, *A Mercy* shows Morrison figuratively working alongside Edward P. Jones, author of the 2003 novel *The Known World,* to rethink the history of slavery as we know it.[27] Both novels show that both white and black races featured slave owners; that not only African Americans but Native Americans, too, were slaves; and that the neo-slave narrative of the new century requires us to rethink what we mean by a slave and to rethink how traditional ideas of race have come to determine who can present that narrative of slaves or who can be represented within it. Works of political and intellectual culture such as Morrison's and Jones's novels advise us to hedge against apocalyptic tales that we have reached the end of African American literature, or of African American studies, for that matter. Lowering the alarm, I urge us to continue to envision—if not in classrooms and reading groups, then on our own, but always in deliberate and critical fashion—what the "politics" of African American literature and African American studies will be, despite and because of race.

Notes

NOTES TO THE PREFACE AND ACKNOWLEDGMENTS

1. Gene Andrew Jarrett, *Deans and Truants: Race and Realism in African American Literature* (Philadelphia: University of Pennsylvania Press, 2007), 9.

NOTES TO THE INTRODUCTION

1. I borrow the phrase "the life of the mind" from Hannah Arendt, *The Life of the Mind* (New York: Harcourt Brace Jovanovich, 1978): "In other words, when the philosopher takes leave of the world given to our senses and does a turnabout (Plato's *periagoge*) to the life of the mind, he takes his clue from the former, looking for something to be revealed to him that would explain its underlying truth" (23).

2. See the "postidentitarian" arguments of Walter Benn Michaels in *The Shape of the Signifier: 1967 to the End of History* (Princeton, NJ: Princeton University Press, 2006) and Kenneth W. Warren in *So Black and Blue: Ralph Ellison and the Occasion of Criticism* (Chicago: University of Chicago Press, 2003).

3. Garry Wills has called the three-fifths compromise an "economic and political calculus" designed mainly by Southern legislators of the era to preserve slavocratic representation in the halls of government. Garry Wills, *"Negro President": Jefferson and the Slave Power* (New York: Mariner Books, 2005), 9. The three-fifths compromise so adversely affected the future of African American civil rights that, aside from the momentum of the Civil War, only amendments were able to begin overturning the act seventy-seven years later. First, the Southern states successfully inscribed the federal ratio into constitutional law. Next, by empowering slaveholders politically, the compromise protected their economic and cultural interests, including the preservation of slavery. Third, the compromise's electoral advantage solidified the South's claims to national representation, even though the controversy over slavery was exacerbating regional conflict between the North and South. Finally, the compromise precipitated a wave of congressional and presidential victories, benefiting a quarter of the presidents between George Washington and the Civil War, including, in 1800, Thomas Jefferson himself. Whether Jefferson was the first "Negro president," because his election to office exploited the South's slave power in the halls of federal government, has fueled a present-day controversy that may not end anytime soon. For the economic protection and extension of slave power, see ibid., xvi, 4, and 11; for the language of populism, see ibid., xvii and 1 (regarding the 1800 election as a "Second Revolution"); and for the congressional and presidential victories, see ibid., 5, 6, and 59. For the academic debate over whether Jefferson was elected to office in these terms, see ibid., xi–xv.

4. In a recent article reflecting on Obama's electoral victory, a reporter further noted, "Obama's election also broke new ground in the mechanics of campaigning. His campaign used the Internet, e-mail, and social-networking sites as community-organizing tools more effectively than any campaign in history. On fundraising, Obama opted out of public financing—the first nominee to do so since the advent of the system in 1976—and raised at least $600 million from more than 3 million donors, another feat that defied expectations." Linda Feldman, "Obama Victory Signals New Push for Unity," *Christian Science Monitor* (November 6, 2008): 25. For the certified statistics of the popular vote, see Federal Election Commission, "2008 Official Presidential General Election Results," http://www.fec.gov/pubrec/fe2008/2008presgeresults.pdf. For a sample of statistics of the African American vote, see Lawrence D. Bobo and Michael C. Dawson, "A Change Has Come: Race, Politics, and the Path to the Obama Presidency," *Du Bois Review* 6.1 (Spring 2009): 3.

5. Christine Smallwood, "Back Talk: Toni Morrison," *Nation* (December 8, 2008), http://www.thenation.com/doc/20081208/smallwood2.

6. John Adams to John Penn, March 27, 1776, quoted in Eric Slauter, *The State as a Work of Art: The Cultural Origins of the Constitution* (Chicago: University of Chicago Press, 2009), 130, 131.

7. Thomas F. Gossett, *Race: The History of an Idea in America* (New York: Oxford University Press, 1997), 3–31.

8. Regina Bendix, *In Search of Authenticity: The Formation of Folklore Studies* (Madison: University of Wisconsin Press, 1997), 15.

9. Waldo E. Martin Jr., *No Coward Soldiers: Black Cultural Politics in Postwar America* (Cambridge, MA: Harvard University Press, 2005), 4. Martin states that the "wide-ranging political consciousness revealed both in the musics and in the larger expressive culture are intimately connected to important individual and collective forms of black struggle, to important varieties of black cultural politics" (ibid., 2). Herman S. Gray also asserts the importance of nonliterary forms of cultural media when he states that "we need to critically scrutinize cultural projects like continuing struggles for cultural visibility, recognition, and inclusion in the national media, especially commercial 'network' television. Politically and historically, my argument is that the cultural politics of recognition rooted in the presumed discursive stability of black cultural representation . . . has given way to new cultural logics and technologies." Gray, *Cultural Moves: African Americans and the Politics of Representation* (Berkeley: University of California Press, 2005), 188–89.

10. Adolph L. Reed Jr., *W. E. B. Du Bois and American Political Thought: Fabianism and the Color Line* (New York: Oxford University Press, 1997), 130, 152.

11. Warren, *So Black and Blue,* 20, 21, 31, 33–34.

12. Adolph Reed Jr. and Kenneth W. Warren, introduction to *Renewing Black Intellectual History: The Ideological and Material Foundations of African American Thought,* ed. Reed and Warren, vii–xi (Boulder, CO: Paradigm, 2010), i.

13. Reed and Warren, introduction to *Renewing Black Intellectual History,* viii–ix. Examples of the payoffs include the essays published in *Renewing Black Intellectual History,* such as an essay by Warren on the revelation of Frederick Douglass's assumptions and anxieties about serving as a political representative of an inherently fragmented African American collectivity; and an essay by Judith Stein on the economic and labor circumstances, not merely the racial circumstances, that distinguished Booker T. Washington's promotion of African American industrial education.

14. In both their earlier and recent works, Reed and Warren tend to cite and critique the notable scholarship of Henry Louis Gates Jr. and Houston Baker Jr., above all. Gene Andrew Jarrett, "New Negro Politics," *American Literary History* 18 (Winter 2006): 836–46. This essay states that William Maxwell, Barbara Foley, Marlon B. Ross, Anne Elizabeth Carroll, and Martha Jane Nadell have connected cultural politics to political culture to make sense of the trope of the "New Negro" between Reconstruction and World War II.

15. Russ Castronovo, *Beautiful Democracy: Aesthetics and Anarchy in a Global Era* (Chicago: University of Chicago Press, 2007), 114.

16. A recent news report in the *Chronicle of Higher Education* notes that, at the annual meeting of the American Political Science Association in Philadelphia in September 2006, the main topic was "Power Reconsidered," which aimed to "remind" "political scientists [that they] own the franchise on the topic." *Chronicle Review* (August 11, 2006): B6. However, when I refer to studies of politics, I am referring not only to political science but to political history and political theory as well.

17. Jodi Dean, "Introduction: The Interface of Political Theory and Cultural Studies," in *Cultural Studies and Political Theory*, ed. Dean (Ithaca, NY: Cornell University Press, 2000), 1, 5.

18. Ibid., 5, 6. Though Dean talks about "cultural studies," I am focusing on its subdivision of literary studies, which deals with an analogous but specialized set of artifacts to examine.

19. Michael C. Dawson, *Black Visions: The Roots of Contemporary African-American Political Ideologies* (Chicago: University of Chicago Press, 2001), 4.

20. See ibid., 11, and Steven Hahn, *A Nation under Our Feet: Black Political Struggles in the Rural South from Slavery to the Great Migration* (Cambridge, MA: Harvard University Press, 2003).

21. Robin D. G. Kelley, *Race Rebels: Culture, Politics, and the Black Working Class* (New York: Free Press, 1994), 13, 33.

22. For a profound theoretical discussion of the relationship between black popular culture and black politics, see Richard Iton, *In Search of the Black Fantastic: Politics and Popular Culture in the Post–Civil Rights Era* (New York: Oxford University Press, 2008), 1–29. Political sociologist Eva Etzioni-Halevy, in her introduction to *Classes and Elites in Democracy and Democratization: A Collection of Readings*, ed. Etzioni-Halevy (New York: Garland, 1997), distinguishes "state elites" from "nonstate elites":

> [E]lites in modern capitalist societies are commonly divided into state and nonstate elites. The state elites include political leaders, whose power flows primarily from political and organizational resources, and the heads of large-scale state-based organizations, such as the government bureaucracy, the military, and the police, whose power is based primarily on that of their organizations. The nonstate elites include the economic elite (or the captains of business and industry), whose power rests primarily on the control of economic enterprises and thus of economic resources; the elite of the media and the academic and cultural elites, whose influence lies in their command of symbols; trade union leaders, who rely for their power on political and organizational resources, and leaders of social movements, where personal resources (which are important for the other elites as well), in conjunction with political resources of popular support, most clearly come into play. (xxv–xxvi)

23. David Lionel Smith, "The Black Arts Movement and Its Critics," *American Literary History* 3.1 (Spring 1991): 93, 102. I talk more about Smith's essay and the field of Black Arts Studies in Jarrett, "The Black Arts Movement and Its Scholars," *American Quarterly* 57.4 (2005): 1243–51. A host of scholars have now researched the complexities and connections of the Black Arts, Black Power, and Black Studies Movements, and the following citations, despite their number, represent only a fraction of the work of this growing field. See William L. Van Deburg, *New Day in Babylon: The Black Power Movement and American Culture, 1965–1975* (Chicago: University of Chicago Press, 1992); idem, *Black Camelot: African-American Culture Heroes in Their Times, 1960–1980* (Chicago: University of Chicago Press, 1997); Madhu Dubey, *Black Women Novelists and the Nationalist Aesthetic* (Bloomington: Indiana University Press, 1994); Eddie S. Glaude, ed., *Is It Nation Time? Contemporary Essays on Black Power and Black Nationalism* (Chicago: University of Chicago Press, 2002); Adolph L. Reed Jr., *Race, Politics, and Culture: Critical Essays on the Radicalism of the 1960s* (Westport, CT: Greenwood, 1986); James C. Hall, *Mercy, Mercy Me: African-American Culture and the American Sixties* (New York: Oxford University Press, 2001); Jerry Gafio Watts, *Amiri Baraka: The Politics and Art of a Black Intellectual* (New York: New York University Press, 2001); K. Komozi Woodard, *A Nation within a Nation: Amiri Baraka (Leroi Jones) and Black Power Politics* (Chapel Hill: University of North Carolina Press, 1999); Wahneema Lubiano, "'But Compared to What?': Reading Realism, Representation, and Essentialism in *School Daze, Do the Right Thing,* and the Spike Lee Discourse," *Black American Literature Forum* 25.2 (Summer 1991): 253–82; Phillip Brian Harper, *Are We Not Men? Masculine Anxiety and the Problem of African-American Identity* (New York: Oxford University Press, 1996); Winston Napier, "From the Shadows: Houston Baker's Move toward a Postnationalist Appraisal of the Black Aesthetic," *New Literary History* 25.1 (Winter 1994): 159–74; Cheryl Clarke, *"After Mecca": Women Poets and the Black Arts Movement* (New Brunswick, NJ: Rutgers University Press, 2005); James Edward Smethurst, *The Black Arts Movement: Literary Nationalism in the 1960s and 1970s* (Chapel Hill: University of North Carolina Press, 2005); and Amy Abugo Ongiri, *Spectacular Blackness: The Cultural Politics of the Black Power Movement and the Search for a Black Aesthetic* (Charlottesville: University of Virginia Press, 2010). Most recently, Lisa Gail Collins and Margo Natalie Crawford, eds., *New Thoughts on the Black Arts Movement* (New Brunswick, NJ: Rutgers University Press, 2006), has appeared to demonstrate further the development of the field. For exemplary books documenting the rise of Black Studies in relation to Black Power, see Fabio Rojas, *From Black Power to Black Studies: How a Radical Social Movement Became an Academic Discipline* (Baltimore: Johns Hopkins University Press, 2007); Noliwe Rooks, *White Money/BlackPower: The Surprising History of African American Studies and the Crisis of Race in Higher Education* (Boston: Beacon, 2007); and Jacqueline Bobo, Cynthia Hudley, and Claidine Michel, eds., *The Black Studies Reader* (New York: Routledge, 2004). A thorough metascholarly analysis of contemporary "Black Power Studies" appears in Peniel E. Joseph, "The Black Power Movement: A State of the Field," *Journal of American History* (December 2009): 751–76; his coining of the term appears on 752. The article finds full demonstration in Joseph's recently authored books, *Waiting 'Til the Midnight Hour: A Narrative History of Black Power in America* (New York: Henry Holt, 2006) and *Dark Days, Bright Nights: From Black Power to Barack Obama* (New York: Basic Books, 2010), and in his edited books, *Neighborhood Rebels: Black Power at the Local Level* (New York: Palgrave Macmillan, 2010) and *The Black Power Movement: Rethinking the Civil Rights and Black Power Era* (New York: Routledge, 2006).

24. Joseph, "The Black Power Movement," 752.

25. Martin Luther King Jr., "Next Stop: The North" (1965), reprinted in *A Testament of Hope: The Essential Writings and Speeches of Martin Luther King Jr.*, 189–94 (New York: HarperCollins, 1986), 193. King talked further about Black Power in his classic June 11, 1967, essay for the *New York Times Magazine*, "Black Power Defined," expanded as the chapter "Black Power," in his 1968 book *Where Do We Go from Here: Chaos or Community?* (Boston: Beacon, 2010), 23–69. In this book, King stresses that "[w]hat is most needed is a coalition of Negroes and liberal whites that will work to make both major parties truly responsible to the needs of the poor. Black Power does not envision or desire such a program. Just as the Negro cannot achieve political power in isolation, neither can he gain economic power through separatism" (50).

26. Joseph, "The Black Power Movement," 753.

27. Eddie S. Glaude Jr., *In a Shade of Blue: Pragmatism and the Politics of Black America* (Chicago: University of Chicago Press, 2007), xii, 10.

28. George Hutchinson and James Edward Smethurst have researched periodicals and regarded them as major features of the cultural and political nationalism of the Harlem Renaissance of the 1920s and the Black Arts Movement of the 1960s and 1970s, respectively. In doing so, they explicitly cite and critique Harold Cruse's disparagement of various sorts of interpersonal contact and ideological cooperation between blacks and whites in his 1967 book *The Crisis of the Negro Intellectual*. Hutchinson and Smethurst go on to argue that the institutional emergence of an African American cultural movement may be attributed to this interracialism. Especially admirable is the critical maneuver of Smethurst, who wrests himself from the epistemology of the literary politics that the 1960s and 1970s have entrenched, even as he describes this period in detail. For discussions of the ideological dynamics of these movements that made certain political themes more valuable than others, see Gene Andrew Jarrett, *Deans and Truants: Race and Realism in African American Literature* (Philadelphia: University of Pennsylvania Press, 2007), 169–74; and Smethurst, *The Black Arts Movement*. Also see George Hutchinson's superb *The Harlem Renaissance in Black and White* (Cambridge, MA: Harvard University Press, 1995). For their critique of Cruse, see Hutchinson, *The Harlem Renaissance in Black and White*, 16–17 and Smethurst, *The Black Arts Movement*, 126–32.

29. In paraphrasing a statement by James Weldon Johnson in 1922, Gates states, "In their efforts to prove Jefferson wrong, in other words, black writers created a body of literature, one with a prime political motive: to demonstrate black equality." Henry Louis Gates Jr., *The Trials of Phillis Wheatley* (New York: Basic Civitas Books, 2003), 66. Though stated recently in Gates's 2003 book, this relatively unchanged political story of Wheatley traces back to his earlier books, including an edited collection of scholarly essays in 1982, a part of an acclaimed monograph published by a university press in 1989, an introduction to a bestselling and definitive anthology of African American literature in 1996 and 2003, an essay in a mainstream cultural magazine in 2003, and an honorary lecture in 2002, all of which culminated in the 2003 book.

30. Eric Sundquist, *To Wake the Nations: Race in the Making of American Literature* (Cambridge, MA: Harvard University Press, 1993), 83–93, 635n. 84.

31. Cynthia A. Young benefits from this expansion in her own analysis of the 1960s and 1970s in *Soul Power: Culture, Radicalism, and the Making of a U.S. Third World Left* (Durham, NC: Duke University Press, 2006), 1–17.

32. Madhu Dubey, *Black Women Novelists and the Nationalist Aesthetic* (Bloomington: Indiana University Press, 1994), 13. Dubey elaborates this point about the threat of women to the Black Aesthetic and surveys previous scholarship that has examined the masculinity of the Black Arts Movement (1–13, 19).

33. William J. Maxwell, *New Negro, Old Left: African-American Writing and Communism between the Wars* (New York: Columbia University Press, 1999), 5.

34. Walter Johnson, "On Agency," *Journal of Social History* 37.1 (Fall 2003): 113–14, 120.

35. Stephen G. Hall, *A Faithful Account of the Race: African American Historical Writing in Nineteenth-Century America* (Chapel Hill: University of North Carolina Press, 2009), 188–226.

36. Johnson, "On Agency," 118.

37. Reed and Warren, introduction to *Renewing Black Intellectual History,* ix.

38. John Ernest, *Chaotic Justice: Rethinking African American Literary History* (Chapel Hill: University of North Carolina Press, 2009), 4–5.

39. David Kazanjian, *The Colonizing Trick: National Culture and Imperial Citizenship in Early America* (Minneapolis: University of Minnesota Press, 2003), 27.

40. Michael Millner, "Post Post-Identity," *American Quarterly* 57.2 (June 2005): 542. These phrases come from Millner's summation of the "post-identitarian" arguments of Walter Benn Michaels in *The Shape of the Signifier* and Kenneth W. Warren in *So Black and Blue.* My book diverges from these arguments in subtle ways.

41. Glaude, *In a Shade of Blue,* 1–2.

42. I am paraphrasing Clifford Geertz's original anthropological definition of culture as "an historically transmitted pattern of meaning embodied in symbols, a system of inherited conceptions expressed in symbolic forms by means of which men communicate, perpetuate, and develop their knowledge about and attitudes toward life." Geertz, *The Interpretation of Cultures* (New York: Harper Torchbooks, 1973), 89.

43. Suzanne Gearhart, "Psychoanalysis, Transnationalism, and Minority Cultures," in *Minor Transnationalism,* ed. Françoise Lionnet and Shu-Mei Shih (Durham, NC: Duke University Press, 2005), 27.

44. Frederick Douglass, "The Need for Continuing Anti-Slavery Work," in *The Life and Writings of Frederick Douglass,* vol. 4, ed. Philip S. Foner (New York: International, 1975), 169.

NOTES TO CHAPTER 1

1. Thomas Jefferson, *Notes on the State of Virginia* (1785; reprint, New York: Penguin, 1999), 147–48. Further citations to this work are to this edition and are given in the text.

2. Henry Louis Gates Jr., *The Trials of Phillis Wheatley* (New York: Basic Civitas Books, 2003), 51, 66. I refer to Gates's description of Wheatley's relationships to the "founding fathers," captured in his imagination of a scene in which Boston "gentlemen" cross-examine Wheatley to verify the authenticity of her poems, which she started publishing in 1767, at the age of fourteen and with little formal education, and which culminated in 1773 as *Poems on Various Subjects, Religious and Moral,* "the first book of poetry published by a person of African descent in the English language, marking the beginning of an African-American literary tradition" (Gates, *Trials,* 22). The book began to cement Wheatley as "the Toni Morrison of her time" (ibid., 31). Gates describes the luminous cast of Boston gentlemen in ibid., 7–15.

3. See Kenneth W. Warren, "Delimiting America: The Legacy of Du Bois," *American Literary History* 1.1 (Spring 1989): 172–89. In addition to Gates's *Figures in Black: Words, Signs, and the "Racial" Self* (Oxford: Oxford University Press, 1989), Warren reviews Bernard W. Bell's *The Afro-American Novel and Its Tradition* (Amherst: University of Massachusetts Press, 1987) and Melvin Dixon's *Ride Out the Wilderness: Geography and Identity in Afro-American Literature* (Urbana: University of Illinois Press, 1987). Note that Warren resuscitates part of his critique of Gates in *So Black and Blue: Ralph Ellison and the Occasion of Criticism* (Chicago: University of Chicago Press, 2003); see, in particular, 28–32, for the relevant section.

4. David Kazanjian, "'When They Come Here They Feal So Free': Race and Early American Studies," in "Historicizing Race in Early American Studies," *Early American Literature* 41.2 (2006): 331.

5. Frances Smith Foster, "A Narrative of the Interesting Origins and (Somewhat) Surprising Developments of African-American Print Culture," *American Literary History* 17.4 (2005): 714; hereafter abbreviated as "A Narrative."

6. Eric Slauter, *The State as a Work of Art: The Cultural Origins of the Constitution* (Chicago: University of Chicago Press, 2009), 178, 194; for the full history of this critical discourse on black imitation, see ibid., 174–95.

7. Stephen G. Hall, *A Faithful Account of the Race: African American Historical Writing in Nineteenth-Century America* (Chapel Hill: University of North Carolina Press, 2009), 17–48.

8. David Kazanjian, *The Colonizing Trick: National Culture and Imperial Citizenship in Early America* (Minneapolis: University of Minnesota Press, 2003), 9.

9. Henry Highland Garnet, preface to *Appeal in Four Articles: An Address to the Slaves of the United States of America,* by David Walker (New York: Cosimo Classics, 2005), iii. Further citations to this work are to this edition (which is an 1848 reprint of Walker's *Appeal*) and are given in the text. In *Appeal,* Walker anticipates the suppression of the book:

> I am fully aware, in making this appeal to my much afflicted and suffering brethren, that I shall not only be assailed by those whose greatest earthly desires are, to keep us in abject ignorance and wretchedness, and who are of the firm conviction that Heaven has designed us and our children to be slaves and *beasts of burden* to them and their children. I say, I do not only expect to be held up to the public as an ignorant, impudent and restless disturber of the public peace, by such avaricious creatures, as well as a mover of insubordination—and perhaps put in prison or to death, for giving a superficial exposition of our miseries, and exposing tyrants. But I am persuaded, that many of my brethren, particularly those who are ignorantly in league with slave-holders or tyrants, who acquire their daily bread by the blood and sweat of their more ignorant brethren—and not a few of those too, who are too ignorant to see an inch beyond their noses, will rise up and call me cursed—Yea, the jealous ones among us will perhaps use more abject subtlety, by affirming that this work is not worth perusing, that we are well situated, and there is no use in trying to better our condition, for we cannot. (12)

For historical evidence of this suppression, see Peter P. Hinks, *To Awaken My Afflicted Brethren: David Walker and the Problem of Antebellum Slave Resistance* (University Park: Pennsylvania State University Press, 1997), 138.

10. For thumbnail sketches of racial uplift and other black political ideologies beginning in the early and antebellum eras, see Richard Newman, Patrick Rael, and Philip Lapsansky, introduction to *Pamphlets of Protest: An Anthology of Early African-American Protest Literature, 1790–1860*, ed. Newman, Rael, and Lapsansky, 1–31 (New York: Routledge, 2001); also see Patrick Rael, *Black Identity and Black Protest in the Antebellum North* (Chapel Hill: University of North Carolina Press). For a continuation of these sketches in the postbellum era, see Kevin K. Gaines, *Uplifting the Race: Black Leadership, Politics, and Culture in the Twentieth Century* (Chapel Hill: University of North Carolina Press, 1996); and Michael C. Dawson, *Black Visions: The Roots of Contemporary African-American Political Ideologies* (Chicago: University of Chicago Press, 2002).

11. David Ramsey, quoted in John Shuffelton, introduction to *Notes on the State of Virginia*, by Thomas Jefferson (New York: Penguin, 1999), xxix.

12. Contrary to the roundtable's emphasis, the semantics of race in the conversation between Jefferson and Walker may not invite much disagreement. As mentioned earlier, in *Notes* Jefferson condemns the "race of Negroes brought from Africa" as inferior, while the Romans belong to "the race of whites," whose "*nature* . . . produced the[ir] distinction" (77, 149). In *Appeal*, David Walker cites these very lines as he refutes them.

13. Sandra M. Gustafson, introduction to "Historicizing Race in Early American Studies," *Early American Literature* 41.2 (2006): 310. In this roundtable, see Gustafson, introduction, 305–11; Joanna Brooks, "Working Definitions: Race, Ethnic Studies, and Early American Literature," 313–20; Philip Gould, "What We Mean When We Say 'Race,'" 321–27; David Kazanjian, "'When They Come Here They Feal So Free.'"

14. Brooks, "Working Definitions," 315; Gould, "What We Mean," 322–23. I subordinate Kazanjian in my discussion, for he does not grapple as much as Brooks and Gould do with the determinacy or indeterminacy of race. Rather, he takes a more abstract view of race's central role in nationalist expressions of citizenship, claiming that "U.S. citizenship came to embody a formal and abstract notion of equality that was deeply, indeed constitutively entangled with emergent, imperial conceptions of race and nation." More to the point, "equality was animated by and articulated with racial nationalism" (Kazanjian, "When They Come Here," 331–32).

15. Gould, "What We Mean," 325–26; Brooks, "Working Definitions," 319.

16. Gustafson warns, "If problems of 'fit' plague early American literary studies as they relate to the later periods vis-à-vis definitions of the literary, established critical narratives, and genealogies of race, an even more salient challenge has been that of relating theoretical models developed to address contemporary concerns (ethnic studies, postcolonialism, feminism, poststructuralism, and so forth) to a period that predated many of the concepts that organize these theoretical fields" (introduction to "Historicizing Race," 310).

17. Slauter, *The State as a Work of Art*, 9, 11.

18. For an example, see the promising dissertation by Alice M. Kracke, "Representing Themselves and Others: Black Poets as Lay-Lawyers in the Early Transatlantic" (Tufts University, 2009).

19. I borrow the definition from Newman, Rael, and Lapsansky, introduction to *Pamphlets of Protest*, 2.

20. Foster, "A Narrative," 715.

21. Gould, "What We Mean," 325; Brooks, "Working Definitions," 315.

22. For more information about this interracial antagonism, see Newman, Rael, and Lapsansky, introduction to *Pamphlets of Protest*, 4–7.

23. Jordan Alexander Stein, "'A Christian Nation Calls for Its Wandering Children': Life, Liberty, Liberia," *American Literary History* 19.4 (Winter 2007): 853.

24. John Ernest, "Liberation Historiography: African American Historians before the Civil War," *American Literary History* 14.3 (Fall 2002): 421.

25. Shuffelton, introduction to *Notes on the State of Virginia*, xiv.

26. Henry Louis Gates Jr. has written most extensively and influentially on this topic. See the following works by Gates: "Phillis Wheatley and the Nature of the Negro," in *Critical Essays on Phillis Wheatley*, ed. William H. Robinson (Boston: G. K. Hall, 1982), 215–33; *Figures in Black*; introduction to *The Norton Anthology of African American Literature* (New York: Norton, 1997, 2003); "Phillis Wheatley on Trial," *New Yorker* (January 30, 2003): 82–87; "Mr. Jefferson and the Trials of Phillis Wheatley," Jefferson Lecture in the Humanities (March 22, 2002), available online at http://www.neh.gov/whoweare/gates/lecture.html; and *Trials*, 57–65. A couple rigorous studies are John Ernest, *Liberation Historiography: African American Writers and the Challenge of History, 1794–1861* (Chapel Hill: University of North Carolina Press, 2004), 85–88; and Hinks, *To Awaken My Afflicted Brethren*, 178–221.

27. The exceptional studies of Walker include Hinks, *To Awaken My Afflicted Brethren*; Ian Finseth, "David Walker, Nature's Nation, and Early African-American Separatism," *Mississippi Quarterly: The Journal of Southern Cultures* 54.3 (Summer 2001): 337–62; and Robert S. Levine, "Circulating the Nation: David Walker, the Missouri Compromise and the Rise of the Black Press," in *The Black Press: New Literary and Historical Essays*, ed. Todd Vogel, 17–36 (New Brunswick, NJ: Rutgers University Press, 2001).

28. See Newman, Rael, and Lapsansky, introduction to *Pamphlets of Protest*, 10, 14.

29. See Hinks, *To Awaken My Afflicted Brethren*, 178–79, 201, 206–9, 221.

30. For more information about our need to recognize the transatlantic breadth of black identity in the late eighteenth and early nineteenth centuries, see Vincent Carretta and Philip Gould, introduction to *Genius in Bondage: Literature of the Early Black Atlantic*, ed. Carretta and Gould (Lexington: University Press of Kentucky, 2001). The results of this scholarly intervention explain a small but crucial issue of terminology in this chapter: "African American" makes little sense in early America, particularly before the amendments to the Constitution declared the entitlement of African descendants to citizenship in 1868. I use the term "black," and alternatively, to a lesser degree, such terms as "African descendants," "African-descended," or "African diaspora," where appropriate; while, in contrast, I use the term "African American" for the postbellum period. A couple more items regarding usage: although white and Native American slaves existed, my discussion of slavery concerns African descendants exclusively, a group that early American intellectuals deemed a race all its own. Such racial classification raises the issue of the continued impact of the "one-drop rule." Across the eighteenth and nineteenth centuries, the popular application of this metaphor—one drop of African blood makes one black—alleged racial purity, even though that purity had been as unquantifiable and provisional as it had been, ironically, the basis of empirical genealogy. Here, my strategic acknowledgment that "race" is a metaphorical construction does not totally exonerate me from sometimes subscribing to its essentialism. But, in this chapter, my initial enclosure of the word in quotation marks (particularly, in Jefferson's phrase, "the race of Negroes

brought from Africa") states my awareness of both its discursive traction as well as its continuing theoretical pitfalls.

31. Matthew Cordova Frankel, "'Nature's Nation' Revisited: Citizenship and the Sublime in Thomas Jefferson's *Notes on the State of Virginia*," *American Literature* 73.4 (December 2001): 698.

32. Ibid., 701–2.

33. For more information about Jefferson's focus on the "intellectual reconstruction of Virginia," see Jack P. Greene, "The Intellectual Reconstruction of Virginia in the Age of Jefferson," in *Jeffersonian Legacies*, ed. Peter S. Onuf, 225–53 (Charlottesville: University of Virginia Press, 1993).

34. Shuffelton, introduction to *Notes on the State of Virginia*, xxv.

35. In a footnote, Jefferson lambastes the deceptive eloquence of Buffon, who influenced the next two generations of naturalists, Jean Baptiste-Lamarck and Charles Darwin: "No writer, equally with M. de Buffon, proves the power of eloquence and uncertainty of theories. He takes any hypothesis whatever, or its reverse, and furnishes explanations equally specious and persuasive" (*Notes*, 308n. 11). Also see David Waldstreicher, introduction to *Notes on the State of Virginia by Thomas Jefferson, with Related Documents* (Boston: Bedford/St. Martin's, 2002), 31, for the premise of racial climatology for French naturalists.

36. "The Declaration of Independence," in *Foundations of Freedom* (Radford, VA: Wilder, 2007), 38.

37. For more information on these laws, see Shuffelton, ed., *Notes on the State of Virginia*, 319n. 172.

38. See Stein, "A Christian Nation," 851. Also see Kazanjian, *The Colonizing Trick*, 96–102, for evidence of Jefferson's particular influence over the African colonization movement.

39. Frankel, "'Nature's Nation' Revisited," 719.

40. Jefferson puts it bluntly in "Query XIV": "The improvement of the blacks in body and mind, in the first instance of their mixture with the whites, has been observed by every one, and proves that their inferiority is not the effect of their condition of life," as it is in the case of Native Americans (148).

41. Thomas Jefferson to Benjamin Banneker (August 31, 1791), in *Wheatley, Banneker, and Horton: With Selections from the Poetical Works of Wheatley and Horton, and the Letter of Washington to Wheatley, and of Jefferson to Banneker*, ed. William G. Allen (Boston: Press of Daniel Laing Jr., 1849), 35.

42. Jefferson to Coles, August 25, 1814, quoted in Andrew Burstein, *Sentimental Democracy: The Evolution of America's Romantic Self-Image* (New York: Hill and Wang, 1999), 244.

43. Bruce Dain, *A Hideous Monster of the Mind: American Race Theory in the Early Republic* (Cambridge, MA: Harvard University Press, 2002), 4.

44. For more information about the Afro-Protestant Press and the Afro-Protestant Church, see Foster, "A Narrative," 715–22.

45. For more information about the political uses of religion, see John Ernest, "Liberation Historiography: African American Historians before the Civil War," *American Literary History* 14.3 (Fall 2002): 415, 422; and Gary S. Selby, "Mocking the Sacred: Frederick Douglass's 'Slaveholder's Sermon' and the Antebellum Debate over Religion and Slavery," *Quarterly Journal of Speech* 88.4 (August 2002): 326, 327, 329.

46. Finseth, "David Walker," 353.

47. Willie J. Harrell Jr., "A Call to Consciousness and Action: Mapping the African-American Jeremiad," *Canadian Review of American Studies* 36.2 (2006): 151.

48. Ibid., 161.

49. See Stein, "A Christian Nation," 853–54.

50. Finseth, "David Walker," 339.

51. Ibid., 343.

52. Tunde Adeleke, "Violence as an Option for Free Blacks in Nineteenth-Century America," *Canadian Review of American Studies* 35.1 (2005): 89.

53. For Frederick Douglass's encounters with and understanding of John Brown, see Douglass, *The Life and Times of Frederick Douglass* (1892; reprint, Mineola, NY: Dover, 2003), 339–96.

54. Adeleke, "Violence as an Option," 93–95.

55. Hinks, *To Awaken My Afflicted Brethren*, 241.

56. David Kazanjian spends time in "Racial Governmentality: The African Colonization Movement," the second chapter of his award-winning book, *The Colonizing Trick*, examining the writings of Jefferson to answer these introductory questions: "[H]ow did 'fervent egalitarianism' 'lead directly' to colonization? How did colonization come 'to be regarded' as 'the logical outcome of manumission'? How, in effect, did colonization come to be valued 'directly,' 'logically,' and self-evidently emancipatory?" (95). My chapter does not refute but complements his fascinating study, which focuses on Jefferson's actual involvement in and inspiration of the emergence of colonization as an alternative to the emancipation of blacks on American soil. For complete coverage of this subject, see Kazanjian, *The Colonizing Trick*, 89–138.

NOTES TO CHAPTER 2

1. In *The Life and Writings of Frederick Douglass*, vol. 4, ed. Philip S. Foner (New York: International, 1975), 256. All further references to Douglass's writings come from this volume and appear parenthetically in the text, unless otherwise cited.

2. See Elizabeth McHenry's invaluable *Forgotten Readers: Recovering the Lost History of African American Literary Societies* (Durham, NC: Duke University Press, 2002) for an exceptional study of the literary and political stakes of African American literacy and reading communities in the nineteenth century.

3. Madhu Dubey, *Signs and Cities: Black Literary Postmodernism* (Chicago: University of Chicago Press, 2003), 84, 85.

4. Ibid., 55.

5. According to Dubey, although postmodern black intellectuals tend to resuscitate the very racial essentialism, black nationalism, and anti-Western universalism of the Black Arts and Black Studies Movements, these intellectuals consistently question print culture's social relevance in an advanced age of multimedia consumption. For more information, see ibid., 31–40. The next step of this argument would be to apply this postmodern skepticism to determining the very social relevance of print culture in African American political history, a topic that is taken up, albeit obliquely, in the introduction to a recent collection that includes an excerpt from Dubey's *Signs and Cities*: Adolph L. Reed and Kenneth W. Warren, eds., *Renewing Black Intellectual History: The Ideological and Material Foundations of African American Thought*, vii–xi (Boulder, CO: Paradigm, 2010).

6. Thomas Jefferson, *Notes on the State of Virginia* (1785; reprint, New York: Penguin, 1999), 68.

7. By "any level of government," I am referring to Jefferson's discussion of Wheatley and Sancho in the context of revising Virginia law, the initial topic of "Query XIV."

8. Steven Hahn, *A Nation under Our Feet: Black Political Struggles in the Rural South from Slavery to the Great Migration* (Cambridge, MA: Harvard University Press, 2003), 3.

9. "The U.S. Constitution," in *Foundations of Freedom* (Radford, VA: Wilder, 2007), 415, 416.

10. For a thorough study of the Reconstruction era, see Eric Foner, *Reconstruction: America's Unfinished Revolution, 1863–1877* (New York: Harper and Row, 1988).

11. See Caroline Gebhard and Barbara McCaskill, introduction to *Post-Bellum, Pre-Harlem: African American Literature and Culture, 1877–1919*, ed. McCaskill and Gebhard, 1–14 (New York: New York University Press, 2006).

12. Leon F. Litwack, *Trouble in Mind: Black Southerners in the Age of Jim Crow* (New York: Knopf, 1998), 53. He goes on to say that after emancipation,

> employers, landlords, and storekeepers, among others, seized every opportunity to exploit black illiteracy for personal gain. . . . To know how to read, write, and cipher, to calculate rates of interest, to command a knowledge of prices, to be familiar with the most fundamental methods of accounting—these skills were deemed increasingly essential if blacks were to carve out for themselves a larger degree of independence in the workplace, if they were to cast off the remaining vestiges of slavery that made them economically dependent on whites. (54)

13. Heather Andrea Williams, *Self-Taught: African American Education in Slavery and Freedom* (Chapel Hill: University of North Carolina Press, 2005), 7. The South Carolina statute is quoted in ibid., 207; the antiliteracy and regulatory statutes of the other states listed are reprinted in Williams's appendix, on 203–213.

14. Frederick Douglass, *Narrative of the Life of Frederick Douglass, an American Slave* (1845), in *Frederick Douglass: Autobiographies* (New York: Library of America, 1994), 37.

15. C. Vann Woodward, *The Strange Career of Jim Crow* (New York: Oxford University Press, 1955), 67. Also see Litwack, *Trouble in Mind*, 224–225, for information on these intellectual qualifications and their overall impact on the shape of the electorate.

16. David Walker, *Appeal in Four Articles: An Address to the Slaves of the United States of America* (New York: Cosimo Classics, 2005), 25.

17. Jefferson, *Notes on the State of Virginia,* 169.

18. William Wells Brown, *Clotel, or, The President's Daughter* (1853; reprint, New York: Penguin, 2003), 131. For a superb analysis of the importance of Benjamin Banneker's letter as the first response to Jefferson's precepts, see William L. Andrews, "Benjamin Banneker's Revision of Thomas Jefferson: Conscience versus Science in the Early American Antislavery Debate," in *Genius in Bondage: Literature of the Early Black Atlantic,* ed. Vincent Carretta and Philip Gould (Lexington: University Press of Kentucky, 2001), 218–41.

19. John Ernest, "Liberation Historiography: African American Historians before the Civil War," *American Literary History* 14.3 (Fall 2002): 421.

20. In *The Works of James McCune Smith: Black Intellectual and Abolitionist,* ed. John Stauffer, 264–90 (Oxford: Oxford University Press, 2006).

21. For Douglass's discussion of state versus federal constitutions, see "The Need for Continuing Anti-slavery Work," 167, and "Reconstruction," 199.

22. For "ballot," see Douglass, "The Need for Continuing Anti-Slavery Work," 167; for "elective franchise," see "Reconstruction," 200; for men's, as opposed to women's, "suffrage," see "Letter to Josephine Sophie White Griffing" (1868), 212–13; for the right to bear arms, see "The Need for Continuing Anti-slavery Work," 168, and "Letter to Major Delany" (1871), 278; for desegregation, see "Letter to W. J. Wilson" (1865), 172–73.

23. Douglass privileged the struggle of black men over the struggle of white women for elective franchise. The black men's endurance of slavery, in his eyes, entitled them to vote more than white women, who already possessed indirect elective representation through their fathers, brothers, and husbands. See "Letter to Josephine Sophie White Griffing," 212–13.

24. For a discussion of racial uplift, see chapter 2 of Gene Andrew Jarrett, *Deans and Truants: Race and Realism in African American Literature* (Philadelphia: University of Pennsylvania Press, 2006), 54–59.

25. For Douglass on the lack of law enforcement against whites, see "Reconstruction," 203; for his approach to the labor question, including class inequity and the labor movements of the time, see "The Labor Question" (1871), 282.

26. Deak Nabers, *The Victory of Law: The Fourteenth Amendment, the Civil War, and American Literature, 1852–1867* (Baltimore: Johns Hopkins University Press, 2006), 7.

27. Michael C. Dawson, *Black Visions: The Roots of Contemporary African-American Political Ideologies* (Chicago: University of Chicago Press, 2002), 10.

28. Ibid. For discussion of the variety of grassroots mobilization in meetings, see Hahn, *A Nation*, 2, 174, 328; for the conventions, see ibid., 199, 262.

29. On the importance of written communication and the prevalence of literacy in black communities, see Hahn, *A Nation*, 3, and McHenry, *Forgotten Readers*, 5.

30. For Douglass's experiences with the black press, see the essay "A Year with the *Era*" (1871), 254–76, and the interview, "The Negro Press" (1891), 468–69. Excellent essays demonstrating Douglass's critical tendencies include his pieces "The Southern Convention" (1871), 251–52, and "The Macon *Union*" (1871), both of which target the *Union* editorship; and "*The Evening Star* on Social Equality," 300–301.

31. See Eric Sundquist, *To Wake the Nations: Race in the Making of American Literature* (Cambridge, MA: Harvard University Press, 1993), 83–112.

32. Dawson, *Black Visions*, 15.

33. The most well-known example of such scholarship is Henry Louis Gates Jr., *Figures in Black: Words, Signs, and the Racial Self* (Oxford: Oxford University Press, 1989). Gates has argued that "the Afro-American literary tradition was generated as a response to eighteenth- and nineteenth-century allegations that persons of African descent did not, and could not, create literature" (25).

34. McHenry, *Forgotten Readers*, 151.

35. Douglass, "The Race Problem" (1890), Library of Congress, "American Memory," http://memory.loc.gov/cgibin/query/r?ammem/murray:@field(DOCID+@lit(lcrbmrptoc13div1)), 3. Further citations to this work are to this version and are given in the text.

36. W. E. B. Du Bois, *The Souls of Black Folk* (1903), in Du Bois, *Writings* (New York: Library of America, 1996), 363.

37. For the discussion of "kinship, labor, and circuits of communication and education," see Hahn, *A Nation*, 7; for the policy of emigrationism, see Douglass, "The

United States Cannot Remain Half-Slave and Half-Free," 320, 361; for the right of blacks to bear arms, see "Douglass, "The Need for Continuing Anti-slavery Work," 168. While Douglass acknowledged the social importance of the black church, he was quite critical of theological hypocrisy.

38. For the ideological "gulf" between Douglass and Booker T. Washington, see Philip S. Foner, "Frederick Douglass," in *The Life and Writings of Frederick Douglass,* 4:149–50.

39. Dawson, *Black Visions,* 8, 25, 26.

40. Douglass, *The Life and Times of Frederick Douglass* (1892; reprint, Mineola, NY: Dover, 2003), 290. Further citations to this work are to this edition and are given in the text.

41. W. E. B. Du Bois, *Black Reconstruction: An Essay toward a History of the Part Which Black Folk Played in the Attempt to Reconstruct Democracy in America, 1860–1880* (1934; reprint, Notre Dame, IN: University of Notre Dame Press, 2001).

42. For a closer look at the paradox of Douglass's representation of the race, see Kenneth W. Warren, "Frederick Douglass's *Life and Times*: Progressive Rhetoric and the Problem of Constituency," in *Frederick Douglass: New Literary and Historical Essays,* ed. Eric J. Sundquist, 253–70 (New York: Cambridge University Press, 1990).

43. Philip Dray, *Capitol Men: The Epic Story of Reconstruction through the Lives of the First Black Congressmen* (Boston: Houghton Mifflin, 2008), 353–54.

44. The final edition of *Life and Times* in 1892 incorporates revised versions of *Narrative of the Life* and *My Bondage and My Freedom* in its first part (chapters 1 to 21) and in the opening of its second part (chapters 1 through 6). However, *Life and Times* also goes well beyond 1855, covering the wartime and postwar periods of Douglass's life, up until his appointment as minister-resident and general consul to the Haitian government from 1889 to 1891.

45. See John Stauffer, *Giants: The Parallel Lives of Frederick Douglass and Abraham Lincoln* (New York: Grand Central, 2008).

46. See Herbert J. Storing, "Frederick Douglass," in *American Political Thought: The Philosophic Dimension of American Statesmanship,* ed. Morton J. Frisch and Richard G. Stevens (New York: Scribner, 1971), 145–66.

NOTES TO CHAPTER 3

1. For further discussion of the Old Negro iconography and the counteractive emergence of racial-uplift discourse, see Gene Andrew Jarrett, "'Entirely Black Verse from Him Who Would Succeed': Minstrel Realism and William Dean Howells," *Nineteenth-Century Literature* 59.4 (March 2005): 494–535; and idem, "'We Must Write Like the White Men': Race, Realism, and Dunbar's Anomalous First Novel," *Novel: A Forum on Fiction* 37.3 (Summer 2004): 303–25.

2. Available online at the Ohio Historical Society website, "The African-American Experience in Ohio, 1850–1920," http://dbs.ohiohistory.org/africanam/page.cfm?ID=13906; capitalization in the original, italics mine.

3. Since the publication of Henry Louis Gates Jr.'s landmark "The Trope of a New Negro and the Reconstruction of the Image of the Black" (*Representations* 24 [Fall 1988]: 129–55), the most notable examples of scholarship specifically about the New Negro include Wilson Moses, *The Golden Age of Black Nationalism, 1850–1925* (New York: Oxford

University Press, 1988); George Hutchinson, *The Harlem Renaissance in Black and White* (Cambridge, MA: Belknap Press of Harvard University Press, 1995); Jon Michael Spencer, *The New Negroes and Their Music: The Success of the Harlem Renaissance* (Knoxville: University of Tennessee Press, 1997); J. Martin Favor, *Authentic Blackness: The Folk in the New Negro Renaissance* (Durham, NC: Duke University Press, 1999); William J. Maxwell, *New Negro, Old Left: African-American Writing and Communism between the Wars* (New York: Columbia University Press, 1999); and Rebecca Carroll, ed., *Uncle Tom or New Negro? African Americans Reflect on Booker T. Washington and Up from Slavery 100 Years Later* (New York: Broadway Books, 2006).

4. Eric Slauter, *The State as a Work of Art: The Cultural Origins of the Constitution* (Chicago: University of Chicago Press, 2009), 129–30.

5. Caroline Gebhard and Barbara McCaskill rightly assert that blacks' "high aesthetic experimentation and political dynamism" bolstered "the vocal press and spiritual institutions they had organized during slavery," erected "new educational institutions," and forged "networks of political and social leadership to resist both the illegal and legal violence aimed at keeping them from full and equal participation in the nation's life." Caroline Gebhard and Barbara McCaskill, introduction to *Post-Bellum, Pre-Harlem: African American Literature and Culture, 1877–1919*, ed. McCaskill and Gebhard, 1–14 (New York: New York University Press, 2006), 2.

6. See Gene Andrew Jarrett, *Deans and Truants: Race and Realism in African American Literature* (Philadelphia: University of Pennsylvania Press, 2006), 14–17.

7. Michele (Birnbaum) Elam, "Towards Desegregating Syllabuses: Teaching American Literary Realism and Racial Uplift Fiction," in *Teaching Literature: A Companion*, ed. Tanya Agathocleous and Ann C. Dean, 58–70 (New York: Palgrave, 2003), 59. A perfect example of the kind of analysis Birnbaum calls for occurs in her "Racial Hysteria: Female Pathology and Race Politics in Frances Harper's *Iola Leroy* and W. D. Howells's *An Imperative Duty*," *African American Review* 33.1 (1999): 7–23.

8. "The poet *in every reader* does not experience the same disjunction from what he reads that the critic in every reader necessarily feels. What gives pleasure to the critic in a reader may give anxiety to the poet in him, an anxiety we have learned, as readers, to neglect, to our own loss and peril. This anxiety, this mode of melancholy, is the anxiety of influence, the dark and daemonic ground upon which we now enter." Harold Bloom, *The Anxiety of Influence* (New York: Oxford University Press, 1973), 25.

9. Hannah Arendt, *The Human Condition* (1958; reprint, Chicago: University of Chicago Press, 1998), 26.

10. Virginia Sapiro, "Seeking Knowledge and Information as Political Action: A U.S. Historical Case Study," longer version of a paper delivered at the Meeting of the European Consortium for Political Research, Turin, March 2002, 2. I thank Sapiro for sharing with me this work-in-progress.

11. Marc Howard Ross, "Culture and Identity in Comparative Political Analysis," in *Culture and Politics: A Reader*, ed. Lane Crothers and Charles Lockhart (New York: St. Martin's, 2000), 48.

12. Anna Julia Cooper, "One Phase of American Literature," in *A Voice from the South*, 175–227 (Xenia, Ohio: Aldine, 1892), 223.

13. Kevin Gaines, *Uplifting the Race: Black Leadership, Politics, and Culture in the Twentieth Century* (Chapel Hill: University of North Carolina Press, 1996), xiv.

14. Du Bois argued that the most intelligent tenth of the African American population should be the leaders. See W. E. B. Du Bois, *The Souls of Black Folk* (1903; reprint, New York: Penguin, 1989), 87.

15. Marlon Ross, *Manning the Race: Reforming Black Men in the Jim Crow Era* (New York: New York University Press, 2004), 16. Race tracts and albums that Ross considers include, respectively, William Pickens's *The New Negro* (1916) and Booker T. Washington (et al.)'s *A New Negro for a New Century* (1900); personalized narratives include Pickens's *Bursting Bonds* (1923) and Walter White's *The Fire in the Flint* (1924); and sociological studies include C. Johnson's *The Negro in Chicago* (1922).

16. For the best information about the writings of Du Bois and Washington in the context of their concerns with literary aesthetics and racial uplift, see Arnold Rampersad, *The Art and Imagination of W. E. B. Du Bois* (Cambridge, MA: Harvard University Press, 1976), and Donald B. Gibson, "Strategies and Revisions of Self Representation in Booker T. Washington's Autobiography," *American Quarterly* 45.3 (September 1993): 370–93.

17. Frederick Douglass, *Life and Times of Frederick Douglass* (1893), in *Frederick Douglass: Autobiographies* (New York: Library of America, 1994), 715–33.

18. For a traditional comparative reading of Du Bois's and Washington's divergent political philosophies through these texts, see Henry Louis Gates Jr. and Terri Hume Oliver, preface to *The Souls of Black Folk: Authoritative Text, Contexts, Criticism,* ed. Gates and Oliver, ix–xli (New York: Norton, 1999). For a brilliant critique of the Washington–Du Bois philosophical polarity, see chapter 8 of Adolph L. Reed Jr., *W. E. B. Du Bois and American Political Thought: Fabianism and the Color Line* (New York: Oxford University Press, 1997).

19. W. E. B. Du Bois, "Opinion by W. E. B. Du Bois," *Crisis* 18.1 (May 1919): 12, 14; italics in the original. People at the time referred to this essay as "Returning Soldiers," since Du Bois wrote it upon his return to the United States in 1919 from a summit in Paris. For example, see Claude McKay, *A Long Way from Home* (New York: Harcourt, 1970), 110.

20. Hubert H. Harrison, "The New Politics," in *When Africa Awakes: The "Inside Story" of the Stirrings and Strivings of the New Negro in the Western World,* 39–53 (New York: Porro, 1920), 40; italics in the original.

21. Ibid., 43.

22. Gustavus Adolphus Stewart, "The New Negro Hokum," *Social Forces* 6 (March 1928): 441.

23. George S. Schuyler, "The Negro-Art Hokum," *Nation* (June 16, 1926): 662–63. Schuyler argues that since Negroes are not peculiarly racial, they do not produce peculiarly racial art. "Negro art," or what Schuyler calls art whose creators are identified as "Negro," bears the cultural imprint of the nation, a pattern discernible in art created by Anglo-Americans, generally called "American art." The idea of considering Negro art "true"—or an authentic, singular tradition—is a hokum.

24. Barbara Foley, *Spectres of 1919: Class and Nation in the Making of the New Negro* (Urbana: University of Illinois Press, 2003), 5.

25. Gates, "The Trope of a New Negro," 147.

26. Foley, *Spectres of 1919,* 31–32.

27. For more information about Locke's earlier writings, see ibid., 205–17; for the subtext of his editing of *The New Negro,* see ibid., 224–44. My sentence in the text plays

on Locke's line in "'The New Negro," the introductory essay in *The New Negro*, that "the mainspring of Negro life" is "radical in tone, but not in purpose." Alain Locke, "The New Negro," in *The New Negro*, ed. Locke, 3–16 (1925; reprint, New York: Simon and Schuster, 1997), 1.

28. According to Barbara Foley, Locke's version of the New Negro coincided with the fact that "the production of literature inflected with revolutionary politics had slowed to a near-trickle by the last half of the decade" (*Spectres of 1919*, 76).

29. Jarrett, *Deans and Truants*, 34–38.

30. W. E. B. Du Bois, "The Younger Literary Movement," *Crisis* 28 (February 1924): 161–63.

31. Alain Locke, "Art or Propaganda?" *Harlem* 1 (November 1928): 12.

32. Alain Locke, "Propaganda—or Poetry?" *Race* 1 (Summer 1936): 70–76, 87.

33. Eric Walrond, "Art and Propaganda," *Negro World* (December 31, 1921): 4; Willis Richardson, "Propaganda in the Theatre," *Messenger* 6.11 (November 1924): 353–54.

34. Some of the best critical and bibliographic scholarship addressing this issue includes Abby Arthur Johnson and Ronald Maberry Johnson, *Propaganda and Aesthetics: The Literary Politics of Afro-American Magazines in the Twentieth Century* (Amherst: University of Massachusetts Press, 1979); Carolyn Fowler, *Black Arts and Black Aesthetics: A Bibliography* (Atlanta: First World, 1981); Lynn Moody Igoe, "Aesthetics," in *250 Years of Afro-American Art: An Annotated Bibliography*, ed. Igoe, 233–39 (New York: Bowker, 1981).

35. Amy L. Blair, "Rewriting Heroines: Ruth Todd's 'Florence Grey,' Society Pages, and the Rhetorics of Success," *Studies in American Fiction* 30.1 (2002): 105. I am applying this paradigm, overcoming the historical "absence of 'race' as a concern in this success literature," the "presumed whiteness of the reading manuals' and mass market magazines' target audience," and "the problems racial categories posed for the [Anglo] U.S. culture of success" (105).

36. Johnson and Johnson, *Propaganda and Aesthetics*, v.

37. Pauline Hopkins, "Editorial and Publishers' Announcements," *Colored American Magazine* 5 (May 1902): 76.

38. Sigrid Anderson Cordell, "'The Case Was Very Black Against' Her: Pauline Hopkins and the Politics of Racial Ambiguity at the *Colored American Magazine*," *American Periodicals: A Journal of History, Criticism, and Bibliography* 16.1 (2006): 56.

39. Amy L. Blair, "Misreading the House of Mirth," *American Literature: A Journal of Literary History, Criticism, and Bibliography* 76.1 (2004): 150, 151.

40. William Braithwaite, "Book Reviews," *Colored American Magazine* 4 (November 1901): 73.

41. For many black intellectuals, African American literature written in dialect, such as the writings of Paul Laurence Dunbar, bore the linguistic stigma of minstrelsy. For example, an article in *A.M.E. Church Review* worried that, in the wake of William Howells's 1896 review of Dunbar's *Majors and Minors*, "titillated" editors, "with the commercial side well developed[,] will besiege [Dunbar] for a copy in a 'minor' [or allegedly black-dialect] view." H. T. Kealing, review of *Majors and Minors*, *A.M.E. Church Review* 13 (October 1896): 256.

42. Pauline E. Hopkins, *Contending Forces: A Romance Illustrative of Negro Life North and South* (1900; reprint, New York: AMS, 1971), 13–14; italics in the original. Further citations to this work are to this edition and are given in the text.

43. The sentimentalism of Hopkins's work corresponded to the generic trait of antebellum domestic novels and cheap magazine literature that "still dripped with the didactic sentiment that had been established, principally by lady poets and novelists, before the war." Scully Bradley, "The Emergence of Modern American Literature," in *The American Tradition in Literature*, 3–13 (New York: Grosset and Dunlap, 1974), 6.

44. Hazel V. Carby, introduction to *The Magazine Novels of Pauline Hopkins*, ed. Carby, xxix–xlix (New York: Oxford University Press, 1988), xxxiv–xxxv.

45. See Steven Hahn, *A Nation under Our Feet: Black Political Struggles in the Rural South from Slavery to the Great Migration* (Cambridge, MA: Harvard University Press, 2003), 325–26.

46. In Paul Laurence Dunbar, *Majors and Minors* (Toledo, Ohio: Hadley and Hadley, 1896), "Frederick Douglass," "Ode to Ethiopia," and "The Colored Soldiers" are a few of his earliest and most famous racial-uplift poems. Dunbar's collected stories include *Folks from Dixie* (1898), *The Strength of Gideon and Other Stories* (1900), *In Old Plantation Days* (1903), and *The Heart of Happy Hollow* (1904). Dunbar also wrote stories that did not appear in these collections and that were published either in periodicals or went unpublished. See Gene Andrew Jarrett and Thomas Lewis Morgan, introduction to *The Complete Stories of Paul Laurence Dunbar*, ed. Jarrett and Morgan, xv–xlv (Athens: Ohio University Press, 2005). In total, Dunbar's political short stories include "The Trial Sermons on Bull-Skin," "Aunt Mandy's Investment," and "At Shaft 11," in *Folks from Dixie*; "The Ingrate," "One Man's Fortunes," "Mr. Cornelius Johnson, Office-Seeker," "A Mess of Pottage," "The Finding of Zach," and "A Council of State," in *The Strength of Gideon and Other Stories*; "A Judgment of Paris," in *In Old Plantation Days*; and "The Scapegoat," "One Christmas at Shiloh," "The Mission of Mr. Scatters," and "Cahoots," in *The Heart of Happy Hollow*. See Dunbar's essays "England as Seen by a Black Man," *Independent* 48 (September 16, 1897); "Recession Never," *Toledo (Ohio) Journal* (December 18, 1898); and "The Negroes of the Tenderloin," *Columbus (Ohio) Dispatch* (December 19, 1898).

47. Gaines, *Uplifting the Race*, xv.

48. For more information, see Julie Cary Nerad, "Slippery Language and False Dilemmas: The Passing Novels of Child, Howells, and Harper," *American Literature: A Journal of Literary History, Criticism, and Bibliography* 75.4 (2003): 813–41.

49. Frances Ellen Watkins Harper, *Iola Leroy, or Shadows Uplifted* (1899; reprint, Boston: Beacon, 1987), 246.

50. Ibid., 251–52.

51. See Hazel Carby, introduction to Harper, *Iola Leroy*, xvi. For the chapters "Open Questions" and "Friends in Council," Harper interspersed sections from the articles "Colored Women of America" (1878) and "Duty to Dependent Races" (1891) and from "Women's Political Future," the address to the 1893 World's Congress of Representative Men.

52. Sutton Elbert Griggs, *Imperium in Imperio* (1899; reprint, Miami: Mnemosyne, 1969), 203.

53. Louis Harlan, introduction to *Up from Slavery*, by Booker T. Washington, vii–xlviii (New York: Penguin, 1986), xx, xli. Noteworthy is that the biblical qualities conveyed in Washington's prose justify its link, at least on this rhetorical ground, with Du Bois's *The Souls of Black Folk*.

54. Arlene A. Elder, "Griggs, Sutton E.," in *The Oxford Companion to African American Literature*, ed. William L. Andrews, Frances Smith Foster, and Trudier Harris, 328–29 (New York: Oxford University Press, 1997), 328.

55. Stephen Knadler, "Sensationalizing Patriotism: Sutton Griggs and the Sentimental Nationalism of Citizen Tom," *American Literature* 79.4 (December 2007): 676, 688. The plantation tradition of Anglo-American literature includes, most notably, the postbellum fiction of Joel Chandler Harris and George Washington Cable, whose many portrayals of African Americans were not unlike those of Harriet Beecher Stowe's Uncle Tom.

56. Booker T. Washington, *Up from Slavery* (1901; reprint, New York: Penguin, 1986), 220–22.

57. Booker T. Washington, *The Future of the American Negro* (Boston: Small, Maynard, 1902), 129–31.

58. Knadler, "Sensationalizing Patriotism," 677.

59. Washington, *The Future of the American Negro*, 131–32. In *Up from Slavery*, Washington disparages, by associating them, the intellectual and political byproducts of Reconstruction: "During the whole of the Reconstruction period two ideas were constantly agitating the minds of the coloured people, or, at least, the minds of a large part of the race. One of these was the craze for Greek and Latin learning, and the other was a desire to hold office" (80).

60. Cathryn Bailey, "Anna Julia Cooper: 'Dedicated in the Name of My Slave Mother to the Education of Colored Working People,'" *Hypatia: A Journal of Feminist Philosophy* 19.2 (2004): 57.

61. Sean McCann, "'Bonds of Brotherhood': Pauline Hopkins and the Work of Melodrama," *English Literary History* 64.3 (Fall 1997): 791–92.

62. For more information about Chesnutt's travel to the Wilmington site and his response, see Bryan Wagner, "Charles Chesnutt and the Epistemology of Racial Violence," *American Literature: A Journal of Literary History, Criticism, and Bibliography* (2001): 311–37; and Jae H. Roe, "Keeping an 'Old Wound' Alive: *The Marrow of Tradition* and the Legacy of Wilmington," *African American Review* 33.2 (1999): 231–43.

63. Ryan Jay Friedman, "'Between Absorption and Extinction': Charles Chesnutt and Biopolitical Racism," *Arizona Quarterly* 63.4 (Winter 2007): 52–53. Note that Friedman conducts a comparative reading of *The Marrow of Tradition* and Chesnutt's 1900 essay "The Future American" to detail this assumption.

64. Charles W. Chesnutt, *The Marrow of Tradition* (1901), in *Charles W. Chesnutt: Stories, Novels and Essays,* ed. Werner Sollors, 463–718 (New York: Library of America, 2002), 489.

65. Wagner, "Charles Chesnutt and the Epistemology of Racial Violence," 213.

66. Werner Sollors, *Neither Black nor White yet Both: Thematic Explorations of Interracial Literature* (New York: Oxford University Press, 1997), 247–48.

67. On the other hand, as Werner Sollors and Julie Cary Nerad note, there have been occasions when blacks did not intend to pass; they inadvertently passed in situations in which people had mistaken them for whites, or they involuntarily passed because, for example, they were too young to understand the complex issue of racial identity. See ibid., 250. Also see Nerad, "Slippery Language and False Dilemmas."

68. Kenneth Warren, "As White as Anybody: Race and the Politics of Counting as Black," *New Literary History* 31.4 (Autumn 2000): 712.

69. Michael Borgstrom, "Face Value: Ambivalent Citizenship in *Iola Leroy*," *African American Review* 40.4 (2006): 781.

70. Arendt, *The Human Condition*, 23.

71. James Weldon Johnson, *The Autobiography of an Ex-Coloured Man* (1912; reprint, New York: Vintage, 1989), 158.

72. Ibid., 168.

73. Ibid., 211.

74. Margaret Nash, "'Patient Persistence': The Political and Educational Values of Anna Julia Cooper and Mary Church Terrell," *Educational Studies: A Journal of the American Educational Studies Association* 35.2 (2004): 133.

75. On partisanship during the Harlem Renaissance, see David L. Lewis, *When Harlem Was in Vogue* (New York: Oxford University Press, 1989), 47–48; for discussion of Charles S. Johnson's "The Social Philosophy of Booker T. Washington," *Opportunity* 6 (1928): 105, see Hutchinson, *The Harlem Renaissance in Black and White*, 179.

76. Reed, *W. E. B. Du Bois and American Political Thought*, 62–63.

77. For more information about Hopkins's dismissal from *Colored American Magazine*, see Cordell, "'The Case Was Very Black Against' Her," 57–61.

78. Nella Larsen, *Quicksand and Passing* (1928; reprint, New Brunswick, NJ: Rutgers University Press, 1986), 1.

79. Ibid., 4.

80. Ibid., 5.

81. For more information about the sexuality and power dynamics of patronage, see chapter 5 of Ross, *Manning the Race*.

82. Jessie Redmon Fauset, *There Is Confusion* (1924; reprint, Boston: Northeastern University Press, 1989). Further citations to this work are to this edition and are given in the text. *Birthright* is the story of a light-skinned, mixed-race, Harvard-educated young man, Peter Siner, who returns to the town of his birth, Niggertown, Tennessee. He is disgusted by the unrefined, backward, and "queer" ineptitude of African American society and culture. His defiant racial–political spirit wanes against the incessant microaggressions of skeptical white bigots, public threats from the Ku Klux Klan, and the duress and jealousies of an African American community at once captivated and resentful of his higher learning. Siner overcomes his misfortunes in Niggertown by repudiating his black blood. He marries a troubled childhood girlfriend, an octoroon who has been impregnated by a local white rapist, and flees with her to Cairo, Illinois. After reading Stribling's novel about Niggertown, Fauset lamented, "Nella Larsen and Walter White were affected just as I was. We could do it better." She went on to say, "Here is an audience wanting to hear the truth about us. Let us who are better qualified to present that truth than any white writer, try to do so." Fauset, quoted in Thadious Davis, foreword to Fauset, *There Is Confusion*, xxii.

83. Rudolph Fisher, *The Walls of Jericho* (1928; reprint, Ann Arbor: University of Michigan Press, 1994), 73. Further citations to this work are to this edition and are given in the text. Other Harlem Renaissance, African American novels that include such major club scenes are Claude McKay's *Home to Harlem* (1928) and Wallace Thurman's *The Blacker the Berry* (1929).

84. Phillip Brian Harper, "Passing for What? Racial Masquerade and the Demands of Upward Mobility," *Callaloo: A Journal of African-American and African Arts and Letters* 21.2 (1998): 395.

1. Claude McKay, *A Long Way from Home,* ed. Gene Andrew Jarrett (1937; reprint, New Brunswick, NJ: Rutgers University Press, 2007), 247. Further citations to this work are to this edition and are given in the text.

2. Langston Hughes to Claude McKay, July 25, 1925, and March 5, 1928, quoted in Wayne F. Cooper, *Claude McKay: Rebel Sojourner in the Harlem Renaissance* (Baton Rouge: Louisiana State University Press, 1987), 243.

3. Langston Hughes, *I Wonder as I Wander* (New York: Hill and Wang, 1993). The most notable essays are "The Negro Art and Claude McKay" (1931), "Claude McKay: The Best" (circa 1933), and "Negroes in Moscow: In a Land Where There Is No Jim Crow" (1933), which are explained and reprinted in *The Collected Works of Langston Hughes,* vol. 9, *Essays on Art, Race, Politics, and World Affairs,* ed. Christopher C. De Santis (Columbia: University of Missouri Press, 2002), 46, 53–56, and 65–71, respectively. Note that in his 1940 autobiography, *The Big Sea,* which covers his life from birth in 1902 to circa 1931, Hughes sounds very much like McKay when he remarks that the black critics and intellectuals of the Harlem Renaissance "were always about the educated Negro—but my poems, or Claude McKay's *Home to Harlem* they did not like." Langston Hughes, *The Big Sea: An Autobiography* (New York: Hill and Wang, 1993), 267. In *The Big Sea,* Hughes refers to McKay on 165, 190, 228, and 242; in *I Wonder as I Wander,* on 86, 262, and 313.

4. Michelle Ann Stephens, *Black Empire: The Masculine Global Imaginary of Caribbean Intellectuals in the United States, 1914–1962* (Durham, NC: Duke University Press, 2005), 131.

5. For the historical prevalence of black international writing, see Wendy W. Walters, *At Home in Diaspora: Black International Writing* (Minneapolis: University of Minnesota Press, 2005). But it should be noted that Walters focuses on Chester Himes, Michelle Cliff, Caryl Phillips, Simon Njami, and Richard Wright, while writing comparatively little about Claude McKay.

6. McKay stressed his disaffiliation from the Communist Party more than once: "I was not a member of the Communist Party"; "Not being a party member, I was unaware of what was going on inside the organization" (*A Long Way from Home,* 121, 126). McKay made those statements in the context of a "dominant urge" to examine objectively the social, political, class, and racial implications of communist radicalism during his tour of Russia.

7. I borrow the term "rebel sojourner" from the subtitle of Cooper's still-definitive biography of McKay, *Claude McKay: Rebel Sojourner in the Harlem Renaissance.*

8. Langston Hughes, "The Negro Artist and the Racial Mountain," *Nation* (June 23, 1926): 692–94.

9. These books include Frederick Douglass, *Narrative of the Life of Frederick Douglass* (1881); Booker T. Washington, *Up from Slavery* (1901); William Pickens, *The Heir of Slaves* (1911) and *Bursting Bonds* (1923); Zora Neale Hurston, *Dust Tracks on a Road* (1942); and Richard Wright, *Black Boy* (1945).

10. This genre muses on the racial politics of the United States versus, say, those of Europe in William Wells Brown, *Three Years in Europe* (1852) and Frederick Douglass, *The Life and Times of Frederick Douglass* (1881); those of Africa and Spain in Richard Wright, *Black Power* (1954) and *Pagan Spain* (1957); those of the Caribbean in Audre Lorde, *Zami* (1982); and those of Cuba in Assata Shakur, *Assata* (1987).

11. Although a literary critic would usually talk about the narrative of *A Long Way from Home* in the present tense of literary criticism, I talk about it instead in the past tense. Here and there I use historical markers to synchronize the autobiographical temporality with the biographical and historical chronologies for the benefit of readers, even though in certain places there are discrepancies between McKay's autobiographical rendition of his life and biographical and historical facts.

12. For a discussion of the discrepancies in McKay's works, see Kate A. Baldwin, *Beyond the Color Line and the Iron Curtain: Reading Encounters between Black and Red, 1922–1963* (Durham, NC: Duke University Press, 2002), 29; and for those in Hughes's works, see ibid., 86–87.

13. I thank William J. Maxwell for this suggestion.

14. In 2007, I attempted to recover *A Long Way from Home* by publishing it in Rutgers University Press's "Multi-ethnic Literatures of the Americas" series, which aims to reintroduce literature that has been unavailable for a long time. *A Long Way from Home* has been stuck between in-print and out-of-print status. The book was reprinted only twice, in 1969 by Arno and in 1970 by Harcourt Brace and World. Since then, the Arno edition has fallen out of print, and Harcourt Brace has sold off its copies and shifted responsibility for publishing the book to Ingram/Lightning Print, which specializes in print-on-demand. What made, and continues to make, such reprints possible was the failure of the original copyright claimant of *A Long Way from Home* to renew the book's copyright in 1965 and, in so doing, to delay its irrevocable transmission to the public domain. While this reprint works to sustain the autobiography's commercial accessibility, this chapter seeks to reaffirm its intellectual value in current literary and cultural studies.

15. See the ever useful and representative works: Arnold Rampersad, *The Life of Langston Hughes,* 2 vols. (New York: Oxford University Press, 1986–1988); Langston Hughes, *The Collected Works of Langston Hughes,* vols. 9 and 10, ed. Christopher C. De Santis (Columbia: University of Missouri Press, 2001–2002); David Chioni Moore, "Colored Dispatches from the Uzbek Border," *Callaloo* 25.4 (2002): 1115–35; idem, "Local Color, Global 'Color': Langston Hughes, the Black Atlantic, and Soviet Central Asia, 1932," *Research in African Literatures* 27.4 (1996): 49–70; Baldwin, *Beyond the Color Line and the Iron Curtain.*

16. For *Appeal to Reason,* see Hughes, *The Big Sea,* 22; and for the *Socialist Call* and the *Liberator* and the lack of Americanism among students, see ibid., 31.

17. See Arnold Rampersad, *The Life of Langston Hughes,* vol. 1, *1902–1941* (New York: Oxford University Press, 1986), 29-30.

18. For general information on the U.S. radical, left-wing organizations from World War I through the Cold War—information that I have necessarily restricted to the backdrop of my stories about McKay and Hughes—see Anthony Dawahare, *Nationalism, Marxism, and African American Literature between the Wars: A New Pandora's Box* (Jackson: University Press of Mississippi, 2003); William J. Maxwell, *New Negro, Old Left: African-American Writing and Communism between the Wars* (New York: Columbia University Press, 1999); James E. Smethurst, *The New Red Negro: The Literary Left and African American Poetry, 1930–1946* (New York: Oxford University Press, 1999); Alan M. Wald, *Exiles from a Future Time: The Forging of the Mid-Twentieth-Century Literary Left* (Chapel Hill: University of North Carolina Press, 2002); Michael Thurston, *Making Something Happen: American Political Poetry between the World Wars* (Chapel Hill: University of

North Carolina Press, 2001); and Robert Shulman, *The Power of Political Art: The 1930s Literary Left Reconsidered* (Chapel Hill: University of North Carolina Press, 2000).

19. Note that aside from a passing reference to a "beloved teacher at Tuskegee" late in *A Long Way from Home* (208), McKay does not discuss his enrollment at the institute founded by Booker T. Washington, where he enrolled prior to attending Kansas State College to study agronomy. For more information about this period, see Cooper, *Claude McKay*, 55–56.

20. See chapter 21 of *A Long Way from Home*, in which McKay describes the notion of a distinctive American art and the distinction between bourgeois and proletarian art.

21. According to Cooper, McKay was reading and writing political material in Jamaican newspapers and in the United States while enrolled at Kansas State College from fall 1912 through spring 1914, when he began his personal involvement with radical politics. See Cooper, *Claude McKay*, 18–49, 68.

22. For more information on McKay's reading of Marx, see Maxwell, *New Negro, Old Left*, 76–88, which conducts an excellent close reading of McKay's 1923 book, *Negry v Amerike* (*The Negroes in America*), in terms of African American approaches to Marxism.

23. So anxious was McKay over his role that, in a political forum, he quibbled over the exact translation of his words from English to Russian. For this episode, see chapter 16 of *A Long Way from Home*.

24. Barbara Foley, *Spectres of 1919: Class and Nation in the Making of the New Negro* (Urbana: University of Illinois Press, 2003), vii.

25. Maxwell, *New Negro, Old Left*, 77–91.

26. For more information, see chapters 16 and 29 of *A Long Way from Home*.

27. See chapter 21 of *A Long Way from Home*, in which McKay states that he relishes lived experience as a means of authenticating literary expression.

28. For more information on the origin of the line "if we must die" in Shakespeare's *Measure for Measure*, see William J. Maxwell, ed., *Complete Poems: Claude McKay* (Urbana: University of Illinois Press, 2004), 333.

29. McKay's own admiration of the poem compelled him to talk about it in five different chapters of *A Long Way from Home* and to reprint it in its entirety in chapter 20, "Regarding Radical Criticism." See chapters 2, 9, 13, 19, and 20 of *A Long Way from Home* for discussions of "If We Must Die." The version of "If We Must Die" in *A Long Way from Home* appears in *Harlem Shadows* (1922). In line 4 of the poem as it was reprinted in *A Long Way from Home*, however, the word "accursed" is missing an accent mark ("accursèd"); in lines 5 and 9, the word "Oh" was originally "O"; and in line 13, "murderous cowardly pack" is missing a comma between "murderous" and "cowardly." For information about the poem, see Maxwell, ed., *Complete Poems: Claude McKay*, 332–33.

30. Quite simply, McKay did not yet have enough undistracted time to think about and write prose. But he did have such free time while traveling abroad, and, unsurprisingly, beginning in 1923, he became a prolific writer of fiction and nonfiction. McKay published *The Negroes in America* (1923), *Home to Harlem* (1928), *Banjo* (1929), *Gingertown* (1932), *Banana Bottom* (1933), *A Long Way from Home* (1937), and *Harlem: Negro Metropolis* (1940).

31. See Lee M. Jenkins, "'If We Must Die': Winston Churchill and Claude McKay," *Notes and Queries* 50 (September 2003): 334–35.

32. This is the crux of Stephens's persuasive argument in *Black Empire,* in which she extrapolates a complex theory of global gender and racial politics, as a result of and response to empire, by examining the texts and contexts of three Caribbean intellectuals: Marcus Garvey, Claude McKay, and C. L. R. James.

33. Baldwin, *Beyond the Color Line and the Iron Curtain,* 27.

34. In *Beyond the Color Line and the Iron Curtain,* Baldwin implies that the authors of Russian literature whom I have mentioned appealed to McKay, who inscribes and praises them in *Home to Harlem* (Baldwin, *Beyond the Color Line and the Iron Curtain,* 25).

35. Note that Locke repeated the emendation in *Four Negro Poets* (1927) (Maxwell, ed., *Complete Poems: Claude McKay,* 309).

36. Cooper, *Claude McKay,* 314. For a detailed discussion of Locke's harsh 1937 review of *A Long Way from Home* ("Spiritual Truancy," *New Challenge* 2.2 [Fall 1937]: 63–64), see chapter 5 of Gene Andrew Jarrett, *Deans and Truants: Race and Realism in African American Literature* (Philadelphia: University of Pennsylvania Press, 2006). For more information about the tense relationship between Locke and McKay, see Cooper, *Claude McKay,* 225, 261, 320; and George Hutchinson, *The Harlem Renaissance in Black and White* (Cambridge, MA: Belknap Press of Harvard University Press, 1995), 131.

37. Hughes, *I Wonder as I Wander,* 47. Further citations to this work are given in the text.

38. For more information about the context of these poems, see Hughes, *I Wonder as I Wander,* 44–60. The Scottsboro Boys consisted of nine African American teenagers who, in March 1931, were accused of raping two white women in Scottsboro, Alabama. The conflicting views that the boys were either falsely accused or undeniably guilty fueled the controversy surrounding the alleged incident and its aftermath in court. The boys were indicted and sentenced to death; they appealed to the U.S. Supreme Court, which overturned their initial convictions. Eventually they were all acquitted, paroled, or pardoned.

39. See Rampersad, *The Life of Langston Hughes,* 1:176–80.

40. Hughes discusses this history in *I Wonder as I Wander,* 26–29.

41. Touching on similar themes, Hughes invests a significant amount of time in *I Wonder as I Wander* to his time in Spain (321–400).

42. Eventually the essays formed the core of Hughes's *A Negro Looks at Soviet Central Asia* (Moscow: Co-operative Publishing Society of Foreign Workers in the USSR, 1934), reprinted in *The Collected Works of Langston Hughes,* 9:71–102.

43. For Hughes's references to the similarities of conditions for "coloreds" in Soviet Central Asia and those of the Negro in the United States, see Hughes, *I Wonder as I Wander,* 119, 144, 172–73, and 211–12.

44. Brent Hayes Edwards, *The Practice of Diaspora: Literature, Translation, and the Rise of Black Internationalism* (Cambridge, MA: Harvard University Press, 2003), 5.

45. I have come to this analysis by looking at the work of Penny M. Von Eschen, *Race against Empire: Black Americans and Anticolonialism, 1937–1957* (Ithaca, NY: Cornell University Press, 1997); and Kate A. Baldwin, *Beyond the Color Line and the Iron Curtain.*

46. For references to Charlotte Mason, the patron described at the end of *The Big Sea,* see Hughes, *I Wonder as I Wander,* 3–4.

47. Rampersad, introduction to Hughes, *The Big Sea,* xxiii.

48. For example, David Chioni Moore repeatedly asserts this point of Hughes's tonal geniality in *I Wonder as I Wander.* See Moore, "Colored Dispatches from the Uzbek Border," 1119; and idem, "Local Color, Global 'Color.'"

49. John Armstrong, "Mobilized and Proletarian Diasporas," *American Political Science Review* 70.2 (1979): 393.

50. Seth Moglen, "Modernism in the Black Diaspora: Langston Hughes and the Broken Cubes of Picasso," *Callaloo* 25.4 (2002): 1191–92.

51. Françoise Lionnet and Shu-Mei Shih, "Introduction: Thinking through the Minor, Transnationally," in *Minor Transnationalism,* ed. Françoise Lionnet and Shu-Mei Shih (Durham, NC: Duke University Press, 2005), 5.

52. Wai Chee Dimock, *Through Other Continents: American Literature across Deep Time* (Princeton, NJ: Princeton University Press, 2006), 3.

53. Lionnet and Shih, "Introduction," 2, 11.

54. Behdad, "Postcolonial Theory and the Predicament of 'Minor Literature,'" 232, 234.

55. William Andrews, *To Tell a Free Story: The First Century of Afro-American Autobiography, 1760–1865* (Urbana: University of Illinois Press, 1988), 16.

56. Moore, "Local Color, Global 'Color,'" 50.

57. Jill Dolan, *Utopia in Performance: Finding Hope at the Theater* (Ann Arbor: University of Michigan Press, 2005), 10, 14.

58. William H. Sewell Jr., *A Rhetoric of Bourgeois Revolution: The Abbé Sieyes and What Is the Third Estate?* (Durham, NC: Duke University Press, 1994), 1, 5, 7, 29.

59. Brent Hayes Edwards, "The 'Autonomy' of Black Radicalism," *Social Text* 67.2 (Summer 2001): 3–4.

NOTES TO CHAPTER 5

1. The derivative works of *Gone with the Wind* for which the Stephens Mitchell Trust owns the copyright include the 1939 film version (*Gone with the Wind,* dir. Victor Fleming; perfs. Clark Gable, Vivien Leigh; Metro-Goldwyn-Mayer, 1939); Alexandra Ripley's novel *Scarlett* (New York: Warner Books, 1991), a sequel to Mitchell's original novel; and Donald McCaig's novel *Rhett Butler's People* (New York: St. Martin's, 2007), a second sequel.

2. For the discussion of *The Wind Done Gone* in these terms, see Eve Allegra Raimon, *The "Tragic Mulatta" Revisited: Race and Nationalism in Nineteenth-Century Antislavery Fiction* (New Brunswick, NJ: Rutgers University Press, 2004), 154–58.

3. In contrast to the preponderance of legal articles, a search of the *MLA International Bibliography* (in 2009) reveals that about ten literary articles have appeared in which the novel is a main subject. I would say, however, that some of the best articles and book chapters to appear on the novel with equal emphases on the 2001 case, legal precedent, and African American literary history have been Richard Schur, "The Wind Done Gone Controversy: American Studies, Copyright Law, and the Imaginary Domain," *American Studies* 44.1–2 (Spring–Summer 2003): 5, 18–25; Raimon, *The "Tragic Mulatta" Revisited,* 154–58; and Lovalerie King, *Race, Theft, and Ethics: Property Matters in African American Literature* (Baton Rouge: Louisiana State University Press, 2007). Houghton Mifflin made the court documents available online at http://www.houghtonmifflinbooks.com/features/randall_url/courtpapers.shtml. Finally, the three appellate judges presiding over this case were the honorable Stanley F. Birch Jr., Stanley Marcus, and Harlington Wood Jr., a judge for the Seventh Circuit sitting by designation.

4. A slew of legal articles have appeared on *SunTrust v. Houghton* since the settlement between the plaintiff and defendant. According to a search on LexisNexis (in 2009), over three hundred articles published in law reviews, journals, and magazines have referred to the case since 2001. Based on my review, the legal article that has most substantively applied the methods of literary criticism to the case, while appreciating the importance of African American literary history, is Zahr Said Stauffer, "'Po-mo Karaoke' or Postcolonial Pastiche? What Fair Use Analysis Could Draw from Literary Criticism," *Columbia Journal of Law and the Arts* 43 (Fall 2007): 43–88. Although Stauffer's essay focuses mostly on postcolonial literature and literary studies, she opens the door to a more sustained analysis of law and African American literature, "where themes and linguistic effects exist in such dialectical fashion with the political and social inequities" (48n. 21).

5. Keith Byerman, *Remembering the Past in African American Fiction* (Chapel Hill: University of North Carolina Press, 2008); and Daniel Grassian, *Writing the Future of Black America: The Literature of the Hip-Hop Generation* (Columbia: University of South Carolina Press, 2009).

6. Darryl Dickson-Carr, *African American Satire: The Sacredly Profane Novel* (Columbia: University of Missouri Press, 2001), 1.

7. Linda Hutcheon, *A Theory of Parody: The Teachings of Twentieth-Century Art Forms* (London: Methuen, 1985), xv, 78.

8. Rosemary J. Coombe reiterates this point in *The Cultural Life of Intellectual Properties: Authorship, Appropriation, and the Law* (Durham, NC: Duke University Press, 1998), 25, 42, 86–87, 134.

9. Note that Melissa J. Homestead, in her book *American Women Authors and Literary Property, 1822–1869* (New York: Cambridge University Press, 2005), connects the implications of *Stowe v. Thomas* to the way that *Uncle Tom's Cabin* itself is a parable of Stowe's concerns with intellectual property (107, 137–44). I am suggesting, however, that this kind of supratextual correspondence between law and literature is not necessary to determine the political potential of *The Wind Done Gone* in *SunTrust v. Houghton*. Indeed, less important is the *actual intention* of Randall, though the ironic authenticity of *The Wind Done Gone* was confirmed by the depositions that she, Houghton Mifflin, and literary experts presented to the court. Hutcheon notes that "irony is not necessarily a matter of ironist intention (and therefore of implication), though it may be; it is always, however, a matter of interpretation and attribution." Linda Hutcheon, *Irony's Edge: The Theory and Politics of Irony* (London: Routledge, 1994), 45.

10. Jennifer Travis talks about distinctive methodologies in "The Trials of Law and Literature," *American Literary History* 21.2 (Summer 2009): 346. Richard A. Posner, a pioneer of this field, identifies the approaches of law in literature, law as literature, and law on literature; he also institutes a fourth category, the "literary turn in legal scholarship." See Richard A. Posner, *Law and Literature: Revised and Enlarged Edition* (Cambridge, MA: Harvard University Press, 1998), 305–77.

11. William Moddelmog, *Reconstituting Authority: American Fiction in the Province of the Law, 1880–1920* (Iowa City: University of Iowa Press, 2000), 17, 224n. 14.

12. Travis, "The Trials of Law and Literature," 346.

13. "The U.S. Constitution," in *Foundations of Freedom* (Radford, VA: Wilder, 2007), 405.

14. For a concise sketch of copyright history in relation to the Romantic notion of genius and to its legal and cultural repercussions, see Paul K. Saint-Amour, *The Copywrights: Intellectual Property and the Literary Imagination* (Ithaca, NY: Cornell University Press, 2003).

15. Olufunmilayo B. Arewa, "From J. C. Bach to Hip Hop: Musical Borrowing, Copyright and Cultural Context," *North Carolina Law Review* 84.2 (January 2006): 550, 565. For the distinction between copyright law and trademark and patent laws, see Kembrew McLeod, *Owning Culture: Authorship, Ownership, and Intellectual Property Law* (New York: Peter Lang, 2001), 3–6.

16. For the quotations, see Hutcheon, *A Theory of Parody*, 6; and Hutcheon, *Irony's Edge*, 58, 99, 100, 101.

17. Russ Versteeg, "Intent, Originality, Creativity, and Joint Authorship," *Brooklyn Law Review* 68 (Fall 2002): 134.

18. E. Nathaniel Gates, "Volume Introduction," in *The Judicial Isolation of the "Racially" Oppressed*, ed. Gates, vii–ix (New York: Garland, 1997), viii.

19. Cornel West, foreword to *Critical Race Theory: The Key Writings That Formed the Movement*, ed. Kimberlé Crenshaw, Neil Gotanda, Gary Peller, and Kendall Thomas, xi–xii (New York: Free Press, 1995), xi. In addition to this seminal volume, the building of Critical Race Theory beyond legal scholarship is discussed in Richard Delgado and Jean Stefancic, *Critical Race Theory: An Introduction* (New York: New York University Press, 2001).

20. See Schur, "*The Wind Done Gone* Controversy"; Arewa, "From J. C. Bach to Hip Hop"; King, *Race, Theft, and Ethics*; and Saint-Amour, *The Copywrights*. A range of other cultural studies are useful: Joanna Demers, *Steal This Music: How Intellectual Property Law Affects Musical Creativity* (Athens: University of Georgia Press, 2006); Lawrence Lessig, *Free Culture: The Nature and Future of Creativity* (New York: Penguin, 2004); Kembrew McLeod, *Freedom of Expression: Resistance and Repression in the Age of Intellectual Property* (Minneapolis: University of Minnesota Press, 2007). I would note that "borrowing" is not exclusive to African American culture but, as Arewa has noted, has historically been highlighted as such in law, even though it has been important to other kinds of cultural expressions, such as classical music ("From J. C. Bach to Hip Hop," 550).

21. Dickson-Carr, *African American Satire*, 1.

22. See Glenda R. Carpio, *Laughing Fit to Kill: Black Humor in the Fictions of Slavery* (New York: Oxford University Press, 2008), 13.

23. "Declaration of Henry Louis Gates Jr.," *SunTrust Bank v. Houghton Mifflin Company*, 136 F. Supp. 2d 1357 (N.D. Ga. 2001), 1.

24. Homestead, *American Women Authors*, 107.

25. While Article I, Section 8, of the U.S. Constitution includes a provision regarding copyright, the details are fleshed out in U.S. copyright law, found in chapters 1 through 8 and 10 through 12 of Title 17 of the United States Code. In section 101 of chapter 1, we have the definition of a "derivative work":

> A "derivative work" is a work based upon one or more preexisting works, such as a translation, musical arrangement, dramatization, fictionalization, motion picture version, sound recording, art reproduction, abridgment, condensation, or any other form in which a work may be recast, transformed, or adapted. A work consisting of editorial revisions, annotations, elaborations, or other modifications, which, as a whole, represent an original work of authorship, is a "derivative work."

U.S. Copyright Office, "Copyright Law of the United States of America," http://www.copyright.gov/title17/92chap1.html#101.

26. *Stowe v. Thomas,* 23 F. Cas. 201, 206, 208 (C.C.E.D. Pa. 1853), in *Primary Sources on Copyright (1450–1900),* ed. Lionel Bentley and Martin Kretschmer, http://www.copyright-history.org/cgi-bin/kleioc/0010/exec/ausgabe/%22us_1853b%22.

27. For more results of the research, see Homestead, *American Women Authors,* 129–37. For elaborations of this relationship between race and property as well as racial representation and literary property, see King, *Race, Theft, and Ethics,* 3; and Stephen M. Best, *The Fugitive's Properties: Law and the Poetics of Possession* (Chicago: University of Chicago Press, 2004), 14, 16, 118.

28. Robert S. Levine, *Martin Delany, Frederick Douglass, and the Politics of Representative Identity* (Chapel Hill: University of North Carolina Press, 1997), 80.

29. Schur, "*The Wind Done Gone* Controversy," 11, 18.

30. Margaret Mitchell to Alexander L. May, July 22, 1938, in *Margaret Mitchell's "Gone with the Wind" Letters,* ed. Richard Harwell (New York: Macmillan, 1976), 217.

31. Saint-Amour, *The Copyrights,* 4–5, 206, where he begins to sketch the relevance of *SunTrust v. Houghton* in terms of the notion of "working-though."

32. For more information about this literary and scholarly tradition of critique, see Elizabeth Young, *Disarming the Nation: Women's Writing and the American Civil War* (Chicago: University of Chicago Press, 1999), 236.

33. Certain white characters in *Gone with the Wind* make cameo appearances in *The Wind Done Gone*: they include not only Scarlett and Rhett, who reappear as Other and R., but also Gerald, as Planter; Ellen, as Lady; and Philippe, as Cousin or Feleepe. Although the temptation to interchange the names of the characters in *The Wind Done Gone* with those of *Gone with the Wind* is difficult to resist, I have elected, in my close reading of Randall's novel, to respect and refer to the names she has imagined for them.

34. Note that the defense played down the novel's ironic subplot of Scarlett's biracial ancestry and its broader ideological critique of the racial purity of whiteness. In contrast, it played up the argument that Randall successfully humanized the black characters in *Gone with the Wind*. Of course, this argument makes legal sense. Court documents presented by Professor Henry Louis Gates Jr. of Harvard University, Associate Professor Barbara McCaskill of the University of Georgia, and Alice Randall herself supported Houghton Mifflin's claim that the genre of fiction, along with Randall's well-grounded knowledge of U.S. history, had authorized her to revise the portraiture of blacks in *Gone with the Wind*. See *SunTrust,* 136 F. Supp. 2d 1357, Gates declaration, exhibit B; and Alice Randall declaration.

35. Thomas F. Haddox, "Alice Randall's *The Wind Done Gone* and the Ludic in African American Historical Fiction," *MFS: Modern Fiction Studies* 53.1 (Spring 2007): 123; Patricia Yaeger, "Circum-Atlantic Superabundance: Milk as World-Making in Alice Randall and Kara Walker," *American Literature* 78.4 (December 2006): 780.

36. Margaret Mitchell, *Gone with the Wind* (1936; reprint, New York: Warner, 1993), 46, 47; hereafter *GWTW*. Further citations to this work are to this edition and are given in the text.

37. The tale of contrasts between Gerald and Ellen also includes their religious differences (the Robillards were Catholic, Gerald was not) and the age disparity (he was "old enough to be her father!") *GWTW,* 56.

38. Eliza Russi Lowen McGraw, "A 'Southern Belle with Her Irish Up': Scarlett O'Hara and Ethnic Identity," *South Atlantic Review* 65.1 (Winter 2000): 124.

39. Diane Roberts, *The Myth of Aunt Jemima: Representations of Race and Region* (London: Routledge, 1994), 178–79.

40. For more information about Rhett's symbolic hybridity, see Young, *Disarming the Nation*, 237, 257–63.

41. McGraw, "A 'Southern Belle,'" 124.

42. By one estimate, *Gone with the Wind* sold one million copies in the United States in less than one year after its initial publication and over twenty-five million since then, placing it second all-time, behind only the Bible. For more information about the novel's commercial sales in the 1930s, see Darden Pyron, *Southern Daughter: The Life of Margaret Mitchell and the Making of* Gone with the Wind (Athens, GA: Hill Street, 2004), 336; for sales since then, see Helen Taylor, *Scarlett's Women:* Gone with the Wind *and Its Female Fans* (London: Virago, 1989), 1.

43. The title is "'Trust Me, I Am Not the Same / As in the Reign of Cinara, Kind and Fair,'" which comes from lines 3–4 of book 4, poem 1, of *Odes* (13 BC) of Quintus Horatius Flaccus (Horace); see *The Odes and Carmen Saeculare of Horace,* trans. John Conington (London: George Bell and Sons, 1882). For the entire poem, see Ernest Dowson, *Verses* (London: Leonard Smithers, 1896), 17–18.

44. One example of numerous textual similarities and allusions between Mitchell's and Randall's novels is the beginning sentences of the books. *Gone with the Wind* has this as its first sentence: "Scarlett O'Hara was not beautiful, but men seldom realized it when caught by her charm" (5). *The Wind Done Gone,* in reference to Other, who represents Scarlett, has this as its seventh sentence: "She was not beautiful, but men seldom recognized this, caught up in the cloud of commotion and scent in which she moved." Alice Randall, *The Wind Done Gone* (New York: Houghton Mifflin, 2001), 1. The plaintiff had identified close to one hundred other credible instances of textual similarity and allusion.

45. Alice Randall, *The Wind Done Gone* (New York: Houghton Mifflin, 2001), 148; hereafter *TWDG.* Further citations to this work are given in the text.

46. Motoko Rich, "Rhett, Scarlett and Friends Prepare for Yet Another Encore," *New York Times* (May 16, 2007).

47. Throughout *The Wind Done Gone,* Randall addresses this idea—for example, in her constant references to the interchangeability of those who breastfeed and those who are breastfed, regardless of the racial differences that may otherwise, in other social contexts, segregate them.

48. Philip Dray, *Capitol Men: The Epic Story of Reconstruction through the Lives of the First Black Congressmen* (New York: Houghton Mifflin, 2008).

49. *SunTrust,* 136 F. Supp. 2d 1357, Randall declaration, 5.

50. *SunTrust,* 136 F. Supp. 2d 1357, trial transcript, 61 (April 18, 2001).

51. See *Campbell, a.k.a. Skywalker v. Acuff-Rose Music,* 510 U.S. 569, 569–70, 579 (1994); italics mine.

52. *SunTrust,* 136 F. Supp. 2d 1357, Houghton Mifflin memorandum, 15, 17 (March 28, 2001).

53. *SunTrust,* 136 F. Supp. 2d 1357, trial transcript, 10 (March 29, 2001).

54. Ibid., at 20.

55. Ibid., at 27.

56. Ibid., at 27–28.

57. Ibid., at 50; italics mine.

58. *SunTrust Bank,* 136 F. Supp. 2d at 1386.

59. Ibid., at 1368.

60. See *SunTrust,* 136 F. Supp. 2d 1357, SunTrust reply (April 25, 2001).

61. See *Cable News Network v. Video Monitoring Services,* 940 F.2d 1471 (11th Cir. 1991), *vacated and rehearing en banc granted,* 949 F.2d 378 (11th Cir. 1991), *appeal dismissed,* 959 F.2d 188 (11th Cir. 1992) (en banc).

62. Paul A. Stewart, "Extraordinary Injunctions in Copyright Cases," Knobbe Martens Olsen & Bear website, http://www.kmob.com/pdf/Extraordinary%20Injunctions%20 in%20Copyright%20Cases%20-%20August%202004.htm.

63. The "idea/expression dichotomy" "strikes a definitional balance between the First Amendment and the Copyright Act by permitting free communication of facts while still protecting an author's expression." See *SunTrust,* 136 F. Supp. 2d 1357, SunTrust brief, 45 (May 18, 2001).

64. Ibid., at 1.

65. Aside from the Microsoft brief, which discouraged focus on First Amendment issues, there was one brief for SunTrust Bank and four for Houghton Mifflin.

66. *SunTrust,* 136 F. Supp. 2d 1357, Houghton Mifflin brief, 3 (May 23, 2001).

67. *SunTrust,* 136 F. Supp. 2d 1357, brief of amici curiae, 5; italics mine.

68. *SunTrust Bank v. Houghton Mifflin Company,* 252 F.3d 1165, 1166 (11th Cir. 2001).

69. Note that the copyright-infringement argument of SunTrust Bank is possible mainly because *Gone with the Wind* is *not* in the public domain. Thus, the leverage is arbitrary; see *SunTrust,* 136 F. Supp. 2d 1357, trial transcript, 54 (March 29, 2001); see also Georgia First Amendment Society amicus brief, 18.

70. *SunTrust Bank v. Houghton Mifflin Company,* 268 F.3d 1257, 1277 (11th Cir. 2001). This is the citation for the final decision of the United States Court of Appeals for the Eleventh Circuit, issued October 10, 2001.

71. *SunTrust,* 268 F.3d at 1268–69.

72. See *Campbell, a.k.a. Skywalker,* 510 U.S. 569.

73. According to the Houghton Mifflin website,

> Both sides continue to maintain the correctness of their respective legal positions taken since the outset of the litigation. The parties have entered into a confidential settlement agreement under which the novel *The Wind Done Gone* will continue in distribution labeled "An Unauthorized Parody," and a financial contribution will be made at the Mitchell Trusts' request to Morehouse College on behalf of Houghton Mifflin, but the rights of the Parties are reserved with respect to the future creation or publication of dramatic or any other adaptations of the book, including motion pictures, television movies or miniseries, sequels, prequels, and stage productions. The rights of Alice Randall with respect to any such adaptations of the book are not affected by the settlement.

Houghton Mifflin Books, "Information about SunTrust Bank v. Houghton Mifflin Company" (May 9, 2002), http://www.houghtonmifflinbooks.com/features/randall_url/ may9pr.shtml. Houghton Mifflin has also usefully assembled the court papers from the case; these are available online at http://www.houghtonmifflinbooks.com/features/ randall_url/courtpapers.shtml.

74. Ibid. As the appellate court put it, "we have found that to the extent SunTrust suffers injury from [*The Wind Done Gone*'s] putative infringement of its copyright in *Gone With the Wind,* such harm can adequately be remedied through an award of monetary damages." *SunTrust,* 268 F.3d at 1277.

75. Haddox, "Alice Randall's *The Wind Done Gone,*" 121.

76. *SunTrust,* 136 F. Supp. 2d 1357, Toni Morrison declaration, 3; italics mine.

77. *SunTrust,* 136 F. Supp. 2d 1357, SunTrust memorandum, 5 (March 23, 2001).

78. Jed Rubenfeld, "The Freedom of Imagination: Copyright's Constitutionality," *Yale Law Journal* 112.1 (October 2002): 9. For Rubenfeld's discussion of why he wishes to put copyright law and copyright scholarship on trial, see ibid., 3–4, 7–8, 10; for the favoritism of parody and criticism in fair use, see ibid., 6–7, 17. Rubenfeld goes so far as to call current copyright law "unconstitutional in that it permits courts to issue injunctions or grant damages in cases of derivative works and live performances" (ibid., 58).

79. Ibid., 4, 17.

80. *SunTrust,* 136 F. Supp. 2d 1357, complaint addendum. There is, however, a counterargument by the acquisition editor that "parody" was the term employed all along: see Anton Mueller declaration, 9.

81. *SunTrust,* 136 F. Supp. 2d 1357, trial transcript, 10 (March 29, 2001); plaintiff memorandum, 6 (April 9, 2001).

82. It is worth mentioning that an overemphasis on parody has another consequence. As Zahr Said Stauffer notes,

> Yet stressing the allegedly parodic nature of Randall's rewriting puts too much pressure on both legal and literary definitions of parody, and risks diffusing the category beyond recognition because of a non-literary distinction the law draws between parody and satire. . . . As more postcolonial and postmodernist writers set their sights on copyrighted texts for the purposes of comment and criticism, we can expect to see parody continue to lose precision as a category.

See Stauffer, "'Po-mo Karaoke' or Postcolonial Pastiche?" 44.

83. Rubenfeld, "The Freedom of Imagination," 4, 33, 35, 36; Alexander Meiklejohn quoted on 33.

84. Ibid., 38, 39, 42, 43.

85. See Arewa, "From J. C. Bach to Hip Hop," stating that a "difference between music and literature arises in part from the nonrepresentational nature of musical notes and the fact that such notes do not involve everyday world phenomena" (578). I would argue that the "notes" are a form of representation as well, and it is not clear how Arewa is determining the immunity of "notes" from "world phenomena."

86. Louis A. Montrose, "New Historicisms," in *Redrawing the Boundaries: The Transformation of English and American Literary Studies,* ed. Stephen Greenblatt and Giles Gunn (New York: Modern Language Association, 1992), 396.

87. The respective cases are *IFG Network Securities, Inc. v. Rex T. King and Rua L. King,* 2003 U.S. Dist. LEXIS 21200; *Sun-Sentinel Co. and Miami Herald Publishing Co. v. City of Hollywood,* 2003 U.S. Dist. LEXIS 15610; *Goldman, Sachs & Co. v. Robert C. Bolster, et al.,* 2004 U.S. Dist. LEXIS 5623; *Calvary Chapel Church, Inc. v. Broward County Board of County Commissioners, et al.,* 2003 U.S. Dist. LEXIS 24101.

1. Barack Obama, *Dreams from My Father: A Story of Race and Inheritance* (New York: Crown, 2004), 196, 198. Further citations to this work are to this edition and are given in the text.

2. Michael Eric Dyson, *Making Malcolm: The Myth and Meaning of Malcolm X* (Oxford: Oxford University Press, 1995), 80.

3. Ibid., 22–24, 132.

4. Melanye T. Price, *Dreaming Blackness: Black Nationalism and African American Public Opinion* (New York: New York University Press, 2009), 3–4, 19.

5. David Remnick, *The Bridge: The Life and Rise of Barack Obama* (New York: Knopf, 2010). Remnick, on 80, 234, and 239, decodes the biographies of Rafiq and other characters mentioned in Obama's *Dreams from My Father*; on 230–31, he also talks about the discrepancies between the information in the memoir and historical facts.

6. Some of the most exceptional pieces in mainstream writing that usefully address these issues, but which I do not quote from in this chapter, include Jabari Asim, *What Obama Means* (New York: William Morrow, 2009); Michiko Kakutani, "From Books, New President Found Voice," *New York Times* (January 19, 2009); William Finnegan, "The Candidate: How the Son of a Kenyan Economist Became an Illinois Everyman," *New Yorker* (May 31, 2004); the staff-written essay "The Choice," *New Yorker* (October 13, 2008); Zadie Smith, "Speaking in Tongues," *New York Review of Books* (February 26, 2009); "The Obama Canon," *New Yorker* (February 18, 2009); an Amazon.com interview with Obama on literature: http://www.amazon.com/Audacity-Hope-Thoughts-Reclaiming-American/dp/0307237699; Christine Smallwood, "Back Talk: Toni Morrison," *Nation* (November 19, 2008); Rebecca Mead, "Obama, Poet," *New Yorker* (July 2, 2007); James Wood, "Verbage," *New Yorker* (October 13, 2008); David Remnick, "The Joshua Generation," *New Yorker* (November 17, 2008). Of course, the list could go on.

7. Janny Scott, "The Story of Obama, Written by Obama," *New York Times* (May 18, 2008).

8. Marjorie Perloff, "The Audacity of Literary Studies," paper presented at the Modern Language Association Conference, December 2008; available online on the *Chicago Blog* (January 5, 2009), http://pressblog.uchicago.edu/2009/01/05/audacity_of_literary_studies.html.

9. Rampersad, quoted in Scott, "The Story of Obama."

10. For more information about these instances of Obama's engagement of literature, see Remnick, *The Bridge*, 77, 79 113, and 263.

11. Andrew Ferguson, "The Literary Obama," *Weekly Standard* (February 12, 2007).

12. Brent Hayes Edwards, "Pebbles of Consonance," *Small Axe* 9.1 (2005): 140.

13. For more information on Obama's writing poetry for Punahou's literary magazine, see Jennifer Steinhauer, "Charisma and a Search for Self in Obama's Hawaii Childhood," *New York Times* (March 17, 2007).

14. I thank Robert Stepto, professor of English and African American studies at Yale University, for the notion of a "bookshelf scholar," which is how he described himself before the advent of African American literary studies as an academic discipline, at a time when the writings were available only on his personal bookshelves, not yet in the libraries or the classrooms. Stepto talked about these issues in his honorary W. E. B. Du

Bois Lectures, "Reading the Classics in the Age of Obama," at Harvard University (April 27–29, 2009).

15. Malcolm X and Alex Haley, *The Autobiography of Malcolm X* (1965; reprint, New York: Ballantine Books, 1992), 210. Further citations to this work are to this edition and are given in the text. For Malcolm X's reflective time in prison, see 151–90; for the first exposure to Islam, see 155; for the "whitening" of history, see 162–81, 202, 212; for racial brainwashing, see 220.

16. In *The Autobiography of Malcolm X,* for the limits of the Nation of Islam, see 289, 316; for the trip to Mecca, see 318; for the beginning of Malcolm X's divorce from the Nation of Islam, see 309; and for the possible redemption of whites, see 341, 355, and 362.

17. Dyson persuasively marks the Black Power Movement with "the emergence of Stokely Carmichael as leader of the Black Power movement, until the demise of the Black Panthers" (*Making Malcolm,* 81). For an overview of this movement, also see James Smethurst, *The Black Arts Movement: Literary Nationalism in the 1960s and 1970s* (Chapel Hill: University of North Carolina Press, 2005).

18. Even now, Obama recalls the importance of Malcolm X, though in different terms. In a very recent interview between Obama, in his office as U.S. president, and his biographer, David Remnick, Obama connects the cultural and political meanings of Malcolm X. An excerpt from this interview serves as a perfect companion to the passage about the deceased leader that is quoted from *Dreams of My Father* in the text:

> I think that I find the sort of policy prescriptions, the analysis, the theology of Malcolm full of holes, although I did even when I was young. I was never taken with some of his theorizing. I think that what Malcolm X did, though, was to tap into a long-running tradition within the African-American community, which is that at certain moments it's important for African-Americans to assert their manhood, their worth. At times, they can overcompensate, and popular culture can take it into caricature—blaxploitation films being the classic example of it. But if you think about it, of a time in the early nineteen-sixties, when a black Ph.D. might be a Pullman porter and have to spend much of his day obsequious and kow-towing to people, that affirmation that I am a man, I am worth something, I think was important. And I think Malcolm X probably captured that better than anybody.

Obama, quoted in Remnick, *The Bridge,* 233–34.

19. Ralph Ellison, *Invisible Man* (1952; reprint, New York: Vintage, 1995), 275. Further citations to this source are to this edition and are given in the text.

20. Ironically, the Founder is also arguably an allegory of Washington himself, who, in his varying portrayals since his death in 1915 as a heroic or antiheroic legend, has come to represent someone outside history.

21. Jim Neighbors, "Plunging (outside of) History: Naming and Self-Possession in *Invisible Man,*" *African American Review* 36.2 (2002): 230–31.

22. Paul Allen Anderson, "Ralph Ellison on Lyricism and Swing," *American Literary History* 17.2 (2005): 288.

23. H. William Rice, *Ralph Ellison and the Politics of the Novel* (Lanham, MD: Lexington Books, 2003), 91–95.

24. Ralph Ellison, "Introduction to the Thirtieth-Anniversary Edition of *Invisible Man,*" in *The Collected Essays of Ralph Ellison,* ed. John F. Callahan (New York: Modern Library, 1995), 482.

25. As Kenneth W. Warren puts it in *So Black and Blue: Ralph Ellison and the Occasion of Criticism* (Chicago: University of Chicago Press, 2003), Ellison "was able to expose as tendentious distortions the apparent truths conveyed in these representations [of "the Negro"]. But while Ellison was able to 'see' this dynamic, he could not necessarily arrest it. That is, what his writing also demonstrated was that attempting to represent 'the Negro' outside the political realm of direct representation—whether one did so literarily, sociologically, philosophically, administratively, or philanthropically—was to enter a hall of mirrors, from which one was most likely to emerge with only misshapen images of oneself" (20).

26. David Samuels, "Invisible Man: How Ralph Ellison Explains Barack Obama," *New Republic* (October 22, 2008). Samuels is correct that "the author's extreme isolation as a child and as a young man and his dislike for the company of other people" is a theme in Obama's early life and "a familiar theme in the lives of writers but an unusual element in the biography of an American politician." I would say, however, that this theme does not exist throughout the memoir, especially not in the "Chicago" section, which relates a time when he sows the seeds of his desire to organize communities on behalf of social change.

27. For another example of this belief, in the wake of Obama's controversial statement on white "bitterness," see Michael Gerson, "Better than the Bitter," *Washington Post* (April 16, 2008): A15.

28. Neighbors, "Plunging (outside of) History," 231.

29. For Ellison's discussion of Ras and Garvey, see Ellison, "The Art of Fiction: An Interview," in *Shadow and Act* (1964; reprint, New York: Vintage, 1995), 181.

30. For more references in *Invisible Man* to being inside and outside history, see 439, 441, 443, and 499.

31. Barack Obama, *The Audacity of Hope: Thoughts on Reclaiming the American Dream* (New York: Crown, 2006), 10. Further citations to this work are to this edition and are given in the text.

32. For more information about his restless personality, see *Dreams from My Father*, 226, and *Audacity of Hope*, 3, 203; for his transnational sensibility, see *Audacity of Hope*, 53, 271; for the rhetorical importance of stories and storytelling to campaigning, see *Audacity of Hope*, 8, 359; and for the importance of reading literature and language to grasping the political world, see *Audacity of Hope*, 52–53; on the impact of written laws on the world, see *Dreams from My Father*, 437–38, and *Audacity of Hope*, 77–100; and for the reaffirmation of the role of culture in social change, *Audacity of Hope*, 63, 244–45. Finally, in a review of *The Audacity of Hope*, Mary Fitzgerald states, "Of course, you don't need to look far into the past to find a would-be president making a similar case. Obama tells us America must rid itself of its 'either/or' thinking, in much the same way that Clinton wanted to break free from the 'zero-sum game.' Clinton felt people's pain, Obama wants to fill the 'empathy deficit.'" Fitzgerald, "Great Non-white Hope," *New Statesman* (May 14, 2007).

33. For his discussion of affirmative action, see *Audacity of Hope*, 28, 33, 244–47.

34. David A. Hollinger, "Obama, the Instability of Color Lines, and the Promise of a Postethnic Future," *Callaloo* 31.4 (2008): 1033.

35. For more information, see Henry Louis Gates, Jr. and Donald Yacovone, eds., *Lincoln on Race and Slavery* (Princeton, NJ: Princeton University Press, 2009). For

more information about Lincoln's disagreements with Douglass on these issues of race, slavery, and the Civil War, see Paul Kendrick and Stephen Kendrick, *Douglass and Lincoln: How a Revolutionary Black Leader and a Reluctant Liberator Struggled to End Slavery and Save the Union* (New York: Walker, 2007); also see John Stauffer, *Giants: The Parallel Lives of Frederick Douglass and Abraham Lincoln* (New York: Grand Central, 2008).

36. Scott Horton, "Best of the '08 Campaign: The Effective Use of History," *Harper's Magazine,* (November 3, 2008), http://harpers.org/archive/2008/11/hbc-90003799.

37. Barack Obama, *Change We Can Believe In: Barack Obama's Plan to Renew America's Promise* (New York: Random House, 2008), 15. Further citations to this work, particularly for "Declaration of Candidacy" and "A More Perfect Union," are to this edition and are given in the text.

38. Lawrence D. Bobo and Michael C. Dawson believe there are "at least seven references to race." See their article "A Change Has Come: Race, Politics, and the Path to the Obama Presidency," *Du Bois Review* 6.1 (Spring 2009): 2.

39. Darryl Pinckney, "Obama and the Black Church," *New York Review of Books* (July 17, 2008).

40. Interestingly, Obama's memoir of conversion is more of a throwback to an earlier, eighteenth-century black tradition of spiritual autobiography, in which the religious deliverance of such authors as Britton Hammon, James Albert Ukawsaw Gronniosaw, John Marrant, and, most notably, Olaudah Equiano complemented their desire to be literate enough to read the Bible and thereby interpret the real world. For more information, see the introduction by Vincent Carretta to *Unchained Voices: An Anthology of Black Authors in the English-Speaking World of the Eighteenth Century,* ed. Carretta (Lexington: University Press of Kentucky, 2003).

41. Wright, quoted in Pinckney, "Obama and the Black Church."

42. Examples of the term "race speech" are in Asim, *What Obama Means,* 127; and Hollinger, "Obama, the Instability of Color Lines," 1036.

43. "The U.S. Constitution," in *Foundations of Freedom* (Radford, VA: Wilder, 2007), 403.

44. The paragraph appears on 220 in *Change We Can Believe In.*

45. William Faulkner, *Requiem for a Nun* (1951; reprint, New York: Random House, 1968), 92.

46. Ellison, "The World and the Jug," in *Shadow and Act,* 139–40.

47. Warren, *So Black and Blue,* 18.

48. For more information on the depth of Obama's choice of Lincoln to establish an American political lineage, see Paul Schwartzman, "A Role Model So Much Larger than Life," *Washington Post* (January 20, 2009): AA35. For Lincoln versus Douglass in this lineage, see Henry Louis Gates Jr. and John Stauffer, "A Pragmatic Precedent," *New York Times* (January 19, 2009): A25.

49. Pinckney, "Obama and the Black Church." For more information on Obama's resignation from Trinity Church, see Michael Powell, "Following Months of Criticism, Obama Quits His Church," *New York Times* (June 1, 2008). For more information on Obama's religious faith and its political implications, see Jodi Kantor, "A Candidate, His Minister and the Search for Faith," *New York Times* (April 30, 2007).

1. Eddie S. Glaude Jr., *In a Shade of Blue: Pragmatism and the Politics of Black America* (Chicago: University of Chicago Press, 2007), xii.

2. Harold Cruse, *The Crisis of the Negro Intellectual: A Historical Analysis of the Failure of Black Leadership* (New York: Morrow, 1967), 100 ("civil writers"), 103 ("the Negro point of view"), 110 ("Negro creative intellectual"), and 452 ("Afro-American Nationalism"). One example of the more eviscerating and egregious statements appears in chapter 23, "Role of the Negro Intellectual—Survey of the Dialogue Deferred," when Cruse implores the African American intellectual to "tell this brainwashed white America, this 'nation of sheep,' this overfed, overdeveloped, overprivileged (but culturally pauperized) federation of unassimilated European remnants that their days of grace are numbered" (455–56). That said, for more information about the kind of Marxist revisionist historiography that Harold Cruse was conducting in attacking the African American bourgeoisie, see Cedric J. Robinson, *Black Marxism: The Making of the Black Radical Tradition* (Chapel Hill: University of North Carolina Press, 2000), particularly chapter 11, "Richard Wright and the Critique of Class Theory," about Cruse on Wright's Marxism. For more specific readings of the text and context of Cruse's *The Crisis of the Black Intellectual,* see the scholarly essays collected in Jerry G. Watts, ed., *Harold Cruse's* The Crisis of the Negro Intellectual *Reconsidered* (New York: Routledge, 2004).

3. For more information on how the academic field of African American studies represents an evolutionary stage of the crisis of the African American intellectual, see Hortense J. Spillers, "*The Crisis of the Negro Intellectual*: A Post-Date," *boundary 2* 21.3 (Autumn 1994): 108–16. Although Spiller's essay opens as a reassessment of the silver anniversary of Cruse's 1967 book, it also appears spurred on by a momentous debate in Boston. Eugene Rivers, the pastor of Azuza Christian Community Church in Dorchester, Boston, published an essay, "On the Responsibility of Intellectuals in the Age of Crack," in the *Boston Review* 17.5 (September–October 1992): 3–4, holding preeminent African American professors accountable for, in his view, their lack of involvement in local black neighborhoods. This essay led to the convening of public discussions at Harvard University on November 30, 1992, then at the Massachusetts Institute of Technology on November 17, 1993, featuring Rivers and these very professors, among others, about the responsibilities of the African American intellectual. For more information, see Spillers, "*The Crisis of the Negro Intellectual,*" 69–70n. 3.

4. Harold Cruse poignantly identifies a possible contradiction: "[T]he Negro intelligentsia . . . have sold out their own birthright for an illusion called Racial Integration. Having given up their strict claim to an ethnic identity in politics, economics and culture, they haven't a leg to stand on. They can make no legitimate claims for their group integrity in cultural affairs. They take the *illusion* of the integrated world of creative intellectuals as the social *reality,* and do not know how to function within its cultural apparatus" (Cruse, *The Crisis of the Negro Intellectual,* 111).

5. Nikhil Pal Singh, "Negro Exceptionalism: The Antinomies of Harold Cruse," in Watts, *Harold Cruse's* The Crisis of the Negro Intellectual *Reconsidered,* 80.

6. Melissa Harris-Lacewell, "Commentary: Don't Hold Obama to Race Agenda," CNN. com (June 5, 2009), http://www.cnn.com/2009/POLITICS/06/05/lacewell.race.agenda/.

7. Darryl Pinckney, "Obama and the Black Church," *New York Review of Books* (July 17, 2008).

8. Ibid.

9. For more information on how Trinity Church was a black "power base," see David Remnick, *The Bridge: The Life and Rise of Barack Obama* (New York: Knopf, 2010), 169–76.

10. For more information about Obama's struggle against Bobby Lee Rush, see ibid., 307–33; for his battles against Jesse Jackson Sr., see ibid., 487–92, 533–35.

11. W. E. B. Du Bois, *The Souls of Black Folk* (1903; reprint, New York: Penguin Books, 1989), 8.

12. Martin Luther King Jr., "Nobel Prize Acceptance Speech" (1964), in *A Testament of Hope,* ed. James W. Washington, 224–26 (New York: HarperCollins, 1986), 224, 226.

13. Du Bois, *The Souls of Black Folk,* 1.

14. One could argue that Michael Steele, a Republican, former lieutenant governor of Maryland, and former chairman of the Republican National Committee, belongs in this group of new black politics.

15. Booker was born in 1969; Patrick, in 1956; Davis, in 1967; Ford, in 1970; Nutter, in 1957; and Obama, in 1961. Booker earned his degrees from Stanford University, Oxford University (as a Rhodes Scholar), and Yale University Law School; both Patrick and Davis earned theirs from Harvard College and Harvard Law School; Ford, from the University of Pennsylvania and the University of Michigan Law School; Nutter, also from the University of Pennsylvania; and Obama, from Occidental College, Columbia University, and Harvard Law School.

16. Peter J. Boyer, "The Color of Politics," *New Yorker* (February 4, 2008): 38.

17. According to Thomas J. Sugrue in *Not Even Past: Barack Obama and the Burden of Race* (Princeton, NJ: Princeton University Press, 2010),

> In the three decades after [Edward] Brooke's election [as a Republican to the U.S. Senate from the state of Massachusetts in 1966], sixty-seven cities with populations over fifty thousand elected black mayors, nearly all of them members of the Democratic Party. Most of those cities were majority white. Many black leaders— even those with origins in the controversial community control and black power movements of the 1960s—forged political coalitions across racial lines, although the admixture of racism and antiliberalism kept most of them from winning a white majority. (27)

18. Remnick, *The Bridge,* 23–24.

19. Matt Bai, "Is Obama the End of Black Politics?" *New York Times* (August 10, 2008).

20. Amiri Baraka, quoted in Boyer, "The Color of Politics," 43.

21. Sugrue, *Not Even Past,* 25–26.

22. Frederick Douglass, "The Need for Continuing Anti-slavery Work," in *The Life and Writings of Frederick Douglass,* vol. 4, ed. Philip S. Foner (New York: International, 1975), 169.

23. "Obama's Path," special issue, *Du Bois Review: Social Science Research on Race* 6.1 (Spring 2009); the pertinent essays include the editorial introduction by Lawrence D. Bobo and Michael C. Dawson, "A Change Has Come: Race, Politics, and the Path to the Obama Presidency," 1–14; Henry Louis Gates Jr., "A Conversation with William Julius Wilson on the Election of Barack Obama," 15–23; Rogers M. Smith and Desmond S. King, "Barack Obama and the Future of American Racial Politics," 25–35; Richard Thompson Ford, "Barack Is the New Black: Obama and the Promise/Threat of the Post–Civil Rights Era," 37–48.

24. Hazel Rose Markus and Paula M. L. Moya, preface to *Doing Race: 21 Essays for the 21st Century*, ed. Markus and Moya, ix–xvi (New York: Norton, 2010), ix–xi.

25. Brent Hayes Edwards, *The Practice of Diaspora: Literature, Translation, and the Rise of Black Internationalism* (Cambridge, MA: Harvard University Press, 2003), 14.

26. James Edward Smethurst, *The Black Arts Movement: Literary Nationalism in the 1960s and the 1970s* (Chapel Hill: University of North Carolina Press, 2005), 17.

27. Other acclaimed contemporary African American novels about slavery include Ishmael Reed's *Flight to Canada* (1976), Sherley Anne Williams's *Dessa Rose* (1986), and Charles Johnson's *Middle Passage* (1991). For more information about this genre of the "neo-slave narrative" and the debates surrounding it, see Madhu Dubey, "The Neo-Slave Narrative," in *A Companion to African American Literature*, ed. Gene Andrew Jarrett, 332–46 (Malden, MA: Wiley-Blackwell, 2010). The literary debate over the topic of slavery corresponds with the debate among academic historians I mentioned earlier, in the introduction.

Index

2 Live Crew, 149, 155
1876 presidential election, 53
2008 presidential election, 11, 202–203, 204, 207, 212n4

Adams, John, 5
"Address before the Pennsylvania Augustine Society, An" (Saunders), 30
Adeleke, Tunde, 42
"African American" (the term), 219n30
African American cultural expression, 131–133
African American historiography: elitism of, 8; in era of Black Studies, 16, 197; Marxist revisionist historiography, 246n2; paradigm of, proposed, 17–18; racism in, 8, 93; slavery in, 8, 16
African American intellectual history: Jefferson and, 12; political activism, contributions to, 10; racial representation in, 11; Reed and Warren on, 7–9; renewal of, 8
African American intellectuals, 198, 221n5, 246n3, 246n4
African American literary studies, 7, 9
African American literature, 1–47, 74–99; 1960s and 1970s, 13–15; agency of, 15–19; autobiography, tradition of, 189; Black Arts Movement, assumptions of, 13–14; Black Power Movement, assumptions of, 13–14; challenges representing racially defined communities, 4; copyright law (see *Sun Trust v. Houghton Mifflin Company*); dialect in, 227n41; double standard applied to, 132; in early America, 21–47; electoral and governmental events, 4, 201; function of, debate about, 82–83;

geopolitics of, 123–126; informing society, 75; Jefferson and, 3, 30, 197; neo-slave narratives, 209; New Negro criticism, 75–81; *Notes on the State of Virginia* and, 3, 21–22; Obama and, 3, 12–13; pamphlets/pamphleteers in, 28, 30; parody in, 133 (see also *Wind Done Gone*); passing for white theme in, 92–94; plantation tradition of, 229n55; political nature/value of, vii–viii, 1, 4–5, 9, 13–14, 22–28, 74–75, 128–129, 197, 209; in post-Obama era, 201–203, 208; in postemancipation period, 40; race relations, direct influence on, 126; racial identities of authors, 28–29; racial representation in, 25, 203; racial uplift theme in, 74–76, 81–99; social change/transformative effects, 4–5, 6, 11, 12, 51, 75, 129, 155–160; *Sun Trust v. Houghton Mifflin Company,* 12; transnationalism, 103; universal appeal, aspirations toward, 114; white critics of, 194
African American periodicals, 81–84, 215n28
African American political activism: agency, 15–16; antiwhite hatred, 162; Black Studies Movement, 4; "direct political action" *vs.* "indirect cultural politics," 7, 9; elected black mayors, 247n17; intellectual culture, 198–199; intergenerational conflict, 204–205; "Joshua generation," 204; "Moses generation," 204, 206; multiracial coalitions, 198, 247n17; parody and, 133; periodicals, role of, 81–84; race in new African American politics, 206–208; racial cynicism in African American political history, 206–208; sewing circles, role of, 88–89; Washington and, 86–87, 88

African American studies, "post-soul" paradigm of, 14

African Americans: agency of, 8; in antebellum period, 60–61; anti-literacy laws, effect of, 53–55; conventions in empowering, 61; Decades of Disappointment (the "Nadir"), 53–55; Democratic Party, 52; early America, 14; electoral power, 2; literary societies in empowering, 63–65; portrayals in Anglo-American literature, 80; Reconstruction, 49–50, 51–53, 69–70, 222n12; Wilmington, North Carolina, massacre (1898), 90

agency, 8, 15–19

Allen, Richard, 30

American Colonization Society (ACS), 35–36

American Lazarus (Brooks), 26

ancestor-relative analogy, 194–195

Anderson, Paul Allen, 177

Andrews, William, 124

Angelou, Maya, 189

Anglo-African Magazine, 81

Anxiety of Influence (Bloom), 225n8

Appeal in Four Articles (Walker), 217n9

Appeal to Reason (newspaper), 104

Appeal to the Colored Citizens of the World (Walker), 38–47; 1st article ("Our Wretchedness in Consequence of Slavery"), 40–41; 2nd article ("Our Wretchedness in Consequence of Ignorance"), 41–45; audience and readership, gap between, 44; black abolitionism, 40, 42; black violence against whites, 42–43; on Christian proslavery advocacy, 38–40; critique of Jefferson's *Notes on the State of Virginia,* 23–25, 30–31, 38–43, 46–47, 55–56; educational differences among African Americans, 43–45; ethical stance, 39–40; historical context, 23, 24–25, 30, 217n9; intellectual condescension in, 44–46; militancy, 42–43; pamphleteering tradition, 30; racial uplift, 29–31, 44

Arendt, Hannah, 2, 75, 93

Arewa, Olufunmilayo B., 131, 132–133

Armstrong, John, 122

art, representational *vs.* "nonrepresentational," 159

"Art or Propaganda" (Locke), 81

Audacity of Hope (Obama): African American writers, references to, 3; *Dreams from My Father* (Obama), 182–184; funeral for Rosa Parks, 183; literary quality, 166; title, 188; transformative moment of publication, 164; U. S. Constitution, creation of, 184–185, 190; year published, 2

"Audacity of Hope" (Wright), 188–189

Autobiography of an Ex-Coloured Man (Johnson), 93–94

Autobiography of Malcolm X (Malcolm X and Haley), 161–164, 169–170, 172–176

Bai, Matt, 204–205

Bailey, Cathryn, 88

Baldwin, James, 178, 189, 194

Baldwin, Kate A., 113

Banneker, Benjamin, 37

Baraka, Amiri, 205

Barbaric Traffic (Gould), 26

Behdad, Ali, 124

Beloved (Morrison), 209

Bendix, Regina, 6

Benjamin, Walter, 17

Bergstrom, Michael, 93

Best, Stephen M., 135

Bethel Historical and Literary Association, 63–65

Bethune, Mary McLeod, 116–117

Big Sea (Hughes), 104, 116, 120–121, 231n3

Birch, Stanley F., Jr., 151

Birthright (Stribling), 96, 230n82

"black" (the term), 219n30

Black and White (film), 121–122

Black Arts Movement, 13–14, 174, 215n28, 221n5

Black Arts Movement (Smethurst), 208

"Black Arts Movement and Its Critics" (Smith), 13

Black Boy (Wright), 109

black liberation theology, 200

copyright law (*continued*): derivative works, 127, 134, 136, 237n25; fair use doctrine, 149, 154; First Amendment issues, 152–154, 157–159; originality, 131–132; parody and, 130, 131–132; racial representation, 133–134, 135–136, 157, 160; *Stowe v. Thomas,* 129, 134–135; Title 17 of the U.S. Code, 237n25; translations and, 134–135

Craig, Donald, 157

Crèvecoeur, St. Jean de (John Hector St. John), 34

Crisis (magazine), 78

Crisis of the Negro Intellectual (Cruse), 198–199, 215n28, 246n2, 246n4

Critical Race Theory, 132

"Cross" (Hughes), 117

Crusader, African Blood Brotherhood's, 80

Cruse, Harold, 198–199, 215n28, 246n2, 246n4

Cullen, Countee, 105

cultural politics, 6

cummings, e.e., 106

Dain, Bruce, 38

Davis, Artur, 203, 247n15

Davis, Frank Marshall, 170–171

Dawson, Michael C., 10–11, 16, 60–61, 66–67

Dean, Jodi, 9–10

Decades of Disappointment (the "Nadir"), 53–55

Declaration of Independence, 29, 31, 35

Delany, Martin, 43, 135

Democratic Party: African Americans, 52; Compromise of 1877, 53; Douglass and, 49, 57–58; elected black mayors, 247n17; electoral power, 2; Reconstruction, 57–58

Dewey, John, 18

"Dialogue between a Virginian and an African Minister" (Coker), 30

Dickson-Carr, Darryl, 129, 133

Dimock, Wai Chee, 123

Doing Race (Markus and Moya), 207

Dolan, Jill, 125

Douglass, Frederick, 49–71; Brown and, John, 42; Christian church, critique of, 189; citizenship and color, 59; constitutional egalitarianism, 59–60; conventions in empowering African Americans, 61; cultural monuments, importance of, 62–63; Democratic Party, 49, 57–58; development of political consciousness, 55; elected office, invitations to run for, 67–70; enfranchisement as a goal, 58–59, 223n23; in England, 70; as forerunner of African American political philosophy, 62; Founding Fathers, 190; idealism of, 65; informal political action, 66, 68; "late Douglass," 62; Lincoln and, 58, 62–63, 68–69, 71; literacy and literary skill, 50, 54, 69; literary societies in empowering African Americans, 63–65; Obama and, 3; political power of, 68–70; politicians admired by, 70–71; in postbellum era, 197; power, theory of, 59; race, 206; racial injustice, reason for, 60; as racial leader, 69; racial radicalism, 62; racism, need for African Americans to confront, 66; Republican Party, 58; schools, political meaning of, 63; slavery, 12, 19, 57–66; statesmanship of, 69, 70–71; Stowe and, 71; truth, 64–65; *Uncle Tom's Cabin* (Stowe), 135; unwritten law in the South, 49; *Wind Done Gone* (Randall), 146–147; women's suffrage, 58–59, 223n23

Douglass, Frederick, writings and speeches of: "Howard University," 63; *Life and Times of Frederick Douglass,* 42, 67–70, 224n44; *My Bondage and My Freedom,* 70; *Narrative of the Life of Frederick Douglass,* 14, 70; "Need for Continuing Anti-slavery Work," 60, 206; "Negro Press," 62; "New Party Movement," 49; "Oration in Memory of Abraham Lincoln," 63; "Politics an Evil to the Negro," 58; "Race Problem," 64, 66, 75–76; "Reconstruction," 59, 62; "Seeming and Real," 60; "Southern Convention," 61; "Woman and the Ballot," 59; "Woman Suffrage Movement," 58–59; "Work before Us," 57

252 | *Index*

Hurston, Zora Neale, 189
Hutcheon, Linda, 130, 131–132
Hutchinson, George, 215n28

"I, Too, Sing America" (Hughes), 117
I Am the American Negro (Davis), 170
I Wonder as I Wander (Hughes), 102–105,
    116–124; as case study for theories of
    autobiography, 124; color discrimination
    in foreign countries, 117–120; "color line"
    in, 123; discrepancies between rendition
    and historical record, 103; transnational
    genre, 103, 123; years covered by, 101, 102
ideology: definition, 10; racial passing,
    92, 229n67; racial uplift, 79–80; scripts
    provided by, 66–67; Western categories,
    racialized, 77; white supremacy, 129, 134
"If We Must Die" (McKay), 102, 105,
    110–113, 125–126
Imperium in Imperio (Griggs), 85–88
In a Shade of Blue (Glaude), 14, 18, 197
information, 75
intellectual culture, social reach of, 198–199
intellectual property law, 131–133
Invisible Man (Ellison), 166, 176–181, 195
Iola Leroy, or Shadows Uplifted (Harper),
    84–85, 93
"Is Obama the End of Black Politics?"
    (Bai), 204–205

Jackson, Jesse, Sr., 200–201
Jacobs, Harriet, 50, 55
James, Sharpe, 205
Jefferson, Thomas: African Ameri-
    can intellectual history, 12; African
    American literature and, 3, 30, 197; as
    "black" president, 2–3, 211n3; on Buffon,
    220n35; *Notes on the State of Virginia* (see
    Notes on the State of Virginia); Obama
    compared to, 1–4; parents, 2; Sancho,
    disparagement of, 3, 12, 21, 37, 46, 51;
    three-fifths compromise, 211n3; Wheat-
    ley, disparagement of, 3, 12, 21–22, 23, 24,
    37, 38, 46, 47, 48, 51
Jim Crow, 53, 117–118
Johnson, Abby Arthur, 82

Johnson, Charles S., 94–95
Johnson, James Weldon, 93–94, 102, 115
Johnson, Ronald Maberry, 82
Johnson, Walter, 15–16
Jones, Absalom, 30
Jones, Edward P., 209
Joseph, Peniel E., 13

Kaufman, Marty, 172
Kazanjian, David: on "articles," 24; *The
    Colonizing Trick*, 26, 221n56; "flash-
    points," 17; on race, 218n14; on slavery
    and race, 22–23
Kelley, Robin D. G., 10–11, 16
Kennedy, Anthony M., 158
King, Lovalerie, 132–133, 135
King, Martin Luther, Jr.: black nationalism,
    13; Douglass and, 62; Nobel speech, 202;
    nonviolence, 13; Obama and, 176; *Testa-
    ment of Hope*, 215n25; Thurman and,
    Howard, 200
Knadler, Stephen, 86, 87
Known World (Jones), 209
Koestler, Arthur, 118–119, 121

Larsen, Nella, 95–96
law, 130–133, 159. *See also* copyright law
Lee, Spike, 162, 174
Lenin, Vladimir Ilyich, 107, 109
Lepansky, Philip, 28
Liberator (newspaper): Eastman and, 112;
    McKay and, Claude, 104, 106, 110–111;
    New Negro, portrayals of, 79–80
Life and Times of Frederick Douglass (Doug-
    lass), 42, 67–70, 224n44
Lincoln, Abraham: Douglass and, 58,
    62–63, 68–69, 71; Obama and, 3, 185–186
literature, 130–131, 159, 165. *See also* African
    American literature
Litwack, Leon F., 53, 222n12
Locke, Alain: ambassadorial status, 79; on
    art and propaganda, 81; Du Bois and,
    80–81, 91; Hughes and, 102; McKay and,
    105, 114–115; *New Negro*, 79–81, 105, 114;
    turn from racial antagonism to amelio-
    ration, 80

Long Way from Home (McKay), 105–115; apolitical literature, vision of, 121; as case study for theories of autobiography, 124; "color line" in, 122–123; critical hostility toward McKay, 101; discrepancies between rendition and historical record, 103, 104–105, 232n11; reprints of, 232n14; transnational genre, 103, 123; years covered by, 102

Lynch, James Roy, 70

Making Malcolm (Dyson), 162–163

Malcolm X, 161–164, 169–176; *Autobiography of Malcolm X* (with Haley), 161–164, 169–170, 172–176; black nationalism, 163–164, 174, 176; Christian church, critique of, 189; intellectual attention paid to, 162; Muhammad and, 172–173; myths surrounding, 162–163; name change, 173; Nation of Islam, 172, 173; Obama and, 15, 163–164, 172–174, 243n18; racial uplift, 173; reading by, 172–173; self-creation, repeated acts of, 172–173; whites, stance toward, 173

Malcolm X (film), 162, 174

Marbois, François, 21

Marcus, Stanley, 151

Markus, Hazel Rose, 207

Marrow of Tradition (Chestnutt), 89–91

Martin, E. Waldo, Jr., 6, 212n9

Mason, Charlotte, 120

Maxwell, William J., 15, 109

McCain, John, 2

McCann, Sean, 89

McCaskill, Barbara, 225n5

McGraw, Eliza Russi Lowen, 139

McHenry, Elizabeth, 63

McKay, Claude, 101–115, 122–125; Braithwaite and, 110, 113–114; Churchill and, 112; Communist Party, 102, 107–108, 110, 231n6; daily work/jobs, 112; Du Bois and, 114; geopolitical activism, 12; Harlem, 105–106; Harlem Renaissance, 102, 104, 105, 115, 231n6; Harrison and, 115; Hughes and, 101–104, 122; International Club (London), 107,

109; internationalism, 108, 112, 115; Jamaica, 105; Kansas State College, 106, 233n19, 233n21; on Lenin, 107; *Liberator* (newspaper), 104, 106, 110–111; Locke and, 105, 114–115; in Moscow, 107, 108, 112–113; Pankhurst and, Sylvia, 107; politics, disenchantment with, 115; politics, racial, 109–110; politics, radical, 102, 105, 107–108, 109–110, 233n21; proletarian authors, view of, 106–107; racial uplift, 115; self-understanding, 106; as transnational figure, 123–124, 197; travels, 105, 106, 108, 111–112, 113, 115; Trotsky and, 110; Tuskegee Institute, 233n19; *Workers' Dreadnought* (newspaper), 107

McKay, Claude, writings of: *Constab Ballads*, 113; *Harlem: Negro Metropolis*, 104; *Harlem Shadows*, 105, 113; *Home to Harlem*, 101, 115; "If We Must Die," 102, 105, 110–113, 125–126; *A Long Way from Home* (see *Long Way from Home*); *My Green Hills of Jamaica*, 104; *Negroes in America* (*Negry v Amerike*), 103, 109; *Songs of Jamaica*, 113; *Spring in New Hampshire*, 113; *Trial by Lynching*, 103; "White House" ("White Houses"), 114

Meiklejohn, Alexander, 158–159

Mercy, A (Morrison), 209

Messenger (magazine), 80

Miller, Loren, 116

minority cultures, power and, 18–19

minority transnationalism, 123–124

Mirror of Liberty (periodical), 81

Mitchell, Margaret, 127, 135. See also *Gone with the Wind*

Moddelmog, William E., 130

Moglen, Seth, 122

Montrose, Louise A., 159

Moore, David Chioni, 124

Morrison, Toni, 3, 156–157, 209

Moya, Paula M. L., 207

Muhammad, Elijah, 172–173

My Bondage and My Freedom (Douglass), 70

My Green Hills of Jamaica (McKay), 104

Nabers, Deak, 60
Narrative of the Life of Frederick Douglass (Douglass), 14, 70
"Narrative of the Proceedings of the Black People during the Late Awful Calamity in Philadelphia" (Allen and Jones), 30
National Association for the Advancement of Colored People, 114
National Reformer (periodical), 81
Native Son (Wright), 194
Natural History (Buffon), 33, 34
"Need for Continuing Anti-slavery Work" (Douglass), 60, 206
"Negro-Art Hokum" (Schuyler), 79, 226n23
"Negro Artist and the Racial Mountain" (Hughes), 102
"Negro Mother" (Hughes), 117
"Negro Press" (Douglass), 62
Negro World (newspaper), 80
Negroes in America (Negry v Amerike) (McKay), 103, 109
Neighbors, Jim, 177, 179
Nerad, Julie Cary, 229n67
New National Era (newspaper), 62
New Negro (Locke), 79–81, 105, 114
"New Negro" (Ransom), 73
New Negro criticism, 75–81
"New Negro Hokum" (Stewart), 79
New Negro politics, 12, 73–74, 80. *See also* racial uplift
"New Party Movement" (Douglass), 49, 58
New Social History, 15–16
Newman, Richard, 28
"Non Sum Qualis Eram Bonae Sub Regno Cinarae" (Dowson), 141–142
Not Even Past (Sugrue), 247n17
Notes on the State of Virginia (Jefferson), 21–25, 30–43; African American literature and, 3, 21–22; black political enfranchisement denied, 21, 24, 29, 31–32, 35–36, 46, 51, 201; blacks' abilities to reason and imagine, dismissal of, 21, 23–25, 31, 33–34, 36–38, 40–41, 46, 218n12, 220n40; colonization as alternative to emancipation of blacks, call for, 35–36, 221n56; European Alps claim, 34–35; Gates, Jr. on, Henry

Louis, 21–22; on human inequality, 34–35; importance, 29; on Native Americans, 32–33, 34, 37, 51; "Query VI," 32, 34, 36, 51; "Query XIV," 21–22, 33–36, 41, 57, 220n40; "Query XVIII," 56–57; racial premises, 57; racial separatism, 36; Sancho, disparagement of, 3, 12, 21, 37, 46, 51; on slavery, 32, 56–57; Walker's critique in *Appeal to the Colored Citizens of the World,* 23–25, 30–31, 38–43, 46–47, 55–56; Wheatley, disparagement of, 3, 21–22, 23, 24, 37, 38, 46, 47, 48, 51; worldview, 29; year published, 1
Nutter, Michael, 203, 247n15

Obama, Barack, 161–199; 1960s to, 163; African American literature, 3, 12–13; alma maters, 165; "appeal" of, 203; autobiographical imprisonment, 182; *Autobiography of Malcolm X* (Malcolm X and Haley), 161–164, 169–170, 172–176; baptism, 189; being "inside" or "outside" history, 166, 176–177, 180; birth, 166; black nationalism, 15, 161–163, 174, 176, 181, 189, 192, 197; Black Power Movement, 163, 200–201; as "black" president, 2–3; Black Studies Movement, 200; blackness of, 175; in Chicago, 168, 171; childhood/early life, 244n26; City College of New York, 172; Civil Rights Movement, 163, 201; Columbia University, 165, 167; as community organizer, 168, 171–172, 179, 187; conversion, memoir of, 245n40; core features, 182; Davis and, Frank Marshall, 170; Developing Communities Project (DCP), 161; Douglass and, 3; election as president, 11, 202–203, 204, 207, 212n4; empathy, political theory of, 177–178; faith of, 187–190, 195; father (Barack Sr.), 2, 167–168, 169; grandfather (Stanley Dunham), 167, 169, 170; grandmother (Madelyn Dunham), 167; Harvard Law School, 165, 168, 188; in Hawaii, 167, 174; identities, 167; in Indonesia, 174; *Invisible Man* (Ellison), 176–181, 195; Islam, 173; Jefferson compared to, 1–4; Kaufman and, Marty, 172; in Kenya, 167; King and, Martin Luther, Jr., 176; Lincoln and, 3, 185–186;

and, 171, 199; "one-drop rule," 85, 89, 92,
144, 219n30; passing for white, 92–94,
229n67; political behavior and, 92–93;
political cynicism of, 207; political
genealogy of, 25–31, 218n16; political
monopoly over, 208; politics of, 201;
slavery, 22–23; in uplift literature, 92–93
"Race Problem" (Douglass), 64, 66, 75–76
race relations, influence of African American literature on, 126
racial genius in nineteenth century, 51–57
racial integration, 198, 246n4
racial realism as proxy for "racial progress,"
vii
racial reconciliation in *Invisible Man*
(Ellison), 180
racial representation: "actual" *vs.* "virtual," 5; in African American intellectual history, 11; in African American
literature, 25, 203; agency, 15; copyright
law, 133–134, 135–136, 157, 160; misrepresentation in acts of, 69; Obama and,
164; politics of, 5–11, 31; transition from
"Old" to "New" Negro, 73
racial uplift, 73–99; African American
critiques of, 91–92; African American
intellectuals, 74; African American
literature, 74–76; *Appeal to the Colored
Citizens of the World* (Walker), 29–31,
44; art *versus* propaganda debate, 80–81;
class analysis framework, 79–80; debate
about function of African American
literature, 82–83; Du Bois and, 77–79,
94, 95; education, 50; as elite-driven
movement, 95; in fiction, 81–99; gradual,
accommodationist brand of, 78, 94;
ideological conflict within program of,
79–80; leaders of, 45–46; Malcolm X,
173; McKay and, 115; New Negro criticism, 75–81; periodicals, role of, 81–84;
as a political enterprise, 75; postemancipation nineteenth century, 25;
"reading up" strategy, 82; social change,
197; success or failure of, 94; "Talented
Tenth" and others, tension between, 77;
"trickle down" version, 44; Washington

and, 77–78, 94–95; Western ideological
categories, racialized, 77; white involvement in, 95–98
racism: in African American historiography, 8, 93; Critical Race Theory, 132;
of Enlightenment, 21, 24; intellectual
culture and, 50; in language, 75–76;
political genealogy of, 25–31; in postbellum period, 66; racial identities of early
American authors, 29; of Washington,
Booker T., 66
Rael, Patrick, 28
Rafiq al-Shabazz, 161–162, 181
Rampersad, Arnold, 104–105, 120, 165
Ramsey, David, 25
Randall, Alice: career, 127; on irony, 148;
oppressive history, overcoming, 135–136;
racial and gender aspects of authenticity,
15; *The Wind Done Gone* (see *Wind Done
Gone*)
Ransom, Reverdy C., 73
Reagan era, 9
Reconstruction: African Americans,
49–50, 51–53, 69–70, 222n12; Democratic
Party, 57–58; rollback of, 68
"Reconstruction" (Douglass), 59, 62
Redemption (to white Southerners), 53
Reed, Adolph L., Jr.: African American
intellectual history, 7–9; agency in African American political history, 15–16;
claims about black collective *mentalite*,
17; "direct political action" *vs.* "indirect
cultural politics," 7, 9; *Renewing Black
Intellectual History* (with Warren), 15;
"rigid disciplinarity" of, 9; on Washington and Du Bois, 95
relative-ancestor analogy, 194–195
Remnick, David, 164, 204, 243n18
Renewing Black Intellectual History (Reed
and Warren), 15
representational *vs.* "nonrepresentational"
art, 159. *See also* racial representation
Republican Party, 53, 58, 79
Requiem for a Nun (Faulkner), 192–193
Rhett Butler's People (Craig), 157
Rice, H. William, 177

Richards, Grant, 113
Ripley, Alexandra, 150
Rivers, Eugene, 246n3
Roberts, Diane, 140
Ross, Marc Howard, 75
Ross, Marlon, 77
Rubenfeld, Jed, 157–158, 159
Rush, Bobby Lee, 200

Saint-Amour, Paul K., 133, 136
Samuels, David, 178–179, 244n26
Sancho, Ignatius: "blackness" of, 31; Jefferson's disparagement in *Notes on the State of Virginia*, 3, 12, 21, 37, 46, 51
Sanctuary (Faulkner), 192–193
Sapiro, Virginia, 75
Saunders, Prince, 30
Scarlett (Ripley), 150
Schur, Richard, 132–133, 135
Schuyler, George, 79, 226n23
"Seeming and Real" (Douglass), 60
"Series of Letters by a Man of Colour" (Forten), 30
Seward, William Henry, 71
Sewell, William H., Jr., 125
Shakespeare, William, 111, 173
Shange, Ntozake, 174
Shih, Shu-Mei, 123–124
Shuffelton, Frank, 29
Sieyes, Emmanuel-Joseph, 125–126
Signifying Monkey (Gates), 133
Singh, Nikhil Pal, 199
Slauter, Eric, 5, 24, 27, 74
slavery, 54–66; in African American historiography, 8, 16; Christianity and, 38–40; Douglass and, 12, 19, 57–66; literacy, 54–55, 245n40; neo-slave narratives, 209; *Notes on the State of Virginia* on, 32, 56–57; race, 22–23; scholarship in 1960s through 1980s, 16; three-fifths compromise, 211n3
Smalls, Robert, 70
Smethurst, James Edward, 208, 215n28
Smiley, Tavis, 18
Smith, David Lionel, 13
Smith, James McCune, 41, 57

So Black and Blue (Warren), 244n25
Socialist Call (newspaper), 104
Soetoro, Lolo, 174
Sollors, Werner, 92, 229n67
Songs of Jamaica (McKay), 113
Souls of Black Folk (Du Bois): artistic forms in, 77; ballots and African Americans, 202; "Of Mr. Booker T. Washington and Others," 78; opening words, 203; racial uplift, resistance to accommodationist brand of, 94
Souter, David H., 149
"Southern Convention" (Douglass), 61
Spanish-American War, 87
Spillers, Hortense J., 198
Spingarn, Joel Elias, 108
Sport of the Gods (Dunbar), 91–92
Spring in New Hampshire (McKay), 113
Stauffer, Zahr Said, 236n4, 241n82
Stein, Jordan, 29
Stephens, Michelle Ann, 102
Stepto, Robert, 242n14
Stewart, Gustavus Adolphus, 79
Stewart, Paul A., 152
Storing, Herbert J., 71
Story of My Life and Work (Washington), 78
Stowe, Harriet Beecher: Douglass and, 71; Mitchell on, Margaret, 135–136; on race and freedom, 29; *Uncle Tom's Cabin* (Stowe), 129, 134–135, 180–181
Stowe v. Thomas, 129, 134–135
Stribling, T. S., 96, 230n82
Styles, Ruby, 174
Sugrue, Thomas J., 205–206, 247n17
Sumner, Charles, 71
Sun Trust v. Houghton Mifflin Company, 127–160; African American literature, 12; amicus curiae briefs, 153; appellate decision, 154–155; *Cable News Network v. Video Monitoring Services (CNN v. VMS)* and, 152–153; *Campbell v. Acuff-Rose Music* and, 149–150, 154–155, 158; copyright law, 151; copyright protection, 151; defense, 137, 148–149, 238n34; District Court for the Northern District of Georgia, 127, 147–151; fair use doc-

About the Author

GENE ANDREW JARRETT is Associate Professor of English and African American Studies at Boston University. He is the author of *Deans and Truants: Race and Realism in African American Literature* and the editor of several scholarly books on African American literature, culture, and history, including *African American Literature beyond Race: An Alternative Reader*, also published by NYU Press. His work has been supported by fellowships from the Radcliffe Institute for Advanced Study at Harvard University, the Woodrow Wilson National Fellowship Foundation, and the Andrew W. Mellon Foundation.